Rationalism, Realism, and Relativism

Rationalism, Realism, and Relativism

PERSPECTIVES IN CONTEMPORARY MORAL EPISTEMOLOGY

Robert L. Arrington

Cornell University Press

ITHACA AND LONDON

First published 1989 by Cornell University Press.

International Standard Book Number 0-8014-2302-3 (cloth)
International Standard Book Number 0-8014-9563-6 (paper)
Library of Congress Catalog Card Number 89-42874

Printed in the United States of America

Librarians: Library of Congress cataloging information appears on the last page of the book.

The paper in this book is acid-free and meets the guidelines for permanence and durability of the Committee on Production Guidelines for Book Longevity of the Council on Library Resources.

To
Margarita

Contents

Acknowledgments

I have many people to thank for their assistance and support in the preparation of this book. First and foremost, I am grateful to Dean Clyde W. Faulkner of Georgia State University, whose commitment to faculty development and whose deep understanding of the academy exemplify the best in academic administration. I am also indebted to Peter Hacker, who read an early draft of the manuscript and made numerous very helpful suggestions. Linda Bell, James Humber, Grant Luckhardt, Ferdinand Schoeman, and Douglas Seanor generously read chapters of the manuscript or discussed the material with me, and anonymous readers for Cornell University Press provided extremely helpful comments and criticisms. Many secretaries worked to type the manuscript at different stages, and I especially appreciate the efforts of Anita Williams, Cindy Noland, Lynn Farnham, Phyllis Hodges, and Mary Nell Stone. During the lengthy period of research and writing, my wife and daughters gave me constant encouragement—and helped keep life in proper perspective.

ROBERT L. ARRINGTON

Atlanta, Georgia

*Rationalism, Realism,
and Relativism*

Introduction

THE study of ethics underwent some dramatic changes in direction during the 1970s and 1980s. During the previous three decades metaethical noncognitivism had been the predominant point of view, and most moral philosophers agreed that moral judgments incorporate a distinctive, nondescriptive form of meaning which prevents them from being true/false statements of fact. As the name implies, noncognitivists maintained that there can be no moral knowledge: after all, the only propositions or judgments that can be known are those that are true. This noncognitivist perspective came under critical scrutiny as early as the late 1950s, and by the 1970s its authority began to be undermined. It also suffered the fate of numerous other established philosophical approaches—philosophers simply lost interest in the issues that inspired it or the methodology that directed it. Either as a result of argument or as the consequence of indifference, the philosophical climate in ethics changed: cognitivist theories began to be put forward with confidence. Applied ethicists purported to solve concrete moral problems; Rawls, Nozick, and others constructed elaborate moral theories about justice and rights; and moral epistemologists brought forth theories on the nature and ground of moral knowledge. Even moral skeptics, who never altogether disappear from view, changed their tactics. No longer appealing to noncognitivist arguments, they opted instead for relativistic considerations or developed novel interpretations of moral judgments such as the error theory. Granting that moral judgments make truth claims, the relativists maintained that these judgments are only relatively true;

the error theorists claimed that in point of fact they are false. It is now widely believed that moral discourse is cognitive in the sense of expressing propositions that have a truth value; there is as yet, however, no consensus on what one is to make of this alleged fact.

The present book surveys the lines of argument that led from noncognitivism to the new cognitivist perspective. It also examines three of the major recent cognitivist positions: rationalism, realism, and relativism. In presenting this material, I have three goals in view. The first is to provide a guide to a portion of the often bewildering scene in moral philosophy during the last two decades or so. Although I attempt to describe this scene in accessible and somewhat synoptic terms, I hope nevertheless to present the theories of rationalism, realism, and relativism fully enough to allow a reader to enter into meaningful debate with the authors I represent. Brief and facile summaries of complex, subtle, and rigorously defended theories serve neither the interests of the theorists nor the need to make the results of recent moral philosophy more widely accessible. A second goal of this book is critical: I hope to show that some of the arguments for cognitivism can be challenged and to demonstrate that all three of the major cognitivist theories we consider have significant flaws. On the basis of our examination of these arguments and theories, I attempt, in pursuit of a third goal, to describe a cognitivist theory that improves upon the alternatives studied here. This is a theory I call *conceptual relativism*, and I devote the last chapter to its development and defense. Conceptual relativism, I argue, is the logical outgrowth of many of the considerations leading to cognitivism, and it succeeds where others have failed in showing how moral judgments have truth values and can express moral knowledge. The criticisms I make of theories discussed in earlier chapters give rise to many of the distinctive features of conceptual relativism.

From Noncognitivism to Cognitivism

The dominant ethical problems of the mid-twentieth century were metaethical, relating to questions about the meanings of moral terms and the nature and structure of moral reasoning. This metaethical debate frequently centered on the issue of whether the theory of emotivism gave an adequate account of meaning and argumentation in the area of moral discourse.[1] Gradually there formed a consensus to the effect that it did not. The theory of prescriptivism, especially as it was articulated in the philosophy of R. M. Hare, came to command widespread respect and to replace emotivism as the approved view.[2] While some philosophers remained uneasy with Hare's prescriptivism, none of them was able to develop an alternative metaethic of equal appeal. Most metaethicists during this period came to endorse something like Hare's view that moral judgments have both evaluative and descriptive meaning and that their function is to commend for choice those objects and actions satisfying the descriptive criteria supplied by general moral standards and principles.

Hare's metaethical theory had much to recommend it. It presented itself as a theory sensitive to the developments in the philosophy of language which encouraged one to look for distinctive uses of language and to break away from the assumption that all or most language functions descriptively. Furthermore, his theory appealed to those who could make no sense of there being moral truths (and falsehoods)—for Hare, one's ultimate moral convictions arise out of personal decisions and, being prescriptive, can hardly be said to correspond to any facts in the world. For this reason, ethical skeptics of various kinds were attracted to prescriptivism. Finally, however, Hare was able to accommodate and illuminate the fact that moral discourse, although prescriptive, nevertheless is constrained by canons of reasoning that permit certain forms of moral debate and rule out others. Giving reason a place in morality allowed Hare to escape the criticism often leveled against emotivism to the effect that it so construes moral language that all debate becomes a

---

1. The standard sources for the theory of emotivism are A. J. Ayer, *Language, Truth, and Logic* (New York: Dover, 1946), and Charles L. Stevenson, *Ethics and Language* (New Haven: Yale University Press, 1944). Important responses to emotivism are found in Stephen Toulmin, *The Place of Reason in Ethics* (Cambridge: Cambridge University Press, 1950); P. H. Nowell-Smith, *Ethics* (Harmondsworth: Penguin, 1954); Paul Edwards, *The Logic of Moral Discourse* (New York: Free Press, 1955); Carl Wellman, *The Language of Ethics* (Cambridge: Harvard University Press, 1961); Kurt Baier, *The Moral Point of View* (Ithaca: Cornell University Press, 1958); and R. B. Brandt, *Ethical Theory* (Englewood Cliffs, N.J.: Prentice-Hall, 1959).

2. Hare's prescriptivism is given its most sustained expression in *The Language of Morals* (Oxford: Clarendon Press, 1952); see also his *Freedom and Reason* (Oxford: Oxford University Press, 1965).

matter of nonrational, emotional persuasion. Hence prescriptivism, while attracting the skeptics, also appealed to many who insisted that "not just anything goes" in morality and that reason and reflection have an important part to play in the unfolding of the moral life.

As a result, however, of accommodating so many different demands and assumptions prescriptivism inevitably began to generate its own critics. Some, most notably Philippa Foot, questioned Hare's account of the meaning of moral terms, especially the notion of an independent evaluative meaning.[3] And others, principally John Searle, challenged Hare's denial that moral judgments can be derived solely from factual premises.[4] Many philosophers found it difficult to accept the view that at bottom our moral convictions are merely decisions of principle, and many remained unconvinced that prescriptivism allowed reason any greater role in morality than did the earlier theory of emotivism. But no new metaethical position was able to command widespread agreement and replace prescriptivism as the dominant view. As noted above, some thinkers lost interest in metaethics as a general approach to ethics; others lost faith in it because of growing doubts concerning linguistic/ conceptual analysis and its ability to characterize the meanings of moral terms and the logical grammar of moral judgments.

The declining fortunes of noncognitivist theories of metaethics coincided with the emergence of an interest in applied, or practical, ethics. Moral philosophers in the metaethical camp had long been criticized for not attending to first-order, normative questions about what individuals and societies ought to do in problematic moral situations. Their close attention to the technical details of meaning and argument, seen by large segments of the general culture as sterile, useless, and irresponsible, did not provide what the public wanted: answers to questions of right and wrong, good and evil, justice and injustice. Of course, the metaethical thinkers had a reply to this charge: their activity, they claimed, was a logically prior, more fundamental one; for only after the metaethical work is done can we know how to answer the first-order questions—if, indeed, we find that they can be answered at all. But this response failed to persuade, and there was a general cultural reaction against the way

3. See Philippa Foot, "Moral Arguments," *Mind*, 67 (1958), 502–13; and Philippa Foot, "Moral Beliefs," *Proceedings of the Aristotelian Society* (1958–59), pp. 83–104.
4. See John Searle, "How to Derive 'Ought' from 'Is'," *Philosophical Review*, 73 (1964).

ethics was pursued by professional philosophers, a reaction supported, in the end, by many of the philosophers themselves.

The urgent moral dilemmas of the early 1970s jolted the public and certainly excited the moral sensibilities of most philosophers: the Vietnam war, the oil crisis and its consequences for world poverty and starvation, Watergate, the problems of abortion and euthanasia, and the multiple issues created by the advance of technology. Many philosophers began to feel not only that these problems are more important than those of theoretical metaethics but also that philosophers *do* have a role to play in resolving them. At a minimum, philosophers trained in logic and epistemology could sort out and clarify the issues and assess the logical validity and epistemological merit of proposed answers. At best, they could take a general normative ethical theory, a theory such as utilitarianism or Kantian deontology, apply it to current issues, and arrive at solutions. Thus concrete, practical normative ethics began to replace metaethics as the domain of many moral philosophers. Little effort was devoted to developing new normative theories; rather, those theories central to the historical tradition were adopted and often revitalized. Philosophers once again were engaged in the task that society always thought they should be engaged in—solving the moral problems of life and death.

An exception to the trend of avoiding theorizing on a general normative level was the work of John Rawls. In a series of early papers, and later in his monumental *Theory of Justice*, Rawls captured the admiration of the philosophical community by his attempt to articulate and defend the principles inherent in our liberal western democracies.[5] Rawls's work showed that normative theorizing can be engaged in with important, defensible results. In support of Rawls's views, or in reaction against them, increasing numbers of philosophers began to turn again to the basic abstract questions of moral theory and to search for first-order answers to them.

Such is the state of affairs that led up to the philosophical activity that is the subject of this book. Ethics at the beginning of the 1970s was

5. John Rawls, *A Theory of Justice* (Cambridge: Harvard University Press, 1971). Important early papers by Rawls include "Justice as Fairness," *Philosophical Review*, 57 (1958); "The Sense of Justice," *Philosophical Review*, 62 (1963); and "Distributive Justice," in Peter Laslett and W. G. Runciman, eds., *Philosophy, Politics, and Society*, 3d ser. (Oxford: Basil Blackwell, 1967).

marked by (a) a loss of interest or faith in the practice of metaethical conceptual analysis, (b) an emerging interest in the problems of applied ethics, and (c) a growing awareness that general ethical theory is, after all, possible. The moral philosophers whose work is studied in the following chapters can be seen as reacting to this complex state of affairs. Furthermore, their reaction can be characterized as a return to metaethical concerns, but with several differences. First, they show little interest in analyzing the meanings of individual moral terms or judgments; instead they focus on the metaethical issue of justification: How, if at all, can moral claims be defended? Second, most of their answers are framed from the point of view rejecting noncognitivism and maintaining that moral claims are true or false and can be known to be one or the other. The success of applied ethics and general normative theory seems to have convinced moral philosophers that some form of cognitivism is true. The effort to show in what this truth consists has led to the re-emergence of moral epistemology, which is the subject of my book.

Intuitionism, Naturalism, and the Open-Question Argument

Perhaps the central complaint against Hare's prescriptivism, and indeed against the entire camp of noncognitivism with which it was affiliated, is that it seems to be at odds with the commonsensical opinion that our moral beliefs can be true or false. This alleged discrepancy between the metaethical theory and our ordinary ways of thinking and talking constitutes a major criticism of prescriptivism, since it was committed to the methodological principle of adhering to and describing the logic of everyday moral discourse. Although Hare and others were able to argue against the earlier emotivists that moral arguments can be valid or invalid, it still remained the case for them that a valid moral argument terminates in a prescription, not a true/false statement of fact. And the major premises of such arguments are general principles that also are prescriptive and thus logically incapable of having truth values. A prescription is something we can choose to formulate and choose to obey. If we refuse to accept a certain prescriptive moral principle, we cannot be accused of error but only, at worst, of disobedience. And if we adopt our own, alternative prescriptive principle, we can hardly claim to have discovered or acknowledged its *truth*. Skepticism seems to attach to prescriptivism; what moral judgments one person or society makes may differ radically from those expressed by another person or society, and if these judgments are no more than prescriptions, we cannot claim to know that ours are true and those of others are false. From the perspective of someone who feels that her moral convictions are true, or at least likely to be true, and that those who disagree with her are simply in error, prescriptivism comes across as a false metaethical theory. And insofar as there is a widespread linguistic practice of judging moral beliefs to be true or false, it is easy to feel that Hare and others have gone wrong in their descriptions of the way moral language functions—that they have misunderstood the "logical grammar" of moral discourse.

But if Hare's prescriptivism and other brands of noncognitivism are unacceptable, what options remain? Most philosophers who were first attracted to emotivism, and then to prescriptivism, felt that their noncognitivist position was clearly and demonstrably superior to the other options available at the time: intuitionism and naturalism. Intuitionism had been given a robust defense by G. E. Moore, the man who might well claim to have initiated metaethical inquiry.[6] Moore felt that we have a special, *nonsensory* faculty of intuition, and that this faculty allows us to perceive the presence of a simple, indefinable, *nonnatural* property of goodness. Most philosophers, however, simply could not accept the reality of such an odd faculty and its exotic subject matter. Moreover, they failed to see how intuitions could ever resolve a moral disagreement. It would appear that all such disagreements could only lead to a standoff in which one party claims to have the appropriate intuition and the other claims not to have it. Thus Moore and his fellow intuitionists in Britain during the first part of the twentieth century were unable to generate much abiding interest in their doctrine.[7]

Moore had arrived at his intuitionism, however, by means of an argument that appeared to many to have substantial and independent

6. Moore's most influential book in ethics is *Principia Ethica* (Cambridge: Cambridge University Press, 1903).

7. Other important intuitionists were W. D. Ross (see his *The Right and the Good* [Oxford: Clarendon Press, 1930]), H. R. Pritchard (see his "Does Moral Philosophy Rest on a Mistake?" *Mind*, 21 [1912]), A. C. Ewing (see his *The Definition of Good* [London: Macmillan, 1949]), and E. F. Carritt (see his *The Theory of Morals* [Oxford: Oxford University Press, 1928] and his *Ethical and Political Thinking* [Oxford: Oxford University Press, 1947]). An early, highly influential critique of intuitionism is given by P. F. Strawson in his "Ethical Intuitionism," *Philosophy*, 24 (1949).

weight: the open-question argument.[8] Using only the most basic techniques of logic, he was able to show by means of this argument that any attempt to equate goodness with some natural or metaphysical property or state of affairs is unsuccessful. Hedonists, for example, are inclined to equate goodness and pleasure; but as Moore pointed out, it is always an open question, that is, a significant one, whether pleasure *is* good. If the hedonists were correct, to ask if pleasure is good would be to ask if pleasure is pleasure—hardly a significant question. But the question is an open one, and hence the hedonist equation is in error. Pleasure may be *a* good, but it is not what is meant by the term 'good'. The same argument can be used against a variety of ethical theories labeled naturalistic—theories, for example, that equate goodness with evolutionary progress or with the fulfillment of human potentialities. It can equally be applied to metaphysical theories equating goodness with, say, the will of God or the perfection of the Absolute. Moore deduced from these uses of the open-question argument that 'good' cannot be defined at all, and he called all efforts to do so instances of the Naturalistic Fallacy.

Moore's use of the open-question argument generally has been accepted by philosophers, although over the years some cogent criticisms have been directed at it.[9] The upshot of this general acceptance, together with the repudiation of intuitionism, was that it came to be widely believed that such moral terms as 'good' and 'right' do not designate any properties at all, and hence that moral judgments in which they are predicated of objects, persons, and actions are not descriptive judgments. And if they are not descriptive, they cannot be true or false. The early emotivists claimed that they serve only to express feelings or attitudes— they were said to have emotive rather than descriptive meaning. Even when more sophisticated emotivists and, later on, the prescriptivists restored some measure of descriptive meaning to moral terms and judgments, it was always depicted as secondary to and dependent on the nondescriptive meaning. What features we descriptively refer to by our

---

8. Moore, *Principia Ethica*, pp. 15–17.

9. A highly influential criticism is given in W. K. Frankena, "The Naturalistic Fallacy," *Mind*, 48 (1939). See also George Nakhnikian, "On the Naturalistic Fallacy," in Hector-Neri Casteñeda and George Nakhnikian, eds., *Morality and the Language of Conduct* (Detroit, Mich.: Wayne State University Press, 1963); and A. N. Prior, *Logic and the Basis of Ethics* (Oxford: Clarendon Press, 1949).

use of 'good' depends on what features we approve of or commend. For this reason moral judgments fail to be objectively true or false for the noncognitivist.

Rejecting Moore's intuitionism while accepting his open-question argument, most metaethical philosophers were committed to the denial of moral knowledge. Moral judgments, they believed, do not record the results of our sensory or nonsensory observations and cannot be tested by appeal to them. These being the most obvious ways in which a moral judgment, or any judgment for that matter, could be known to be true or false, then how, if neither is at work, can we be said to know what is right or wrong, good or evil? Throughout twentieth-century Anglo-American philosophy, there has been a widespread conviction that all knowledge of matters of fact, moral or otherwise, must rest in the end on sensory, scientific observation. But if naturalism is defeated by the open-question argument, such observation cannot account for our presumed moral knowledge. If we are to continue to believe that our moral convictions are true and known to be so, we must explain how this knowledge is possible. We could, of course, repudiate the open-question argument and resurrect naturalism, or we could look for other explanations of moral knowledge. Much of the ethical theorizing since 1970 has been an attempt to do the latter.

Forms of Cognitivism

Two possibilities eventually came to mind. First, there is the traditional alternative to sensory observation as a source of knowledge—rational proof. Of the rationalist moral theories that appeared in the late 1960s and 1970s, the most important are those of Nagel, Gert, Gewirth, and Donagan.[10] These thinkers reject the empiricist conception of practical rationality which limits the role of reason to determining the means to the fulfillment of our present, personal desires. Nagel argues that it is perfectly rational to pursue the interests of others, and Donagan claims that the goal of reason can be the acknowledgment of intrinsic value rather than the production of some end of desire. Gert,

10. See Thomas Nagel, *The Possibility of Altruism* (Oxford: Oxford University Press, 1970); Bernard Gert, *The Moral Rules* (New York: Harper & Row, 1966); Alan Gewirth, *Reason and Morality* (Chicago: University of Chicago Press, 1978); and Alan Donagan, *The Theory of Morality* (Chicago: University of Chicago Press, 1977).

too, offers a "new" conception of rational action, maintaining that some actions, such as those productive of pain for the agent or those reducing the agent's capacities, are irrational per se, whether or not the agent desires their ends (in fact, Gert observes, desiring pain or the reduction of one's capacities makes the act even more irrational). Gert, Nagel, and Donagan use their revised notions of rationality to show how reason alone gives rise to certain moral principles: these principles are such that their denials are irrational. Gewirth uses the same strategy, but he operates with a traditional conception of reason. He argues that we can deductively derive the fundamental principle of morality from necessarily true premises; indeed, he maintains, it is irrational to deny this fundamental principle because such a denial is self-contradictory.

Still other recent theories can be viewed as rationalistic. It is possible to interpret Rawls's philosophy as offering us a procedure for making rational decisions concerning moral matters.[11] A rational choice is one we would make in the original position, behind the veil of ignorance. And in the early 1980s, none other than Hare developed a view that looks suspiciously like rationalism, relying heavily as it does on the logical principle of universalizability.[12] All of these theories, different as they are, agree that moral questions can be decided by determining what it is rational to believe. The canons of logic at work in the area of practical experience and action are thought to provide the insights by which we know the truth of moral judgments.

The second possibility for an alternative, nonnaturalistic conception of moral knowledge is that of revitalizing intuitionism, specifically by providing an understanding of moral intuitions which requires neither a mysterious faculty nor a mysterious subject matter. This has been attempted recently by a group of British moral realists.[13] Their

11. See Rawls, *A Theory of Justice*, sections 25 and 26.

12. See his *Moral Thinking* (Oxford: Oxford University Press, 1981).

13. The most systematic presentation to date of recent British moral realism is given in Mark Platts, *Ways of Meaning*, chap. 10 (London: Routledge and Kegan Paul, 1979); also see John McDowell, "Virtue and Reason," *The Monist*, 62 (July 1979); John McDowell, "Are Moral Requirements Hypothetical Imperatives?" *Proceedings of the Aristotelian Society*, supp. vol. 52 (1978); and Sabina Lovibond, *Realism and Imagination in Ethics* (Oxford: Basil Blackwell, 1983). British moral realism is to be distinguished from American moral realism, the latter being essentially naturalistic. I include a brief section on American moral realism in Chapter 4, but the discussion concentrates on the British version of the theory.

intuitionism-cum-realism is in many ways more elusive and innovative than moral rationalism. To be sure, its basic tenets are clear enough: there are moral facts that exist regardless of whether anyone is aware of them; these facts are not reducible to nonmoral, naturalistic facts that can be observed by the senses; a special moral, perception-like capacity, grounded in the ability to employ a distinctive moral language, is required in order to apprehend and appreciate these facts; and this capacity may be dulled, distorted, or impaired by the influence of self-interest, desire, and so on. What is difficult to see is how these theses can be maintained without admitting the reality of a mysterious faculty of intuition which everyone wishes to repudiate. It also is difficult to understand how moral facts relate to natural facts—how they can somehow be "fixed" by natural facts, as the realists claim, without being reducible to them; and how, if not reducible to facts in the natural realm, moral facts avoid taking on an exotic status.

At this stage of our inquiry, all that can be said is that most of the British realists proceed by raising the issue of what it means to speak of *facts, perceptual capacities, descriptive concepts*, and the like. They call into question the traditional empiricist understanding of these notions, arguing that this tradition has operated with metaphysical assumptions that cannot be defended. Often appealing to the work of Wittgenstein, these realists deny that there is a way of transcending our linguistic practices and determining which of our utterances really describe facts and which of our conceptual abilities really issue in expressions of knowledge. If, on the contrary, we remain within our linguistic practices, then what counts as a fact is the sort of thing it is linguistically correct to call a fact—the sort of thing for which there is an established technique for determining factual status. And what counts as knowledge and perception is the operation of whatever capacities we conceptualize as knowledge/perception, capacities whose conceptualizations contain standards of accuracy and evidential warrant.

Seen in this light, our tendencies to speak of our moral beliefs as true and to speak of our seeing and knowing that someone has a certain moral property take on special significance. They show, for the realist, that our concept of morality includes the concepts of moral facts and moral knowledge. And given the realists' view of the significance of such conceptual truths, the basic tenets of this moral realism easily follow. No exotic faculty need be attributed to moral agents, first because the moral faculty will be thought of as exotic only if we presuppose the empiricists' confused metaphysical prejudices, and second because the moral faculty is no more or less than one of our many abilities to master a conceptual repertoire and use it. Moral facts lose the appearance of being metaphysically suspect, for no longer do we operate with the empiricists' metaphysical standard of a fact or with their conception of the proper relationships among the different orders of fact. Disabused of metaphysical prejudices in this way, we are able to accept, the moral realists believe, the realist opinions of everyday, commonsense morality.

The conviction that as philosophers we must acknowledge and honor the fact that we ordinarily think and speak of moral convictions as true or false has had an enormous impact even on those who continue to advocate one or another form of ethical skepticism. Few thinkers today accept metaethical noncognitivism. But to concede that moral judgments can be true or false is not necessarily to acknowledge that we can have the kind of knowledge of moral truths urged by the rationalists or the realists. Nor is it to admit that moral truths have the properties of objectivity and universality claimed by both rationalists and realists—the properties, that is, of reflecting a realm of independent moral facts and of being binding on all human beings. A number of skeptical or quasi-skeptical theories, recently developed, deny that moral judgments have these properties even while admitting that these judgments have truth values. A quasi-skeptical account is offered by contemporary relativists, a highly skeptical one by the error theory. And closely related to the error theory is a sophisticated form of emotivism: the expressivist, or projectivist, theory.

Relativists do not deny that moral judgments are true or false; they simply deny that moral judgments must be true for all persons and that they reflect moral facts independent of the practices and states of mind of human beings.[14] The truth of a moral judgment is seen by them as relative to the beliefs, customs, or rules of a social group or individual. Most relativists argue that this relativity is built into the very meaning of our moral talk, although they disagree over the way in which this is so.

14. An excellent source of recent writings on relativism is Michael Krausz and Jack W. Meiland, eds., *Relativism: Cognitive and Moral* (Notre Dame, Ind.: University of Notre Dame Press, 1982); also see Gilbert Harman, *The Nature of Morality* (Oxford: Oxford University Press, 1979); and David Wong, *Moral Relativity* (Berkeley: University of California Press, 1984).

Some maintain that moral judgments refer to customs or rules as part of their subject matter; others hold that the logic of moral discourse is such that many if not all moral judgments can be true or false only for those who accept the rules yielding these judgments; and there are still other possibilities. All of these relativists grant that procedures exist for determining that a moral judgment is true or false, but most of them are convinced that no one set of these judgments is true for all human beings. Hence they deny the universality of moral knowledge.

Furthermore, relativists deny that acknowledging the truth or falsity of moral judgments commits us to a realm of moral facts independent of human practices and customs. As they see it, the rules in terms of which truth values are assigned to moral judgments arise out of these practices and customs, and if they vary, so too will the rules and the moral truths they generate. If they do not vary, the truth of moral judgments is still a reflection of only the practices and customs, not of a realm of independent moral facts. Inasmuch as it is based on or expressive of human activities and artifacts, moral truth is therefore not "objective" truth.

Contemporary relativists maintain, however, that it is a perfectly objective matter whether or not an act accords with the rules of an individual or group. Moral judgments need not be subjective in the sense of being based on a speaker's (or group's) biases, emotional reactions, or self-interest rather than on empirical evidence and sound canons of reasoning. To capture the way in which contemporary relativists acknowledge the existence of moral truths, we need a distinction other than the ordinary objective/subjective one. In this book, I propose a set of distinctions among *objectivist*, *subjectivist*, and *nonobjectivist* theories, and I assign recent forms of relativism to the camp of nonobjectivist theories. Whereas objectivist theories like realism and rationalism hold that moral truths reflect facts that are independent of human creation and invention, contemporary forms of relativism deny this. They do not, however, interpret moral judgments as expressing or being based upon the subjective states of mind of human individuals, and for this reason they are superior to many more traditional, subjectivist forms of relativism.

In addition to relativism, still other ways have been devised for acknowledging the fact that moral discourse is permeated with cognitive locutions without at the same time acquiescing in some form of moral objectivism. One way, forcefully and influentially proposed by John Mackie, asserts that although most people use moral language in such a fashion as to mean that objects, persons, and actions have moral features, in fact these objects and so on do *not* have such features.[15] This is the well-known error theory of ethics, which maintains that most people think, in error, that some moral judgments are true. No moral judgments are true because there are no moral properties; all moral judgments are false. We believe that persons, actions, and objects have moral properties because we project our feelings of approval, love, disapproval, and hatred upon them. We have been tricked by this projection into thinking falsely that moral judgments reflect an independent realm of moral facts.

A similar but not identical view is held by Simon Blackburn.[16] Blackburn calls himself an expressivist, or projectivist, and offers us a highly sophisticated form of emotivism. Hence he is committed to a thesis rejected by all the other recent theorists discussed above: the thesis that the basic role of moral judgments is to express attitudes rather than to state facts. Nevertheless, he acknowledges, we often talk of truth and falsity and of validity and invalidity in moral contexts, and with good reason. Such talk is our way of reflecting on the attitudes we express in our first-order moral judgments, criticizing or defending these attitudes, indicating our continuing commitment to them or our rejection of them, tracing out their consequences, and so on. Cognitive discourse about morality thus serves an invaluable function, but it does *not* show that in reality our moral judgments are true or false in the sense of corresponding or failing to correspond to facts, or even that they are descriptive. Blackburn's expressivist theory thus explains the cognitive locutions in moral discourse without placing an objectivist interpretation on them—indeed, it is clearly a subjectivist theory. Whether it merits being called a cognitivist position is debatable, as is the case with Mackie's theory as well. But Mackie allows that we make cognitive moral errors, and Blackburn allows that our use of cognitive idioms has a valuable function. Hence they may be said to propose attenuated cognitivist theories that are highly skeptical and far removed from moral objectivism.

15. Mackie's error theory was developed early on in his "The Refutation of Morals," *Australasian Journal of Philosophy*, 24 (1946); the theory reappeared in his *Ethics: Inventing Right and Wrong* (Harmondsworth: Penguin, 1977), chap. 1.

16. See his "Moral Realism" in J. Casey, ed., *Morality and Moral Reasoning* (London: Methuen, 1971); a more recent presentation of his views is found in *Spreading the Word* (Oxford: Oxford University Press, 1984).

We will not consider Mackie's error theory or Blackburn's expressivist theory any further, although an occasional reference will be made to ways in which expressivism might respond to the moves and claims of objectivists.

The emergence of the cognitivist/objectivist theories of realism and rationalism—and the appearance of cognitivist/nonobjectivist positions such as relativism—did not take place in a vacuum. As indicated above, numerous philosophical attacks on noncognitivism were under way beginning in the 1950s, each concerned to undermine a particular aspect of this theory. These criticisms created a climate in which the acceptance of cognitivism became possible. It is instructive to examine a number of the arguments used against noncognitivism in order to remove some of the prejudices that prevent many philosophers even today from taking cognitivism seriously. Such a survey also allows us to review the once-powerful theory of noncognitivism. Chapters 1 and 2 concentrate, respectively, on criticisms of the noncognitivists' account of moral reasoning and criticisms of their picture of moral judgments. In both instances, these objections frequently amount to demonstrations of striking, significant parallels between moral discourse and nonmoral, factual discourse.

In Chapters 3, 4, and 5, I deal with rationalism, realism, and relativism, respectively, describing these theories in detail and evaluating their claims to have identified the source and ground of moral knowledge. I discuss some of the problems they face by referring to criticisms leveled against them in the literature and by raising objections of my own. Both of the variants of rationalism I consider—those of Gert and Gewirth—have in my estimation serious internal defects: logical gaps in the argument or outright inconsistencies. Such faults are especially embarrassing to rationalist theories, and I mention still other reasons for thinking that rationalism is unsuccessful in providing a cognitive basis for morality. Contemporary British realism is a powerful but highly controversial theory. Special attention is paid to two recent criticisms of realism: Gilbert Harman's claim that moral facts need not be postulated in order to explain moral knowledge, and Blackburn's and Mackie's claim that supervenience poses a serious threat to the doctrine of moral properties. I argue that the realists either do or could offer satisfactory responses to these criticisms, but I go on to question both their metaphysical doctrine of independent moral properties and facts and their perceptual model of moral knowledge. Relativism constitutes a major nonobjectivist but cognitivist alternative to rationalism and realism, and it recently has received significant new expressions in the work of Harman and David Wong.[17] After finding fault with these new theories, I argue that a modified form of relativism offers us an attractive alternative to rationalism and realism. This alternative, conceptual relativism, is developed and defended in Chapter 6. It is, I suggest, the most plausible way of accommodating and interpreting the cognitive locutions in our moral language, and it goes a long way toward illuminating the nature of moral knowledge.

17. See Harman, *Nature of Morality*, and Wong, *Moral Relativity*.

1 / Moral Reasoning

MANY contemporary philosophers grew up in an atmosphere in which the distinction between questions of value and questions of fact was taken for granted. This distinction was given its most refined expression in the noncognitivist theories of the mid-twentieth century. More recently, however, the intellectual atmosphere has begun to change. Many ethical theorists claim to see far more parallels between moral and factual discourse than were acknowledged by the earlier noncognitivists. Although no general cognitivist picture of moral discourse has achieved the kind of consensus commanded by R. M. Hare's noncognitivist picture, recent writers have argued forcefully for specific parallels between moral and nonmoral talk. Many theories claim that moral language possesses one or another cognitive feature or that it shares one or another similarity with the admittedly factual discourse in common sense and science. All of these theories are controversial, and an advocate of a theory proclaiming one parallel might well disagree with the advocate of another proclaiming a different one. My strategy in this and the following chapter is to summarize, coordinate, and evaluate some of these views. I do not attempt to assess every one, but I do indicate where I stand regarding the trends of thought arising out of the arguments and theories examined.

There are two general dimensions to the newly emerging cognitive picture of moral discourse. The first concerns the structure of moral reasoning and argumentation; the second relates to the composition and structure of moral judgments. The two dimensions are coordinate and must fit together—that is to say, the way we view moral arguments must be consistent with the way we view moral judgments. Moral judgments must be such as to be defensible by the type of moral arguments we describe, and the moral arguments must be functions of the type of moral judgments we formulate. Being able to provide a coherent account of moral reasoning *and* moral judgments is a test of any complete cognitive theory of moral discourse. In this study, however, we must approach the two dimensions separately, largely because most of the philosophers who have identified moral/nonmoral parallels in reasoning have not gone on to give us parallels regarding moral and nonmoral judgments, and vice versa. I begin with similarities detected in the area of argumentation and move on in the next chapter to similarities observed with respect to the nature and structure of judgments.

Review of Noncognitivism

Largely as a result of the work of Hare, there gradually emerged during the 1950s and 1960s a widely shared view concerning the canonical form of moral arguments.[1] Whereas some writers had maintained that there are distinctive rules of moral inference,[2] Hare argued forcefully that moral reasoning is deductive in the traditional sense. We might, for example, attempt to justify one of our particular moral convictions or judgments by arguing for it in the following way:

> One ought to keep one's promises.
> I promised to attend John's lecture.
> Therefore I ought to attend John's lecture.

Likewise, we might defend one of our general moral convictions by deductively deriving it from other propositions:

> A state always ought to enforce whatever promotes social stability.

---

1. See R. M. Hare, *The Language of Morals* (Oxford: Clarendon Press, 1952), chaps. 2, 3, and 4. Also see R. M. Hare, *Practical Inferences* (London: Macmillan, 1971), especially pp. 1–21.
2. See Stephen Toulmin, *An Examination of the Place of Reason in Ethics* (Cambridge: Cambridge University Press, 1950); also see Stuart Hampshire, "Fallacies in Moral Philosophy," *Mind*, 61 (1949), 466–82.

Capital punishment promotes social stability.

Therefore a state ought to enforce capital punishment.

In both of these arguments we have a major premise, a minor premise, and a conclusion following deductively from the two premises. The major premises and the conclusions are moral propositions; the minor premises are factual statements. The author of one of these arguments seeks to justify the moral conclusion by subsuming it, via a factual minor premise, under a more general moral proposition serving as the major premise. Moral justification, then, consists in a demonstration of consistency between our contested moral convictions, on the one hand, and the facts and our more general moral convictions, on the other. Against those who maintained that special rules of inference at work in morality permit us to argue directly from factual propositions to moral conclusions, Hare contended that these alleged special rules are in reality suppressed moral principles or standards. As such, they should be thought of as the substantive major premises of deductive arguments, in which case the moral conclusion is always derived from a moral principle or standard in conjunction with a factual minor premise. Moral judgments can never be defended by appeal to facts alone; to defend our judgments we must appeal to the facts *and* our universal moral principles or standards.

According to Hare, the moral propositions that figure as the major premises and conclusions of moral arguments are prescriptive judgments, not descriptive ones. The function of any moral judgment for Hare is to prescribe or commend choices, something he thinks a mere description cannot do. Commands and other imperatives are the vehicles used to prescribe choices, and hence moral judgments must be thought of as having the logical status of prescriptions. Particular moral judgments commend or prescribe particular actions or objects of choice, and general moral principles and standards prescribe general classes of actions or choices. The prescriptive status of moral judgments is particularly evident in the case of a moral disagreement. Such a disagreement often does not reveal a "theoretical" difference of opinion over facts but rather manifests a highly charged and dynamic conflict of prescriptions regarding what some person, some group of individuals, or everyone ought to do or choose. When such a conflict arises, it is part of the concept of morality that all parties to the dispute are required to give reasons for their moral judgments. Such defenses take on the form of the

moral arguments illustrated in the paragraph above. A particular prescription or a prescription of low-level generality is deductively derived
from a more general prescriptive principle or standard and a statement
of fact.

Construing moral judgments as prescriptive does cause a problem,
however, for anyone who thinks of moral arguments as having a deductive form. Prescriptions do not have truth values—it is senseless to say,
for example, that the command "shut the door" is either true or false.
But the very notion of deductive validity is usually defined in terms of
truth values: a deductive argument is valid if its premises cannot be true
while its conclusion is false. By virtue of their prescriptive status, moral
judgments for Hare are incapable of having truth values; they are quasi-
imperatives, not declarative sentences or descriptive utterances. How,
then, can an argument containing them be assessed as valid or invalid?

To surmount this problem, Hare developed an ingenious theory
whereby the logical features of a judgment are functions of a part of it
that is independent of whether the judgment is descriptive or prescriptive. That a judgment is descriptive or prescriptive is, according to this
theory, a matter of its *neustic*, the manner in which its content is "affirmed." But the content, the *phrastic*, can be common to both descriptive and prescriptive judgments—it would simply be affirmed differently in the two cases by different *neustics*. Given that the *phrastic*
determines the logical features of judgments, both of these kinds of
judgment can occur and logically interact within the same argument.
Thus arguments containing both can be valid or invalid. The place of
reason in moral debate is thereby secured, in spite of the fact that moral
judgments contain prescriptive *neustics* and cannot be true or false.

Although Hare's *phrastic/neustic* analysis allows us to understand how
prescriptions can occur in deductively valid arguments, the prescriptive
status of moral judgments generates still another problem for the notion
of a deductive moral argument. With any deductive argument we must
distinguish between its validity and its soundness. The question that
arises, then, is whether it is possible to generate sound arguments in the
moral sphere. And given Hare's view that the major premise and conclusion of a moral argument are prescriptions, it is difficult to see how there
could be sound moral arguments. Soundness attaches to arguments that
are valid *and* whose premises are known to be true, but a prescriptive
moral principle or standard cannot be true (or false). If the purpose of a

moral argument is to defend its conclusion and provide reasons for accepting it, generating a valid argument is not enough. We must provide reasons for accepting the major premise. If we cannot show this premise to be true, how do we justify it?

Hare's answer is that we justify the major premise of a moral argument by subsuming it under a still more general moral principle or standard. Typically this might be done by indicating the consequences of obeying the lower-level principle and pointing out that these consequences accord with or violate a more general, higher-level principle. Or it might be done by showing that the satisfaction of the lower-level principle is a necessary condition for the satisfaction of the higher-level one. In both instances, the argument gives us a reason for accepting the major premise of the original argument and hence a reason for accepting its conclusion. A sound moral argument, then, might be thought of as one whose minor premise is true and whose major premise is subsumable under a more general principle.

But why should we accept the more general principle? Obviously the same problem arises here as in the case of the initial moral argument. Even though our higher-level argument is valid, this fact gives us no reason in itself for believing or accepting the argument's major premise. Once again, however, we can provide such a reason by deducing the principle serving as the major premise from a still more general, higher-level principle. In this way we can continue to give reasons for accepting the moral judgment whose defense generated the moral argument in the first place. At some point in this process, however, we will arrive at a highly general principle that cannot be subsumed under a more general one. According to Hare, these ultimate moral principles reflect our most basic moral commitments. In the nature of the case they cannot be defended by appeal to anything higher or more general, for they constitute the bedrock of a proof. The role of reason in moral arguments, then, is to show the consistency between our basic moral commitments and our lower-level principles and particular moral judgments.

It is easy to feel unsatisfied by Hare's solution to the problem of soundness in moral arguments. One's ultimate moral principle or principles are not and cannot be justified, for they rest on nothing more basic. Are they not, then, arbitrary? And if so, does not this arbitrariness extend throughout one's set of moral beliefs to all those other principles and particular judgments they justify? Hare grants that one's ultimate moral commitments reflect decisions of principle, but this need not, he thinks, show that these commitments or the subordinate principles and judgments following from them are arbitrary. He argues that if we go through the elaborate process of deducing our particular judgments from principles, pointing to the consequences of following these principles and in this way subsuming them under more general and finally ultimate principles, we have done enough to show that our moral beliefs are not arbitrary.[3] We have, as it were, defined a whole way of life and shown how our moral convictions are integrated into this way of life. In light of such an articulate and systematic defense of our moral views, does not the accusation of "arbitrary" lose its sting?

Even if we agree with Hare that the process of argumentation involved in defending a moral judgment is adequate to avoid the charge of arbitrariness, certain consequences still follow from his views with respect to what we can expect from a moral argument. A moral argument as he understands it may under certain circumstances be successful in resolving a disagreement over an issue, but such an argument can break down in several ways. Most important, it is possible for two or more individuals to bring different ultimate principles to bear on an issue. If this happens, although there may be agreement on all the facts surrounding the issue, there will be a fundamental disagreement over the moral significance of these facts. Given that the different principles are ultimate ones, there is no way to overcome the disagreement by appeal to still other facts or other principles. Hence the disagreement is rationally irresolvable. The possibility of arriving at such ultimate, rationally irresolvable disagreement looms over every moral debate, given Hare's analysis of the structure of moral argumentation.

Hare succeeds in showing that reason has a large role to play in moral debate. Under certain circumstances it can be used effectively to win agreement over relevant facts, and it can demonstrate inconsistency and consistency among moral principles. But reason never suffices to provide complete and conclusive proof of a judgment, for in the end its use presupposes moral principles that we accept without proof or reason. If we agree on them, in theory we can come to agreement on more specific moral matters. If we disagree regarding them, we will have to agree to

3. Hare, *The Language of Morals*, pp. 68–69.

disagree, or resort to techniques of nonrational persuasion, or go to war against one another, or . . .

This noncognitivist characterization of moral reasoning and its consequences contrasts with a widely accepted picture of the form of reasoning that occurs in nonmoral contexts, both in common sense and in science. According to this "empiricist" picture, judgments of matters of fact made in these contexts are directly or indirectly justified by appeal to empirical observations. This is obviously the case with answers to such straightforward questions as "Is there any more marmalade in the refrigerator?" and "Who won the 1988 Women's Doubles Championship at Wimbledon?" Here observation not only justifies one answer against the others, it conclusively proves the truth of one of the answers. With more complicated issues, empirical proof is admittedly less direct and conclusive. For example, two historians may disagree over the origins of the Welsh people, and although each has a theory supported by some empirical data, neither is able to establish it beyond doubt and in such a way as to win agreement from the other. In this and similar cases, however, disagreement is viewed as the result of a lack of sufficient empirical evidence, and there is confidence on the part of all concerned that if such evidence were to be forthcoming, proof and agreement would follow. All the evidence is not and may never be available, yet the question is felt to be resolvable in principle.

In those cases in which ordinary people or scientists disagree over some matter of fact, the important thing to note, according to this conception of reasoning, is that in the debate among them nothing comparable to competing moral principles comes to the surface. To be sure, scientists may disagree over the proper methodology to employ in investigating a problem. But (a) these scientists share a general conception of scientific method, and more specific methodological disagreements can usually be resolved in light of this conception and the success or failure of particular methodological strategies; and (b) methodological principles are not substantive in the way in which moral principles are thought to be. There is, it will be granted, one other kind of general statement over which scientists often disagree, and it is substantive—namely, statements of laws of nature. But although general beliefs regarding laws do figure prominently in the sciences and in scientific disagreements, there is nevertheless a radical difference between law statements and moral principles. The latter can be justified only by being deduced from higher, more general principles. The law statements may be deduced from more general, highly theoretical laws, and such a deduction may be enough to convince the scientific community of their truth. But the law statements also are open, at least in principle, to a different kind of justification. They can be supported inductively, first by deducing from them that certain observations should be forthcoming under certain circumstances and then by performing the appropriate experiments and noting that the observations do occur. Such experiments can be repeated until adequate inductive evidence is available to convince all concerned that the law statements are probably true. Furthermore, law statements can be conclusively falsified. Inductive support and observational falsification show that law statements are capable of justification from "below," whereas moral principles can be justified only from "above"— hence their radical epistemic difference.

This is a greatly oversimplified sketch of the highly controversial "empiricist" characterization of what goes on in nonmoral common-sense and scientific debates. Nevertheless, it serves to identify the conception of matter-of-fact justification which distinguished moral from nonmoral discourse in the minds of many of the noncognitivists. Specifically, it highlights the noncognitivists' conception of the importance of moral principles and their deductive derivation from more general moral principles that cannot themselves be justified. These ultimate principles arise out of, and rest on, decisions, attitudes, desires, or some other noncognitive mode of commitment. General scientific and common-sense beliefs, on the contrary, are capable of inductive (or hypothetico-deductive) justification, and they are subject in principle to observational proof or disproof.

Is this empiricist/noncognitivist picture accurate? Although the contrast drawn between moral reasoning and scientific reasoning still seems to many philosophers to be persuasive and definitive, considerable doubt has been cast upon it in recent years. Moral reasoning has come to be seen as much more similar to scientific reasoning. Furthermore, the picture of what goes on in science has come to look more and more like what goes on in morality. In other words, both scientific and moral argumentation have been reassessed. It is time to look at these reappraisals.

An Analogy with Scientific Reasoning

The paradigm of moral reasoning we have been considering has the following structure:

Major premise: Universal moral principle
Minor premise: Statement of relevant facts
Conclusion: Particular moral judgment.

Any attempt to justify the major premise will proceed in like manner until one arrives at a fundamental, unprovable, moral principle of the highest generality. The assumptions operating here are (1) that moral justification is always deductive; (2) that particular judgments are justified by being derived from moral principles; and (3) that justification terminates in a basic, unprovable principle. Each of these assumptions can be and has been challenged—often all three are challenged in the same attack.

J. B. Schneewind and Baruch Brody mount such an attack.[4] They deny that deduction is the primary mode of moral justification, that particular judgments are always derived from principles, and that the process terminates in and is grounded by basic, highly general principles. Positively, they claim that moral discourse incorporates something more akin to the scientific pattern of reasoning. Particular moral judgments are said to give rise to general moral principles, which in turn serve to systematize the particular judgments and to yield new particular judgments for novel or difficult cases. The general moral principles or rules can be used on occasion to criticize particular judgments that do not accord with them, but if enough aberrant particular judgments occur, the general principles have to be adjusted or revised. The parallel with science is close, for in science general theories and laws are developed on the basis of particular observations, the purpose of these general statements being to organize and render coherent the observations

---

4. J. B. Schneewind, "Moral Knowledge and Moral Principles," in *Knowledge and Necessity*, Royal Institute of Philosophy Lectures, 3 (1968–69), 249–62; reprinted in S. Hauerwas and A. MacIntyre, eds., *Revisions* (Notre Dame, Ind.: University of Notre Dame Press, 1983); citations are to the reprint. Baruch Brody, "Intuitions and Objective Moral Knowledge," *The Monist*, 62 (October 1979), 446–56.

and to generate predictions of new observations. Theories can be appealed to in order to repudiate observations that run counter to their requirements, but theories also will be revised or rejected when the observational evidence mounts against them.

According to Schneewind, the scientific model of reasoning shows clearly that there is no a priori order or hierarchy among our empirical judgments. Neither particular observation reports nor general theoretical statements take precedence—logically or epistemically. Each can be used in certain circumstances to criticize the other. We may justify a theory by appealing to observational data, but we also may accept an unexpected, "odd" observation by showing that in fact it is predicted by the theory. Schneewind acknowledges the work of C. S. Peirce and J. L. Austin as showing that there is no "context-free order of dependence" among our judgments. Might not moral discourse also lack a context-free order of dependence? Must particular moral judgments always derive their legitimacy from moral principles? Is it not possible, on the contrary, that moral principles can be justified by showing that they accord with the preponderance of one's particular moral judgments? Perhaps we can even test a proposed moral principle by deducing from it what it would require under certain circumstances and determining whether the "prediction" accords with the actual particular judgment we would make in those circumstances. Schneewind and Brody think that such suggestions actually accord with our real-life moral experience. As Schneewind puts it: "Moral beliefs show the same kind of susceptibility to systematization, criticism, revision, and resystematization that factual beliefs show. There are analogs to theory and data among our moral beliefs, and these can be understood as related in ways like those in which theory and data are related in the sciences."[5]

The relationship between theory and data in the sciences is one of mutual critical dependence: each feeds the other and can be criticized in light of the other. This process of systematization, criticism, and resystematization also occurs among moral principles and particular judgments. Neither has priority—each can be derived from the other, and each can be criticized for its failure to accord with the other.

Both Schneewind and Brody see moral reasoning as beginning with particular moral judgments. Schneewind refers to them as "specific

judgments, rules, and ideas, the correctness of which we have no hesitation in affirming,"[6] and Brody thinks of them as judgments that formulate "fundamental moral intuitions . . . judgments about the rightness or
wrongness of particular actions, the justice or injustice of particular social arrangements, the blameworthiness of particular individuals."[7]
Brody describes the initial judgments as tentative, but Schneewind appears to accord them a higher degree of conviction; still and all, for both
theorists they are fallible and liable to correction. In thinking of moral
reasoning as beginning with these fallible particular judgments, both
Schneewind and Brody appear to mean that temporally they are the first
to be formed: we do not deduce them from principles already in hand.
Both of these theorists also see the next step in the pursuit of moral
knowledge—or in the process of moral development—as the formulation of general moral beliefs analogous to the general theories of science.
In Brody's words: "The next stage is the stage of theory formation. The
goal of this stage is to form a theory as to which actions are right or
wrong, agents blameworthy or innocent, and institutions just or unjust.
The data about which we theorize are the first intuitions; the goal is to
find a theory which systematizes these intuitions, explains them, and
provides us with moral judgments about cases for which we have no
intuitions."[8]

Brody does not elaborate on how theoretical moral statements *explain*
the particular judgments, but presumably the general principle picks out
certain features common to particular situations we judge to be good,
right, or just, hence revealing that it is by virtue of having these features
that the situations are good, right, or just. The moral theory or principle
seeks to locate the essential ingredient that gives rise to the moral character of a situation, just as a scientific theory hypothesizes that certain
factors are what cause or constitute natural events. Schneewind tells us
that general moral beliefs "express the point or rationale of specific
moral convictions,"[9] which I take to be the same claim.

Schneewind adds still another dimension to the structure of moral
reasoning—what he calls a *world outlook*.[10] He makes the important

---

6. Ibid.
7. Brody, "Intuitions," p. 446.
8. Ibid., p. 447.
9. Schneewind, "Moral Knowledge and Moral Principles," p. 121.
10. Ibid.

point that just as scientific laws cannot be tested individually or discretely but rather must be understood in the context of more encompassing scientific theories, so too moral principles or theories must be placed in the wider context in which they occur. This is typically a religious world view, but it also may be a secular metaphysics. The mutual dependence of the particular moral judgments, the principles, and the world view is described by Schneewind in the following manner: "A large part of the terms and beliefs of these general metaphysical views of life and the world are inseparably intertwined with what we think of as distinctively moral beliefs. The very concepts by which we pick out subjects for moral predication may be rooted in religious or metaphysical propositions, and these in turn may be unintelligible without the evaluative and moral implications."[11] Here we have an admirable transfer of the doctrine of holism from the scientific sphere, where it recently has been influential (and about which we shall hear more) to the moral sphere. Moral concepts and judgments are part of a system of concepts and judgments, other components being descriptive factual and metaphysical beliefs. No clear lines of demarcation can be drawn among these components in such a way as to generate discrete, logical categories of judgments. It is the system as a whole that we bring to bear on our experience, and it is the system that has explanatory value. Specifically, it would appear to follow from this view that moral judgments, particular or universal, cannot be expected to face the test of confirmation alone— they cannot be justified or repudiated as isolated, merely "moral" utterances.

One of the epistemological consequences of moral holism becomes apparent in a final point on which Schneewind and Brody insist. This relates to the notion of underdetermination of theory by data. In the philosophy of science it has become a commonplace that observations do not uniquely determine or justify any one scientific theory—they are compatible with any of a number of theories. Moreover, theories are not as vulnerable to straightforward falsification as some philosophers had thought. A well-established scientific theory likely will not be given up just because one of the observations it predicts does not occur. Such a theory may be maintained in spite of such contrary evidence because of its overall predictive power, its simplicity, its relation to other accepted

11. Ibid.

theories, or some other reason. The contrary evidence can be dealt with by developing an ad hoc subsidiary hypothesis or by putting it down to observational error, faulty conditions of observation, and so on. Only when the contrary evidence becomes overwhelming does it usually lead scientists to abandon the theory. Schneewind and Brody maintain that in moral reasoning we find a phenomenon closely parallel to the under-determination of theory by data. Our particular moral beliefs can be systematized in various ways, and a given systematization (for example, utilitarianism) that has developed over time, that provides persuasive organization and coherence to our beliefs, and that has the power to generate new beliefs in novel circumstances is not apt to be given up in the face of recalcitrant moral opinions on particular subjects. Ad hoc adjustments to the moral theory can always be made, and other explanations similar to those in science are available to accommodate the discrepancy. It is only when the particular moral beliefs inconsistent with the theory become sufficiently numerous that they provide enough leverage to ensure falsification.

Schneewind points to some other defects of moral theories which may lead to their abandonment, defects that once again can be seen as parallel to those infecting some scientific theories and that involve pragmatic considerations rather than straightforward falsification.[12] Moral theories or principles may lose their relevance to changing circumstances; they may not yield sufficiently specific guidelines for action; they may issue conflicting guidelines; or the religious/metaphysical background theory may lose its power to convince. In any and all of these circumstances, new moral principles may evolve. Their acceptance does not depend, as the noncognitivist paradigm suggested, on an ungrounded act of will or on free-floating attitudes. The principles or theories are accountable to a vast number of factors—the data of particular moral beliefs and the logical and pragmatic functions of moral theory—and they can be rationally criticized in light of any of these factors.

It should be obvious from the account just given that Schneewind and Brody are operating with a view of scientific reasoning different from the empiricist model that inspired the noncognitivist contrast between moral and nonmoral discourse. Their view has become standard in recent philosophy of science, largely as a result of the work of W. V.

12. Ibid., p. 123.

Quine.[13] Quine argues persuasively that it is a scientific theory as a whole and not individual predictive claims that face the tribunal of experience. As a consequence, observation no longer is seen as having the simple relations of verification and falsification to theory, and pragmatic factors relating to comprehensiveness, coherence, and simplicity are thought to play an important role in theory evaluation. As a result of Quine's work, philosophers have come to challenge the very distinction between observation and theoretical statements, pointing out (perhaps ad nauseam) that observation terms are "theory-laden." The older empiricist, positivist view, accepted by the noncognitivists, that observation affords a clear-cut decision procedure for accepting and rejecting claims about the world is now repudiated by almost all philosophers of science.

In such a context, the feeling that science and morality are categorically different by virtue of the presence in one and lack in the other of verification/falsification procedures begins to lose its persuasiveness. If moral principles are related to particular moral judgments in something like the way described by Schneewind and Brody, and if the new picture of scientific reasoning is placed in the background, the lack of clear-cut verification procedures in morality is a matter of no surprise and not a cause for moral skepticism. The same situation prevails in science. But particular moral convictions do provide a check on moral principles, and principles can be corrective of particular judgments—and so the same kind of reciprocal, nonfoundationalist accountability occurs in moral discourse as in the scientific variety. Disabused of outmoded pictures of science and morality, we can see how very similar they are.

The overlap between the two modes of thought becomes even more obvious if we take into account some other recent developments in the philosophy of science, specifically Thomas Kuhn's well-known work on paradigms in science and his views concerning the evolution of scientific theories.[14] According to Kuhn, scientific research takes place against the background of a paradigm or set of paradigms, these being particular scientific theories or problems that serve to define the kinds of questions scientists may ask and the kinds of methods they may use. Sometimes Kuhn speaks of a paradigm as a widely encompassing world view pro-

13. See W. V. Quine, "Two Dogmas of Empiricism," in his *From a Logical Point of View* (Cambridge: Harvard University Press, 1953, 1961).
14. See Thomas Kuhn, *The Structure of Scientific Revolutions*, 2d ed., enlarged (Chicago: University of Chicago Press, 1970).

vided by a scientific theory such as Newtonian mechanics. Regardless of the ambiguity involved in his notion of a paradigm, Kuhn clearly thinks that paradigms serve as normative models for all standard research. They are unquestioned, and they exercise considerable pressure on scientists to conform by asking the "proper" questions and using the "proper" methods. Additionally, Kuhn and others have pointed to the sociological and cultural factors that shape scientific research, among them publication requirements, the expectations of agencies awarding grants, and the current needs of the culture. Rather than being pure and uncontaminated by normative elements, science rests on the normative support of paradigms and on factors of the "sociology of knowledge." How different is such a state of affairs from that prevailing in morality? Even if the noncognitivists are correct in their assumption that moral discourse presupposes commitments, principles, and attitudes that cannot be given a rational justification, Kuhn's philosophy of science seems to imply that science too rests on such nonrational foundations.

Before leaving the new "scientific" model of moral reasoning, we should look briefly at the related theory propounded by Rawls and at the most recent views of Hare. In fact it was Rawls who, in all likelihood, was initially responsible for the conception of moral methodology sketched above, and he probably has had more influence than anyone else in gaining support for this model. Hare has developed a theory that appears to resemble the model but in the end does not. His thoughts on the role of "intuition," however, raise important questions for the new approach.

In *A Theory of Justice* Rawls propounds two basic principles of justice and argues that they would be chosen by all rational human beings who, in a context guaranteeing a lack of bias and inequality (the "original position"), are drawing up the rules by which they would order their society and their lives. How, he asks, can he justify his description of the original position and of the principles he claims would emerge from it? His answer is: "By seeing if the principles which would be chosen match our considered convictions of justice or extend them in an acceptable way."[15] And he elaborates as follows:

> We can note whether applying these principles would lead us to make the same judgments about the basic structure of society which we now make

15. John Rawls, *A Theory of Justice* (Oxford: Oxford University Press, 1972), p. 19.

intuitively and in which we have the greatest confidence; or whether, in cases where our present judgments are in doubt and given with hesitation, these principles offer a resolution which we can affirm on reflection. . . . We can check an interpretation of the initial situation, then, by the capacity of its principles to accommodate our firmest convictions and to provide guidance where guidance is needed.[16]

The parallel with what Brody and Schneewind have to say is clear.

Rawls also appears to believe that the notion of the original position and the principles emerging from it have some intuitive and/or rational plausibility of their own, such that, even though tested against our initial convictions about justice, they may produce a conception of justice that does not always accord with these convictions. When such discrepancies occur, we face a choice:

We can either modify the account of the initial situation or we can revise our existing judgments, for even the judgments we take provisionally as fixed points are liable to revision. By going back and forth, sometimes altering the conditions of the contractual circumstances, at others withdrawing our judgments and conforming them to principle, I assume that eventually we shall find a description of the initial situation that both expresses reasonable conditions, and yields principles which match our considered judgments duly pruned and adjusted. This state of affairs I refer to as *reflective equilibrium*.[17]

Thus for Rawls the goal of ethical theorizing is to achieve this state of reflective equilibrium between our initial but considered judgments and our principles and theories.[18] Achieving it requires acknowledging as proper the reciprocal influence of initial particular judgments and general principles. Neither are thought of as self-evident or necessary truths.[19] The justification of a concept of justice "is a matter of the mutual support of many considerations, of everything fitting together into one coherent view."[20] Rawls himself points to the parallels between this

16. Ibid., pp. 19–20.
17. Ibid., p. 20, my emphasis.
18. The most sustained and penetrating work on the notion of reflective equilibrium has been done by Norman Daniels. See his "Wide Reflective Equilibrium and Theory Acceptance in Ethics," *Journal of Philosophy*, 76 (1979), 256–82.
19. Rawls, *Theory of Justice*, p. 21.
20. Ibid.

conception of moral methodology and the methodology at work in scientific inquiry—his example is linguistics. And the fascination and influence exerted by *A Theory of Justice* testify to the appeal of this conception. There is a growing conviction among moral philosophers that in science and in morality we seek reflective equilibrium between our considered particular judgments and our theoretical principles.

Hare also has given a more prominent role to particular judgments or intuitions than he was wont to do in his earlier moral philosophy. In *Moral Thinking* (1981), he distinguishes two levels on which we operate morally: the intuitive and the critical.[21] (He also speaks of a third level, the metaethical, which does not deal with matters of moral substance.) On the intuitive level we respond to the events around us on the basis of habit and conditioning. We make quick and ready evaluations with regard to the passing scene by applying relatively simple and highly general principles we have internalized as a result of our conditioning or moral training and experience. The principles we apply in such responses must be simple and uncomplicated enough to be absorbed to the degree that they become intuitive, and they need to be sufficiently unspecific to allow us to respond to a large number and variety of situations. Such immediate, intuitive responses are valuable, for often there is not enough time to think things through, and in any event many of us are incapable of a much higher degree of reflection. Moreover, insofar as our responses involve the application of general principles, we are less exposed to the temptation of special pleading—hence the desirability of having these principles inform the intuitions and dispositions ingrained in our characters and motivations.

On the level of critical thinking, we no longer rely on such set responses. We think things through, using a pattern of reasoning that Hare believes is built into the very concepts we employ in the moral domain. In doing this we formulate universal (but perhaps highly specific) principles to which we can give overriding strength relative to other principles such as those of etiquette. Moreover, in our critical thinking we seek those principles we can universalize with respect to all agents, by which Hare means that we would accept them even if we were the individuals affected by their implementation. Armed with such principles, we are in a position to correct judgments made at the intui-

21. R. M. Hare, *Moral Thinking* (Oxford: Clarendon Press, 1981), chap. 2.

tive level and to resolve conflicts among intuitions. We are also able to develop the principles that we teach to others (and ourselves) until they become intuitive.

Hare's two levels of critical thinking bear only a superficial resemblance to the two levels discussed by Schneewind, Brody, and Rawls. For one thing, Hare's acknowledgment of the intuitive level is a grudging one. He grants that it has value, but his heart is with critical thinking. Critical thinking not only corrects intuitive judgments, but ideally it also provides the principles that, through training and education, become intuitive. Intuitive judgments never are used to refute or modify the general principles formulated critically. And these principles are decidedly not viewed as following inductively from the intuitive judgments or as, in analogy with science, organizing and systematizing the intuitive judgments. In the end, Hare's distinction between levels of moral thinking does not break away from the epistemic paradigm we discussed at the beginning of this chapter, a paradigm for which he was largely responsible. He acknowledges that moral thinking does not always follow this paradigm, and often for good reasons, but in difficult situations—or in an ideal world—it should.

In pointing to the deficiencies of the intuitive level, Hare identifies some concerns philosophers are likely to have with the scientific model of moral reasoning.

> The appeal to moral intuitions will never do as a basis for a moral system. It is certainly possible, as some thinkers even of our times have done, to collect all the moral opinions of which they and their contemporaries feel most sure, find some relatively simple method or apparatus which can be represented, with a bit of give and take, and making plausible assumptions about the circumstances of life, as generating all these opinions; and then pronounce that it is the moral system which, having reflected, we must acknowledge to be the correct one. But they have absolutely no authority for this claim beyond the original convictions, for which no ground or argument was given. (The 'equilibrium' they have reached is one between forces which might have been generated by prejudice, and no amount of reflection can make that a solid basis for morality. It would be possible for two mutually inconsistent systems to be defended in this way; all that this would show is that their advocates had grown up in different moral environments.)[22]

22. Ibid., p. 12.

Here Hare is posing the question of the *causation* and *authority* of moral intuitions or specific moral judgments made at the intuitive level. Why, he asks, should we accord them authority? They may be nothing more than the product of prejudice or the result of our upbringing and therefore of social mores. Accordingly, they may vary from person to person and society to society. Even if the intuitive judgments are the product of our previous experience in making decisions, we can question these previous decisions, we can question whether the principles they generated were the right ones, and we can question whether those principles, even if previously valid, apply to our new cases. In all of these cases, "to use intuition itself to answer such questions is a viciously circular procedure; if the dispositions formed by our upbringing are called into question, we cannot appeal to them to settle the question."[23]

It is not our purpose to settle this dispute, but we may be able to clarify it. The scientific model of moral reasoning characterizes moral judgments only from the standpoint of the structure of the process of reasoning and debate within which they occur, not with regard to their origins. Rawls occasionally speaks of our particular judgments as expressing our moral sentiments, but no theoretical weight, I think, attaches to this. Schneewind, Brody, and Rawls place importance on the fact that we initially attach great conviction to these intuitive judgments. This conviction obviously is thought to count for something, epistemically speaking. Starting with the judgments possessing it, they proceed to describe a procedure whereby these judgments enter into an epistemic structure yielding other, general judgments and, *in mediis rebus* as well as in the end, allowing for the correction of some of the initial judgments. It is in terms of the internal mechanics or logic of this epistemic system that philosophically we are to determine epistemic authority. The initial particular judgments have a provisional (Rawls's term) authority, but it is only as a part of the overall process of theory construction and validation that they are to be accorded final, philosophical authority. Because of the initial conviction attaching to particular moral judgments *and* because some of them yield moral principles successful in organizing and explaining the particular judgments (and capable of correcting some of them), we are justified in our reliance on them. Such, these theorists might suggest, is equally the source of the

23. Ibid., p. 40.

authority we give observation statements in science. We have here a coherentist, nonfoundationalist, holistic interpretation of both science and morality.

But is the coherentist story the only one we can tell about observation statements in science? Some philosophers say that we can also give a scientific account of the *origin* of these observation statements which will reinforce our conviction that they tell us something about the world. It will do this by incorporating the truth of the observation statements into the explanation of the statements themselves. We will see in Chapter 4 how it can be argued that a convincing genetic story of this sort cannot be told about our particular moral judgments. Without it, the thinking goes, the scientific model of moral reasoning is essentially incomplete. Without it, for all we know, our particular moral convictions may reflect only prejudice and custom, even if they do have the place and role in a system of moral proportions of the kind discussed by the advocates of the scientific model of moral discourse.

We also can question whether Schneewind, Brody, and Rawls are correct with respect to the degree of conviction they attribute to particular moral judgments. To be sure, some may carry substantial conviction, but many are made with reservations and uncertainty and are subject to considerable doubt. Moral situations, as the realists point out, are frequently complex and puzzling, and to claim certainty, or even great conviction, in the face of the twisted detail of these situations is out of place. Occasionally we may encounter a lie or an act of cruelty that is straightforwardly and obviously wrong, but often questions will arise as to whether the consequences of the lie justify it, or whether what looks to be an act of cruelty is not in fact something else, the act, say, of a stern taskmaster who has at heart the interests of those he commands. Are we not, in fact, more certain of the proposition that generally, or prima facie, it is wrong to lie than we are certain that a particular instance of lying is wrong? It is plausible enough to think that we first are taught, and accept, general moral rules and that acceptance of these rules constitutes the first step in moral thinking and moral development. It is possible, then, that Schneewind et al. have misidentified the moral propositions that initially command the greatest degree of certainty or that come first in the process of moral development. Instead of particular moral judgments, it may be such basic rules or principles as "It is wrong to tell a lie" and "Cruelty is wrong" which carry the most conviction. Such, at any rate, is the position developed later in this study.

Renford Bambrough: A Critique of Deduction

Let us shift ground a bit and consider a different kind of attack on the noncognitivist picture of moral reasoning. This attack results from some basic and subtle philosophical investigations into the nature of justification itself and consequently into the nature of logic and deductive inference. The source I have in mind is Renford Bambrough's *Moral Skepticism and Moral Knowledge*.[24] In this book Bambrough attempts to show that the deductive model of justification is wrong not only for moral discourse but for most other forms of thought and inquiry as well. Even in logic, he thinks, we often misinterpret the significance of deduction.

As Bambrough sees it, the deductive model opens the door to skeptical doubts concerning our ability to know anything. If particular propositions can be known only by deducing them from general propositions or principles along with appropriate minor premises, the proof carries conviction only if we have reason to accept the general propositions. So they in turn must be deduced from still other general propositions, and those from still others. In this process of justification, either we generate an infinite regress in the succeeding steps of the proof or we stop at some general proposition not deduced from anything else. In the latter case, how can we be said to know this proposition? Unless it is self-evident—a most unlikely status, given the history of what has been thought to be self-evident—this end-point proposition stands both without proof and in need of it, in which case we cannot be said to know it. And if we pursue the endless steps of an infinite regress, we never reach a point where we can declare that final and complete proof has been achieved. Hence the deductive procedure in neither case can yield proof and knowledge. If deduction is alleged to be the paradigm of justification, we are in deep trouble.

Bambrough points out an additional problem with the deductive model which arises when we attempt to use it to justify problematic kinds of beliefs such as moral ones. A skeptic wants to know how we can ever prove a moral proposition to be true. If we proceed to offer a proof in the deductive mode, one of our premises inevitably will be a moral one: a particular moral judgment, for instance, is deduced from a moral principle and a statement of fact. But this, the skeptic objects, begs the

24. Renford Bambrough, *Moral Skepticism and Moral Knowledge* (London: Routledge and Kegan Paul, 1979).

question. If we want to know how *moral* claims can be defended, we cannot appeal to moral claims in our alleged proof. Consider, however, what happens if our proof does not introduce moral propositions into the premises. In this case the proof, as a deduction, is invalid. No moral proposition follows deductively from nonmoral propositions. Thus the deductive proof is either circular or invalid. Skepticism seems inevitable. No *ought* can be deduced from an *is*, and to deduce one *ought* from another fails to show how *ought* statements are justified.

Bambrough initiates his attack on the deductive model by attempting to show that skeptical considerations of this sort apply to logic itself as well as to morality and other modes of discourse.[25] To this end he cites a "story" told by John Wisdom in which a child asks her father to provide a justification for the following inference: all men are mortal; Socrates is a man; therefore Socrates is mortal. When the father responds by offering a rule of inference—If all A is B, and X is A, then X is B—the sagacious, if somewhat repellent, child raises an objection. She points out that citing the rule involves the claim either that *every* argument with this form is valid (including the inference at issue about Socrates and mortality) or that every argument with this form *other than* the specific argument in question is valid. In the first case, citing the rule simply begs the question—it amounts to saying that the inference at issue is valid because *it* and all others of the same form are valid. Furthermore, if the rule is to cover all instances of arguments having the form given by the rule, the rule is no more acceptable than the particular inference we are trying to justify—and if this inference needs justification, so too does the rule. In the second case, citing the rule involves an invalid argument: namely, all arguments of this form other than the one at issue are valid, therefore this one is valid. If we do not beg the question in the way described above, the rule can only be said to govern all other arguments of the given form, from which claim it is invalid to deduce that it applies in this instance.

Another way of expressing the child's objections, according to Bambrough, is to point out that if we try to justify a logical inference by appeal to logic—to logical rules—we beg the question, and if we try to justify the inference without begging the question—by appeal to a set of non-normative facts about the form of the argument—we end up with a non sequitur. Our predicament in attempting to justify a logical in-

25. Ibid., chap. 8.

ference is precisely the same as the one we encounter in attempting to justify a moral claim. In both cases, either we deduce the problematic notion from an idea of the same sort—hence begging the question and failing to convince—or we deduce it from a notion of a different sort—hence arguing invalidly and failing to convince. If skepticism is justified for these reasons in morality, it is also justified in the realm of logic.

Skepticism, of course, is not justified in the realm of logic. Any skeptical reasoning designed to cast doubt on logic would have to be logically coherent in order to be convincing. Therefore it would presuppose the validity of the inferences sanctioned by logic. But if the credentials of logic cannot be underwritten by our providing deductive justification for the inferences we take to be valid (as Wisdom's story demonstrates), such justification cannot be seen as a requirement for rational acceptability. The fact, then, that moral inferences and judgments cannot be justified deductively should not be thought, in and of itself, to cast doubt on them.

Bambrough is convinced that Wisdom's story not only shows the bankruptcy of the deductive model but also justifies Wisdom's well-known methodological dictum that at the bar of reason the final appeal is always to cases—that examples are the final food of thought.[26] This advice, he points out, coincides with Mill's claim (violated by Mill himself in *Utilitarianism*) that reasoning is always from particulars to particulars and that rules and principles serve only as memoranda. Bambrough sees this methodology at work in both logic and morality. For instance, we take particular inferences with a specific form to be valid, and we accept a rule of inference embodying this form because it summarizes our initial convictions. The rule "is not the justification of our judgment on the particular instances; on the contrary, the particular instances, the character they display when inspected one by one, are the justification that the rule is sound."[27] Likewise, our acceptance of particular moral judgments is primary, and moral principles are accepted on the basis of particular convictions.

If we are to escape from the mazes and dilemmas of traditional epistemology, whether in its general form or in its specifically moral variant, we must follow the arrow that points upwards to the top of the blackboard

26. John Wisdom, *Paradox and Discovery* (Oxford: Oxford University Press, 1965), p. 102.
27. Bambrough, *Moral Skepticism and Moral Knowledge*, p. 113.

from the particulars to the principles, and not the arrow of deductive logic that points downward from the so-called axioms or principles to the particulars. To escape from the skeptical implications of the standard assumptions about proof and explanation, meaning and justification, we need to recognize that the question 'are all things of this sort good or bad?' cannot be answered by somebody who does not know the answer to any question of the form 'is this thing good or bad?' We must abandon the idea that to justify a moral or any other conclusion about an instance of an action or person or character or motive is to apply to that instance a principle from which, together with a description of the instance, the conclusion about the instance logically follows. If the question 'is this *x* good?' has not been answered, the question 'are all *x*s good?' has not been answered. The mistake that philosophers have made in ethics is the mistake that they have made in all other branches of epistemology: they think that the foundations of our knowledge are to be looked for in the sky and not in the soil.[28]

Bambrough's rejection of the deductive model of justification and his positive theory concerning the role that particular judgments play in the process of justification give us a new way of responding to the skeptical charge that we cannot derive a normative *ought*-claim from a descriptive *is*-claim. In fact we frequently engage in such derivations both in logic and in morality. In justifying a logical inference we have made, we may point to the form of the argument. In doing so we describe the form of this particular argument—not the form of a general class of arguments (including or excluding this one)—and we cite this description as a reason for treating the argument as valid. But this is a case of deriving a normative conclusion (about validity) from a descriptive premise (about the form of the argument). If such a process of justification works in logic, why can it not also work in morality? Surely we have as much right to justify an *ought*-statement by referring to a description of an action as we have to justify a validity claim by reference to a description of the form of an argument. In neither case is our process of justification a deductive one. In neither case does it help to "reconstruct" the justification by putting it into a deductive form with a general logical or moral principle as a first premise; such deductive derivation fails (as we have seen) to improve the credentials of our justification. In both the moral and logical cases, our actual mode of justification involves an appeal to the prop-

28. Ibid., p. 137.

erties of a particular case (of action or argument) from which we immediately derive a normative conclusion. If this process is deemed invalid in the case of morality, it must also be deemed invalid in the case of logic. But what standard of justification could the skeptic use in calling one or both of these processes into question? Certainly not the concept of deductive validity, for we have seen that as a model of justification deduction never works. Is there some other ideal or standard of justification that our inferences from *is* to *ought* fail to meet? The skeptic surely fails to tell us what this standard is.

Bambrough warns against taking his appeal to particular cases as another kind of foundationalism, one in which particular moral judgments are thought to be intuitively or self-evidently true, or incapable of being doubted. Although particular moral judgments are prior to general principles, they can be questioned just as the principles can: "any conclusion . . . can at any stage or at any time be rationally questioned and criticized."[29] At a particular time and in a particular context we accept certain judgments as true, and we use them as a basis for criticizing or defending others. In other contexts, these same convictions might be criticized or defended by appeal to other concrete beliefs we hold fast to on those occasions. All proofs require premises that are accepted,[30] but what is accepted on a particular occasion has no general epistemological priority: "there are no canonical starting points."[31]

What we accept on a given occasion without proof and without the need of proof are those particular judgments commanding our assent. In logic we assess validity and draw up rules for it on the basis of our convictions that certain particular inferences are valid. In morality we engage in an analogous process, going from particular moral judgments to rules or principles. It is simply a fact of human nature, Bambrough claims, that people respond normatively to arguments having certain forms by calling them valid.[32] Likewise, human beings respond to certain natural features of actions, such as the fact that an act is cruel, by judging normatively that actions having these features are wrong and immoral. Human nature being what it is, people *agree* in their "logical" reactions and in their "moral" ones. In Bambrough's eyes, it is these

29. Ibid., p. 143.
30. Ibid., pp. 23–26.
31. Ibid., p. 142.
32. Ibid., pp. 86–88, 146.

shared responses that are at the heart of morality and logic, not general rules and the model of deduction. We cannot prove—deductively—that a particular act of cruelty is wrong, but nothing could be more certain for us. Here we have reached bedrock; we have arrived at a basic conviction that in turn generates our principles and itself has no justification. But nothing is missing; no opening exists for the skeptic. For the very principles of logic themselves are grounded in our basic convictions that particular inferences are valid. If skepticism succeeds in morality, it succeeds in all inquiry whatsoever—including logic—and therefore self-destructs. But if we put aside the deductive model that generates the skeptical doubts, we have no basis for moral or logical skepticism.

Bambrough's argument is deep and provocative. It has a Wittgensteinian air to it; indeed, it seems to move, although on different grounds, toward the popular rule-skepticism interpretation of Wittgenstein which sees him as challenging the role of rules in our thought.[33] Bambrough's position also encapsulates much that remains persuasive in the approaches of G. E. Moore and John Wisdom to other topics. No attempt will be made here fully to assess this argument, but certain reservations do come readily to mind. One can, I think, admit many of the points Bambrough makes and come up with different conclusions. Let me explain.

As we have seen, Bambrough thinks of himself as showing that logical and moral justifications are similar and that both assume the priority of particular judgments over general principles. But admitting that the mode of justification is similar, may we not explain this similarity in a different way? Assume for a moment that, as the traditional view Bambrough criticizes has maintained, we do in fact derive particular judgments from general principles or rules. Must the principles or rules be understood in such a way as to generate the problems Bambrough sees in the deductive method? To begin with, if, as Bambrough argues, something must simply be accepted in any proof, why not principles or rules as well as, or in place of, particular judgments? Why can it not be our response to certain basic principles or rules that is bedrock rather than our response to certain particular states of affairs? If the answer is— as it seems to be for Bambrough—that we cannot be sure of the princi-

33. See Saul Kripke, *Wittgenstein on Rules and Private Language* (Oxford: Basil Blackwell, 1982).

ple or rule until we are sure of its instances, this is to conceive of (and misconceive) the nature of a principle or rule as a generalization. Generalizations, to be sure, rest on their instances. But a principle need not be thought of this way, and certainly a rule is not a generalization. A rule guides our individual actions and our particular judgments; it is neither guided by them nor produced by them. A rule can be compared with a yardstick, which allows us to make measurements of particular objects and to assess measurements that have been made of these objects. But we do not need to measure the yardstick; in fact, it makes no sense to do so, for the yardstick determines or defines what a yard is. Likewise, logical and moral rules, or principles understood as rules, can be thought of as instruments we use to determine what to do in particular circumstances—what conclusions to draw or what actions to engage in. We also use them to check on the validity of inferences or the rightness of actions already performed. We do not need to prove that what the rule tells us is valid or right is actually so, for the rule is definitive; it defines what is valid or right.

According to this way of looking at rules, when we appeal to a rule to justify the claim that a certain act is right, we do not beg the question, for the rule is not a summary statement about all acts that are right, including this one. Nor does the rule cover all other acts except this one, so that its application to this one is invalid. The rule is neither a partial nor a complete generalization. The same can be said, *mutatis mutandis*, for rules of inference. Hence we do not get trapped in the dilemma of Wisdom's story.

Bambrough passes on to us Wittgenstein's advice that the propositions we simply accept and subsequently use as the premises of our arguments are often those we are taught.[34] If this is true, we need to remember that we are often taught basic moral rules or principles. Following this line of thought, we see that it is the moral rules that are basic, not particular moral judgments. When the skeptic asks for a justification of the rules, he fails to understand (a) that it is in principle impossible to prove everything in a proof and that the demand is therefore absurd (Bambrough's point), *and* (b) that rules, having a distinctive role, cannot and need not be justified in the way particular judgments are justified. In fact, if something in a proof must go without proof, and if rules

34. Bambrough, *Moral Skepticism and Moral Knowledge*, p. 137.

are basic, the demand that rules be justified is absurd. Skepticism is thus defused, but deduction from moral rules still has a role to play in moral reasoning.

In defending deduction as a mode of moral reasoning, I do not intend to show that the noncognitivists were right after all in their construal of moral reasoning. To be sure, they were not wrong simply by relying on a deductive model, but it remains possible that they misunderstood the nature of the principles that operate as premises in a moral deduction. My argument is framed in terms of the distinctive nature of a rule, and it is by no means clear that noncognitivists—even prescriptivists—had a clear notion of moral rules. Once we have a better understanding of rules (something I hope to provide in Chapter 6), we may find that the simple, straightforward notion of deduction the noncognitivists used is too simple to fit the facts about moral reasoning.

Bambrough's position has many affinities to that of Rawls, Schneewind, and Brody. All of them place initial emphasis on particular moral judgments and derive moral principles from them. Is this the way moral justification actually proceeds in our moral life, or is the alternative picture just sketched—in which moral principles are bedrock rules from which particular judgments are derived—a more accurate representation? This question can be settled only by attending more closely to the actual operation of moral justification. The new approach to moral reasoning gives us an interesting new possibility, but it cannot at this stage be seen as totally convincing. In Chapter 6, I present a view of the relationship between particular moral judgments and moral principles that improves on both the traditional notion of subsuming particular judgments under general principles and the more recent idea studied here of deriving general principles from particular judgments.

2 / Moral Judgments

THE metaethical discussions of the 1950s and 1960s produced not only a standard view of the structure of moral reasoning but also a paradigm conception of the nature of moral judgments. These judgments were viewed as possessing a distinctive mode of meaning by virtue of which they performed certain dynamic, noncognitive functions and as a result failed to express propositions having a truth value. Just as much recent ethical theorizing has repudiated the noncognitivist model of reasoning, so too has it rejected the noncognitivist account of judgment. It is now widely believed that moral judgments do in fact express propositions having truth values. In this chapter we consider a variety of arguments that have been brought against the older view and that point to the new cognitivist perspective. We begin, however, with a review of the noncognitivist characterization of moral judgments.

Noncognitivist Analysis of Moral Judgments

As noted in the Introduction, ethical theorists responding to G. E. Moore's work found themselves in a difficult position. Many of them accepted Moore's open-question argument and the repudiation of naturalism that went along with it, but they refused to endorse Moore's intuitionism.[1] Given that the description of either intuitions or empiri-

---

1. Moore developed the open-question argument in his *Principia Ethica* (Cambridge: Cambridge University Press, 1902), pp. 15–17. Typical responses to this argument are found in A. J. Ayer, *Language, Truth, and Logic* (New York: Dover, 1946), chap. 6; and in R. M. Hare, *The Language of Morals* (Oxford: Clarendon Press, 1952), pp. 30, 83, and passim, esp. pp. 170–72.

cal observations (of natural facts) seemed to be the only cognitive function moral judgments could have, just what is to be made of them if, as
most philosophers concluded, they are not descriptive of either the one
or the other? It followed for many of these theorists that moral judgments do not have any meaning at all. Lacking descriptive content, such
judgments were thought to lack cognitive sense and hence to be meaningless. This conclusion resulted from strict adherence to one of two
influential conceptions of meaning: the logical positivists' verifiability
criterion or the early Wittgenstein's picture theory.[2]

But moral judgments do not *seem* to be meaningless. They certainly
are not gibberish. Yet how can one attribute meaning to them without
rendering them descriptive and thereby either embracing intuitionism
or committing the Naturalistic Fallacy?

At about the time moral philosophers struggled with this problem, a
number of new theories of meaning were being developed that did not
equate meaningfulness with verifiability or with descriptive picturing.
Bertrand Russell, and later C. K. Ogden and I. A. Richards, proposed a
causal theory according to which meaning was understood in terms of
the capacity of words to cause certain reactions in an agent.[3] Charles
Stevenson, who articulated what is perhaps the most thoughtful and
elaborate theory of emotivism, used a sophisticated form of this causal
theory to show that moral propositions have emotive as well as descriptive meaning.[4] Soon thereafter, the influence of the later Wittgenstein
began to be felt.[5] Wittgenstein urged philosophers to give up the descriptive, representational model as a paradigm for all language, the paradigm he himself had accepted in his earlier work, and he showed how
language has a variety of nondescriptive uses—to tell jokes, to engage in

2. On verifiability, see Ayer, *Language, Truth, and Logic*; on the picture theory of
meaning, see Ludwig Wittgenstein, *Tractatus Logico-Philosophicus*, trans. D. F. Pears and
B. F. McGuinness (London: Routledge and Kegan Paul, 1961).

3. See Bertrand Russell, "On Propositions: What They Are and How They Mean,"
Proceedings of the Aristotelian Society, supp. vol. 2 (1919), and *The Analysis of Mind* (Lon-
don: George Allen and Unwin, 1921), chap. 10; also see C. K. Ogden and I. A.
Richards, *The Meaning of Meaning* (London: Kegan Paul, 1923).

4. Charles L. Stevenson, *Ethics and Language* (New Haven: Yale University Press,
1944).

5. See Ludwig Wittgenstein, *The Blue and Brown Books* (New York: Harper & Row,
1965), and *Philosophical Investigations*, ed. G. E. M. Anscombe and R. Rhees, trans. G. E.
M. Anscombe, 3d ed. (New York: Macmillan, 1969).

play-acting, to express orders, and to engage in such activities as "asking, thanking, cursing, greeting, praying."⁶ Equating meaning with *use*, Wittgenstein compared the words of our language with tools: "Think of the tools in a tool box: there is a hammer, pliers, a saw, a screwdriver, a rule, a glue-pot, glue, nails, and screws. The functions of words are as diverse as the functions of these objects. (And in both cases there are similarities.)"⁷ Following this advice, ethical theorists began to look for nondescriptive uses of moral language, and as soon as they looked in this direction the distinctive nature and meaning of moral discourse seemed to stare them in the face. Moral language obviously has a very close connection with our feelings, emotions, and attitudes and an equally close connection with our actions. Perhaps, as the emotivists claimed, the function of this language is the dynamic one of expressing and/or evoking feelings and attitudes, in which case this function should be incorporated into the very meaning of moral judgments. Prescriptivists soon emerged and maintained that the role or use of moral language is primarily one of guiding choices, of commending objects and actions, and of committing oneself to certain modes of action and life—hence R. M. Hare's view that the very meaning of a moral judgment involves an imperative. For them, "One ought to do *x*" implies "Do *x*," which is an answer to the practical question generating a moral discussion, namely, "What shall I *do*?"⁸

The emphasis on the emotive or prescriptive nature of moral judgments gave the noncognitivists a means of understanding why the open-question argument works. If we describe an object as pleasant or an action as commanded by God, it is still an open question whether the object is *good* or the action one that we *ought* to perform. The reason for this is that the descriptions have only descriptive meaning and serve only to state what is the case. But the evaluations using 'good' and 'ought' are not descriptive, or not primarily so; rather they are emotive or prescriptive and have expressive or commendatory functions. 'Good', let us say, expresses the speaker's approval of whatever he applies it to. Thus to say of something that it produces pleasure is merely to describe it as having this property; but to call it good is to express one's approval of it. The

---

6. Wittgenstein, *Philosophical Investigations*, Part I, § 23.
7. Ibid., I, § 11.
8. See Hare, *Language of Morals*, pp. 1, 29, 46.

two functions are quite different, and hence when it has been said descriptively that an object produces pleasure, it remains an open question whether the speaker wishes to express approval of the object (or the pleasure). Similar considerations show why it is an open question whether actions described as commanded by God are actions a speaker wishes to commend and hence prescribe.

Although maintaining that some form of nondescriptive meaning is primary, most of the noncognitivists granted that value judgments do have some descriptive meaning. The descriptive component might be something as simple and subjective as "I approve of x" (Stevenson's first pattern of analysis) or as elaborate and objective as "X has properties a, b, and c" (Stevenson's second pattern of analysis).[9] Hare argued that to call something good is, in addition to commending it, to say that it has certain properties by virtue of which it is commended.[10] He called these the "good-making characteristics" of the object. Hence for both Stevenson and Hare, to judge an object to be good is to evaluate *and* describe it; evaluative judgments have *both* evaluative and descriptive meaning.

Hare also maintained that the good-making characteristics vary as the class of objects commended varies—what leads us to commend cacti is not what leads us to commend cars or human beings. At the same time, however, the evaluative meaning of 'good' remains constant across these classes: the word always has a commendatory, prescriptive function. Furthermore, what the good-making characteristics of a class of objects are depends on what properties we wish to commend. In this way, the constant evaluative meaning of 'good' is construed as having primacy over its variable descriptive meaning, just as for Stevenson the properties we describe a good object as having are those toward which we express our approval. Whatever features an object or action possesses, we will not call the object good or the action right unless we approve of its features or wish to commend them. The descriptive meaning of the normative term is therefore contingent on its emotive or prescriptive meaning. Moreover, the descriptive content is relative to the specific group of language users employing the term, depending as it does on what characteristics they approve of or commend. Given this dependency, the descriptive component or meaning of a value judgment may be quite vari-

9. Stevenson, *Ethics and Language*, pp. 81–110 and 206–26.
10. Hare, *Language of Morals*, chaps. 6 and 7.

able across groups, even for a given class of objects or actions. If different individuals wish to commend different features of automobiles or human beings, the descriptive meanings of their uses of 'good auto' or 'good human being' will be different.

Hare argued that any person who calls an object good is under a logical obligation to furnish a reason for doing so. This reason will consist in the fact that the object has a certain property or set of properties. Moreover, saying that the object is good for this reason commits one to saying that any other object of the same class that is just like it in this respect will also be good. This being so, every particular judgment that commends an object for having a certain property implies a universal proposition to the effect that all objects (of the same class) having this property are good. This universal proposition is a standard that itself commends a subset of the general class of objects: the subset whose members possess the property or properties in question. A particular value judgment, then, implies a universal standard. This standard identifies the good-making properties of the general class of objects. Moreover, these properties become the descriptive meaning of the term 'good' as it applies to instances of this class. The standard essentially defines the descriptive meaning of the value term with regard to this class of objects. Because the descriptive meaning is defined by a commendatory, prescriptive standard, the descriptive meaning of the term is dependent on its evaluative meaning. The standard tells us in effect to describe as good those objects we would commend or choose.

Most of the noncognitivists were basically empiricists, and they saw their new notion of evaluative meaning as perpetuating and illuminating an empiricist thesis propounded by Hume: reason is but the slave of the passions.[11] This notion could equally be used to express the Aristotelian notion that theoretical reason alone *moves* nothing.[12] These traditional convictions could now be cast in more acceptable linguistic dress: descriptive statements that can be known by observation or "reason" to be true or false do not logically entail any expression of emotion or any prescription to act in a certain way, or any other judgment with a conceptual/logical relation to our affective, conative, and practical nature. Moral judgments, on the contrary, do entail expressions of emotion or

11. See David Hume, *An Inquiry Concerning the Principles of Morals*, Appendix I.
12. See Aristotle, *Nicomachean Ethics*, 1139a36.

prescriptions to act. These emotions and the commitments and decisions reflected in prescriptions are the sorts of thing that move us to act. It follows that moral judgments by their very function and meaning have an essential connection to action which is not shared by descriptive judgments. Descriptions and the thoughts they express may provide us the psychological basis for our emotional responses or decisions and commitments, but the descriptions cannot themselves express these emotions and decisions. Hence descriptions, the product of "reason," move nothing; they function merely to serve the "passions," which alone move us to act.

The essential or logical connection between evaluation and action was given clear expression by Hare when he reflected on the functional role of evaluations. "One ought to do x" and "X is good," he claimed, are answers to the practical questions "What shall I do?" and "What shall I choose?"[13] Such evaluative judgments are *proper and complete answers* to these questions because they entail the imperatives "Do x" and "Choose y." Anything other than such an imperative—a description, for instance, to the effect that action x will produce such and such consequences— does not tell one what to do. It may describe a possible action, one of the available options, but no matter how extensive the description, it is nothing *but* a description of the action and its consequences. It does not amount to saying: take this action. Consequently it is not an answer to the practical question "What shall I do?" The prescriptive evaluation, entailing as it does an imperative, does provide an answer. Thus descriptions by their very linguistic nature are incapable of performing the practical role of evaluative judgments.

It is easy to see how the noncognitivists' analysis of the nature of moral judgments joins hands with their analysis of moral reasoning as discussed in the last chapter. The separability of descriptive and evaluative meaning and the dependence of the former on the latter are given succinct expression in the claim that particular moral judgments imply universal standards or principles that commend classes of objects or actions and define their good-making or right-making properties. The particular judgments can then be seen as following deductively from the universal standards or principles implied by them (in conjunction with appropriate factual premises). The principles/standards themselves may

13. Hare, *Language of Morals*, pp. 29, 46.

imply more general ones, and this series of implications continues until we reach a set of ultimate principles or standards. The latter are expressed in judgments that are prescriptive or emotive and hence incapable of having truth values. There being nothing one can appeal to in order to justify or criticize these ultimate commitments, disagreement at this level becomes rationally irresolvable.

Because of the harmonious fit between its picture of moral reasoning and its picture of moral judgments, the noncognitivist theory as a whole possessed enormous appeal. We have seen, nevertheless, that its characterization of moral reasoning has come to be challenged; now we must examine the reasons many philosophers have given for repudiating its conception of moral judgments. In doing so we concentrate on two elements of this conception: (1) its identification of the meanings of moral terms and judgments with their expressive and practical functions; and (2) its distinction between descriptive and evaluative meaning and its interpretation of the former as dependent on the latter, thereby allowing for widespread, cognitively irresolvable moral disputes.[14]

Classic Responses

Several factors have contributed to the declining fortunes of the noncognitivist analysis of moral judgments, among them (a) closer attention to the details of moral discourse and the parallels it exhibits with factual discourse, (b) a perception of a limit to which speech-act and meaning-as-use characterizations of language can be carried, and (c) the influence of Fregean and truth-conditional semantics. These factors are not mutually exclusive, and considerations regarding one are often mixed with reflections on the others. In what follows, I survey some of the more influential arguments that have been directed against the noncognitivist

14. An additional reason for abandoning the noncognitivists' conception of moral judgments results from the work philosophers have done on the concepts of such psychological states as desires and attitudes. They have demonstrated that these states frequently are not the free-floating, noncognitive eruptions the noncognitivists often took them to be, but rather are reflective responses amenable to rational discussion and assessment. The work of Thomas Nagel has been particularly influential in this area—see his *The Possibility of Altruism* (Oxford: Oxford University Press, 1970). Also see John Finnis, *Fundamentals of Ethics* (Oxford: Oxford University Press, 1983), chap. 2; and Mark Platts, "Moral Reality and the End of Desire," in Mark Platts, ed., *Reference, Truth, and Reality* (London: Routledge and Kegan Paul, 1980).

picture. The result is a collage of views, some of which, as we shall see, are subject to grave reservations. But the collage as a whole expresses an intellectual atmosphere in which cognitivism reasserts itself vigorously.

We should begin by taking note of Philippa Foot's well-known objection to the noncognitivist picture—specifically, to its portrayal of the relationship between the descriptive and evaluative components of a moral judgment.[15] As we have seen, noncognitivists regarded a moral judgment's descriptive meaning as being secondary to and dependent on its evaluative (emotive or prescriptive) meaning. According to Foot, such a theory implies that a person could accept a standard of goodness which incorporated *any* descriptive properties whatsoever, no matter how odd they are or how irrelevant we normally would think them to be to the goodness of the type of thing at issue. A person could do this, the theory suggests to her, simply by commending those properties. "On this hypothesis a moral eccentric could be described as commending the clasping of hands as the action of a good man, and we should not have to look for some background to give the supposition sense. That is to say, on this hypothesis the clasping of hands could be commended without any explanation; it could be what those who hold such theories call 'an ultimate moral principle.'"[16] This strikes Foot as absurd. There must be, she thinks, some constraint on what the object of moral approval can be, that is, on what the good-making properties can be. The relationship between these properties and moral approval cannot merely be "external" in such a fashion that the approval could attach itself to any object and need not do so to any particular one. Rather, the relation must be "internal": the attitude and a certain set of properties must be necessarily connected. If this is so, it follows that we can understand the attitude of moral approval and the evaluative meaning of a moral term only by grasping the appropriate object of this attitude. For example, one cannot feel *pride* in just anything, because the feeling of pride is internally related to a certain kind of object or class of properties—namely, those characteristics of a person that constitute an achievement or advantage. Likewise, Foot argues, one can morally approve of a person and evaluate her as morally good only if this person acts in a way that bears intelligi-

15. See Philippa Foot, "Moral Arguments," *Mind*, 67 (1958); and "Moral Beliefs," *Proceedings of the Aristotelian Society*, 59 (1958–59); both are reprinted in her *Virtues and Vices* (Berkeley: University of California Press, 1978); all citations are to the reprints.
16. Foot, "Moral Beliefs," p. 112.

bly upon human well-being. Without an elaborate explanation linking the clasping of hands three times an hour with the avoidance of harm or the promotion of well-being, one cannot convert this feature into a good-making characteristic. One certainly cannot do so simply by approving of it or commending it. In Foot's view, the features a good person must possess are built into the very concept of a good person. It is the logical or conceptual relation between the attitude and its object that makes the connection between the two an internal one. And it is this internal relation that prevents us from playing fast and loose with moral terms in the manner of the noncognitivist. The descriptive content of 'good person' is to a large extent fixed and hence not dependent on the variable feelings and whims of individual evaluators or groups. It follows that whether someone is a good person is an objective matter of fact—a matter of whether he or she has the properties built into the very meaning of 'good person'.

Foot's position, often referred to as *neo-naturalism*, is rendered appealing by her attention to a number of specific moral or evaluative concepts—for instance, rudeness. 'Rude', she points out, is certainly an evaluative word; its use involves the expression of both attitudes and imperatives. But its "evaluative meaning" is not something that can associate itself with just any rude-making properties: "It is obvious that there is something else to be said about the word 'rude' beside the fact that it expresses, fairly mild, condemnation: it can only be used where certain descriptions apply. The right account of the situation in which it is correct to say that a piece of behavior is rude, is, I think, that this kind of behavior causes offense by indicating lack of respect."[17] Whether or not an act is rude is a matter of whether it causes this kind of offense. If it does, there can be no question but that it is rude—there is no further question of whether or not the person observing or talking about the act approves of it. For a person to admit that the descriptive meaning of rude is satisfied by an act but still to deny that the act is rude is to reveal a failure on his part to understand the concept of rudeness. Hence the descriptive content of "*x* is rude" and the attitudes expressed by this judgment do not divide into two separate conditions that could be met independently. Even less is it the case that the descriptive content is determined by the attitudes or decisions of the speaker. The total (eval-

17. Foot, "Moral Arguments," p. 102.

uative and descriptive) meaning of 'rude' is fixed, and it is public. If one uses the concept of rudeness at all, it is incumbent on one to admit that whether certain acts are rude is an objective matter of fact and at the same time a fact to which we normally express adverse attitudes.

By concentrating on such specific concepts as rudeness—the kind most often involved in actual moral judgments—rather than attending exclusively to the more abstract moral terms like 'good' and 'ought', we will be able to see, Foot maintains, that moral language is far more descriptive than we were led earlier to believe. This thesis has been adopted recently by a group of thinkers who call themselves *moral realists*. John McDowell, for instance, asks us to think of judgments of kindness, and Mark Platts recommends that we examine terms such as 'sincere', 'loyal', and 'compassionate'.[18] These realists give to moral judgments a descriptive meaning that is not a naturalistic one, but they agree with Foot in seeing these judgments as being both objectively descriptive and evaluative.

Two other well-known arguments also attempt to show that moral language is fundamentally descriptive and fact-stating. The first is John Searle's famous (infamous) derivation of *ought* from *is*. The second is Peter Geach's influential distinction between attributive and predicative uses of adjectives like 'good'. Space permits only a brief look at each of these classic philosophical maneuvers.

In discussing rudeness, Foot casts her remarks in terms of the old question of whether one can derive an evaluative judgment (about rudeness) from a factual judgment (about the descriptive conditions of rudeness). Her answer is that the conceptual grammar of 'rude' not only permits but requires this inference. Likewise, Searle argues that from the patently descriptive claim "Jones uttered the words 'I hereby promise to pay you, Smith, five dollars'" we are able to derive the judgment "Jones ought to pay Smith five dollars."[19] Once all the intermediate steps and their conditions are filled in—none of which, Searle claims, involves evaluative statements or moral principles—the *is*-statement can be seen to entail the *ought*-statement.

Searle's alleged derivation of *ought* from *is* has been the subject of

18. See John McDowell, "Virtue and Reason," *The Monist*, 62 (July 1979); and Mark Platts, *Ways of Meaning* (London: Routledge and Kegan Paul, 1979), p. 246.
19. John Searle, "How to Derive 'Ought' from 'Is'," *Philosophical Review* (1964), 43–58.

great controversy, and a large volume of literature has been devoted to it. It would be of little value for us to go into this controversy, for the issue can be decided only after a careful examination of each step of the proof and of the various critical responses to it.[20] For our purposes, it is enough to note that Searle's argument introduced into recent moral theory the idea of an institutional fact.[21] That Jones promised to pay Smith five dollars is an institutional fact, one constituted by the rules of the institution of promising. These rules likewise permit the derivation of the institutional fact that Jones ought to pay Smith five dollars. Institutional facts are no less facts for being institutional. There are truth conditions for statements made about them, and whether or not these truth conditions hold is a public, objective matter. Some people may not participate in the institution of promising, just as some may not use the concept of rudeness, but those who do are constrained to admit the legitimacy of inferences from factual statements (to the effect that promises have been made) to normative statements of obligation (with respect to the fulfillment of these promises). There is more in the world than brute facts about nature; there are social facts as well, including ones about moral obligation. As language is employed within social institutions, many concepts like promising are both normative and descriptive.

Next we need to see how the noncognitivists' sharp distinction between descriptive and evaluative meaning can be challenged by reference to Peter Geach's distinction between attributive and predicative uses of adjectives.[22] Consider the following: (a) George is a yellow cat; (b) George is a large flea. In the case of (a) we can deduce that George is yellow and that he is a cat. Here the adjective 'yellow' is being used predicatively. In the case of (b), we cannot infer that George is large and that George is a flea, since George, although a large flea, is not large at all but rather small, as all fleas are. In this case 'large' is being used attributively. When an adjective is used attributively we must look

20. For a collection of essays dealing with Searle's argument, see W. D. Hudson, ed., *The Is/Ought Question* (London: Macmillan/St. Martin's Press, 1969), pp. 135–72. Also see J. R. Searle, "Reply to 'The Promising Game,'" in K. Pahel and M. Schiller, eds., *Readings in Contemporary Ethical Theory* (Englewood Cliffs, N.J.: Prentice-Hall, 1970), pp. 180–82.
21. Searle, "How to Derive 'Ought' from 'Is'," pp. 55–58.
22. Peter Geach, "Good and Evil," *Analysis*, 17 (1956), 33–42.

for the meaning of the entire phrase of which it is a part; we cannot grasp the meaning of the phrase by joining together the separate meanings of the constituent terms, as is the case with adjectives used predicatively. Comprehending 'large flea', for instance, requires mastering the meaning of this complete phrase and is not accomplished by understanding the meaning of 'large', understanding the meaning of 'flea', and then conjoining these meanings.

How are we to characterize "George is a good man"? Is 'good' being used attributively or predicatively in this judgment? Considerations such as the following lead Geach to conclude that the use of 'good', and that of its opposite, 'bad', is attributive. We say, for instance, that someone is a good burglar, but we surely do not mean that this person is a burglar and is good. And when we speak of bad money, we cannot infer that it is money and is bad—bad money is not money at all. Finally, knowing that someone is a good man is not something we could accomplish by pooling the separate bits of information that (a) he is a man and (b) he is good. We could not know that he was good independently of knowing that he was a man.

The implication of Geach's argument is that the sense of 'a good x' must be grasped as a whole. There is no independent evaluative meaning of 'good'—such as commendatory force—that could be grasped apart from knowing what x is. To think there is such a meaning is to treat 'good' as predicative rather than attributive. To be sure, 'good' is not systematically ambiguous in such a manner as to ensure that 'a good man', 'a good knife', and 'a good serve' have nothing in common. But what they have in common need not be an identical and independent evaluative meaning. According to Geach, 'good' could have a common abstract descriptive meaning, but one that gets fleshed out only in relation to the particular kind of thing that is called 'good'. It could be a common function, like the squaring function, that gets its concrete meaning only in relation to its specific values.

If 'good' is used attributively, the noncognitivist bifurcation of evaluative and descriptive meaning is a false one. We do not first learn to use the word 'good' to commend things (in general) and then proceed to apply it to particular things whose properties we have decided to commend. Consequently, we do not have to worry about the skeptical possibility that different people, all equally masters of the evaluative meaning of 'good', will decide to commend different properties as the good-making characteristics of a certain class of object. We do not have to worry that agreement cannot be reached on the good-making properties of good persons because the evaluators have different attitudes or make different decisions of principle. The meaning of 'good person' is fixed *as a whole*. To master it is to learn what everyone else using the language calls a good person. Having mastered it, we are constrained to admit that those individuals satisfying the semantic conditions of 'good person' are in fact good. We do not have the liberty, as the noncognitivists thought, of admitting that these conditions hold but refusing to apply the words because we do not commend the person or her properties. The commendation is not a separate and independent aspect of the meaning of 'good person' such that it could fail to be satisfied even though the descriptive component is satisfied.

The attempt to give the word 'good' an evaluative meaning along the lines of commendatory force has been subjected to still other criticisms. Some philosophers began in the mid-1960s to question the "meaning as use" perspective and to reject extreme speech-act or use-analyses of words like 'good', analyses that equate the meaning of this term with its nondescriptive uses. A leader in this effort was once again Peter Geach, whose essay "Assertion" contains a classic criticism of such speech-act analyses.[23] In this essay Geach identified what he called the *Frege point*, which is: "A thought may have just the same content whether you assent to its truth or not; a proposition may occur in discourse now asserted, now unasserted, and yet be recognizably the same proposition."[24] Geach shows how many philosophical analyses associated with the meaning-as-use approach to philosophy miss the Frege point and consequently, in his opinion, go astray. With regard to ethics, the theory he opposes is the one maintaining that "To call a kind of act bad is not to characterize or describe that kind of act but to condemn it."[25] Against this, he notes that we use 'bad' not just in simple declarative sentences such as 'stealing is bad', but also in complex sentences such as hypotheticals—we may say, for instance, "If stealing is bad, it ought to be punished," or "If doing a thing is bad, getting your little brother to

23. Peter Geach, "Assertion," *Philosophical Review,* 74 (1965); reprinted in his *Logic Matters* (Berkeley: University of California Press, 1972), pp. 254–69; all references are to the reprint.
24. Ibid., pp. 254–55.
25. Ibid., p. 267.

do it is bad." In the antecedents of these hypothetical propositions, 'bad' is not being used by the speaker to condemn anything. As Geach points out with regard to his second example, "one could hardly take the speaker to be condemning just *doing* a thing."[26]

And yet—here is the Frege point—the word 'bad' must have the same content or meaning in the hypothetical proposition as in the simple one. As a proof of this, Geach points to the fact that we can and often do construct arguments like the following, arguments in which a word like 'bad' occurs both in a simple declarative sentence and in a hypothetical context:

> If doing a thing is bad, getting your little brother to do it is bad.
> Tormenting the cat is bad.
> Ergo, getting your little brother to torment the cat is bad.

If the word 'bad' had different meanings in the first and second premises, the argument would be guilty of the fallacy of equivocation. Conversely, the fact that the argument obviously is valid proves that 'bad' does not have different meanings in the two premises. But in the major premise it cannot have a condemnatory meaning, because it is not being used to condemn anything. Hence it does not have such a meaning in the minor premise either. On the contrary, in both premises its meaning is its contribution to the content of the propositions in which it is involved. Although Geach does not put it this way, more recent analysts honoring the Frege point have claimed that its meaning is its contribution to the truth conditions of the propositions in which it figures.

Geach concludes his argument by granting that when we assert a proposition containing 'bad' or 'good' we may be said to engage in some evaluational speech act of condemnation or praise. This concession, however, does not entail that in asserting that something is bad or good we fail to make a true-or-false statement: "Of course an *asserted* proposition in which 'bad' is predicated may be *called* an act of condemnation. But this is of no philosophical interest, for there being an act of condemnation is nothing that can be put forward as an *alternative* to being a proposition."[27] The nondescriptive functions that use analysts and speech-act analysts often claim for words like 'good' are really *uses of*

26. Ibid., p. 269.
27. Ibid.

propositions. And because what it used is a proposition, it can be true or false. A moral proposition may be used to condemn or commend, but this in no way threatens its fact-stating role or, therefore, its cognitivity and objectivity.

John Searle is one of the philosophers who has accepted the Frege point, and he uses it to define what he calls the Speech Act Fallacy.[28] Searle grants, as Geach did, that sentences in which 'good' occurs may be used to commend. He thinks, however, that philosophers have drawn the wrong conclusion from this fact. "*Calling* something good is characteristically praising or commending or recommending it, etc. But it is a fallacy to infer from this that the meaning of 'good' is explained by saying that it is used to perform the act of commendation."[29] It is this faulty inference that Searle calls the Speech Act Fallacy.

Searle's identification and criticism of the Speech Act Fallacy is but one application of his general theory of language. This theory provides a basic explanation of how language can be both evaluative and descriptive and at the same time shows how the evaluative status of a judgment need not threaten its cognitivity and objectivity. Moreover, it reflects the type of approach to language found in many followers of Frege as well as in the influential work of J. L. Austin.[30] And it is close in perspective to the truth-conditional semantics currently so popular.[31] It will be helpful to review Searle's general theory, for it or something like it informs many recent cognitivist views. This review also will provide us an opportunity to take note of one way in which it can be challenged and hence to warn against too ready acceptance of this particular kind of cognitivist turn.

The broad outlines of Searle's theory, at least those pertinent to his conception of evaluative language, are as follows. The basic unit of analysis for the investigation of language is the speech act, the utterance of a sentence as an act incorporating subsidiary acts of referring and predicating and additionally having a certain point.[32] Thus if one says, "Sam smokes habitually," one is (a) performing an act of uttering words, (b)

---

28. Searle, *Speech Acts* (Cambridge: Cambridge University Press, 1969), pp. 136–41.
29. Ibid., p. 137.
30. See J. L. Austin, *How To Do Things with Words* (Oxford: Oxford University Press, 1962).
31. For a systematic introduction to truth-conditional semantics, see Platts, *Ways of Meaning*, chap. 1.
32. Searle, *Speech Acts*, chaps. 1 and 2.

performing propositional acts of referring to Sam and predicating 'smokes habitually' of him, and (c) performing an illocutionary act of stating, which is the point of the utterance. If instead one says, "Does Sam smoke habitually?" one would once again perform an utterance act (using some of the same words), the same propositional acts, and the different illocutionary act of asking. Likewise, "Sam, smoke habitually!" involves a similar utterance act, the same propositional acts, and the different illocutionary act of commanding.

It is important to note that in the above examples the propositional acts of referring and predicating are the same in spite of the fact that the illocutionary acts are not. The propositional acts of referring to Sam and predicating habitual smoking of him provide all three illocutionary acts with the same propositional content. Consequently, according to Searle, all these examples express the same proposition. The different illocutionary acts are three different ways of expressing this proposition—by asserting that it is true, by asking if it is true, and by commanding that it be true. In fact, the speech act of predication, as analyzed by Searle, is the act of "raising the question of the truth" of the predicate term with respect to the entity singled out by the referring term.[33] Predication and truth are essentially connected, for "to know the meaning of a general term (the predicate) is to know under what conditions it is true or false of a given object."[34] The illocutionary acts are, accordingly, different ways of answering the question posed by the predication act, different ways of relating the predicate to the referent. Assertion amounts to claiming that the predicate does apply to it, interrogation asks whether it applies, and commanding demands that it apply. But common to all these acts is their propositional content—reference to an object and predication of a term with regard to this object. Hence "*a proposition is to be sharply distinguished from an assertion or statement of it.*"[35]

Applying this mode of analysis once again to evaluative utterances such as "John is a good person," it is easy to see why Searle thinks the noncognitivists have misunderstood them. Insofar as "John is a good person" involves the propositional acts of reference and predication, it expresses a proposition. And surely in uttering this sentence we are re-

33. Ibid., p. 122.
34. Ibid., p. 125.
35. Ibid., p. 29.

ferring to John and predicating 'is a good person' of him. We are also, of course, praising him. Given Searle's conception of the notion of predication, we are raising the question of the truth or applicability of 'is a good person' with respect to John, and we are praising him for its being a fact that he is a good person. Praising is what we do with respect to the utterance's content, which is determined by what object is referred to and what term is predicated of it.

What, for Searle, is the meaning of the predicate 'good'? Searle suggests that the term really has a family of meanings, among which we find "meets the criteria or standards of assessment or evaluation," "satisfies certain interest or needs," and "fulfills certain purposes."[36] In uttering "John is a good person" we may mean one or another of these, but in any event we are propositionally raising the question of whether this predicate applies to John, and we are illocutionarily praising John by saying that it does.

Wittgenstein on Frege

Theories of language distinguishing the propositional content of an utterance from its illocutionary force are, as noted above, common today. Dummett has suggested that this type of distinction—which he refers to as the distinction between sense and force—is basic to any general theory of language.[37] In spite of its popularity, however, such an approach is open to question, and we pause at this point to consider some criticisms of it.[38] One of the philosophers who does not accept the sense/force distinction is Wittgenstein. In fact, Wittgenstein levels an attack against it which has considerable power and which has not been adequately rebutted by sense/force theorists. He writes in the *Philosophical Investigations*:

> Frege's idea that every assertion contains an assumption, which is the thing that is asserted, really rests on the possibility found in our language of writing every statement in the form: "It is asserted that such and such is

36. Ibid., p. 152.
37. Michael Dummett, *Truth and Other Enigmas* (Cambridge: Harvard University Press, 1978), p. 450.
38. The most sustained criticism of the sense/force distinction is found in G. P. Baker and P. M. S. Hacker, *Language, Sense, and Nonsense* (Oxford: Basil Blackwell, 1984), chaps. 2 and 3.

the case."—But "that such and such is the case" is *not* a sentence in our language—so far it is not a *move* in the language-game. And if I write, not "It is asserted that. . . . ", but "It is asserted: such and such is the case," the words "It is asserted" simply become superfluous.

We might very well also write every statement in the form of a question followed by a "Yes"; for instance: "Is it raining? Yes!" Would this show that every statement contained a question?[39]

Three important questions are being raised here. First, is the component that supposedly serves as the propositional content really capable of being the carrier of truth values? In Wittgenstein's discussion, "that such and such is the case" (e.g., that the cat is on the mat) is taken to express the propositional content. But as he points out, a clause like "that the cat is on the mat" is not a complete, meaningful sentence in English, not a move in a language-game. Hence it cannot be used to say something that is true or false, for certainly our truth claims are moves in a language-game. Philosophers using something like a sense/force distinction often specify the sense of an utterance by means of a verbal noun like 'the door being open'—it is this, they say, that is common to the different illocutionary acts of stating that the door is open, commanding that it be open, and asking if it is open. Given this analysis, Wittgenstein's point can be expressed by noting that "the door being open" *says* nothing, and hence nothing that is true or false. A component of an utterance, Wittgenstein suggests, is not what is true or false; rather it is what one says by means of the utterance as a whole which is true or false.

A second question concerns whether it is necessary to add an assertion marker, or some illocutionary force, to a sentence in order to turn it into an assertion. If, in "It is asserted: such and such is the case," the clause "it is asserted" is superfluous, one is already asserting something when one says "such and such is the case." Saying "the door is open" is already to make an assertion, which means that one makes an assertion simply by using the subject term to refer to the door and using the predicate term 'is open' to say something of it. In other words, Searle's acts of reference and predication add up to an assertion. There is no need for another component, an illocutionary force, to be added to the acts of reference and predication in order to generate an assertion.

These reflections raise doubts in particular about Searle's notion of an

---

39. Wittgenstein, *Philosophical Investigations*, I, § 22.

act of predication. It will be recalled that he interprets this act as "raising the question" of the truth of the predicate with respect to the referent. Predicating 'is open' of the door is not raising a question, however, but rather asserting that the door *is* open. Searle's act of predication is already a complete speech act, not a part of one of the components of a speech act. Furthermore, he has mischaracterized it—it is the speech act of assertion, not "raising the question." If one wanted to raise the question of the truth of 'is open' with respect to the door, one would *ask* "Is the door open?" Once again, however, this "raising of the question" would not be a *part* of a speech act; it would be the complete speech act of asking.

Putting these two points together, we see that the attempt to isolate a component of every speech act that could carry a truth value is confronted with some difficulties. The propositional content often put forward as fulfilling this role seems incapable of doing so. Furthermore, the carrier of truth values seems to be the conjoined acts of referring and predicating, but they add up to the act of assertion. Only assertions have truth values. Unless it can be shown that value judgments are assertions, it cannot be demonstrated that they have truth values. The attempt to find a component within them which is neutral with respect to illocutionary force and which could provide them with truth values even if they are not assertions is highly problematic.

The third question Wittgenstein raises points to the grammatical basis of the sense/force analysis of utterances and warns against inferring anything significant from it. Why not analyze an assertion, he asks, as a conjunction of a question and an affirmative illocutionary force? We could come up with a grammatically acceptable paraphrase of this sort for every assertion. But what would that prove? Surely it would show only that there are various ways, all grammatically acceptable, of saying the same thing. We can say that it is raining by writing, "I assert that: it is raining" or "Is it raining? Yes!" But if both of these ways are grammatically acceptable, neither of them should be taken as providing an analysis of what is really going on in the utterance. We cannot read the real nature of an assertion from its grammatical features, for they are variable and conventional.

I would like to raise one other issue concerning theories distinguishing between the sense and force of utterances. Even though they allow moral judgments to be both descriptive and evaluative, they bifurcate the two dimensions of meaning in a way that may unwittingly promote a noncognitivist construal of the relationship between them. If the sense of an utterance is a proposition, and the meanings of its components are given in terms of the contributions they make to the truth conditions of the proposition, the propositional or descriptive meaning of the utterance is distinct from any illocutionary forces it may have. And indeed we have seen how sense/force theorists claim that one and the same proposition could be uttered with a variety of different illocutionary forces. It must be possible, therefore, for us to comprehend the descriptive content or meaning of a moral judgment, or a moral term, independently of our grasping the evaluational force that attaches to the judgment, or the term, on a given occasion of its use. It would seem, then, to be a contingent matter whether or not one decides to attach an illocutionary force of an evaluative nature to the descriptive content. And this means that we could refuse to assert the moral proposition even though we are prepared to affirm the descriptive content in a purely locutionary speech act. We would not assert the evaluative moral proposition unless we were prepared to engage in the illocutionary act of praise or commendation. This generates the sharp separation of descriptive and evaluative meaning the noncognitivists exploited, and it makes the affirmation of a moral judgment dependent on whether one is willing to engage in a certain illocutionary act that is independent of the locutionary acts of referring and describing. It is noteworthy that Hare's distinction between the phrastic and the neustic of an utterance is just another variation of the sense/force distinction, the phrastic being the content of an utterance and the neustic the way in which this content is "affirmed."[40] Hare's separation of descriptive and evaluative meaning goes hand in hand with his use of a sense/force mode of analysis. If such a separation is to be avoided, as the arguments by Geach (regarding attributive adjectives), Searle (regarding concepts such as promising), and Foot suggest, we should be wary of any theory advocating a distinction of sense and force.

Furthermore, we should be wary of the claim that there *is* a Speech Act Fallacy. Concepts as well as utterances seem to have both evaluative and descriptive meaning. To my mind, the idea that there are concepts used to designate elements of institutional facts, and that these concepts

---

40. See Hare, *Language of Morals*, chap. 2.

necessarily have both descriptive content and evaluative import, is an important one. Likewise, I am persuaded by Foot that concepts like *rude* and *pride* are essentially both descriptive and evaluative and that there is an internal connection between their two dimensions. And I take it that Geach's notion of attributive adjectives shows that there are phrases whose descriptive and evaluative meanings cannot be separated. None of these ideas requires a sense/force distinction; indeed, as just noted, they seem incompatible with such a distinction. This suggests that we can best understand terms like 'rude' and 'pride', and phrases like 'a good person', not by separating sense and force but by insisting that the terms "sense" and "force," as well as the categories "descriptive" and "evaluative," do not designate mutually exclusive linguistic elements or kinds of utterance. The descriptive/evaluative distinction is a philosopher's invention, not a fact about our actual use of language.

Descriptions, Wittgenstein reminds us, come in many different forms, with many different functions.[41] One of the functions of a description, I suggest, can be to convey morally significant information about a person or an action. An utterance can be used to describe the moral features of a person or action, features that essentially require praise, commendation, disapproval, or disgust. Likewise, some terms are such that we learn to use them to pick out the features of objects, persons, or actions which are to be condemned, applauded, or otherwise evaluated. Insofar as they do pick out these features, they are descriptive; insofar as the features picked out essentially have evaluational import, the terms are also evaluative. Furthermore, there is no reason to believe that the descriptive import of these terms could be identified other than by using the terms themselves or their evaluative synonyms. McDowell has asked whether we have access to the dimensions descriptively picked out by the use of a term like 'courage' other than through the use of this very term.[42] Can we identify the factual dimensions of courage by using words with no evaluative import? There is, McDowell thinks, no reason to believe we can.

To grant that some terms and judgments have both evaluative and descriptive meaning and that these dimensions are inseparable need not

41. Wittgenstein, *Philosophical Investigations*, I, § 24.
42. McDowell, "Non-cognitivism and Rule-Following," in S. Holtzman and C. Leich, eds., *Wittgenstein: To Follow a Rule* (London: Routledge and Kegan Paul, 1981), pp. 144–45.

run afoul of Geach's argument in "Assertion." He points to complex sentences in which an evaluative sentence occurs as one of its parts, and he argues that in this context the component sentence could not be used to command, praise, and so on. For example: "If stealing is wrong, it ought to be punished." Here 'stealing is wrong' is not used to command or to engage in any type of evaluational act, and hence its meaning, Geach concludes, cannot be characterized in terms of such an evaluational act. In response, we might note that, although it is true that in this context the clause is not being used to condemn or command, it can be understood in relation to such an act. We might paraphrase the antecedent in the following way: "If stealing is x, y, and z, and hence something to be condemned, then. . . ." This paraphrase characterizes the word 'wrong' as having descriptive meaning (x, y, and z) and a resultant evaluative one (something to be condemned). In a declarative sentence—for example, "Stealing is wrong"—the word 'wrong' can be taken to have the same descriptive meaning and the same evaluative meaning, and hence the sentence as a whole can be taken to mean "Stealing is x, y, and z, and hence something to be condemned." It follows that an argument in which the declarative sentence and the hypothetical sentence occur together can be, as Geach demands, a valid argument, no fallacy of equivocation being committed.

Characterizing the meaning of 'wrong' as 'x, y, and z, and hence something to be condemned' exhibits the close connection between the descriptive and the evaluative dimensions of the term. Depending on how one understands the 'hence', it is possible to see the two dimensions as fused. The moral realists we study in Chapter 4 take the 'hence' to designate a noncontingent, albeit nonentailing, relation of supervenience, and this notion can be used to generate a particular understanding of how the descriptive and the evaluative dimensions of moral discourse are essentially and inextricably connected. In Chapter 6, I interpret the 'hence' as indicating a criterial relation, and this too serves to fuse evaluation and description. Rather than attempt to show, then, that evaluations can have truth values by analyzing them into independent propositions and illocutionary forces, we might do better to probe ways in which moral and other normative concepts unite their descriptive and evaluative dimensions.

Obviously no pretense is made here to have discussed fully or adequately the many complex issues surrounding the sense/force distinction. I wished merely to show that the distinction can be challenged and therefore that the type of cognitivist analysis of evaluative judgments presented by Searle and Geach on the basis of such a distinction rests on questionable assumptions. And I leave the issue with the suggestion that much of what Geach, Searle, and Foot have to say about specific concepts that are both evaluative and descriptive can be retained even if we jettison the general theory of meaning that separates propositions and illocutionary forces.

Analogies between Moral and Nonmoral Discourse

Still another approach leading to a cognitivist interpretation of moral discourse, but one without the trappings of a general and questionable theory of language, is found in Renford Bambrough's *Moral Skepticism and Moral Knowledge*.[43] Bambrough tries to show that many of the features of moral discourse responsible for noncognitivist analyses also can be found in what is admittedly factual discourse. He grants that the acceptance of a moral judgment expresses attitudes and commitments; it also leads, other things being equal, to action. It is these expressive and practical functions that the noncognitivists made central to the very meaning of moral and other evaluative utterances. But, Bambrough argues, the acceptance of a factual judgment also expresses an attitude, the propositional attitude of belief.[44] Moreover, the utterance of a proposition may express an attitude of doubt or fervent conviction. If it is questioned whether these are properly called attitudes, it can be asked in return whether we are able to distinguish the propositional attitudes from emotional attitudes in a way that bears on the factual/nonfactual dichotomy. What, after all, Bambrough asks, is the approval that the emotivists make so much of? Is not approving something thinking that it is good, just as believing a proposition is thinking that it is true?[45] If so, approval and belief are not distinguishable in an interesting way for the question at hand—both are, as it were, modes of thought. Moreover, common speech implies that just as we can think a proposition to be true when it is not, we can think a person to be good when she is not.

43. Renford Bambrough, *Moral Skepticism and Moral Knowledge* (London: Routledge and Kegan Paul, 1979).
44. Ibid., p. 111.
45. Ibid., p. 22.

In other words, the appearance/reality distinction works as well with attitudes of approval as with attitudes of belief.[46] This suggests that the attitude of approval is just as "factual" and "propositional" as the attitude of belief.

Bambrough is especially persuasive when dealing with the logical relation allegedly existing between moral judgments and actions but claimed by the noncognitivists not to exist between factual judgments and actions. He maintains that the noncognitivist thesis results from a failure to take a large enough view of what belongs in the camp of actions.[47] Are not assent, assertion, and denial actions? And is there not a logical relation between accepting a factual judgment and assenting to it or asserting it? In fact, the usual criterion of a person's acceptance of a factual proposition is whether, under appropriate circumstances and other things being equal, he asserts it or assents to it. So actions *are* logically bound up with factual judgments. If it is not the factual proposition itself that is logically connected to the action but rather the acceptance of the proposition, the same could be said about a moral proposition.

Another way of putting Bambrough's point is the following. It is claimed by noncognitivists that theoretical reason does not by itself motivate—it "moves nothing"—but that practical judgments do motivate. But theoretical reason produces *belief* and hence the assertion and denial of propositions. These being actions, it follows that theoretical reason *does* motivate. And if theoretical reason can generate belief, assertion, and denial, why can it not generate approval and moral action? If it can produce the one form of commitment, why not the other?

In addition to drawing a parallel between accepting a value judgment and action, on the one hand, and accepting a factual judgment and asserting it, defending it, and so on, on the other, Bambrough points to a related parallel consisting of the fact that the phenomenon of *akrasia* is found in both areas.[48] Just as a person can acknowledge that an act is his duty and still fail to do it, so too he can acknowledge that a proposition is true and fail to assert it, defend it, or to act on it in other appropriate ways. Because of our desires, hopes, obsessions, and so on we may not

46. Ibid., pp. 21, 55, 111, 159.
47. Ibid., p. 159.
48. Ibid., pp. 112–16.

do our duty, but these very same desires may lead us to refuse to acknowledge what we know to be the case. Indeed, we can refuse even to see certain facts, facts that, in another sense, we surely do see. So the logical connection between assent and action is threatened by weakness of the will in the case of both moral and admittedly factual beliefs.

Bambrough's line of argument suggests to me still another way in which the alleged dichotomy between normative and factual discourse might be challenged.[49] Hare, it will be recalled, distinguished these two forms of discourse on the grounds that the former is able to answer the practical question "What shall I do?" in a way the latter is not.[50] The explanation he gave is that normative judgments entail imperatives—which alone fully answer this question—whereas factual judgments do not. In reply to this argument, we could suggest that factual judgments be construed as answers to the question "What shall I believe?" and we could urge that only an imperative "Believe p" can fully answer this question. Therefore, our response would run, factual judgments entail imperatives no less than moral judgments do, and if this feature does not prevent factual judgments from being true or false, why should it prevent moral ones from having a truth value?

There is an interesting way of supporting the idea that factual judgments entail imperatives of the form "Believe p." Consider a liar, one who, intent on deceiving, asserts p even though he believes not-p. As a result of his lie, the person to whom he spoke comes to believe p. Subsequently, let us imagine, this person finds out the truth and accuses the liar of deceiving him. One thing the liar cannot say is: "I never told you to believe p; I only asserted p." That he cannot say this shows that in asserting p he is in effect commanding "Believe p." If his assertion had not entailed this imperative, the liar could properly deny responsibility for what the other person believes; but we hold the liar directly accountable, thereby acknowledging that he did issue the prescription to believe p.

If a person, in asserting p, simply expressed his own conviction that p—if his assertion merely entailed "I believe p"—he could not in general be held responsible for other people's coming to believe p on the basis of

49. It must be emphasized that, in spite of the influence, this is my argument and not Bambrough's.
50. See Hare, *Language of Morals*, pp. 29 and 46.

his assertion. In simply expressing his own conviction, he would leave it up to them whether to believe *p* or not. If this were all that is involved in an assertion, then the liar could not be held responsible for what others believe as a result of his assertion. To be sure, he might have thought it likely that people would believe whatever proposition he asserted, and he might have exploited this credulity or this trust. In such circumstances, he might be held responsible to some degree for the deception. Circumstances of this sort, however, are relatively uncommon, but deceiving others is *always* wrong, even when a speaker cannot assume it to be likely that his audience will believe what he says because he says it. But if, on any occasion of lying, one of the implications of a liar's asserting *p* is an imperative to his audience to believe *p*, he is responsible for deliberately telling others to believe something he knows to be false. The possibility of lying as a phenomenon that is always morally wrong depends, therefore, on factual assertions entailing imperatives. But lies are false and therefore true-or-false propositions—otherwise they would not be lies. Entailing imperatives, then, has nothing to do with whether an utterance is true or false.

It might be objected that it makes no sense to speak of commanding belief, belief not being something within our voluntary control. This claim, however, is questionable. Some beliefs clearly are not within our control, but others surely are. Frequently our beliefs are formed on the basis of reasons, and this suggests that we exercise voluntary control over them. We *decide* to believe that S is *p* because of other beliefs of ours that imply that S is *p*. When we "make up our minds" we frequently come to believe something, and this expression suggests that we could have come to believe otherwise.

Looking at the issue of voluntary control from the standpoint of a speaker, certain assumptions seem to govern the assertion of a proposition. Normally we assert a proposition with a particular audience in mind, and we assume that the audience can come to believe what we assert. Implicit in our assertion is the conviction that the audience can be led to form the belief either because of the fact that we assert the proposition (their having faith or confidence in us) or because they will accept the reasons we provide in defense of the proposition. We do not, except perhaps in rare instances, think that our audience will come to believe in an involuntary manner what we say; specifically, we do not think that our asserting the proposition will causally bring about the belief without any reasoning going on in the mind(s) of the audience.

In asserting the proposition that S is p we are affirming that S *is* p rather than conjecturing that S may be p, wondering whether S is p, or doubting or denying that S is p. And we could affirm a proposition, or engage in any of the other cognitive acts with regard to it, without having an audience. But when we do have an audience, and when we affirm a proposition in front of it, we are doing something in relation to the individuals in question. We are *telling* them something, telling them *what to believe*, and such telling might well be characterized by the imperative "Believe that S is p." This imperative converts our affirmation into an assertion. It is reasonable to think, then, that assertions entail imperatives.

To substantiate this claim further, we need to define what attitude someone brings, qua audience, to the context of assertion. There is no one such attitude. A person may be curious to know what the speaker believes; hence she would bring to the utterance the question, "What do you believe?" But equally she might, as audience, attend to an utterance in light of the question, "What am I to believe?" or "What are we to believe?" The speaker in turn can be seen as responding to these questions. If the speaker's utterance is in the confessional or manifestational mode, he can be taken to answer the audience's "What do you believe?" question. If his utterance is in the argumentative or assertorial mode, the speaker can be taken to answer the audience's "What am I to believe?" question. Obviously a speaker could respond to both questions simultaneously. But to the extent that his utterance is an assertion, it would appear to be primarily a response to the question "What are we (the audience) to believe?"

To the extent that the value judgment "S is good" is a way of commending S and telling people what to choose, it might well be characterized, as Hare claimed, as entailing the imperative "Choose S." It is equally plausible to think that asserting "S is p" to an audience is a way of telling people what to believe and hence can be characterized as "Believe that S is p." *If* Hare's analysis works with commendations, it would be applicable just as well to assertions. This shows, once again, that the fact that an utterance entails an imperative has nothing to do with whether it is true or false. Assertions of propositions describing matters of fact entail imperatives to just the extent that commendations entail imperatives. If we are so inclined, we can grant the prescriptivists' characterization of moral judgments and maintain nevertheless that these judgments have truth values.

Cognitivist Options

We have seen how some philosophers argue that moral judgments can have truth values even if they express emotions or commitments, even if they entail imperatives, or even if they have an illocutionary force different from or in addition to the force of assertion. This claim can be defended by appeal to a general theory of language involving a sense/force distinction (as Searle and others would prefer) or simply by pointing to the many parallels between moral and nonmoral discourse (as Bambrough and I would prefer).

I have shown how theories involving sense/force distinctions can be criticized on Wittgensteinian grounds, and I have argued that such theories unwittingly may lend more support to a noncognitivist perspective than to the cognitivist point of view (the point of view held by many of those who would apply the sense/force analysis to moral discourse). Following what Foot, Geach, and Searle have said about *specific* normative concepts such as rudeness, good person, and promising, I have urged that moral concepts be understood as having a *fused* descriptive and evaluative meaning. The two dimensions of meaning cannot be separated so as to allow one of them, the descriptive meaning, to be made dependent on the other, the evaluative meaning. Such concepts are necessarily both descriptive and evaluative, and a person does not have mastery of one of these concepts unless she uses it to express both a certain descriptive content and a certain normative character. It remains to be seen how such concepts actually work—how, that is to say, the descriptive and evaluative dimensions are joined or fused. Later in this work we shall see how the realists offer one interpretation of this connection through their theory that (subvenient) nonmoral properties fix the (supervenient) moral ones. Conceptual relativism provides a different interpretation of the connection in terms of a criterial relation between the descriptive elements (the grounds of assertion) and the normative dimension (the moral character).

Following a lead suggested by Bambrough, I also have argued in this chapter that the fact that moral judgments can be interpreted as entailing imperatives does not distinguish them from nonmoral, descriptive judgments. The latter, I have contended, can equally well be interpreted as entailing imperatives—imperatives to believe what is asserted. Or, more modestly, I have claimed that to the extent that Hare's prescriptive analysis applies to moral judgments, a prescriptive characterization can also be given of matter-of-fact assertions. Such an argument connects with the general pattern of thinking of many philosophers who urge that there are significant parallels between moral discourse and nonmoral common-sense and scientific discourse.

The various arguments considered in the first two chapters were not entertained with a view to deciding with any finality whether or not they are correct. I have tried to give a picture of some of the reasons that have led philosophers to abandon what was once the canonical position of analytical philosophy toward moral discourse—noncognitivism—and to adopt a new cognitivist perspective. I have criticized some of these arguments, not with the intent of reestablishing noncognitivism but with the aim of pointing to new ways in which cognitivism might be defended. It is now time to turn to an examination of several full-blown theories committed to the cognitivity of moral discourse, theories that attempt to explain the specific way in which we come to know the truth of our moral judgments.

3 / Moral Rationalism

THE impact of noncognitivism during the mid-twentieth century convinced most philosophers that it is impossible to justify moral judgments by showing through some form of observation that they correspond to the facts. Moore's open-question argument, the Naturalistic Fallacy, and the arguments of the emotivists and prescriptivists led to the rejection of the view that moral judgments are susceptible of empirical confirmation, and the majority of philosophers repudiated any notion of an intuitive "observation" of metaphysical properties and states of affairs. Consequently, the noncognitivists and their followers denied that there are any true or false moral propositions—lacking empirical and intuitive verification, moral judgments were deemed to lack truth values.

There is, however, another option, one that hardly occurred to the noncognitivists. Moral judgments might be open to confirmation, not by observation, but by means of procedures comparable to logical and mathematical proof. In other words, moral judgments might be shown to be true or false by the exercise of reason alone. Our knowledge of right and wrong, on this analysis, would be a priori instead of a posteriori. Such a suggestion would undoubtedly have seemed absurd to most noncognitivists, largely because of their view that a priori propositions are mere formal tautologies and therefore empty of content.[1] But this conception of the nature of a priori propositions has itself seemed ab-

1. See A. J. Ayer, *Language, Truth, and Logic* (New York: Dover, 1946), chap. 4.

surd to many others: after all, mathematical and logical propositions are generally thought to be a priori, but they are not obviously empty of content. And if we have knowledge of mathematical and logical truths, why not of moral ones as well?

Such a suggestion has been taken up and developed during the last decade, largely by a number of American philosophers. They claim to show that moral propositions are indeed capable of rational proof. Many also maintain that our moral discourse and beliefs have a structure resembling that of a logical/mathematical system. That is to say, they view the acquisition of moral knowledge as a matter of deductively deriving moral judgments from a rationally validated first principle or set of first principles. Once we have a proof of the fundamental principle(s), the main problem remaining, as they see it, is to provide whatever factual propositions are needed in order to deduce specific moral precepts from the first principle(s).

The agreement just characterized is a very general one, open to significant variations in the specific theories of different rationalists. Especially variable is their conception of how the fundamental principle of morality is validated. Alan Gewirth opts for the strongest possible proof—a demonstration that the denial of his principle is self-contradictory.[2] Hence he uses such obvious deductive techniques as *reductio ad absurdum* arguments. Bernard Gert attempts to show that it would be irrational to reject the fundamental moral principles or rules because doing so would express irrational desires and would commit one to irrational actions.[3] For Gert, rejecting the moral rules involves a distinctive, *practical* form of irrationality that cannot be reduced to formal inconsistency. Other rationalists have identified still other ways of justifying the fundamental principle or principles of morality. Alan Donagan, an important rationalist we shall not study for lack of space, has argued that the fundamental principle—for him the principle that it is impermissible not to respect every human being as a rational creature—is justified because reason determines it to be the proper response to the free, autonomous nature *of reason itself*.[4] Just by being rational, human beings are creatures of the sort that reason requires us to respect. In Donagan's analysis,

2. Alan Gewirth, *Reason and Morality* (Chicago: University of Chicago Press, 1978).
3. Bernard Gert, *The Moral Rules* (New York: Harper & Row, 1966).
4. Alan Donagan, *The Theory of Morality* (Chicago: University of Chicago Press, 1977).

reason gives us not only a proof of the fundamental moral principle but also its ground.

Given these differences in the conception of a rational justification of morality, it is difficult to discuss rationalism as a general theory. We must proceed by examining specific theories in their own terms and assessing them in that way, and for this purpose I have selected the theories of Gewirth and Gert. They represent two quite different rationalist approaches to moral epistemology. In examining them, however, we shall be able to observe some common merits and faults in the rationalist approach. It may be helpful to have in advance some indication of what they are.

On the positive side, rationalism should be given high marks for identifying and accurately describing the content of morality. Many of Gert's "ten moral rules" are indeed basic moral principles, and Gewirth's emphasis on basic human rights (and, we might add, Donagan's emphasis on respect for persons) accords well with our contemporary, western conception of morality. We can learn much about this conception by studying the rationalists. Moreover, rationalism alerts us to the possibility of there being necessary (as opposed to contingent) propositions in morality, a breakthrough that in the end allows us to get a grip on the cognitive status of moral discourse. The rationalists, of course, think that certain moral propositions are necessary because it would be self-contradictory, or irrational in some other way, to deny them. In Chapter 6 I reject this explanation of the necessity of selected moral propositions, but I argue that, in a different way, these propositions are indeed necessary.

On the negative side of the picture, our discussion reveals three problems with the rationalist approach. (1) The efforts of the two rationalists we study to prove the truth of a basic moral principle or set of principles turn out to be in vain. Problems endemic to each proof are identified and lead us to reject it. Obviously, the two theories considered here do not exhaust rationalist approaches to moral philosophy, but insofar as they are representative and among the best of the kind available at this time, their failure does not bode well for the rationalist enterprise in general. (2) Gewirth attempts to define and justify a moral principle underlying all other moral principles and hence serving as the fundamental principle of morality. I argue that his principle is ambiguous and that its different interpretations can be used to derive quite different and opposing specific principles. This raises the question whether in fact there is a basic principle underlying, unifying, and justifying more specific principles. In Chapter 6 I argue that there is an irreducible *variety* of basic moral principles and that each is necessary on its own merits, not by virtue of being derived from a very general, fundamental principle. Finally, (3) I conclude this chapter by questioning whether the rationalist view of morality as a set of principles imposed by reason itself is an accurate picture. I argue that it misinterprets the role of reason, and the concept of a rational person, in moral experience.

Bernard Gert

Bernard Gert's *Moral Rules* is an admirable attempt to provide "a new rational foundation for morality."[5] Whether or not it succeeds, it contributes many important insights to our understanding of morality and the cognitive and psychological dimensions surrounding it. Gert argues that reason can be seen to require acceptance of ten moral rules—*require* in the strong sense that it would be irrational not to accept them. He does not think that reason is capable of demonstrating that we must *act* morally, but in his eyes it does fully justify the moral rules. Rules such as "Do not kill" and "Do not cause pain" are objective "truths" that cannot, except on pain of irrationality, be denied. Our goal here is to understand this alleged justification of the moral rules and to see whether the limit placed on reason—its inability to prove that we should act morally—is of any epistemological consequence.

As Gert himself acknowledges, the key to his defense of the moral rules is his conception of reason. According to this conception, desires and actions as well as beliefs can be rational or irrational. Furthermore, rational action is not defined in terms of belief; an irrational action is not, as Hume claimed (on Gert's interpretation of him), an action based on a false belief. Indeed, Gert maintains that rational belief is to be defined in terms of rational action, a rational belief being one that generally leads to a rational action. It is difficult to see, however, that he makes a case for this claim of dependency, and in fact he offers us an excellent analysis of irrational belief which makes no mention of irrational action.[6] Moreover, it is not so much rational action as rational

---

5. This is the subtitle of the book.
6. Gert, *Moral Rules*, p. 21. Further page and chapter references to this work are indicated parenthetically in the text.

(and irrational) *desire* that plays the central role in his defense of the moral rules. But these are minor quibbles. The main thrust of his analysis is clear: there is such a thing as having irrational desires and engaging in irrational actions, and these facts about practical rationality and irrationality constitute a basis for defending the moral rules.

Gert brings to bear on belief, desire, and action a tripartite vocabulary of rational assessment: there are beliefs, desires, and actions *required by reason*; there are those *prohibited by reason*; and there are those *allowed by reason* (chap. 2). A belief is required by reason if it would be irrational not to have it. It would be prohibited by reason if it would be irrational to have it. And it would be allowed by reason if it is neither required nor prohibited by reason, that is, if it would not be irrational either to have the belief or not to have it. Likewise, a desire is required by reason if it would be irrational not to have it, prohibited by reason if it would be irrational to have it, and allowed by reason if it would not be irrational either to have it or not to have it. Rational beliefs and desires are those required or allowed by reason. We will see momentarily how this vocabulary of rational assessment applies to actions.

Gert grants that there will be numerous disagreements over how to classify various beliefs and desires; moreover, what is irrational with respect to belief is relative to a social context of shared knowledge. To overcome these problems, he opts for the weakest possible claim: he will call irrational only those beliefs and desires that "everyone" would be willing to call irrational—or, more precisely, those beliefs and desires that all who are sufficiently intelligent and knowledgeable to be moral agents would call irrational (p. 21). "Thus when I talk about irrational beliefs, I shall mean beliefs which would be irrational to anyone with enough knowledge and intelligence to be subject to the moral rules" (p. 23). Likewise, only those desires that everyone would call irrational are placed in this category. If some individuals would think a belief or desire rational and others would think it irrational, Gert classifies this belief or desire as allowed by reason. He realizes that this procedure will result in the labeling of fewer desires as prohibited by reason than most people think to be the case, but this fact, he correctly notes, only strengthens his case. If he can show that the moral rules prohibiting certain actions derive their justification from the fact that these actions express desires that everyone (qualified as above) would consider to be prohibited by reason, the moral rules cannot be viewed as contestable.

Gert claims to make no attempt to distinguish rational from irrational *persons*, noting that this distinction is generally held to be a matter of degree (p. 20). He does, however, often speak of rational persons. Given his analysis of rational and irrational beliefs, desires, and actions, I think we can safely say that he takes a rational person to be one who usually, or on a particular occasion, engages in rational actions and has rational beliefs and desires (i.e., those allowed or required by reason). At times he implicitly identifies a rational person with one who is intelligent and knowledgeable enough to be subject to the moral rules.

What are some irrational desires? The following is typical of Gert's thought on the matter:

> We can, as with beliefs, provide a list of desires that it would be irrational for anyone (with sufficient intelligence to be subject to moral judgment) to act on simply in order to satisfy them. The desire to be killed is irrational. Unless one has some reason, it is irrational to act on this desire. Even if, in a cool moment, one decides that he would like to be killed more than he would like to do anything else, we would not say he was rational if he acted on this desire. . . . This does not mean it is always irrational to kill oneself; one may have a reason for doing this. Being killed may be the only way to escape constant severe pain. But to do this for no reason, simply because one desires to be killed, is irrational. There may be some dispute as to what constitutes an adequate reason for killing oneself—that is, a reason sufficient to make the action rational; but there can be no dispute that one needs some reason. It is not enough simply to desire to do so. Thus the desire to be killed or to kill oneself is quite different from most of our desires. If we desire to wear pink shirts, we need no reason, and acting on this desire will not be irrational. Thus even if we have not decided what is an adequate reason for killing oneself, we can still distinguish the desire to kill oneself from most other desires. (pp. 30–31)

In addition to (1) the desire to kill oneself, irrational desires include (2) the desire to have pain inflicted on oneself, (3) the desire to be disabled, (4) the desire to restrict one's freedom and opportunity, and (5) the desire to deprive oneself of pleasure. In each case, the irrational desire must be understood as one for which there is no good reason. A masochist's desire for pain, for example, is not irrational, according to Gert, because masochists have a good reason for wanting pain: they enjoy having pain inflicted upon them (p. 31).

Why are the above five desires irrational? This is a crucial question, and the novelty of Gert's approach lies in the way he answers it. First, he claims, these desires are *not* irrational because we would decide in a cool moment that they conflict with other, more important desires of ours. The emphasis here should be on the notion of *deciding*: it is not one's decision that makes a desire irrational. The desire to kill oneself (just because one wants to) is irrational even if someone decides in a cool moment that she wants to do so. In fact, Gert tells us, it would be even more irrational if decided on in a cool moment.

Second, irrational desires are not necessarily irrational because they conflict with self-interest. Reason *allows* one to kill oneself in order to prevent death to others or to prevent them from suffering extreme pain (i.e., at least some rational people would accept the idea of doing so), but such acts are surely contrary to self-interest. Moreover, the concept of self-interest itself needs explanation, and likely we will have to unpack it in terms of avoiding death, pain, dismemberment, and so on—that is, in terms of avoiding all those things it is irrational to desire. So the notion of self-interest can hardly be used to define rational and irrational desires.

If desires are not irrational because they conflict with self-interest or would be seen in a cool moment to conflict with more important desires, why are they irrational? "My answer is, 'Because they are.' We just do regard anyone who acts on any one of these desires simply because he wants to as acting irrationally" (p. 37). Gert admits that this may seem unsatisfactory, insufficiently self-evident, but he is content to rest with it. And in this he appears to be justified, given his avowed method. Prima facie, it seems undeniable that all individuals intelligent and knowledgeable enough to be subject to the moral rules would agree that it is irrational to desire to kill oneself for no reason. It seems, although this is to put words into Gert's mouth, a paradigm case of an irrational desire, the kind of example serving to define this term. If the unmotivated, unreasoned desire to kill oneself is not irrational, nothing is; if this desire is not irrational, what does 'irrational desire' mean? I take this "ordinary language philosophy move" as a way of expressing Gert's claim that "we just do regard anyone who acts on any one of these desires simply because he wants to as acting irrationally" (p. 37). If the five irrational desires he lists are built into the very meaning of 'irrational desire', he is quite correct to think of this notion as designating an objective fact that is not dependent on human choice or decision.

Having listed and "argued for" five irrational desires, Gert is in a position to identify five irrational actions. Any action undertaken merely in order to fulfill an irrational desire is an irrational action. Hence there is an irrational action corresponding to each of the five irrational desires. But the scope of irrational action is wider than the scope of actions expressing and seeking to fulfill irrational desires. One may do something that it is not irrational to desire to do but nevertheless act irrationally. This would be the case if one knew that the consequences of acting in this manner would involve a significant risk to oneself of death, pain, disability, loss of freedom or opportunity, or loss of pleasure—and there was no good reason for acting this way in spite of these probable consequences. Hence an obsession with washing one's hands, with full knowledge that one likely will suffer some stigmatization because of this action, can be said to be an irrational action.

Gert refers to death, pain, disability, loss of freedom or opportunity, and loss of pleasure as *evils* (chap. 3). An evil is any object of an irrational desire (p. 45), and we have seen that it is irrational to desire death, pain, and so forth. Using this notion of evil, we can say that an irrational action is one a person carries out to achieve an evil or knows is likely to cause him to suffer some evil. Of course, one might seek to bring an evil upon oneself for a good reason—for example, to avoid a greater evil or to prevent someone else from suffering an evil. In this case, one would not be acting irrationally.

To complete our categorization of actions in terms of the tripartite vocabulary of rational assessment, we can now define actions that are required by reason and allowed by it. Any action taken to avoid one of the five evils is required by reason (unless there is a good reason not to avoid it). And any action that is neither prohibited nor required by reason is allowed by reason. Rational actions are those allowed or required by reason.

An important question presents itself: Is it irrational to act on a desire to harm others simply because one wants to? Gert's answer is no. There are, he admits, cases of what we call senseless killing, but he thinks we condemn these actions as irrational because the agent undertakes them with a knowledge that they are likely to bring harm to himself. It is possible, however, to harm others on occasion with little or no risk to oneself, and such actions are not thought by everyone to be irrational— some would consider them perfectly rational. Thus we must conclude that harming others, however distasteful, is not necessarily irrational.

Again, Gert insists that this conclusion does not amount to equating rational action with self-interested action. Although reason does not prohibit harming others on some occasions, and does prohibit harming oneself on most occasions, it allows harming oneself in order to benefit others. So the relationship of rational action, self-interest, and altruism is more complicated than it is often made out to be.

So far we have seen how Gert deals with rational and irrational desires and actions. How can these facts about what reason prohibits, requires, and allows be used to justify the moral rules?

Before answering this question, we must have some conception of the moral rules. Gert proceeds here both by way of noting generally accepted cases of moral rules—what I shall call *paradigm cases*—and by arguing that there are certain necessary and sufficient conditions for something's being a moral rule (chap. 4). "Do not kill," "Do not cause pain," and "Do not deprive of freedom" are paradigm cases—rules that would be admitted by everyone to be moral. Such rules have certain formal characteristics and certain aspects of content setting them apart from other rules and hence serving to identify them as moral. Formally, they are universal in that they apply to all rational persons; they are understandable by all rational persons and require no specialized knowledge for their comprehension; they can be followed and broken by all persons in all circumstances; they are unchangeable; they are discovered rather than invented; and they admit of exceptions. As for their content, moral rules require one *to avoid evil*; they do not demand that one promote good. This fact is important, for it shows how they can meet the formal requirements. A rule prohibiting us from causing evil is one that can be obeyed by all persons at all times in regard to all other persons— usually it is obeyed simply by doing nothing. But a rule requiring one to promote good is not one that all human beings can obey at all times and with regard to all others. Following it requires proper occasions and special capacities and opportunities. Hence, according to Gert, there is no moral rule requiring us to promote good. In fact, no positive action whatsoever is required by the moral rules, not even that of preventing evil. What Gert calls the moral *ideals* encourage us to prevent evil. But such actions are only allowed, not required, by the moral rules. The rules require only that we avoid certain kinds of action. One implication of this view is that it is always wrong to cause evil in order to promote good.

With these conditions in hand, Gert is still unable to draw up a list of the moral rules. In order to know whether a rule is moral, he thinks it is necessary additionally to ascertain whether a certain attitude—he calls it the *moral attitude*—would be required by reason to be taken up toward it. In order for a rule "to be a moral one, all rational men must agree in taking a certain attitude toward it, an attitude that involves the view that it should be universally obeyed" (p. 75). The moral attitude and the requirements listed above provide a set of conditions individually necessary and jointly sufficient for a rule to be moral. Getting a clear picture of this moral attitude is very important, for if it turns out that this attitude is in fact required by reason to be directed at certain rules, this will amount for Gert to a rational justification of those rules.

Let us begin by asking what attitude rational persons would take toward the rule "Do not kill" (chap. 5). They would want the rule obeyed by others with respect to themselves, and also with respect to persons they care about (e.g., family and friends). They would not, however, want the rule obeyed in this way without exception, for it is possible to imagine circumstances in which they would wish it broken with regard to themselves or those they care about, circumstances such as those in which by being killed they prevent others they care about from being killed. And those they care about might have similar reasons for not wanting the rule obeyed with regard to themselves. Thus the attitude of rational persons toward the rule "Do not kill" would be the following: "I want all other people to obey the rule 'Don't kill' with regard to anyone for whom I am concerned (including myself), except when they have a good specific reason for thinking that either that person or myself (possibly the same) has (or would have if he knew the facts) a rational desire that the rule not be obeyed with regard to him" (p. 80).

Rational persons must form this attitude toward "Do not kill," but they need not want to obey the rule *themselves*. Nor need they wish that it be obeyed with regard to *all persons* equally. They have the above attitude toward the rule because they want themselves and those they care about protected from the evil of death. "It is an attitude required by those who want to avoid the consequences that all rational men want to avoid" (p. 87). Similar attitudes will be taken up by rational individuals toward the rules prohibiting the causing of pain and disability, deprivation of freedom and opportunity, and deprivation of pleasure. But in all these cases, as above, reason requires only that the attitude favor the rule's being followed with respect to those about whom one is concerned, namely, oneself and one's family and friends. Such an attitude is *not* a moral attitude. As we have seen, in order for a rule to be a moral one, all rational persons must adopt toward it the attitude that it be obeyed universally—*by all* and with regard *to all* rational persons. The attitude we have just considered does not bestow such universality upon a rule. How can we pass from this limited-obedience attitude to a moral one?

What if a person expressed the "limited" attitude in public? The consequences might be disastrous. All persons who fall outside the circle of her concern would have no reason whatsoever to respect her attitude. In fact, such an attitude might well provoke a hostile response from them. This is precisely what the person expressing the attitude does not want. How, then, can she get the people for whom she is not concerned to agree to follow the rule with regard to those for whom she is concerned? She must realize that these other persons, being rational, have the same attitude toward the rule against killing, and so on, that she has. If she were to express approval of their rule, they might well express approval of hers. But this means that she must publicly express the attitude that "Do not kill" be obeyed by all and with respect to all persons. Other rational agents could be expected, for the same reasons, to express publicly the same "universal" attitude. Hence to protect herself and those for whom she is concerned, a rational person will publicly express the following attitude: I want all people to obey the rule "Do not kill" with regard to every other person (including myself) except when they have a good specific reason for thinking that either that person or myself (possibly the same) has (or would have if she knew the facts) a rational desire that the rule not be obeyed with regard to her. Here we have an attitude that can claim to be moral, for it is universal in scope.

Gert introduces the technical term *public advocacy* to convey the ideas we have just traced (p. 89). To advocate publicly is to express an idea or attitude with a view to reaching agreement with all rational persons; furthermore, "one is publicly advocating . . . when and only when one regards all rational men as potential listeners and believes that they all could accept the attitude being advocated" (p. 89). From this condition it follows that one cannot publicly advocate an idea or attitude one knows cannot be advocated by all rational persons. Hence it must be an attitude allowed by reason. The attitude just described *is* allowed by reason. Furthermore, the public advocacy of this attitude seems to be *required* by reason. Not to advocate it publicly would sharply increase one's chances of suffering evil at the hands of others, whereas publicly advocating it greatly improves one's chances of avoiding this evil. It is required by reason to believe that all rational human beings will take action to avoid an evil and that they will inflict evil on those they believe will try to cause them this evil. Hence the rational person *must* publicly advocate that the rule "Do not kill" be obeyed by all with regard to all. "Since he increases his chances of suffering evil by not advocating this attitude, and has no reason for not advocating it, I conclude that it would be irrational for him not to advocate it" (p. 90).

Gert reminds us again that public advocacy of the rule against killing requires, from the standpoint of reason, that exceptions be permitted. But the exceptions must be those cases in which one has a good reason not to want the rule followed with respect to oneself. Every rational person must publicly advocate that the rule *not* be followed in such cases. Hence the attitude that a rational person must publicly advocate toward the rule "Do not kill" is the following: "Everyone is to obey the rule with regard to everyone except when he would publicly advocate violating it" (p. 92).

This, then, is the rationally required, universal attitude—the *moral attitude*—toward the rule "Do not kill." It is easy to see that the moral attitude also must be publicly advocated by all rational individuals toward those rules prohibiting the other four evils. And so we arrive at a list of five rules, which, insofar as they would have the moral attitude publicly advocated toward them by all rational persons and insofar as they fulfill the other requirements for moral rules, can all be called moral rules:

(1) Do not kill;
(2) Do not cause pain;
(3) Do not disable;
(4) Do not deprive of freedom or opportunity;
(5) Do not deprive of pleasure. (p. 86)

Gert goes on to show that five additional rules also command public advocacy of the moral attitude (chap. 6). Showing this is more complicated than is the case with the first five, involving as it does a demonstration that not following these rules, even though frequently leading to no direct evil, stills puts at risk practices we value, practices without which we run a high risk of suffering evil. We need not go into the details of this more elaborate demonstration. Its result is to add to our list of moral rules the following:

(6) Do not deceive;
(7) Keep your promises;
(8) Do not cheat;
(9) Obey the law; and
(10) Do your duty. (p. 125)

All ten moral rules would be publicly advocated in the manner described above by all rational individuals. Public advocacy of all ten rules would prevent evils that all rational persons wish to avoid. Hence reason *requires* public advocacy of the ten moral rules.

Gert claims that the fact that reason requires public advocacy of the ten moral rules amounts to a justification of them: "Showing that reason publicly requires the moral attitude toward a moral rule is what I call justifying that moral rule" (p. 101). It does not amount, however, to a proof that rational persons must *act* morally. In fact, Gert appears to concede that rational persons need not even publicly advocate the moral rules: they may keep quiet, expressing no public attitude. But if they make judgments at all, speaking to what we ought to do and what rules we ought to follow, they *must* publicly advocate the moral attitude toward the moral rules. If, having done so, they turn around and violate the rules, they may be accused of hypocrisy but not of irrationality. Reason allows us to act morally, but it does not require it. It equally allows us to act immorally.

It might be objected that if a person acts immorally, if, say, he kills someone or causes her pain, he also increases the risk of suffering evil himself at the hands of others. But this may or may not be the case. If one sees that in killing another his own chances of suffering an evil are increased, it would be irrational for him to act this way. But if he is careful and runs no such risk, reason permits him to do the act. It is hard to imagine, however, that expressing an attitude toward the moral rules which is not the moral attitude would result in anything other than harm to oneself and those for whom one is concerned. Hence reason requires one to publicly advocate the moral attitude even while it allows one to act immorally on certain occasions.

Has reason failed us here? Has it failed to do something that it must do if it is to give a rational foundation to morality? Gert thinks not. As he sees it, the view that reason ought to be able to justify moral action rests upon the mistaken belief that reason *can* justify *another* type of action—namely, self-interested action (chap. 10). If reason could justify acting in that way, but could not justify acting morally, it would indeed have slighted morality. But reason *cannot* justify acting self-interestedly in the sense of requiring it. As we have seen, it is not irrational to sacrifice one's self-interest to the interests of others. Reason does not require this sacrifice, but it allows it. And thus it does not require self-interested action but at best allows it. Hence from the standpoint of reason, acting self-interestedly and acting morally are, in general, on a par. Reason does not provide a superior foundation for self-interest and hence does not fail to provide a standard in the area of morality.

This concludes my presentation of Gert's moral rationalism. By way of assessment, I wish to point out several problems I have with his theory.

First, Gert's concept of an irrational action is too demanding. A person is said to act irrationally if she acts on an irrational desire without having a good reason to do so. For instance, a person would act irrationally if she tried to kill herself just because she wanted to. But does anyone *ever* do this? It seems most unlikely. Does anyone cause herself pain, or dismember herself, just because she wants to—that is, for no other reason, including even the bizarre one that she enjoys it? If these possibilities are merely theoretical and not occasionally actualized, we must conclude either that all people are always rational or that Gert's concept has not captured what really counts as irrational action. But Gert admits that "all of us act irrationally some of the time" (p. 20). Hence he has failed to identify what an irrational action is. His concept requires or demands too much—what no person can be imagined to do.

On the other hand, Gert's concept of irrational action is also too lenient. People act irrationally if they know that in doing so they run a substantial risk of causing themselves to suffer some evil (and have no reason to wish to do so). But what counts as "a substantial risk"? There is little chance that we can quantify this, and hence little chance that we can separate irrational persons from rational ones willing to take high risks. The notion of "running a substantial risk," then, is so loose as to allow us to capture altogether too many actions under the caption "irrational."

Looking next at Gert's notion of irrational desires, we can raise the same question we raised regarding irrational actions: are there any such desires of the sort described? If a person wants to kill himself, and does not want to do this in order to avoid some evil like pain, the desire would be irrational. We must ask, however, whether anyone ever *just* wants to kill himself (for no reason at all). If not, Gert has not identified an instance of an irrational desire that leads someone to act irrationally. In fact, it is highly doubtful that anyone ever acts on the basis of one of the desires Gert calls irrational. He has not, therefore, accurately characterized the source of our not-infrequent irrational actions.

To be sure, we can imagine cases in which people want to kill themselves and have no reasons of the sort described by Gert which would convert their desires into rational ones. Hence for Gert they would act irrationally. But in fact we would not consider their desires or their actions irrational at all, because they have *another* kind of reason for what they want to do. Consider the case of a person who came to believe that life is absurd and hence not worthwhile. He is not suffering, and his perception of the absurdity of life does not cause unbearable *angst*. But, he argues, life not being worthwhile, he wants to kill himself. He does not have a reason in Gert's sense for doing so—he is not avoiding an evil or even seeking a good. He has certain thoughts that prompt him to wish to kill himself. How is such a person irrational? His desire is "based on" his reflections, and his reflections are surely allowed by reason. We can, if we have read enough existential philosophy, understand this type of person, and though we might find him odd, oversensitive, melancholic, and in many ways absurd, it is unlikely we would think him irrational. But his desire seems to satisfy all the conditions that Gert would think sufficient to render it irrational.

These reflections cast doubt on whether Gert is correct in saying that his examples are the kinds of things we take irrational actions and desires to be. It seems more likely that our paradigms of irrational action are those based on irrational beliefs, in precisely the sense in which Gert takes this term: they are actions based on beliefs that are patently inconsistent with what the agent is intelligent enough to know (pp. 20–21). This seems to be the case, for instance, with the fly-catcher who catches all the nonexistent flies she believes are surrounding her. Her intellectual and perceptual capacities are adequate to allow her to realize that there are no flies in the room (she is not blind, nor is she necessarily of limited intelligence). On this occasion, however, her intellectual or perceptual equipment is not working properly, and as a result she believes there are flies in the room and consequently tries to catch them.

If Gert's appeal to paradigm cases of irrational desire and action does not work because his examples are not paradigms—even worse, are merely hypothetical and never in fact exist—his entire argument loses much of its plausibility. His defense of the moral rules consists in showing that in refusing to advocate them publicly a person would be acting irrationally. But Gert has not identified the kind of irrational desire that could do the job of revealing this refusal to be irrational.

There is also a real question, as has been pointed out by Donagan, whether Gert's defense of the moral rules is a *moral* defense of them.[7] Gert argues that we must advocate them in order to protect ourselves and those we care about from suffering evil. Even if this argument is successful, all it shows is that we have *personal* reasons for advocating morality. To be sure, these are not just self-interested reasons, for they include our concern for the welfare of others, but only the others *we* care about. If we happen not to care equally for all human beings, and surely most of us fall into this camp, our reasons for advocating morality could accurately be called personal and prejudicial. How different it would be to defend the moral rules—as Donagan himself does—by saying that obedience to them expresses our respect for all other human beings. This is not a personal, prejudicial reason, but a moral one. Gert argues against utilitarianism that it fails to defend the *moral* rules and instead defends nonmoral ones; he might be accused in turn of not *morally* defending the moral rules.

Moreover, has he justified, one way or another, the moral rules? He seeks to show that reason requires that they be publicly advocated because it is in our personal interest to express this attitude. But one might admit this fact even while believing that the moral rules are *false*; such would be the position of the personal egoist. Publicly advocating the moral rules does not require, then, that we see them as true or justified. But does it make sense to say that the moral rules have been shown to be justified if this does not entail thinking that they are true? Defending the public advocacy of the moral rules as Gert does seems to be a matter of saying that we should make it *appear* that we believe them to be true,

7. Donagan, *Theory of Morality*, p. 239.

that we should act *as if* we think them true. This view appears to involve a bit of dishonesty. Would it not be more frank to say, at least to oneself, "I don't know if the moral rules are justified or not, but I am going to publicly advocate them because it is in my and my loved ones' interest to do so"?

Furthermore, in claiming to have justified the moral rules, Gert maintains that he has shown them to be objective. Indeed, for him one of the defining features of a moral rule is that it is discovered, not invented. But what bearing does showing that reason requires the public advocacy of moral rules have on their objectivity? If one really believes that moral rules are discovered and not invented, one might express this by saying that they are true or valid *whether or not they are known by human beings to be so*. But to demonstrate that all rational people must publicly advocate them in order to avoid suffering evil hardly amounts to a demonstration of the truth of the subjunctive conditional that they would be true even if they were never asserted or advocated.

Gert believes that a sense of guilt, among other things, leads a person to act morally after learning that reason requires the public advocacy of the moral rules. If a person accepts what Gert calls the rational answer to the question "Why be moral?" (namely, that reason requires the public advocacy of the moral rules), then, he tells us, "feeling guilty is unavoidable when he acts immorally" (p. 206). And again, "the desire to avoid feeling guilty may provide a strong motive for acting morally" (p. 206). But why should anyone feel guilty for acting immorally? After all, immorality is allowed by reason. That I am required by reason to publicly advocate the moral rules should not cause me to feel guilty when I break them, for I know *why* I must publicly advocate them—namely, to protect myself—and if I feel that I can act immorally without running a significant risk of harming myself, there is nothing whatsoever inconsistent about publicly advocating the moral rules and also breaking them in practice. If I feel any uncomfortable emotion as a result of violating what I have publicly advocated, it is likely to be a sense of embarrassment or shame that I have been caught, that my actions might show my public advocacy of the rules was not sincere, that I really did not believe that I ought to refrain from, for example, causing others to suffer pain. If I am lacking in temerity, this sense of embarrassment may cause me to act morally, but then again it may lead me to take no public stand on the moral rules. The latter possibility is permitted by reason, and it allows me to avoid my rather minor discomfort.

Put another way, feeling guilty for breaking the moral rules—something we *do* feel, and often intensely so—cannot be explained in terms of Gert's analysis. Its most obvious explanation is that we feel we have *done* something that we ought not to do. Gert shows only that we ought to publicly advocate not doing it. On his view, reason does not require that we not break the moral rules; it allows us to do so. But being permitted to break the moral rules and being obligated *not* to break them are different matters indeed!

Accepting for the sake of argument Gert's conception of irrational desires and actions, we note that reason *can* demand or require certain actions of us. It does not require that we act in our self-interest, but it does require that we avoid doing anything that would bring evil on us or on the ones for whom we care. And this often entails a requirement that we *do* certain things—for instance, the requirement that we publicly advocate the moral rules. Let us say that reason requires us to act to defend our *personal* interests—when these include our self-interest and our interest in the welfare of others—and let us call these required actions *personal actions*. There is, then, a significant contrast between what reason cannot do with regard to moral action and what it can do with regard to personal actions. And its inability to provide the justification for moral action, coupled with the fact that it can provide justification for personal actions, should make us very skeptical of morality. Furthermore, a reason that supports what we want (our personal desires), but not moral action, appears very much to be a slave of the passions. It is questionable, then, whether Gert's conception of reason is a new one after all.

I must conclude that Gert's attempt to provide "a new rational foundation for morality" (as the subtitle of his book suggests) fails. The distinctive feature of Gert's conception of reason—the notion of desires that are in themselves irrational—is highly dubious. And without it, his conception of reason would turn out to be philosophy's old "instrumental reason." Public advocacy of the moral rules would be required by reason because it is an effective means to avoid many of the evils we wish to avoid. This would make the rules *contingent*: they would be justified *if* publicly advocating them helped us avoid these evils, and conceivably it might not have this effect. One of the appealing features of Gert's theory is that it gives the impression of there being something irrational about not accepting (or at least not publicly advocating) a rule such as "Do not kill." It is not just that we would turn out to be defeating our goals if we do not advocate the avoidance of killing, the theory suggests, but rather that the desire leading us to refuse to advocate this would be irrational. This approach promises to provide the rule with a kind of necessity. But if we must reject Gert's notion of an irrational desire, it appears that the only justification he gives us for advocating a moral rule is that doing so in fact promotes our goals. This does not seem strong enough (in some instances it may not even be true). In fact there is, I suggest (and argue for in Chapter 6), something necessary about "One ought not to kill others" and "It is wrong to tell a lie." Many of the other rules identified by Gert also have a sense of necessity; they are not binding on us because, as it turns out, advocating them avoids bad consequences. Gert appears to acknowledge and explain this necessity, but in the end his explanation does not work.

Nevertheless, there is something very positive we can take away from our discussion of Gert. This is his insistence on the centrality of moral rules in the moral domain. We noted in Chapter 1 that some philosophers who oppose a deductive model of moral reasoning denigrate or at least deemphasize the role of principles and rules in the moral life. In response, I argued that some of these critics of rules tend to misconceive their nature, taking them incorrectly to be generalizations. I also urged that we reflect more deeply on how central and fundamental rules are to us in the moral life. Gert's elaboration of ten specific moral rules assists us greatly in this task. Even if we reject his proposed justification of these rules, we can welcome his concrete specification of them, for with examples in hand it is easier to see their central function. Rules prohibiting us from killing or causing pain or injury to others figure prominently in our moral lives. We appeal to them, we teach them to our children, we remind ourselves of them, we celebrate them. Furthermore, most of the rules Gert identifies as moral are rules on which there would be widespread agreement—many people, in many and perhaps most cultures, would accept them as moral requirements. And, as noted, the suggestion that a necessity attaches to them is valuable. Also valuable is the idea that our moral practices rest on basic judgments with no deeper, more fundamental justification. Perhaps the notion that we *just do* find certain desires and actions irrational should be revised to suggest that we *just do* find certain actions right and wrong. We do not normally try to justify our basic moral rules: that task is assumed by that insignificant minority, the philosophers. Perhaps these moral rules cannot be justified. Perhaps their role is to justify our acting in one way rather than another and in this fashion to define what is right and wrong, good and evil. Can such "constitutive" rules be justified, or are they propositions without a deeper foundation? We return to this question in Chapter 6.

Finally, Gert's identification of ten moral rules alerts us to the diversity of moral thinking. Gert does not attempt to derive these rules from a single, fundamental one, although his "moral reason" for being moral—that it avoids harm to others—comes close to it (p. 201). But he makes no effort to show how this harm to others is anything distinct from the particular evils he identifies as resulting from violations of the ten moral rules. We do well to remember the pluralism and particularity involved in Gert's account.

Alan Gewirth

In one of the most ambitious projects of recent moral philosophy, Alan Gewirth has attempted in his book *Reason and Morality* to provide a rigorous demonstration of the necessary truth of what he considers to be the fundamental principle of morality. Such uncompromising rationalism is a rarity in any field; in ethics it is practically unprecedented, at least since the time of Spinoza and Kant. Gewirth's moral outlook is very similar to Kant's, but his method is reminiscent of Spinoza. Step by step, through several hundred pages, he proceeds to deduce his fundamental principle from premises he regards as necessary and attempts to prove are necessary. Each step of the deduction is carefully and thoroughly defended. Objections are considered—endlessly, it sometimes seems—and are dealt with in a manner that satisfies the highest philosophical scruples. After constructing the proof of his first principle, Gewirth turns to the task of applying it, showing what concrete results can be derived from it and how moral conflicts can be resolved by the use of it. The entire effort is salutary and worthy of serious consideration by anyone interested in the problems of ethics. One may feel in the end, as so often happens with rationalistic systems, that much has been demonstrated and little proved. But to avoid Gewirth's conclusions one must enter into debate with him in the deepest and most serious of terms. He is thoroughly knowledgeable in contemporary philosophical argument, and he is prepared to give any critic a good round.

Gewirth's fundamental principle of morality is what he calls the Principle of Generic Consistency (PGC). He expresses it as follows: "Act in accord with the generic rights of your recipients as well as of yourself."[8] The generic rights of oneself and one's recipients turn out to be rights to well-being and freedom, so the PGC amounts to an enjoinder not to interfere with the freedom and well-being of agents. (A *recipient* is defined by Gewirth as any person whose capacity to behave freely and maintain well-being is affected by one's actions.) To obey the PGC involves showing respect for oneself and others as rational and autonomous beings, and in this way Gewirth's ethical perspective is linked with that of Kant.

Rejecting a number of contemporary ways of justifying moral judgments, Gewirth argues that the only alternative is to pursue the more traditional approach of attempting to prove a first, or fundamental, moral principle (chap. 1). Furthermore, he maintains, the first principle of morality must be shown to be necessarily true, that is, "logically necessary so that its denial is self-contradictory" (p. 23). If the first principle of morality is logically necessary, we *must* follow it on pain of sacrificing our rationality. Action in accordance with the principle then becomes "categorically obligatory" (p. 23).

But how can it be shown that the principle is logically necessary? It is not, Gewirth both admits and insists, *self-evident*. Thus it must be entailed or deductively implied by other premises that are self-evident or inescapable in some other way. These premises cannot be moral ones, for if they were, the fundamental principle would not be "first." Where are we to find premises that are nonmoral, that are necessarily true and self-evident, and that entail the Principle of Generic Consistency?

Gewirth's ingenious answer to this question is that the concept and fact of human action provide what is needed. Human beings frequently are agents, and their agency and actions have a certain structure. This structure is articulated in the concept of action. Each and every action *must* fulfill the necessary and sufficient conditions set forth in this concept. We might refer to the necessary conditions of actions as their *generic features*, these being "invariant features that pertain generically to all actions" (p. 25). If it can be shown that the existence of one or more of these features entails the PGC, every agent must, in realizing that he is

8. Gewirth, *Reason and Morality*, p. 135. Further page and chapter references to this work are indicated parenthetically in the text.

acting, realize that he must accept the PGC. This connection between acting and its necessary conditions is self-evident, so that every agent must acknowledge the reality of these conditions. The necessary conditions or generic features in turn entail the PGC. Hence every agent must also acknowledge the PGC.

What does this have to do with morality? According to Gewirth, action is the inevitable subject matter of morality (pp. 25–26). Frequently in making moral judgments we are directly assessing the moral qualities of actions; at other times we command people to perform or refrain from certain actions in order that some other morally significant state of affairs be realized. Hence directly or indirectly all moral judgments are concerned with action. If actions have certain generic features, all moral considerations must take these features into account. And if these features logically imply a moral principle, then as agents or as moral assessors of actions we must accept this principle. The inevitable subject matter of morality—action—would then entail a moral principle that, following deductively from the necessary structure of action, would itself be necessary. This is, according to Gewirth, exactly the case: "It is from the generic features of the actions that are the common objects of all such moral and other practical precepts that the supreme principle of morality is logically derived" (p. 28).

Before we look at what Gewirth considers to be the generic features of action, it is necessary to examine a crucial aspect of the method he uses in deriving the PGC from these features. He calls his method the "dialectically necessary method" (pp. 42–47). By *dialectical* he means that "the method proceeds from within the standpoint of the agent, since it begins with statements or assumptions he makes" (p. 44). The dialectical method deals with what some agent or other *takes* to be the case, *believes* to be true, or *claims* to be justified in accepting. It concentrates on the logical relationships holding among these assumptions or claims, attending to what else an agent must logically take to be the case if accepting a certain proposition as true. The dialectical method does not pass judgment on the truth or falsity of the assumptions or claims with which it deals, in contrast with what Gewirth calls the *assertoric method*. If we employ the assertoric method, we ourselves assert the propositions with which we are concerned and hence are committed to their being true. As an alternative way of expressing the difference between the two methods, Gewirth states: "Where the assertoric statement is about X, the dialectical statement is about some person's judgment or statement about X" (p. 44). In making dialectical statements, we are not committed to the reality of the subject matter of the judgments we refer to; in making assertoric statements, we make claims about reality, not just about the beliefs or assumptions of agents. Dialectical statements are agent-relative; assertoric statements are not. The importance of this distinction cannot be emphasized too strongly, for many of the criticisms that have been directed at Gewirth's proof fail precisely because they ignore it.

The method is not only dialectical, but also *necessary*. It is concerned, not with thoughts, assumptions, and assertions an agent may or may not have or make, but only with those that, as agent, she *must* have or make. It is not concerned, therefore, with an agent's individual and variable beliefs, desires, interests, purposes, and so on. But if action has a generic structure, all agents—as conscious, rational beings—will be aware (at least dispositionally) of these features. Hence "the statements the method attributes to the agent are set forth as necessary ones in that they reflect what is conceptually necessary to being an agent" (p. 44). The method then proceeds by tracing what logically follows from these statements that an agent qua agent must make. The culmination of this process is the PGC. Thus the dialectically necessary method shows that the agent must accept the PGC.

We may describe as follows the scenario envisaged by the application of the dialectically necessary method to the beliefs of agents qua agents:

(1) An agent S does act a.
(2) Act a has certain generic features.
(3) S is "aware" of these features.
(4) S "expresses" her awareness in proposition p.
(5) Proposition p entails proposition q.
(6) S, being rational, must accept q.

Proposition q, we know, is the Principle of Generic Consistency.

Gewirth raises the question whether it is possible to assert the PGC assertorically as well as dialectically, and he cautiously concludes that it is. Insofar as the PGC follows dialectically from what all agents not only accept but must accept, the PGC must be accepted by all agents. Recalling that action is the direct or indirect subject of interest in all moral considerations, we see that anyone thinking morally must accept the PGC. Thus we can assert the PGC not just relative to this or that agent, but relative to all moral agents and all moral considerations. This is tantamount to asserting it assertorically, since it is unavoidable from the moral point of view.

What *are* the generic features of action that give rise to the fundamental principle of action? Being generic, they are not to be found among the variable purposes, goals, and intentions entertained by individual agents. But to be an agent at all means having some goal, some purpose, and some set of intentions. So purposiveness itself is a generic feature of action (pp. 37–42). If a person does something without intending to do it and without having some end in view in doing it, she has not *acted* at all. Her body may have gone through certain motions, but bodily motions become action only when they express a mental purposiveness and intentionality. Acting purposively involves both having a goal in mind and wanting and trying to obtain it. Gewirth insists that not all wanting and striving is "inclinational" or hedonic—that is, not all action is an attempt to attain a goal the agent thinks will bring her pleasure or an action she enjoys engaging in. On the contrary, many actions aim at the good of others and many are done in spite of the fact that the agent is not inclined to do them or does not enjoy doing them. But all actions have a goal, and an agent always has a favorable attitude (a pro-attitude) toward obtaining the goal of her action—otherwise it would not be her goal. The action itself consists of the agent's movement toward this goal, even if she herself does not anticipate enjoying the fruits of her labors.

The other generic feature of action is its voluntariness. Voluntariness, in Gewirth's words, "comprises the agent's causation of his action" (p. 41).[9] In acting, the agent brings it about that he does certain things with a view to obtaining his goals. Behavior that is not voluntary is not action at all, although instances of "forced choice" constitute difficult borderline cases. For behavior to be voluntary, it must not be the result of external compulsion, internal factors (e.g., reflexes and disease) beyond the control of the agent, or indirect compulsion generated by coercion, threats, and the like. Positively, voluntary behavior or action occurs when an agent's "unforced and informed choice is the necessary and sufficient condition of the behavior" (p. 31). An agent must be aware of

9. On voluntariness, see pp. 31–37.

what he is doing, must grasp and understand (at least dispositionally) his reasons for doing it, and must choose to do so on the basis of these reasons.

With the two generic features of purposiveness and voluntariness in mind, we are ready to begin the use of the dialectically necessary method. What will any and all agents, just by being agents, commit themselves to? What will they be required by the generic features of action to admit?

The first proposition Gewirth attributes to agents seems uncontroversial enough. An agent, being rational and self-conscious, will say to himself (or will be dispositionally inclined to say): "I do act X for purpose E" (p. 49). This statement reflects the conativeness involved in the agent's act—the fact that he is positively inclined toward achieving E and makes an effort to do so. This conativeness is of enormous importance for Gewirth, for it generates the first step in the dialectical process, the derivation of the first implication of "I do act X for purpose E": "From this conativeness it follows that the purpose for which he acts seems to him to be good. Hence, he implicitly makes a value judgment about this goodness. Suppose the fact of the agent's performing a purposive action is expressed by him in such a descriptive statement as 'I do X for purpose E'. Because of the presence of purposiveness in action, from the standpoint of the agent this statement entails 'E is good'" (p. 49). To regard his goal or purpose as good does not mean, Gewirth insists, that the agent thinks it *morally* good. At this stage in the dialectical process, no moral concepts are at work. Moreover, even when the agent uses moral concepts and thinks E is morally *bad*, to the extent that he continues to pursue E he thinks it good or valuable in some way and to some degree. He regards it as good insofar as it is the object of his pro-attitude or positive interest or desire, which is to say, as long as it is his goal.

From "I do X for purpose E," then, it follows for the agent that "E is good." But if the agent is committed to regarding his purpose as good, he also is committed to regarding the necessary conditions for the pursuit of this goal as good. These necessary conditions are, or include, the generic features of action, without which there would be no action at all, no attempt to pursue E. Therefore: "Since his action is a means of attaining something he regards as good, even if this is only the performance of the action itself, he regards as a necessary good the voluntariness or freedom that is an essential feature of his action, for without this he would not be able to act for any purpose or good at all" (p. 52). For him to think E is good entails that he think his freedom to seek E also is good. Likewise, the agent regards the purposiveness of his action as a good, since this too is a necessary condition of his acting at all and hence a condition of his acting to achieve E. Thus the generic features of action turn out to be *generic goods* for the agent. He values his ability to control his actions by his unforced choices, and consequently he values the noninterference of other persons with his actions. Furthermore, the generic purposiveness he values encompasses "those basic aspects of his well-being that are the proximate necessary conditions of his perfor-mance of any and all of his actions" (p. 53). These "basic goods" include life, physical integrity, mental equilibrium, self-confidence, and so on (p. 54). His ability to retain goods already possessed and his ability to increase his purpose-fulfillment also fall under the notion of general pur-posiveness. To value E, therefore, commits the agent to valuing all these aspects of purposiveness—they become for him generic goods. Because no particular purpose can be achieved or realized without them, Gewirth refers to the generic goods involved in purposiveness as *well-being*. It follows, then, that an agent's commitment to "E is good" dia-lectically entails that he accept the proposition "My freedom and well-being are good." And insofar as freedom and well-being are necessary for the attainment through action of any particular purpose whatsoever, this freedom and well-being become *necessary goods* for the agent. Thus we arrive dialectically at the proposition "My freedom and my well-being are necessary goods."

In light of what was said above about the dialectically necessary method, it is important to observe that Gewirth is not making assertoric claims that an agent's freedom and well-being *are* good. Rather, he is claiming that the agent herself, being necessarily committed to "E is good," also and necessarily is committed to "My freedom and well-being are good." The agent would contradict herself by admitting the former and denying the latter. And given that "E is good" follows for the agent from the descriptively true statement "I do X for purpose E," the agent who does X must, upon pain of contradiction, admit that her freedom and well-being are good. No matter what her particular purposes are and no matter what particular things she holds good, she must take the generic features of her action to be good. And this is true of all agents, regardless of their highly variable specific ends.

The next step in the dialectical derivation of the PGC is of crucial importance, and it is also the most controversial. As Gewirth expresses it: "Since the agent regards as necessary goods the freedom and well-being that constitute the generic features of his successful action, he logically must also hold that he has rights to these generic features, and he implicitly makes a corresponding right-claim" (p. 63). In other words, having necessarily committed himself to "My freedom and well-being are necessary goods," the agent is also committed to "I have a right to my freedom and well-being." These rights are called *generic rights* by Gewirth, and claiming them means (dialectically, *from the agent's point of view*) that the agent is entitled to the noninterference of others with respect to his freedom and well-being. This noninterference is what the agent considers (must consider) his due from all other persons. Freedom and well-being are not just things he wants from others. He claims them as an entitlement, for this is what a right is. The ground of this entitlement "is the fact that freedom and well-being are the most general and proximate necessary conditions of all his purpose-fulfilling actions, so that without his having these conditions his engaging in purposive action would be futile or impossible" (p. 65).

Surely, we want to protest, from the fact that an agent holds her freedom and well-being to be goods, even necessary goods, it does not follow that she has a right to them. At most, our protest continues, it follows that she *wants* others not to interfere with her having these goods. This is the objection most often raised against Gewirth.[10] But it contains an important confusion, and it also ignores the way in which Gewirth goes from "My freedom and well-being are necessary goods" to "I have a right to freedom and well-being."

The confusion is easily diagnosed. It is the error of switching from the dialectical to the assertoric mode of argument. *Gewirth* is not claiming that the agent has a right to well-being and freedom; the agent *herself* is committed to claiming this right. But how so? How is this commitment dialectically derived from the previous stage of the argument?

10. See the essays by R. M. Hare, Kai Neilsen, and W. D. Hudson in Edward Regis, Jr., ed., *Gewirth's Ethical Rationalism* (Chicago: University of Chicago Press, 1984).

The passage from "My freedom and well-being are necessary goods" to "I have a right to freedom and well-being" is mediated by the concepts of *ought* and *must*. Consider first the role of *ought*. Realizing that she must have freedom and well-being in order to be an agent at all, the agent affirms that all other persons ought not to interfere with these necessary goods of hers. This is *not* a moral *ought*. Gewirth refers to it as a *prudential* one (p. 71). In the first place, it signifies a necessary connection between having freedom and well-being, on the one hand, and being an agent who entertains purposes and who acts to obtain her purposes, on the other. The former, one might say, is a means (and a necessary means) to the latter. But for an agent to say that she ought to have freedom and well-being (and that others ought to refrain from interfering with them) is not simply for her to remark on a factual means-end connection. Given, as has already been established, that she values her purposes and the generic goods as necessary conditions for the realization of these purposes, the agent *advocates* having these necessary conditions and hence *prescribes* that others not interfere with them. Hence "I ought to have the generic goods" has both a factual and a normative aspect. Just as a prudent person will say, "I ought to go to the dentist," when she realizes that this is the means to good dental health (which she values), so she will say, "I ought to have the generic goods, and others ought not to deny me of them," when she realizes that the generic goods are the means to what she values. In the second case, however, the *ought* is much stronger. There are other ways to maintain dental health than by going to the dentist, and it is possible, even if unlikely, that some people will not value their dental health. But *all* agents must value their freedom and well-being, as these are necessary conditions for everything else an agent values. Hence "I ought to have the generic goods and others ought not to interfere with my having them" has a categorical strength to it that is unmatched by other prudential *ought*s.

The other concept mediating the passage from thinking one's freedom and well-being good to claiming them as rights is that of *must*. "Others ought not to interfere with my freedom and well-being" expresses a necessary link between my having these goods and my being an agent; given that I am committed to the value of my purposes (and hence to the value of my being an agent) and also to their necessary conditions, my advocacy of others' not interfering with my generic goods is expressed in the strongest, most categorical terms (p. 79). I *must* have these things; and if I must have them, you *must* allow me to do so (p. 81). As Gewirth puts it, it would be self-contradictory to say "I must have my freedom and well-being, but you may prevent me from having them if you wish" (p. 80). If I cannot say that you *may* prevent me from having the generic goods, I am required to say that you *must* allow me to have them.

Now we are in a position to see exactly how the right to freedom and well-being is dialectically generated. The link between an agent's *ought*-claim and his right-claim with respect to the generic goods derives from the correlativity of 'ought' and 'rights'. All would agree that from "I have a right to *x*" one is able to derive a statement about what other persons ought to allow me. If an individual has a right to freedom, others have a duty to allow him this freedom and hence ought to do so. Gewirth claims that the entailment holds in the other way as well: "the right-claim takes the correlative form of an 'ought'-judgment addressed to all other persons, that they ought at least to refrain from interfering with the agent's having freedom and well-being. This correlativity amounts to logical equivalence so that there is mutual entailment between the agent's right-claim and this 'ought'-judgment" (p. 66). We have seen that an agent must assert that others ought to allow him freedom and well-being. Given the mutual entailment between *ought*-judgments and right-claims, it follows that the agent must assert his right to these generic goods. Gewirth grants that *ought*-judgments do not always entail right-claims. They do so only "when the person making the 'ought'-judgment regards it as setting for other persons duties that they owe him" (p. 66). This condition is satisfied, he thinks, in the case of the agent who claims that other persons must not interfere with his freedom and well-being. Freedom and well-being are goods that others ought to, indeed *must*, allow him. Hence they are his due. Being his due, his freedom and well-being are the objects of his rights.

Because of the critical importance of this step in Gewirth's argument, let us look briefly at some of the objections raised against it and Gewirth's responses to them. R. M. Hare has clearly identified what I have already referred to as the main objection: "Let us admit for the sake of argument that the agent must *want* his purpose to be achieved (at least want it *ceteris paribus*), and that if one wants the purpose to be achieved, one must *want* whatever is a necessary condition for its achievement. But does it follow that one must therefore think that other persons *ought* to supply these necessary conditions, by refraining from interfering? Can I not want something, without thinking that I ought to have it?"[11] This objection has also been entered by W. D. Hudson and Kai Nielsen.[12] Gewirth responds as follows: "This objection overlooks the crucial role of the 'must'. . . . Hare's and Hudson's references to 'want something' and 'insists upon having something' suggest that the agent's desire for the necessary goods of action is on the same level as any of his contingent, dispensable desires. But this fails to take account of the distinction I have emphasized between necessary and contingent goods."[13] Because as an agent I must have freedom and well-being, I would contradict myself if I said that other persons may interfere with these generic goods. But if I am logically prohibited from saying that they may so interfere, this is equivalent to saying that they *must not* interfere, and this in turn is a way of claiming rights against them.

Second, it has been claimed that Gewirth's argument uses moral notions at this stage and therefore does not succeed in deriving the fundamental principle of morality solely from nonmoral notions. Against Gewirth's claim that he is operating on the prudential level, Hare notes that Gewirth is not maintaining that an agent must demand of other persons that they prudentially seek their own interests—rather, an agent must demand that *other persons* promote *his* (the agent's) own interests, and this is to claim a moral right.[14] Moreover, Hare and D. D. Raphael urge that terms such as 'due' and 'entitlement' are at home only in a moral context, not a prudential one, and hence that Gewirth has smuggled these moral notions into his argument.[15]

Gewirth's reply to this criticism is, first, that moral considerations are by definition those concerned with the interests of other persons.[16] The agent who claims rights against others is not concerned with the interests of those others, but only with her own purposes and their necessary

11. R. M. Hare, "Do Agents Have to Be Moralists?" in Regis, *Gewirth's Ethical Rationalism*, p. 54.

12. W. D. Hudson, "The 'Is-Ought' Problem Resolved?" and Kai Nielsen, "Against Ethical Rationalism," in Regis, *Gewirth's Ethical Rationalism*.

13. "Replies to My Critics," in Regis, *Gewirth's Ethical Rationalism*, p. 207.

14. Hare, "Do Agents Have to Be Moralists?" p. 54.

15. Hare, "Do Agents Have to Be Moralists?" and D. D. Raphael, "Rights and Conflicts," in Regis, *Gewirth's Ethical Rationalism*, p. 88.

16. Gewirth, "Replies to My Critics," p. 208.

conditions. So she is not making moral claims in telling them what they ought to do. She is making prudential claims about what *they* must do to serve *her* interests. Second, this criticism "assumes that the concepts of 'duty' and 'owing' can function only in moral contexts, not prudential ones."[17] Again, the distinction between the prudential and the moral is a matter of whose purposes and interests are to be served. When it is the agent's interests, and when these are necessary interests (as they are in the case of her freedom and well-being), the concepts of 'duty' and 'owing' function just as well as they do in the moral sphere. If others must do something to serve my necessary interests, they have a duty to do so.

At one stage in his argument, Gewirth points to a number of non-moral uses of the term 'rights', specifically its uses in epistemic contexts (pp. 69–70). If a person has accumulated adequate evidence for a theory, we say she has a right to believe it; if she has perceived some state of affairs, she has the right to tell us what happened; if her argument has a certain structure, she has a right to draw its conclusion. In each of these cases, the satisfaction of applicable epistemic standards gives the agent her epistemic right. Similarly, Gewirth thinks, the satisfaction of prudential criteria or standards gives the agent a prudential right. If the noninterference of others is a necessary means to the agent's achievement of her purposes, it satisfies the standards for what is prudentially required, and the agent ipso facto has a prudential right to it. If we can talk of epistemic rights as well as moral rights, we can equally speak of nonmoral, prudential rights.

Third, and finally, it has been objected against this stage of Gewirth's argument that the fact that an agent *claims* that she ought to have freedom and well-being does not entail that she *has* a right to these things.[18] But this objection reflects a failure to stay on the track of the dialectically necessary method. Gewirth's argument is that the agent, having claimed that she ought to have the generic goods, is logically bound to claim the right to these things. At this point, *we* are not saying that she does, or does not, have such a right.

Let us proceed with the dialectical advance. To claim a right requires

17. Ibid., p. 209.

18. Edward Regis, Jr., "Gewirth on Rights," *Journal of Philosophy*, 78 (December 1981), 791; see Gewirth's response in "Why Agents Must Claim Rights: A Reply," *Journal of Philosophy*, 79 (July 1982), 405–6.

conceptually that we have a justifying reason for claiming it. The agent who claims a right to freedom and well-being has as his reason the fact that these generic goods are necessary conditions for the achievement of any purpose whatsoever—necessary conditions, that is, of his agency. At this point, the logical principle of universalizability comes into operation. This principle tells us: "if some predicate P belongs to some subject S because S has the property Q (where the 'because' is that of sufficient reason or condition), then P must also belong to all other subjects $S1, S2,. . . . Sn$ that have Q. If one denies this implication in the case of some subject, such as $S1$, that has Q, then one contradicts oneself" (p. 105). Applying this principle to the case at hand, we see that an agent must extend his right to freedom and well-being to all other agents as well: "Now whatever the description under which or the sufficient reason for which it is claimed that a person has some right, the claimant must admit, on pain of contradiction, that this right also belongs to any other person to whom that description or sufficient reason applies" (pp. 104–5).

The logical principle of universalizability requires that "if one person S has a certain right because he has quality Q . . . then all persons who have Q must have such a right" (p. 106). Given that *all* agents must have freedom and well-being in order to be agents, and given that these generic goods constitute the quality Q that justifies an agent in claiming *his* right to freedom and well-being, it follows that the agent must grant that all agents have the right to freedom and well-being. And if a particular agent must attribute these rights to all other agents, it follows that he must address to himself an *ought*-judgment that requires him not to interfere with their freedom and well-being. Thus we arrive at the Principle of Generic Consistency: Act in accord with the generic rights of your recipients as well as of yourself. Every agent must accept this fundamental principle, and in accepting it he places himself under an obligation not to coerce or harm any other agent. Because the principle speaks to what is required by the interests of others, it is a moral principle. It is fundamental because it is the first moral principle that can be derived by the dialectically necessary method; it in turn is to be used to justify all other moral principles. And it is necessarily true because an agent can deny it only upon pain of contradicting himself.

Let us elaborate a bit on the last point. Consider an agent who grants that she has the right to freedom and well-being but denies that others have it. This denial entails that it is permissible for her to interfere with their freedom and well-being, in spite of the fact that these features are the necessary conditions for their agency. Such a denial amounts to saying that these necessary conditions of agency are not sufficient justifying conditions for attributing rights. But the agent has claimed a right to freedom and well-being for herself *solely* on the grounds that they are necessary conditions for her agency; that is to say, she has maintained that these conditions are the sufficient conditions for her having the right. To claim the right in this way for herself and not to grant it to other agents thus involves the outright inconsistency of both granting and denying that the necessity of freedom and well-being for agency is a sufficient condition for a rights judgment.

This concludes the dialectical proof of the Principle of Generic Consistency. Starting with an agent's affirmation that he does an act for a certain purpose, the method proceeds to show how all agents are committed to the principle requiring them to acknowledge and honor the rights to freedom and well-being of all other agents. Given that *all* agents, and hence all participants in any moral practice, *must* accept the PGC, its relativity to agents is no longer of any significance. It stands alone as a necessary truth that all rational persons must accept. Any agent who denies it contradicts himself, and the obligations it imposes cannot be avoided as a result of the desires, inclinations, or commitments an agent contingently has or fails to have (p. 135). It is a categorical imperative, whose truth can be deduced by the power of reason alone. It takes account of the interests of other persons in addition to those of the speaker, and hence it is a moral principle. It is, in sum, the supreme necessary principle of morality.

Gewirth gives considerable attention to the logical and epistemological status of the PGC (pp. 150–90). Is it, he asks, an analytic truth? He concludes that it is, in spite of the fact that it is not self-evident. Its necessity, he argues, is indirect, not direct, meaning that "a consideration only of the definitions or meanings of its directly constituent terms together with the logical principle of identity" (p. 151) will not reveal that its denial is self-contradictory. Its necessity results from its being entailed by other propositions that themselves are necessary and must be accepted, and hence its necessity is grounded in the logical linkage between its directly constituent terms and the terms occurring in these other necessarily true propositions. These other propositions have to do with the goodness of the purpose at which an agent aims and the good-ness of the generic goods that are the necessary conditions for attaining this or any other purpose. It is because of this indirect, dialectical linkage that an agent may fail to be aware of the necessity of the PGC and may even be led to deny it. Seeing that the denial is in fact self-contradictory requires a grasp of the dialectical argument that leads to the PGC.

Unlike many analytic truths, the PGC possesses material as well as logical necessity. Its truth is not an empty, formal one that deals only with possibilities, not actualities. The PGC, on the contrary, is grounded in the facts of human action. The first step in its dialectical proof is the *true factual statement* "I do X for purpose E." Furthermore, it is grounded in the necessary structure of all action. Hence it has a necessary factual content, or *material necessity*.

Gewirth's proof is ingenious, elegant, and powerful—but for all that it may not work. Space (not to say patience and energy) prohibits our canvassing all the objections that have been raised against the proof and considering Gewirth's responses to them. It is hoped that the above presentation will stimulate the reader to look at the texts themselves and to engage directly in debate with Gewirth. It is difficult, however, for me to resist the temptation to offer one criticism of my own, to attempt, perhaps imprudently, to put the finger on the fatal flaw in the proof. The spirit of optimism declares that where others have failed, there is still room for success; at the same time the counsel of experience warns against making the attempt. So I characterize my criticism only as a problem I have had in fully appreciating Gewirth's proof.

Let us look once again at the stage of the proof that seems to worry most people: Gewirth's deduction of the right to freedom and well-being from the agent's claim that these are his generic and necessary goods. Gewirth maintains that when an agent claims "I have a right to freedom and well-being" he is claiming a prudential right to these goods. I wish to argue that, considered as a matter of prudence, an agent cannot claim such a right. After that, I shall ask whether it is possible for an agent to deduce a *moral* right to freedom and well-being from the fact that they are his necessary goods. Gewirth denies that a moral right can be derived in this way, but he does so, I claim, for the wrong reasons. Having "corrected" Gewirth on this point, I argue that nevertheless there are other, legitimate reasons endemic to his proof which do dis-allow this derivation. My conclusion is that Gewirth cannot use his dialectical method to show that an agent is justified in claiming any right, prudential or moral.

Gewirth maintains that to make a rights claim logically requires having a reason that one considers sufficient to justify it (pp. 65, 104). The agent who makes a prudential rights claim to his own freedom and well-being has, to be sure, what *he* considers a good reason for it—it will help him attain the fulfillment of his purposes. But can he maintain that this reason is one that other persons also can grant to be a good reason for attributing a right to him? When Gewirth's agent claims for himself a prudential right, he is at the same time claiming that other agents have a duty or obligation to him, for rights and obligations are correlative. If the agent thinks he has a good reason to claim his right, he also must think there is a good reason for attributing a duty to others. Moreover, the agent must think that there is a reason for attributing the right (to himself) and duty (to others) which is acceptable not only to him but to the other persons as well. We cannot charge people with obligations whose grounds they do not recognize *and cannot reasonably be expected to recognize*! Do I have any justification for thinking that another agent, *not conceived of as a moral agent but only as a prudential one*, has a reason to recognize my prudential right to my own freedom? Expressed in terms of the correlative notion of duty or obligation, is there any reason to think that another prudential agent has a reason to recognize his duty to respect my prudential right? This is highly doubtful. Why should another agent, acting solely on the motive of prudence, recognize an obligation to me, just because my freedom/well-being are necessary conditions of my agency? But if I cannot attribute to the other person a reason for granting me my freedom, a reason he can be expected as a rational, prudential agent to accept, I cannot attribute to him a duty, not even a prudential one, to respect my freedom/well-being. And if I cannot attribute a prudential duty to him, I can hardly claim a prudential right against him, for again rights and duties are logically correlative.

Indeed, it is unclear what it means to talk about *prudential* duties and obligations owed to others. Perhaps we have prudential obligations to ourselves, but how so to others? What would a prudential duty to others be like? Perhaps it is a requirement that I behave in certain ways toward others in order to maintain and protect *my own* purpose fulfillment. But Gewirth has not shown that agents should respect the freedom and well-being of others in order to protect their own agency. Such a move plays no role in his dialectical proof—perhaps advisedly so, since it is far from certain that an agent necessarily must honor the freedom and well-being of others in order to protect her own. So if we can make no sense of the notion of a prudential duty, it is a notion that Gewirth should not use. But without prudential duties, how can he speak of prudential rights?

As the widely shared critical response to Gewirth reveals, it is tempting to think of the right an agent dialectically claims for herself as being a moral right. Gewirth, of course, denies that it is, for he is attempting to justify the PGC as the fundamental, that is, first, principle of morality. Nevertheless, we might ask whether it is possible to use the dialectically necessary method to prove, first of all, that an agent must claim a moral right to her freedom and well-being. If it is, we might construe the logical principle of universalizability as generalizing this right and attributing it to all other agents. This would not be quite the result Gewirth envisaged, but it would be a formidable accomplishment. The dialectically necessary method would allow an agent to deduce her own moral right to the generic goods and then to derive the moral rights of all other people to these goods as well. Let us see if this reformulation of Gewirth's proof works.

If I claim a moral right to freedom and well-being, and not merely a prudential right, it is much easier to picture me as attributing a correlative duty to others, for moral duties are not nearly as problematic as prudential duties. Gewirth would claim, of course, that it is impossible for his agent to attribute a moral duty to others, for this agent is concerned only with his own interests, and by definition a moral claim is one that takes the interests of others into account. But is this any more than arbitrary linguistic legislation? Perhaps my judgment on this occasion is moral because, although it deals only with my interests, it requires something of other persons in regard to my interests—it attributes obligations to others to respect my interests. Morality is surely as much a matter of considering what obligations others have to me and my interests as it is of considering what obligations I have to the interests of others. If this is so, my firm conviction that I have a right to freedom and well-being and that you have a duty not to interfere with them can be considered a moral judgment. Gewirth might be well advised to abandon his restriction on what constitutes a moral claim. If he did so, would he not, then, be able dialectically to derive a moral right from "My freedom and well-being are necessary goods"?

Before we answer affirmatively, we must ask once again if the agent can understand other agents as having a reason to acknowledge this moral right he would claim and hence a reason to acknowledge a moral duty to him. This would be possible if the agent had what he considered to be a sufficient reason for demanding the right and could take other agents to have the rational capacity to acknowledge this reason. An agent could deliberate in the following way: freedom and well-being are necessary conditions of my agency; other agents can acknowledge this as well as I; it follows for me from this fact that I have a moral right to freedom and well-being; other agents, being rational, also can deduce from the fact that freedom and well-being are necessary conditions of my agency that I have a right to them; accordingly, other agents have a reason to acknowledge their duty to respect my freedom and well-being. If an agent can attribute in this fashion a reason to others for assuming a moral duty to him, he can attribute to himself a moral right.

Unfortunately, this step cannot be taken within the confines of Gewirth's dialectically necessary method. Gewirth does not pass directly from "freedom and well-being are necessary conditions of my agency" to "I have a prudential right to freedom and well-being." There is an additional element in the dialectical background of the rights claim—namely, the agent's pro-attitude toward his own purpose-fulfillment or agency (p. 66). Noting the necessary connection between freedom/well-being and agency and, *additionally*, desiring to fulfill his purposes, the agent demands the right to freedom and well-being. It is this second element that poses a problem for any attempt to attribute a moral duty to others. The agent may attribute to another (rational) person the perception that freedom/well-being are necessary conditions of his (the agent's) agency, but he cannot attribute to her a pro-attitude toward his (the agent's) own agency. That is to say, it is not necessary for an agent to see the other person as having this pro-attitude toward his (the agent's) agency. So even though he can attribute a partial reason to the other person for acknowledging his right—namely, the perception of the necessary connection between his freedom/well-being and his agency—he cannot attribute a complete reason, one that is sufficient. But if he cannot attribute to the other person a sufficient reason to acknowledge his right, and hence a reason to assume a duty toward him, it follows that the agent cannot maintain that he has a moral right to his freedom and well-being.

Of course, an agent might reason dialectically in the following fashion: another person (being rational) can see her own freedom/well-being as necessary conditions of her own agency, and she will have a pro-attitude toward her own agency—therefore she will conclude that she has a right to freedom/well-being. But to attribute to the other person the thought that she has a right is not the same as attributing to her the thought that she has an obligation to someone else. The agent needs to attribute the latter thought to the other person in order to claim his own right to freedom/well-being. And, again, he cannot do this.

What would happen if we omitted the pro-attitude as a condition for deriving a rights claim? What if the agent tried to derive his right solely from the fact that freedom and well-being are necessary conditions of his agency? He certainly can judge that other rational agents would see his freedom and well-being as necessary conditions of his agency. Thus if he appealed to this fact alone to derive his right he could claim that others also will see that these conditions give him a right and accordingly will see that they have an obligation toward him. Thus the agent could claim that others have a good reason for acknowledging his right, and therefore he could claim it for himself.

Were this way of developing the proof available to Gewirth, it would accomplish part of what he desires, but it would convert him from a rationalist into a naturalist. The mere fact that freedom and well-being are necessary conditions of agency would entail the agent's right to these conditions. But then a rights claim would become just a factual claim ("I, in order to be an agent, must have freedom and well-being"), and there would be no need for a dialectical, rationalistic proof of moral propositions. In fact, it is unlikely that a rights claim can be interpreted as no more than a factual claim of this sort. The proposition that Gewirth relies on so heavily in his proof, namely, "I *must* have freedom and well-being," is not equivalent to "There must be freedom and well-being in order for there to be agency." The former involves advocacy, the latter does not, being only a statement of the necessary conditions of agency. This is another way of saying that rights claims cannot be logically derived solely from statements about necessary conditions of agency.

Gewirth is probably correct, then, to insist on something like the expression of a pro-attitude as a component of a rights claim. A rights claim has an ineliminable normativity attached to it. Unfortunately, it is just the presence of this pro-attitude or normative dimension which makes it impossible for an agent, using Gewirth's method, to attribute to others a moral obligation toward him and hence impossible for him to claim for himself a moral right. And he cannot, as argued above, claim a prudential right. Hence the dialectic grinds to a halt. We are unable to pass from "My freedom and well-being are necessary goods" to "I have a (prudential or moral) right to freedom and well-being." What is perhaps the most rigorous rationalistic proof of a fundamental moral principle ever attempted thus fails.

Before leaving Gewirth, we should address two other problems with his theory. The first involves the question whether Gewirth's PGC can lay claim to being the principle underlying all more specific moral precepts. The difficulty arises because different people may see the PGC as yielding different specific precepts. If they do, they will interpret the meaning of this principle differently, each person understanding it to entail her preferred precept. Furthermore, it appears impossible in the nature of the case to specify the meaning of the principle in a way that is independent of a specification of the propositions or precepts following from it. If this could be done, two disputants could assure themselves that they share a first principle and then argue that one and not the other precept follows deductively from it. But if such independent specification of the meaning of the first principle is not possible, neither party to the dispute can prove to the other that her precept follows and the other's does not.

Let us see how such a criticism can be developed with respect to Gewirth's theory. What, we must ask, is contained in the PGC, in the injunction to act in accord with the generic rights of other agents? Gewirth claims that the PGC requires us not only to refrain from interfering with the freedom and well-being of others but also to assist other persons in attaining these necessary conditions of agency (pp. 217–18). We are to help them by providing the benefits needed to attain freedom and well-being, the only limits placed on this requirement being that we need not incur a comparable cost and that our duty is activated only if the other agents cannot attain the generic goods by their own efforts.

Many moralists would reject this idea of a positive duty to promote the freedom and well-being of others. Gert, for example, claims that our only duty is to refrain from causing an evil to befall others; there is for him no moral duty to do good for others.[19] Gewirth, of course, would

19. Gert, *Moral Rules*, pp. 69–75.

reply that those who reject a positive duty are simply wrong, that they have failed to see that the PGC requires this duty and that the duty can be logically deduced from it. But is such a reply convincing?

The issue of positive versus negative duties has been debated for a long time, and the disagreement continues. It is unlikely, although possible, that one party to the dispute has made a logical error. A more probable interpretation of the disagreement is that, in appealing to something like the PGC in order to justify their respective precepts concerning duty, two disputants are not really appealing to the same fundamental principle but rather to two different principles ambiguously expressed in the same way. Or it might be said that they appeal to two different interpretations of the PGC. In defense of this account of the disagreement, one might argue that the only way we have of knowing what the PGC means is to see what follows from it. If one party derives a positive duty from it, and after lengthy discussion can discern no logical mistake in this derivation, we must conclude that for this party the PGC *means* that we should act in accordance with our positive duties toward others. And the same follows for the other party: if she derives only negative duties from the PGC and fails to discern a logical error after lengthy discussion, in all likelihood she takes the PGC to require only negative duties of us. Accordingly, we do not have a disagreement over the same fundamental principle, but rather two appeals to two different fundamental principles.

If individuals who differ over the reality of positive duties and rights operate with different fundamental principles or different interpretations of the PGC, neither party can claim to justify its specific precepts by appeal to the PGC. The PGC becomes just as disputable as the claims that there are, or are not, positive rights and duties. If we get positive duties out of the PGC, it is because we put them there in the first place.

In response, it might be argued that Gewirth's theory affords us a way of establishing the meaning of the PGC which is independent of a consideration of the precepts following from it. We might interpret its meaning in terms of what went into its proof. The PGC, according to this view, enjoins the kind of rights and duties incorporated in the premises used in its proof, duties and rights that therefore can be identified by studying these premises.

But what rights and duties are revealed in Gewirth's proof of the PGC? When an agent claims a right to her own freedom and well-being, is she claiming a positive one or only a negative one? Gewirth apparently takes her to demand both her positive and negative rights. But someone else, who otherwise acknowledges the validity of Gewirth's proof, might take an agent to demand only her negative rights. Nowhere in the proof does Gewirth show that an agent *must* demand her positive rights and not just her negative ones.[20] Hence Gewirth merely assumes that an agent will and must do this, and his assumption has no more surface plausibility than the contrary assumption that only negative rights are claimed. Here, then, we have a standoff. The disagreement over the interpretation of the PGC recurs in essence in the very proof of the PGC, but at this point we have no general principle to appeal to in order to resolve our disagreement. If one interpretation of the proof is correct and the other incorrect, it is fair to say, I think, that Gewirth has not adequately demonstrated this. And if not, an appeal to the proof of the PGC will not decide the issue between those who derive both negative and positive rights from this principle and those who insist on deriving only negative rights from it. More may need to be said on this subject, however, for the idea of a person's demanding her *prudential* rights (upon satisfaction of the criteria of prudence) does seem to suggest that others should assist her as well as not interfere with her in her effort to attain freedom and well-being. But I have questioned whether it makes sense to speak of prudential rights.

Rather than identifying a principle that is to be found in all moral thinking, then, Gewirth has given us a formulation open to at least two radically different interpretations. His proof is unable to resolve the issue and hence unable to demonstrate that there is only *one* fundamental principle operating in moral thinking.[21]

20. Gewirth does say early on that an agent's right-claim "entails, *in a secondary way*, that under certain conditions other persons ought to assist him to have freedom and well-being" (p. 67, my emphasis). He does not, however, explicate or justify this secondary entailment.

21. The same difficulty occurs in the rationalist moral philosophy of Donagan. In *The Theory of Morality*, Donagan defines a principle of respect which he thinks is the fundamental principle of morality and hence the source of other subordinate principles, or what he calls *first-order precepts*. It turns out, however, that there can be extreme differences of opinion as to what follows from this fundamental principle, and reflection on these differences can lead one to hypothesize that what we have in the principle of respect is not a common first principle shared widely within western culture, but rather two or more different principles expressed by means of the same ambiguous terms.

As an illustration, consider the examples of suicide and self-defense (*Theory of Morality*, pp. 77, 72, and 86–87). Donagan argues that respect for oneself as a rational creature is

We also have rejected Gewirth's claim that reason requires the PGC, in either formulation, as a condition of moral rationality. His proof of this first principle of morality does not work. But even if it did, we could question whether it establishes the PGC as the kind of first principle that actually operates in our moral thinking. In not claiming self-evidence for the PGC and in arguing that its necessity is indirect, Gewirth is open to the charge that his first principle does not have the unconditional, indubitable status we accord to basic moral principles in everyday life. The PGC is more like a theorem than an axiom—it requires proof and is derived from other propositions. Hence, even if its proof worked, it would not provide us the kind of bedrock ground we have in the moral sphere. It is conditional upon facts about human agency, and our commitment to it would have to have the following form: *if* human agency is such and such, *then* we should respect the generic rights of others. Furthermore, given the complexity of the proof, we would have to be open to the possibility of having made a logical error along the way. There is, however, something absolutely bedrock and obvious about the basic principles of morality, about telling the truth, not hurting others, and so on. Gewirth's PGC is neither bedrock nor obvious.[22]

---

consistent with the permissibility of committing suicide in certain circumstances. Equally it gives one the right to take the life of another in self-defense or in defense of the life of some other person. Both of these propositions have been heatedly rejected by some members of the Hebrew-Christian tradition, the tradition out of which Donagan thinks the principle of respect emerges. Probably the majority opinion within this tradition has been against suicide, and a significant minority of Quakers and pacifists has rejected the moral permissibility of taking the lives of others. Donagan is well aware of these facts. The first, however, he dismisses by arguing that religious considerations are responsible for it. From a purely moral point of view, he thinks, both it and the second position are arguably wrong. They misconceive what follows from the principle of respect. This, too, is unconvincing. The mere fact that there is a long-standing dispute between pacifists and nonpacifists, and between those opposing suicide and those defending it, makes it likely that any logical errors (or any factual errors in the minor premises) would long ago have been detected. In all probability the arguments between them turn on different conceptions of what it means to respect a rational creature—this difference being built into their first principles. If, after extended discussion and argument, two parties continue to disagree over whether the principle of respect permits or disallows suicide or war, the likelihood is that they start with different interpretations or conceptions of this principle. What each gets out of it deductively is what each put into it in the first place. Only ostensibly, it should be concluded, do they share a first principle.

22. Again, we find the same problem in Donagan's moral rationalism. He does not give us an a priori proof of his principle of respect, and he does not regard it as self-evident. Nevertheless, he thinks that reason requires it, and he claims that we would be

These reflections might suggest that fundamental moral rules must have the kind of necessity attaching to axioms: they must be self-evident. A self-evident rule would require no proof—simply to understand it would be to acknowledge that it is true. If our basic moral rules are unconditional and obvious, are they not self-evident? Is not a self-evident proposition the only kind of ground or starting point that could have these features? In fact, as I show in Chapter 6, there *is* another way for such a starting point to be possible. We can interpret moral principles, or at least some of them, as having a special and distinctive role, in which they are and must be unquestioned. Our moral axioms are unshakable propositions, not because they are necessarily true and self-evident, but because their role is to provide a constant measure for assessing the unconstant moral character of the passing scene. So conceived, basic moral principles stand in contrast to contingent moral judgments, which may be true or false and which require a ground. The ground of these judgments is, in large part, the basic moral principles themselves. The latter are groundless—they are the *given* in the moral life.

---

able to perceive a synthetic necessary connection between respect and the freedom and rationality of human beings if only we had a deep enough insight into reason. This not only opens the door to the skeptic who dismisses such synthetic necessary connections, it also in effect characterizes the basic moral principle in a way that is inconsistent with our ordinary understanding of it. In everyday moral life we accept the principle of respect in an absolute and unconditional way. But for Donagan, this principle has a ground beyond itself, in the fact that human beings are free and rational. We are to grasp the truth of the principle by rationally perceiving the necessary connection between it and its ground. In doing so, surely we could make a mistake—intuitions of necessary connections are not, I take it, infallible (they seem extraordinarily hard to come by in the first place). Although we might be highly confident in thinking that human nature rationally requires respect, we would have to admit that we could be mistaken. If Donagan were correct, we could imagine that, possibly having made a mistake, in fact we are not required to respect other human beings. This is not the attitude we have toward those principles we unconditionally accept. That attitude, as I claim in Chapter 6, sees the principle of respect as one of the essential assumptions of morality and one that could not be given up without abandoning the moral perspective altogether. It is a necessary assumption in the sense that it cannot meaningfully be repudiated while remaining in the moral sphere. It is not, however, grounded in any alleged facts about human nature. Its role, rather, is that of a rule that grounds other, more specific, contingent, and contestable moral judgments.

Conclusion

We have now examined in detail two rationalist theories of morality. Each is impressive in its own way, but each is also open to criticism. If the objections I have leveled against them are valid, neither of these theories provides an adequate account of how we come to know the truth of moral propositions. Neither of them succeeds in proving that one or more moral propositions are necessarily true and the source of all other true moral convictions. It is possible, of course, that my objections can be met, and it is also possible that some other form of rationalistic theory can be developed which would escape criticism. It would be rash to predict otherwise, but as noted earlier, the failure of these exemplary theories should cause us at least to question the entire rationalist enterprise in moral philosophy. I shall conclude with a few observations that cast still another kind of doubt over the rationalist project.

Is the rationalist model of proof actually operative in the moral life? To ask this question is not to call into doubt whether we often seek to deduce our specific moral judgments from more general moral principles, but rather to inquire whether we are attached to these general principles and specific judgments "because reason requires it"—because it would be irrational for us not to accept them. To be sure, we often say that we have a good reason for doing what we do, but it is far less obvious that we speak of *reason* supporting our actions. How many of us would claim to have a reason for doing what we do that is traceable back to logically necessary premises or to premises it would be irrational to deny? If asked why we believe, say, that abortion is wrong, we may proceed to give reasons for doing so, and this defense may involve a deductive component. We may, for instance, appeal to the alleged fact that the fetus is a living person with a right to life, and we may deduce this right from the general principle that all living persons have a right to life, together with the factual claim that the fetus is a living person. But if it is asked why all living persons have the right to life, the answer is likely to be something to the effect that God gave them this right or simply a peremptory and irate "They just do!" It would be very surprising to hear an opponent of abortion say that all living persons have a right to life because it would be self-contradictory or contrary to reason to deny it. So to the extent that deduction does operate in moral justification, it seldom if ever does so from a set of premises perceived to be rationally necessary.

What if the deductive derivation of specific precepts did proceed from rationally necessary premises? It would follow that anyone who does not reach the same moral conclusion as the one that deductively follows from these premises is being irrational or at least making a serious logical error. But just as Gert has denied that reason can require us to behave morally because it would turn too many of us into irrational persons,[23] so too we should deny that reason requires us to believe any given set of fundamental principles and their derivatives, since this also would turn too many of us into irrational persons. Given the great diversity of moral opinion on any particular topic, most of us would turn out to be either irrational or logically blind. Surely this is not the case.

Another way of putting this is to deny that the concept of a rational person (or irrational person) carries much weight in the moral sphere. Gert points out that 'irrational' has numerous colloquial equivalents in our language: 'nutty', 'crazy', 'stupid', and so on.[24] But do we ever say that it would be *nutty* of a person to approve of an abortion? Would we be *crazy* to break a promise, *stupid* to tell a lie? In most instances these expressions would be quite out of place. Likewise, the positive expressions 'the rational thing to do', 'what reason requires', and 'what logic demands' have little application in our ordinary moral discourse. None of this is to deny that in moral practice and moral debate we *reason*, we *justify*, and we even seek to *prove* our convictions. It is to suggest only that the rationalist model for explicating these linguistic facts does not fit certain other aspects of our linguistic and moral practices very well. Reason is a tool of the moral life, yes, but it is unlikely to be its source or its substance.

23. Gert, *Moral Rules*, p. 212.
24. Ibid., p. 21.

4 / Moral Realism

CONTEMPORARY British moral realism is a young and developing movement.[1] The philosophers primarily responsible for it are John McDowell and Mark Platts. McDowell expressed his disenchantment with noncognitivism and simultaneously proposed his realist alternative in a series of brilliant, provocative articles published in the 1970s and early 1980s, notably "Are Moral Requirements Hypothetical Imperatives?" and "Virtue and Reason."[2] Platts gave a brief, more systematic presentation of the theory in the last chapter of his book *Ways of Meaning*.[3] Subsequently, Sabina Lovibond elaborated a distinctive form of realism based on her interpretation of Wittgenstein in her book *Realism and Imagination in Ethics*.[4] All of these thinkers acknowledge a debt to David Wiggins, whose 1976 British Academy Lecture, "Truth, Invention, and the Meaning of Life," has had a powerful impact on recent

1. In this chapter I concentrate almost exclusively on the writings of contemporary British moral realists and devote only the last section to the theories of contemporary American moral realists. The two approaches share some features, but the American thinkers disagree in important ways with their British cohorts, largely with regard to intuitionism and to the non-natural status of moral features and facts. I develop these points of contrast in the last section of the chapter.

2. John McDowell, "Are Moral Requirements Hypothetical Imperatives?" *Proceedings of the Aristotelian Society*, supp. vol. 52 (1978), 13–29; "Virtue and Reason," *The Monist*, 62 (July 1979), 331–50.

3. Mark Platts, *Ways of Meaning* (London: Routledge and Kegan Paul, 1979), chap. 10.

4. Sabina Lovibond, *Realism and Imagination in Ethics* (Oxford: Basil Blackwell, 1983).

moral philosophy.[5] Wiggins describes himself not as a realist but as an anti-noncognitivist, but many of his suggestions lend themselves to a realist interpretation. And all of these realists recognize the inspiration they have received from Iris Murdoch's *Sovereignty of Good*.[6]

The general outlines of the realist theory proposed by these philosophers are easy enough to identify. Moral propositions, or at least many of them, are taken to be straightforward descriptions of moral facts. As such they have truth values, determined by whether they accurately depict the moral facts or not. Moral facts are constituted by situations, persons, and actions possessing irreducible moral features or aspects. Although the moral aspects are in some sense determined by the other features of the situation, person, or act, they are not to be thought of as logically entailed by these other "nonmoral" features—morality is fundamentally autonomous, and moral judgments are not to be assimilated to scientific ones. Nevertheless, moral aspects are objective and independent of human desires and attitudes. Human beings, or most of them, have a perception-like capacity to apprehend and appreciate the moral dimensions of their world. No special moral sense is involved in this apprehension; rather, it is to be understood in terms of the standard operations of perception and reflection together with the capacity to employ a distinctive moral language. A person's moral perceptions on occasion may be nonveridical as a result of desire, wishful thinking, or any of the other standard threats to observational accuracy. Consequently, people may disagree morally, but these disagreements are in principle capable of being resolved. As in other departments of the pursuit of knowledge, what is required for achieving or acknowledging moral truth is carefulness, diligence, and imagination.

The fact that this theory of moral realism is recent and evolving poses a problem for anyone attempting to give a systematic description of it. There are gaps and apparent inconsistencies in the presentations we currently have of the theory. I have no choice but, on occasion, to try to fill in the gaps and to propose ways of reconciling the different accounts. Thus many aspects of my survey must be taken as my own interpretation of what has been, or should be, said about a particular topic. I attempt to flag those occasions on which I go beyond what has been claimed by

5. David Wiggins, "Truth, Invention, and the Meaning of Life," *Proceedings of the British Academy* (1976), 331–78.

6. Iris Murdoch, *The Sovereignty of Good* (London: Routledge and Kegan Paul, 1970).

the realists themselves, and I make every effort to extend or amend the theory in a way that would be acceptable to them. How successful I am is, of course, another matter.

Truth-conditional Semantics

One of the difficulties the realists have faced in making their theory accessible to a wide philosophical audience results from its having been proposed against the background of a highly technical, often obscure semantic theory. McDowell and Platts have advocated and made significant contributions to the truth-conditional semantics developed in Britain and the United States during the 1970s.[7] This approach to semantics is largely the result of Donald Davidson's seminal effort, in his article "Truth and Meaning," to construe the idea of a theory of meaning as a theory of truth.[8] Without some understanding of the truth-conditional semantics resulting from this effort, a reader is unlikely to appreciate the power and novelty of the moral realism that has been built on it. Hence our first task is to come to grips, albeit in a highly general and simplified manner, with the truth-conditional approach to meaning.[9]

Davidson and others view the meaning of a sentence as being articulated by a theory providing a statement of the conditions under which the sentence is true. A complete theory of meaning for a particular language would yield an explication of the truth conditions for each sentence of the language. These statements of truth conditions are patterned after Alfred Tarski's famous "T-sentences," which result from his theory of truth.[10] A Tarskian theory of truth yields, for every sentence of a language, a T-sentence like the following:

7. See Platts, *Ways of Meaning*, and his "Introduction" in Platts, ed., *Reference, Truth, and Reality* (London: Routledge and Kegan Paul, 1980). See the essays by McDowell in *Reference, Truth, and Reality* and also his "Introduction" (with Gareth Evans) and "Bivalence and Verificationism" in G. Evans and J. McDowell eds., *Truth and Meaning* (Oxford: Oxford University Press, 1976).

8. Donald Davidson, "Truth and Meaning," *Synthese*, 7 (1967), 304–23.

9. No effort is made in the following account to be critical of truth-conditional semantics, although the theory is not without its critics. Perhaps the most forceful repudiation of the various notions incorporated into it is to be found in G. P. Baker and P. M. S. Hacker, *Language, Sense, and Nonsense* (Oxford: Basil Blackwell, 1984). I discuss Wittgenstein's criticism of Frege's notion of propositional content, an important component of the theory, in Chapter 2.

10. Alfred Tarski, "The Concept of Truth in Formalized Languages," in his *Logic, Semantics, and Metamathematics*, rev. ed., trans. J. H. Woodger (Indianapolis: Hackett, 1983).

T: 'Reagan is a conservative' is true if and only if Reagan is a conservative.

Most readers immediately respond to such a sentence with incredulity, asking how such an obvious claim could illuminate the notion of truth. The T-sentence appears to be merely a redundant, empty claim. Upon examination, however, it is not empty at all. The clause on the left-hand side of the 'if and only if' sign (the LHS, as it is usually abbreviated) is a sentence about a *sentence*; the sentence on the right-hand side (the RHS) is a sentence about the man Reagan. And the two sentences are materially or extensionally equivalent—that is to say, if the one is true, so is the other, and if the one is false, so again is the other. Moreover, it is intuitively, pre-analytically obvious that the T-sentence does express a true claim about the conditions under which the sentence 'Reagan is a conservative' is true. The T-sentence is not, however, a logical truth; it is a contingent one about the truth conditions, which could have been otherwise, for a particular sentence. Being contingent, the T-sentence is informative, as could be seen more readily if the sentence quoted on the LHS were in a foreign language and the remainder of the LHS and all of the RHS were in English—the sort of situation that would prevail if we were using the T-sentence to articulate in English the truth conditions of the foreign sentence. It is no less informative, however, if we use it to articulate in English the truth conditions of an English sentence, since it is a contingent matter whether the fact described on the RHS is the fact that makes the sentence quoted on the LHS true. Not only is the T-sentence an informative truth, it is a truth that must be acknowledged by any theory attempting to define the notion of truth. Hence for Tarski an adequate conception of truth would have to yield a theory that provided a true T-sentence for every sentence of the language. True T-sentences constitute constraints on acceptable theories of truth.

Davidson used these ideas to suggest that the Tarskian T-sentence illuminates the *meaning* of the sentence quoted on the LHS. Simple sentences such as 'Reagan is a conservative' are to be understood as meaning that the condition described on the RHS of its T-sentence prevails—the condition, namely, under which it would be true. The meaning of more complicated sentences is given recursively, that is, by showing how their truth conditions are truth functions of the truth conditions of the simple sentences composing them. Hence the meaning of

'Reagan is a conservative and Mondale is a liberal' is given by the truth conditions of 'Reagan is a conservative' and 'Mondale is a liberal' as these are related by the logical, truth-functional connective of conjunction. What about the words or constituents making up the simple sentences of the language—how are we to understand their meanings? For truth-conditional semanticists, the meanings of these constituents are to be explicated in terms of the contributions they make to the truth conditions of the sentence as a whole. To understand how this takes place, the Tarskian notions of *reference* and *satisfaction* can be employed. The subject term of a simple sentence is to be interpreted as referring to an object, and this reference is encoded in an axiom of one's theory of meaning. Thus the theory would contain many axioms like:

      R: 'Reagan' refers to Reagan.

The predicate term has its meaning articulated via another axiom specifying its satisfaction condition. Thus the meaning of 'is a conservative' is explicated by means of:

      S: An object x satisfies 'is a conservative' if and only if x is a conservative.

If we want to know the meaning of the simple sentence 'Reagan is a conservative' we can obtain it by deriving its truth condition from the axioms governing its constituent terms. This deduction would allow us to conclude:

      T: 'Reagan is a conservative' is true if and only if Reagan is a conservative.

The axioms R and S show the contributions of the subject and predicate terms of the sentence to the truth conditions of the complete sentence. And theorem T articulates the meaning of the sentence.

Such are the bare outlines of the truth-conditional theory of meaning. For our purposes, further elaboration is unnecessary. It suffices to look at some of the implications of the theory by reflecting on some of the criticisms to which it might appear vulnerable. Let us raise again the charge of vacuity. How can "'Reagan is a conservative' is true if and only if Reagan is a conservative" tell one anything about the meaning of 'Reagan is a conservative'? It does not seem to say enough. Obviously, it might be argued, if one knows the meaning of the expression on the RHS then one knows the meaning of the quoted sentence on the LHS, but *equally*, if one does not know the meaning of the quoted sentence on the LHS, one can hardly be said to know the meaning of the RHS. If the T-sentence is to give one a grasp of the meaning of the sentence quoted on the LHS, this presupposes that one does not already understand the quoted LHS sentence. But if not, how can one understand the RHS either?

In response to this criticism, the truth-conditional semanticist notes that the T-sentence is what one can be said to know *if* one knows the meaning of 'Reagan is a conservative'.[11] And surely, if one knows the meaning of this sentence, one does know (perhaps tacitly) the T-sentence. So the criticism must be that, if one knows the meaning of a sentence, one knows *more* than the corresponding T-sentence. In a sense this is so. One must also know the appropriate axioms governing the sense of the constituent terms of the sentence, axioms of the form R and S. This again may seem inadequate: R and S may appear insufficient as far as representing what one knows in knowing the meaning of a simple sentence. But what more is needed? It is tempting to say that what is wanted is some indication of how one recognizes that 'Reagan' refers to Reagan, and some indication of how one verifies that an object satisfies 'is a conservative'. Having a recognition procedure for applying names and a verification procedure for using predicates may seem essential to understanding the sense of a sentence. But this is just what the truth-conditional semanticists wish to deny!

How is one to provide a recognition procedure for applying names? One suggestion, perhaps the only one available, is that a name is to be applied to an object if the object satisfies certain descriptions. 'Moses' applies to the person who led the Jews out of Egypt; 'Reagan' applies to the first actor to become an American president; and so on. Associated with every name will be a number of such descriptions, and understanding the meaning of the name, so goes the suggestion, is understanding

11. See John McDowell, "On the Sense and Reference of a Proper Name," in Platts, ed., *Reference, Truth, and Reality*.

that one is to apply it when these descriptions, or at least most of them, are true of an object.

This suggestion faces numerous problems. First, as Saul Kripke has argued, a person may understand a name and know to what it refers even if it turns out that the individual named does not have the properties attributed to it by the associated descriptions.[12] Reagan in fact may not be the first actor to become an American president; but if this were the case, one might still know to whom the word 'Reagan' refers. Second, different people using different descriptions for applying a name need not mean different things by it; they simply have different techniques for applying the name to the same object. Their understanding does not vary as their application techniques vary, and hence the application or recognition techniques do not enter into the meaning of the name they use. Third, a person often will understand many names for which he has no recognition procedure of the above type at all. Does one apply the word 'Mother' to someone only after observing whether some descriptions are true of her? And what descriptions do we associate with the name 'red'? Using a name more often than not is noninferential, but it would always have to be inferential were the description theory correct.

Perhaps in light of these difficulties we will come to think better of the proposal that an R-type axiom expresses what we know or understand when we know the meaning of a name. If one's R axiom states that 'Reagan' refers to Reagan, this tells one no more, but also no less, than to whom the term refers. And surely it is the case that anyone and everyone who understands 'Reagan' knows that it refers to Reagan. Thus the axiom captures all that we *must* know to understand the name in question.

Similar considerations apply to the proposal that understanding a predicate like 'is conservative' or 'is green' requires a grasp of a verification procedure for knowing when to apply the predicate. Notoriously, attempts to provide these verification procedures for even simple predicates have been far from satisfactory. Does 'is green' apply when an

---

12. Saul Kripke, "Naming and Necessity," in Donald Davidson and Gilbert Harman, eds., *Semantics of Natural Languages*, 2d ed. (Dordrecht and Boston: D. Reidel, 1972), pp. 253–355.

observer has certain sensations? Which ones? Does a blind person fail in principle to understand the term? If one says that an object is green, is one saying that a given person will have such and such sensations? Surely not, for an object may be green without any particular person's having the sensations in question. In any event, to speak about sensations is to speak of an observer and her experiences; to speak of green is to talk of the color of an object. The verification procedures, even if they could be given, would not amount to the meaning of the predicate.

This last point is even more obviously true when we examine slightly more complex predicates. Under what conditions does one verify that someone "crossed the Rubicon"? One may do so by observing the event, or by reading about it in various books, or by asking an expert. No one of these verification procedures is built into the meaning of the term, for if it were, different people who use different verification techniques would mean different things by it. But a history teacher and his pupil, and an observer on the scene, do not mean different things by 'crossed the Rubicon'.

The failure of verificationism as a theory of meaning is a failure of analysis—the attempt to provide a decompositional account of the necessary and sufficient conditions for applying a term. The history of linguistic philosophy in the twentieth century demonstrates again and again the failure of such attempts. After eighty or so years, we are no closer to having adequate analyses of the propositions concerning us than we were at the beginning of the century. One explanation for this curious history of failure is that the analysts were confused from the start in thinking that simple components, verification procedures, recognition procedures, and so forth are part of the meanings of our terms and sentences. The truth-conditional semantic approach can be understood as urging just this explanation. And pointing to the failure and its likely explanation goes a long way toward showing that in asking for the meanings of terms and sentences we are *not* asking for more than is supplied by T-sentences and R and S axioms.

To employ a T-sentence to articulate the meaning of a sentence is to offer what McDowell and Platts call an *austere* account of the meaning.[13] For the reasons given above, no attempt is made to analyze this

---

13. See McDowell, "On the Sense and Reference of a Proper Name"; and Platts, *Ways of Meaning*, chap. 10.

meaning, and though definitional "glosses" are allowed, they are not to be construed as indicating decompositional necessary and sufficient conditions for applying the *definiendum*. The T-sentence is said to provide us with the literal meaning of the sentence it mentions; and the T-sentence is to be understood as employing the techniques of designation and use. Both of these notions require brief explanation.

T-sentences, according to truth-conditional semanticists, are only a part of a complete theory of meaning for a language. The theory as a whole contains everything needed to interpret the linguistic behavior of language users. The T-sentences are to be thought of as articulating the *senses* of sentences: they tell us *what is said* by speakers who use them. But in addition to expressing a sense, sentences are put to use in the performance of certain speech acts—acts of asserting, asking, ordering, warning, praising, and so on. Thus in addition to having a sense, sentences have an illocutionary *force*. A complete theory of meaning will comprise, then, a theory of sense and a theory of force.[14]

The theory of force will tell us what a speaker, in uttering a sentence with a certain sense, is *doing*. The speech act as a whole is a matter of the particular use to which the sense or literal meaning is put—for example, to assert that something is the case, ask whether it is the case, praise it for being the case, and so on. Obviously, then, the theory of force does not give us the (complete) meaning of a sentence but rather presupposes the sense of the sentence. Something like the Speech Act Fallacy (see Chapter 2) would be involved in restricting a theory of meaning to a theory of force or a theory of use.

Why are T-sentences thought to be the proper vehicles for portraying the sense or literal meaning of sentences? In a T-sentence the RHS is a declarative sentence. Declarative sentences are uniquely qualified to express the truth conditions of sentences, for they themselves can be true or false. Furthermore, declaratives seem capable of embodying more semantic information than other grammatical moods. They can carry, for instance, information about tenses, whereas imperatives cannot.[15] Thus they seem qualified for the task of articulating a sentence's *content*, which can be "acted" on in different ways by the performance of different illocutionary acts: an assertion serves to say that the content does

14. See Platts, "Introduction," in *Reference, Truth, and Reality*.
15. Ibid., p. 3.

apply to the world, an interrogative asks whether it applies, a command demands that it apply, and so forth. All such illocutionary acts need a content, and hence all meaningful sentences need truth conditions. This is not to say that all of them are true or false—only assertions have this property.

To articulate the sense of a sentence by using a T-sentence is said to employ the technique of designation and use.[16] This means simply that the LHS of the T-sentence designates or mentions a sentence, and the RHS uses a sentence. When the T-sentence is formulated in the same language that is employed to formulate the designated sentence, the sentence designated is the same as the sentence used. This has an important implication. If one is explicating the meaning of a sentence in one's own language, one must use this sentence in the very process of explicating it. One's theory of meaning does not place one at a distance from one's language or provide either a neutral perspective from which to view it or a neutral vocabulary to describe it. In characterizing it, one must employ it. And when one uses an English sentence to express the meaning of a sentence in a foreign language, once again one must use the English sentence in order to express the truth conditions of the foreign one. A theory of meaning using T-sentences brings along with it all the presuppositions and commitments, conceptual and perhaps ontological, of the theorist's own language.

This last point has great significance when we attend to the notion of a truth-conditional theory of *moral* language. If one were to articulate the sense of 'breaking promises is wrong', one would have to use this sentence as well as mention it. Thus one would have to express (although not necessarily to assert) the proposition that breaking promises is wrong. The noncognitivist philosophers were always claiming that they were merely analyzing what moral language means and that they were not themselves engaged in normative ethics, in telling people what is right or wrong. Their metaethical analyses, they maintained, entail no normative judgments. If one accepts the proposal for a truth-conditional theory of moral language, this appearance of detached neutrality is deceptive. To say "'Breaking promises is wrong' is true if and only if breaking promises is wrong" requires that one use the moral sentence on the RHS. Of course, the theorist is not required to *assert* that breaking

16. Platts, *Ways of Meaning*, p. 244.

promises is wrong, for the RHS sentence is only part of a hypothetical—biconditional—proposition. Nevertheless, this normative sense must be one the theorist understands and expresses; he does not hold it at a descriptive distance. He must at least *think* the moral proposition. As Wiggins has put it: "If the theorist believes his own theory, then he is committed to be ready to put his mind where his mouth is at least once for each sentence *s* of the object language, in a statement of assertion conditions for *s* in which he himself uses either *s* or a faithful translation of *s*."[17]

A second implication following from the application of truth-conditional semantics to moral discourse is the obvious one that moral judgments have truth conditions. This is unavoidable, given that their sense is explicated in terms of the conditions under which they are true. From this it does not strictly follow that they are true or false, for it might be the case that they are used illocutionarily to do something other than to assert that their truth conditions are satisfied. But it does follow that in understanding a moral claim like "Breaking promises is wrong" one must grasp the notion of its being the case that breaking promises is wrong. One must understand this even if the proposition has the illocutionary force of a prescription and hence is being used to tell someone to bring it about that this is the case, that is, bring it about that breaking promises is wrong. In fact, it makes little sense to say this, which should discourage us from giving a prescriptive account of the illocutionary force of the utterance. The most natural account of the illocutionary act performed on a sentential content like breaking promises is wrong is that this content is *affirmed*. This, of course, would convert the utterance into a true or false assertion.

Finally, by way of considering the general implications of truth-conditional semantics for moral theory, let us reflect on the notion of an austere interpretation of the sense of a moral proposition. That a truth-conditional interpretation offers such an austere account may be seen as one of its greatest attractions. The history of metaethical analysis shows a recurrence of failure and inconclusiveness on a scale at least as large as that in other fields of philosophy. It simply has been impossible to reach agreement on whether a sentence of the form 'x is good' is a statement of subjective feelings, an expression of these feelings, a statement about the

17. Wiggins, "Truth, Invention," p. 355.

natural or metaphysical properties of x, a command to choose x, or a statement that there are good reasons to choose x, and so on. None of these analyses has carried much conviction, and almost all of them have been put forward by their authors as mere approximations to the sense of the sentence, practically an admission that the theorist has not quite gotten it right. Philosophers have been unable to agree whether the Naturalistic Fallacy is a fallacy or not, because they have been unable to decide if moral terms designate natural properties. And emotivists are never quite pleased with their description of the emotion they think is expressed by moral judgments, just as prescriptivists feel the need to insist that moral prescriptions are only similar to commands, being in other respects quite unlike them. Perhaps the time has come to suggest that the entire attempt to analyze the meanings of moral utterances is bankrupt.

In this context, the proposal for an austere account of moral judgments can appear very refreshing. Consider the judgment that betraying a friend is wrong. The austere approach would take understanding this to involve grasping:

R: 'Betraying a friend' refers to betraying a friend; and
S: An object x satisfies 'is wrong' if and only if x is wrong.

Putting these axioms together amounts to understanding:

T: 'Betraying a friend is wrong' is true if and only if betraying a friend is wrong.

Whatever else the speaker is doing—prescribing, expressing a proattitude, and so forth—she is performing this illocutionary act with respect to the sentential content or sense, its being the case that betraying a friend is wrong. One understands the content of what is said by deducing the RHS of the T-sentence from axioms R and S. Furthermore, the most natural account of the illocutionary act is to say that one is affirming or asserting it to be the case that betraying a friend is wrong. The most straightforward answer to the question "What does the sentence 'betraying a friend is wrong' mean?" is that it means that betraying a friend is wrong. It certainly does mean this, and knowing that it means this is sufficient for knowing what it means. Here we have an account of meaning which, in dramatic contrast to the metaethical theories of non-cognitivism and naturalism, looks to be infallible!

The contemporary moral realists' use of truth-conditional semantics is in line with G. E. Moore's claim that the word 'good' means the property of goodness, as well as with his reliance on Butler's famous dictum that a thing is what it is and not another thing.[18] If one says that knowledge is good, one literally means that knowledge is good. One is not saying that it brings pleasure, or promotes the survival of the species, or satisfies God's demands on us. All of these other things may be true of knowledge, but they certainly do not constitute what it *means* to say that knowledge is good. Nor does one's claim mean the same as saying that an impartial spectator would approve of or choose knowledge, or that it would be rational to do so, or that one's conscience tells one to do so. All of these claims may reflect ways in which one comes to believe or to verify that knowledge is good, but how one recognizes this fact is distinct from the fact itself. The recognition and verification procedures merely show how one comes to have, and to confirm, the belief *that knowledge is good.*

The Influence of Wittgenstein

We now turn to some other general and preliminary methodological considerations. In addition to their commitment to truth-conditional semantics, the British realists are under the influence of certain aspects of Wittgenstein's later philosophy.[19] This influence is a limited one, since truth-conditional semantics is, at least prima facie, a repudiation of the Wittgensteinian notion of meaning as use. Perhaps the new semantic theory can accommodate under the rubric of illocutionary force much that is involved in Wittgenstein's descriptions of use, but the Fregean notion of propositional content which plays such a large part in this theory was explicitly rejected by Wittgenstein.[20] (Furthermore, the realist notion

18. See G. E. Moore, *Principia Ethica* (Cambridge: Cambridge University Press, 1903).

19. This is especially apparent in Lovibond, *Realism and Imagination in Ethics*; also see John McDowell, "Non-cognitivism and Rule-Following," in S. Holtzman and C. Leich, eds., *Wittgenstein: To Follow a Rule* (London: Routledge and Kegan Paul, 1981).

20. See L. Wittgenstein, *Philosophical Investigations*, trans. G. E. M. Anscombe (London: Macmillan, 1953), I, §22; see Chapter 2 for a discussion of Wittgenstein's views.

that one can grasp the truth conditions of a proposition without knowing how to confirm that they hold appears to run counter to a verifica-
tionist or constructivist tendency in Wittgenstein.[21]) Be that as it may,
Wittgenstein's insistence on describing how we actually talk and on
grasping the rules and standards involved in actual linguistic practices is
acknowledged and honored by the realists.[22] They too see language as a
social practice with no external justification or warrant—a practice that
defines its own criteria of assessment and that cannot legitimately be
evaluated in terms of criteria originating from some position external to
it. The realists seem to share Wittgenstein's philosophy of mind, as becomes clear when they eschew psychologistic explanations of linguistic
behavior. (McDowell's rejection of the notion of sense as incorporating
a recognition procedure is an example.[23])

The realists also join with Wittgenstein in refusing to see principles or
rules of reasoning in either mechanistic or Platonic terms, denying, for
example, that the principles of deduction operate as causal laws generating valid arguments or that they trace logical connections already and
eternally in existence in some Platonic heaven. Our processes of
reasoning—deductive or otherwise—are human activities, governed
normatively, not causally, by standards we define and employ, and they
cannot be judged consistent and rational, or inconsistent and irrational,
from the standpoint of any external perspective. Likewise, our practices
of classification and description operate on the basis of human interests
and perceptual capacities. We train people to engage in them, and we
formulate criteria and standards to assess when they are performed correctly. There is no perspective external to these practices from which we
can view the world to determine whether or not it contains the like-
nesses and distinctions our descriptive language expresses. There is,
moreover, no neutral, privileged vantage point from which we can wit-
ness our human epistemological adventures and declare them successes
or failures. Knowledge in all its forms can only be expressed in and

21. For this interpretation of realism, see the following writings of M. Dummett:
"Truth," *Proceedings of the Aristotelian Society*, 69 (1968–69); "What Is a Theory of
Meaning?" in S. Guttenplan, ed., *Mind and Language* (Oxford: Clarendon Press, 1975);
"What Is a Theory of Meaning? (II)," in G. Evans and J. McDowell, *Truth and Meaning*.
Also see Platts, "Introduction," in *Reference, Truth, and Reality*, p. 12.

22. See Lovibond, *Realism and Imagination in Ethics*, and McDowell, "Noncognitivism and Rule-Following" and "Virtue and Reason."

23. See his "On the Sense and Reference of a Proper Name."

evaluated in terms of the concepts and standards we actually possess. In sum, the realists share Wittgenstein's contempt for the notion of a transcendent, supposedly "objective" perspective from which we can pass judgment on our language practices, including, most importantly, our moral practices.

Let us reflect on these Wittgensteinian assumptions as the realists apply them to the central questions of moral theory. Are moral utterances to be understood as descriptions having a truth value? If so, by virtue of what are they true or false? And what type of reasoning, or, more generally, what form of cognition goes into the ascertainment of the truth values of moral claims? In answering these questions, the realists see themselves as heeding Wittgenstein's demand that we *look and see* how our language works rather than approach it with a priori preconceptions.[24] Such a direct examination of moral language reveals to them that it is used descriptively for the purpose of ascribing moral properties or aspects to persons, actions, and situations. After all, moral utterances are expressed in declarative sentences, truth values are attributed to these sentences, reasons are demanded and given for the moral beliefs embodied in them, and public, social standards are in operation to determine the correct and incorrect application of moral language.

Of course, moral features and moral facts are highly distinctive, and our talk concerning them often does not fit the mold of much of our talk about nonmoral features and facts. Certainly discourse about the moral domain is not reducible to scientific theorizing about a purely natural domain. But to take this difference as a sign of the noncognitive status of moral discourse is to reveal a metaphysical bias. Noncognitivists bring to the debate an assumption that only scientific facts are real and that only the scientific method yields true knowledge. These metaethical theorists do not look and see—they already "know" that natural, scientifically observable and describable features exhaust reality. But what perspective do the noncognitivists occupy so as to know this? If they occupy the perspective of a scientist, all they can say is that moral facts are not subject to scientific verification—but the moral realist admits this. If they pretend to occupy a perspective from which they can see

24. "The thing to do in such cases is always to look how the words in question *are actually used in our language,*" L. Wittgenstein, *The Blue and Brown Books* (New York: Harper & Row, 1965), p. 56. Also see Wittgenstein, *Philosophical Investigations,* I, §§120–24.

that scientific statements alone describe the world, their pretension can be challenged. How is such a second-order perspective to be achieved, what are its credentials, and how does it relate to the first-order perspectives of science, morality, and so on? It must be able to acknowledge the truths of science without itself occupying the scientific perspective and using the methodology and standards of science, for otherwise it would simply beg the question in favor of science. And it must be able to denigrate the status of moral utterances while appreciating exactly what they mean and what canons of truth and objectivity are endemic to them. The very idea of such a neutral, privileged perspective begins to lose its sense. Surely scientific claims have merit only with respect to scientific standards of inquiry, and moral claims fail to have merit only with respect to moral standards of inquiry. To apply other standards would be to justify science on nonscientific grounds, and what interest do we have in doing that? To criticize morality on nonmoral grounds leaves the moral justification for these claims (surely the important one) untouched.

What if it turns out, as a result of our looking and seeing, that moral inquiry falls into neither the deductive nor the inductive methodological pattern? What would this show, other than that moral thought is neither a matter of logic and mathematics, on the one hand, nor of empirical generalization, on the other? Is there any non-question-begging justification for holding these to be the only adequate methodologies to use in the pursuit of knowledge? What needs to be done, and all that philosophically can be done, is to examine the method of moral inquiry with a view to ascertaining what its structures and standards are. This is something that can be accomplished only by engaging in moral thought itself, grasping at first hand how moral concepts work, when they apply, and how we know that they apply. In turn this means having moral concerns and participating in a moral practice with others who have similar concerns. The strategies of moral argument and investigation finally make sense only in the context of these shared concerns and the interests that go along with them. Our concepts and arguments express our interests and concerns, and so understanding them requires that one be a full-fledged participant in the moral practice of one's community (which may be mankind at large). The distance the noncognitivists alleged to maintain from actual moral practice—the claim that their metaethical theories implied no normative theses—may have brought impartial objectivity. But to the extent that this distance was maintained, it prevented the theorists from understanding what moral talk is all about. It is no small wonder, then, that the noncognitivist descriptions of moral language seem so woefully inadequate and appear to bear little resemblance to the real thing.

It may seem odd to picture the realists as recommending a "look and see" procedure when they already have been described as advocating a general, truth-conditional theory of meaning. It would appear that many of their views about moral language are simply deductions from their theory of meaning, these views reflecting what the independently established theory would say if applied to moral discourse. There can be little doubt that the realist moral theory is implied by the general program of truth-conditional semantics. At the same time, however, the justification for that general theory must involve showing that it "fits" numerous ranges of discourse. A characterization of moral discourse achieved by the "look and see" procedure and also required by the theory would constitute an important substantiation of the theory. And to the extent that the theory had already received independent validation, its consonance with our direct observations of moral language would tend to give them epistemic support. No question need be begged, then, by approaching a domain of language with both a theory in hand and a policy of observing the facts.

Thick Moral Concepts

Let us turn to more specific aspects of the theory of moral realism. First, what are the facts about moral discourse allegedly uncovered by the realists' attention to our actual moral practices? It is important, they think, *where* we begin, where we initially focus our attention. They note that most metaethical theorists have been concerned primarily with general evaluative terms like 'good' and 'right'. These terms occur in nonmoral contexts as well, and they have a high degree of generality and ambiguity built into them. It is unclear what elucidation of distinctively moral discourse can be expected to issue from a study of 'good' and 'right', and there is a real risk that their very generality may mislead the analyst. The realists prefer to begin the study of moral language with specific, undeniably moral concepts, such as courage, kindness, loyalty, and so forth.[25] Even these may have nonmoral uses, but much actual moral discourse and argument is conducted in terms of them, and it is

25. See Platts, *Ways of Meaning*, pp. 243, 246.

easier to see what is going on when we morally praise someone for being courageous than when we praise her for being good. Bernard Williams has referred to these specific notions as *thick* moral concepts, and the label is apt.[26] A great deal of specific detail is built into the concept of courage, whereas the notion of a good person connotes very little.

What is immediately noticeable about the thick concept of courage is that (a) what acts or persons can correctly be called courageous is fairly strictly delimited; and (b) it is a decidable matter of fact that a person acted courageously or not on a given occasion. Less noticeable, but apparent upon reflection, is that (c) the meaning of courage, being given not by the standard verification conditions but by truth conditions, is as rich and complex as the phenomenon itself. Let us consider each of these features.

First, not just any act or person can be called courageous. To say that Casper Milquetoast is courageous is to misuse the term and possibly to reveal that one does not understand it. The concept of courage is a public concept with definite and objective occasions when its use is correct. Although it is obviously the case that in describing someone as courageous one is evaluating the person, the description does not harbor a "primary evaluative meaning" that could attach itself to just any descriptive criteria the speaker wished. This is not possible in principle. The evaluative meaning of 'courageous', if we want to speak this way at all, must be securely tied to the limited public, objective occasions on which the term is applied. There is no separating the two dimensions of meaning, and neither can be thought of as varying independently of the other. Being praiseworthy for possessing certain distinctive features is just as objective and objectively delimited as possessing those features in the first place.

The noncognitivist thinkers who separate descriptive and evaluative meaning imply that a person could understand the conditions of application for a moral term even if he did not share the attitudes or accept the prescriptions built into the evaluative meaning. These conditions of application would be provided by the descriptive meaning, which is itself morally neutral. McDowell has argued that in fact this may not be the case.[27] Can we be sure, he asks, that the conditions for applying a term

26. Bernard Williams, *Ethics and the Limits of Philosophy* (Cambridge: Harvard University Press, 1985), p. 129.

27. McDowell, "Non-cognitivism and Rule-Following," pp. 144–45.

like 'courage' can be identified in morally neutral language? Can we be sure, in other words, that there is a way of classifying things which groups them in the same way we do when we call them courageous, but which could be mastered and understood independently of the concept of courage? McDowell suggests that in using the concept of courage and other specific moral concepts we learn new ways of classifying persons and actions and that we have no descriptive access to these groupings if we do not employ these moral concepts. If this is so, it would demonstrate how tightly the so-called descriptive and evaluative meanings of moral terms are connected. This would short-circuit the attempt to free the evaluative use of moral terms from the public occasions on which it is deemed proper to apply them. These occasions and the evaluative meaning are welded together, so that one cannot even understand the descriptive content of terms like 'courage' without sharing the evaluative sentiments that go along with it. Conversely, the evaluative sentiments become just as public and objective as the occasions and conditions of application.

This leads to the second point. When one learns moral language one is taught to use its terms in definite ways and not in others. There is a Quinean "pull toward objectivity" at work.[28] Mastery of the language requires that, to apply a term correctly, we must do so in ways that meet the approval of the speech community, ways that conform to public usage and that avoid personal idiosyncrasies. We may disagree with others concerning some specific cases, but there must be a general agreement in judgments with the speech community if we are to be accepted as part of it and acknowledged to have competence in its language.

The implication of this "pull toward objectivity" is that most questions concerning specific moral issues can be decided in rational, objective, and factual ways. Social practice and consensus, according to Lovibond, give rise to and ground the notions of rationality and objectivity.[29] A shared form of life defines the standpoint from which a judgment can be made in a public and objective manner rather than in a personal and subjective one. For a participant in this shared form of life, an objective moral judgment will be one in "conformity to the consensual standards of sound judgment."[30] A moral judgment made within

28. See Lovibond, *Realism and Imagination in Ethics*, pp. 58–62.
29. Ibid., pp. 39–40.
30. Ibid., p. 43.

this practice is answerable to public canons of evidence and reasoning. If a judgment satisfies these canons, it is, by definition, objective and rational. This social constitution of rationality and objectivity takes place no less in science than in morality. Scientific and moral judgments are answerable to public, consensual canons of thought generated by the ongoing practices of the moral and scientific communities. There are no practice-transcendent canons of rationality and objectivity. Disabused of the idea of such transcendent standards, we have no basis for thinking that judgments made in accordance with consensual standards are *not* rational and objective.

It is not inconceivable, however, that individuals widely thought to possess a virtue like courage turn out in fact not to possess it. This third feature of thick moral concepts results from their having what Platts calls *semantic depth*.[31] When one masters a term like 'courage', one becomes skilled in applying the term when certain standard conditions are met. These standard conditions are not the same as the truth conditions, but rather are the commonly accepted means of ascertaining that the truth conditions prevail. These verification procedures may not in fact reveal courage, and this possibility allows for an overturning of publicly accepted judgments. Mastery of the verification conditions is consistent with failing to grasp the satisfaction conditions of the predicate 'is courageous'. What is finally constitutive of factuality and objectivity in moral or any other discourse is social consensus concerning truth conditions, not verification conditions.

But there is more to semantic depth than this. One may correctly identify the truth conditions of judgments concerning courage but have a superficial grasp of them. Although competent in the standard use of 'courage', one may still fail to grasp the deep nature of its truth conditions. One may have mastered the use of the term without having known any exceptionally courageous persons or without having experienced those circumstances that require and test courage. More personal and in-depth experience of life, or of courageous persons, may allow one to see previously unknown dimensions and depths of this virtue. In this event, it is not inappropriate to say that one comes to see what courage *really* is. Not that it was not courage one identified before; it was, but one's knowledge of it was superficial. The wiser one becomes, the more one may come to see that some acts and persons superficially appearing

31. Platts, *Ways of Meaning*, p. 249.

courageous are, at bottom, morally ambiguous. And one may come to see that acts that do not appear very courageous are in fact so. Hence one may be led to revise or extend in novel ways some of the judgments of the linguistic community. One is able to do this, however, only because one takes its concept of courage, with the austere truth conditions defining it, and comes to see in greater detail, clarity, or depth what is true of things that fall under it. One enriches the public concept; one does not invent and employ one's own concept. All knowledge of courage, superficial or deep, widely shared or extremely personal, has to be positioned within a public conceptual domain where shared meanings guide discourse. Semantic depth allows for new moral discoveries, even shocking and revolutionary ones, but these discoveries presuppose the sense of propositions (and the reference and satisfaction axioms) provided by the austere account of public meaning. This is the thread connecting the superficial and the deep use of moral terms.

Examination of thick moral concepts with semantic depth allows us to see another aspect of the moral life often obscured in treatments centering on general, abstract terms like 'right' and 'good'—namely, that moral knowledge requires insight and appreciation and that keen penetrating vision is often of greater value than argumentative skill. Given the truth conditions for judgments of courage, ascertaining the presence of this virtue requires attention to the facts and observations of behavior, character, and circumstance. Given the semantic depth of the notion of courage, our initial observations may be crude and partial. Knowledge of the "real thing" will require patience and perseverance in the effort to see more deeply or fully into the complexity of behavior, character, and circumstance. Here we encounter the possibility of the moral sage—and that there are moral sages, although few and far between, is an important feature of the moral realm. Sages see more, and see more clearly, than we do. It is not their skill at argument that impresses us, not their ability to be more consistent and rigorous in their moral views. They show us new things, new dimensions to the familiar and trite world we inhabit.

Moral Facts

But enough! We have been talking blithely of moral facts and moral knowledge as if it were obvious that these are well-understood matters, whereas, as we all know, they have been challenged throughout the history of philosophical reflection on morality. It is time to see in some detail how the new realists come to grips with these problems and how they make good their employment of cognitive terminology. What *are* moral facts? What *is* moral knowledge?

Moral facts are those states of affairs in the world which make moral propositions true or false. As Platts has expressed it, "if a moral judgment is true, it is true by virtue of the (independently existing) real world, and is true in virtue of that alone."[32] If, for example, we judge that Washington's crossing of the Delaware was a courageous act, and our judgment is true, then Washington's act possessed the feature or property of courage. Likewise, a kind person instantiates the property of kindness. Other moral situations will possess aspects that might be described as *requirements*. McDowell has noted that we can come to see that a situation we are in requires or demands kindness or courage of us.[33] Thus moral facts do not have a uniform appearance. The kinds of moral aspects they possess will vary—some being properties, others requirements. Some moral facts, we might say, are facts about how things already are; others are facts about how they ought to be or must be. That some of these features, especially the latter kind, are highly distinctive should be no argument against calling them features or aspects of the world. Only a metaphysical assumption about what kind of features we find in the world could generate such an argument. If, on the contrary, we follow the contours of our ordinary moral talk, we will feel no reluctance to speak of its being a fact that we ought to show more kindness to our children or that the world must do more to eradicate starvation, just as we will feel no impropriety in speaking of a person's outstanding feature as being kindness or courage.

The realists we are studying are avowed pluralists: "there are *many* distinct ethical properties whose occurrence can be detected—sincerity, loyalty, and so on."[34] They reject the view that there is a common denominator to all moral values, a highest genus, and that specific moral features are determinants of this "supervalue." Far from the diverse moral properties being gradations of The Good or The Right, so that they might be weighed on a common scale and a determination made of

32. Ibid., p. 243.
33. "Virtue and Reason," pp. 331–32.
34. Platts, *Ways of Meaning*, p. 246.

which takes precedence, they may in fact be quite incommensurable.[35] Moreover, they may come into deep and tortuous conflict, and their incommensurability entails that no quantitative decision procedure could be invoked to decide among them. In the end, as we shall see in more detail, the decision and choice would lie with perception.

Relying on the austere account of moral judgments requires that we look directly for moral facts. We are not to infer moral facts or features from the presence of more elementary components into which they have been analyzed and which alone can be directly observed. The facts and features at issue are not "logical constructs" out of more elementary and "more real" facts and features. They are real in their own right and immediately observable. We can see that an act is courageous just as immediately as we can see that an object is red or that a figure is square. Moral properties may be more complex than these particular nonmoral ones, but complexity is not the issue. One can observe someone making a promise; one can observe a riot going on; one can observe the swearing in of a president; one can observe a case of extreme cruelty—all of these are surely complex facts but all of them can be directly observed. They are not logical fictions, nor are they hypothetical or inferred entities; to a clear, informed, and attentive mind they are directly evident.

Moral features and facts, however, do have a distinctive character that appears to make them inferential. They have a noncontingent relation to other facts. To know that someone acted courageously—indeed, to see that he acted courageously—requires a grasp of the other features of the act, features of the person himself and the situation in which he acted. One needs to know what happened and in what circumstances; one needs to know something about the risks, the dangers confronted, and the odds on succeeding; also relevant will be information about the agent's frame of mind. Knowing that George Washington's crossing of the Delaware was courageous requires knowing some military, social, and personal history. As Platts puts it, we might, if we only had a clear idea of what the term meant, call these *nonmoral* facts and go on to say that coming to see Washington's act as courageous requires grasping a number of nonmoral facts about it.[36] In some sense, the moral property of being courageous is a function of these other facts.

35. Ibid.; see also Wiggins, "Truth, Invention."
36. *Ways of Meaning*, p. 254.

The considerable problem that begins to emerge here—perhaps the central problem for moral realism—is that the existence of a moral property, though not inferable from nonmoral ones, is still a function of them. Morality is said to be autonomous: moral propositions are not entailed by nonmoral ones. At the same time, it is always appropriate to ask for a person's reasons for claiming that an act has a specific moral character, and these reasons encompass descriptions of the nonmoral character of the act. Furthermore, these reasons appear to be connected to the moral character in a noncontingent manner. They indicate not just how we come to know an act is, say, courageous, but what makes it courageous. How can nonmoral facts be noncontingently related to moral facts and yet not entail them? Is this a coherent and intelligible set of views? We must digress for a moment from our exposition of realism to consider in some detail how the realists can be criticized for holding these views.

The Problem of Supervenience

Simon Blackburn has long been one of the most articulate and forceful critics of moral realism, and he has argued on numerous occasions that the conception of moral facts just described, and particularly the relationship alleged to exist between moral and nonmoral properties, renders realism incoherent or at least mysterious.[37] Blackburn agrees with the realists that moral concepts are related to nonmoral concepts in the way described, and he likes to speak of this relation as one of *supervenience*. Supervenience, he agrees, is a feature of moral discourse, but he argues that the realists' interpretation of moral discourse as descriptive of moral facts cannot explain this supervenience. On the contrary, it converts it into a monstrous, unintelligible mystery. Or to cite John Mackie's problem with supervenience, it makes moral facts unpalatably queer.[38]

37. Simon Blackburn, "Moral Realism," in J. Casey, ed., *Morality and Moral Reasoning* (London: Methuen, 1971); for his more recent thoughts on supervenience and the problems of realism, see his *Spreading the Word* (Oxford: Oxford University Press, 1984), chap. 6, and his "Supervenience Revisited," in Ian Hacking, ed., *Exercises in Analysis* (Cambridge: Cambridge University Press, 1985). Also see R. M. Hare, "Supervenience," *Proceedings of the Aristotelian Society*, supp. vol. 58 (1984), 1–16.

38. John Mackie, *Ethics: Inventing Right and Wrong* (Harmondsworth: Penguin, 1977), chap. 1.

Blackburn provides his own analysis of what supervenience would involve if there were moral properties and moral facts. There are two aspects to it, what one might call a *diachronic* and a *synchronic* aspect. Regarding the diachronic supervenience of the moral properties of a single person, act, or situation, Blackburn offers the following definition:

> (S_1) A property M is supervenient$_1$ upon properties $N_1 \ldots N_n$ if M is not identical with any of $N_1 \ldots N_n$ nor with any truth function of them, and it is logically impossible that a thing should become M, or cease to be M, or become more or less M than before, without changing in respect of some member of $N_1 \ldots N_n$.[39]

The contrapositive of this also will hold, so that an act, person, or situation that remains the same with respect to its nonmoral properties $N_1 \ldots N_n$ will remain the same with respect to its moral property M. Synchronic supervenience with respect to two or more objects is defined by Blackburn as follows:

> (S_2) A property M is supervenient$_2$ upon properties $N_1 \ldots N_n$ if M is not identical with any of $N_1 \ldots N_n$ nor with any truth function of them, and it is logically impossible that two things should each possess the same properties from the set $N_1 \ldots N_n$ to the same degree, without both failing to possess M, or both possessing M, to the same degree.[40]

Blackburn takes the general concept of supervenience to encompass both S_1 and S_2. One important feature of his definitions is that supervenience incorporates the notion of logical necessity. It is not just that entities having the same natural or metaphysical properties in fact have the same moral ones, but rather that they must. Thus, "if someone claimed . . . that an action was absolutely identical in every respect with another, except that it was much worse . . . it would be a logical and not merely a moral mistake that had been made."[41] Moreover, if an entity

---

39. Blackburn, "Moral Realism," p. 106. For the sake of clarity, I have transcribed Blackburn's definition S as S_1.
40. Ibid.
41. Ibid., p. 197.

changes in its moral character, it *must* change in its nonmoral character as well.

Another significant feature of Blackburn's definitions is that the logical connection between possessing moral qualities and possessing nonmoral ones is a one-way connection—that is, it is not a biconditional relationship. It is logically necessary that if an object changes its moral properties it also changes its nonmoral ones. Supervenience does not require, however, that if an object has or comes to have certain nonmoral properties (the base, subvenient ones) then it is logically necessary that it have certain moral ones. In other words, supervenience does not amount to saying that nonmoral qualities entail moral ones (otherwise expressed, it does not amount to saying that a statement ascribing the subvenient nonmoral properties entails a statement ascribing the supervenient moral properties). Hence it is compatible with supervenience that an entity have any set whatsoever of nonmoral properties and not have any supervenient moral ones. Likewise, two entities may possess the same nonmoral qualities and neither of them possess a moral characteristic. Supervenience does require, however, that if two entities have the same subvenient nonmoral qualities, and one has the supervenient moral quality, the other does so as well: "If two things are the same in their naturalistic properties, then it follows that they are identical in their moral qualities, i.e., have the same moral worth."[42]

Blackburn thinks we can begin to see how supervenience poses a problem for realist theories by reflecting on the fact that supervenience is not an entailment relation between nonmoral and moral qualities. The problem is one of understanding why, in circumstances in which a nonmoral description of an entity or entities does not entail a moral description of them, the relation of supervenience should still hold. Consider an act A that possesses the subvenient properties $N_1 \ldots N_n$. The assertion that A is $N_1 \ldots N_n$ does not entail that A is M (e.g., good). Yet if A is $N_1 \ldots N_n$ and M, it cannot cease to be M without ceasing to possess one of the subvenient properties $N_1 \ldots N_n$. Why not?

> It is logically possible that A should be as it is in all naturalistic respects, yet this further state of affairs not exist. But if *that's* a logical possibility, *why* isn't it a logical possibility that A should stay as it is in all naturalistic

42. Ibid., p. 106.

respects, and this further state of affairs cease to exist? If it's a logical possibility that A should be as it is in all naturalistic respects, and not be good, why isn't it a logical possibility that A should stay as it is in all naturalistic respects, when it was once good, and cease to be good?[43]

If an entity continues to have the same nonmoral properties, it must—given supervenience—continue to have the same moral ones it previously had, but the statement to the effect that it has the nonmoral properties does not entail the statement that it has the moral ones. This state of affairs, Blackburn remarks, is "very mysterious."[44]

The mystery becomes even darker when we recall that supervenience constitutes a logical relation between the possession of moral features and the possession of nonmoral ones. This means that we cannot account for the continuation of the moral properties by understanding them as being caused by the nonmoral ones or connected to them in some scientific, lawlike manner. Any causal or lawlike connection would be contingent, not logically necessary. If the nonmoral properties caused an object's goodness, we could still imagine without logical inconsistency that the same nonmoral properties might continue to exist without the goodness. But this is precisely what we cannot do, given the conception of supervenience we are entertaining. Supervenience rules out a lawful, contingent relation between $N_1 \ldots N_n$ and M; lack of entailment rules out a logical connection between them. And yet if the nonmoral properties persist, M also must persist. Again we must ask the question: why? "Supervenience becomes, for the realist, an opaque, isolated, logical fact, for which no explanation can be proffered."[45]

It is considerations like these that give substance to Mackie's claim that the supervenience of moral properties makes them queer: "If there were objective values, then they would be entities or qualities or relations of a very strange sort, utterly different from anything else in the world."[46] Not only, according to Mackie, does supervenience cause metaphysical perplexities concerning the relationship between subvenient properties and the supervenient moral properties, it causes epistemological difficulties as well. How could we know that cruelty is wrong,

43. Ibid., p. 110.
44. Ibid., p. 111.
45. Ibid.
46. Mackie, *Ethics*, p. 38.

if wrongness were supervenient on the natural properties of cruelty? "It is not even sufficient to postulate a faculty which 'sees' the wrongness. Something must be postulated which can see at once the natural features that constitute the cruelty, and the wrongness, and the mysterious consequential connection between the two."[47] We cannot know that cruelty is wrong empirically, for observation reveals only contingent connections. We cannot know this logically or a priori, because the natural features of cruelty do not entail its wrongness. From the standpoint of standard empiricist epistemology, supervenience is unintelligible.

But does the supervenience of moral properties really make them queer, different from "anything else in the universe"? Does the realist theory make supervenience unintelligible? It is time to assess these allegations.

A Realist Response

Platts is foremost among the realists in attempting to come to grips with the problem of supervenience. He has suggested that we can understand and render coherent the supervenience of moral properties on nonmoral ones by interpreting the nonmoral properties as *fixing* the moral ones even though they do not entail them.[48] Let us examine Platts's theory in some detail. He gives us an interesting example to illustrate what he means by the notion of fixing. He asks us to consider a figure of a head composed of many dots. The positions of the dots fix the shape of the head, but we do not deduce the shape from the position of the dots—rather, we directly observe the shape. We might have some description of the position of the dots—in the guise, say, of a grid analysis—and still be totally ignorant of the shape they form. Likewise, we might see the face and be totally ignorant of the grid description. Still and all, if we change the arrangement of the dots, we change the shape of the head, and if we change the shape of the head, we change the arrangement of the dots. The dots fix the shape, but the shape is not inferred from them. Rather, it is something that can be independently and directly observed.

If we follow the analogy, it dictates that we see Washington's courage

47. Ibid., p. 41.
48. *Ways of Meaning*, pp. 244, 253.

as being fixed by such things as his military and political goals, his chances of success and failure, the consequences of failure, and his state of mind. If we change these, we remove or significantly alter the courage he demonstrates. And yet we do not infer his courage from a knowledge of these factors. We can immediately perceive this courage. Moreover, possessing these features does not entail the possession of courage, for it is easy enough to imagine all these circumstances prevailing and his still not being courageous. His state of mind might have been produced, for example, by excessive alcohol.

The analogy has its limitations, some of which Platts mentions.[49] Perhaps its most serious flaw is that it fails to account for the fact that we cannot see or appreciate the courageousness of Washington's act unless we also see and acknowledge some of the other features, those that fix its moral quality. One can see a facial shape and know nothing of the grid arrangement of the dots; one cannot see Washington's courage without knowing considerable detail of the personal, social, and military history surrounding his act. Even if one is unaware of them, the dots and their arrangement may cause one to see them as a head. But the features of Washington's act which fix its courageousness cannot merely, unknown to oneself, cause one to see it as courageous. They must be one's *reasons* for calling it courageous—indeed, the reasons it *is* courageous.

Platts acknowledges the problem and makes some admittedly tentative efforts to resolve it. First, he questions the moral/nonmoral distinction we have used in setting up the problem.[50] Do we have, he asks, a clear and general distinction in mind? It is doubtful that we do. In the absence of an acceptable distinction of this sort, why can we not say that the various features that fix the courageous nature of an act are themselves moral features?[51] To describe the features that fix Washington's courage is to point to such characteristics as steadfastness of purpose in the face of great odds, a high degree of control over emotions of fear, and so forth. Are these morally neutral? They are factual enough, but they reverberate with moral significance. Platts refers to them as "lower level, more concrete moral considerations,"[52] considerations that we use in justifying our higher-level judgment of courageousness. Such lower-

49. Ibid., pp. 244, 251.
50. Ibid., p. 254.
51. Ibid.
52. Ibid.

level features do not entail courage, but they do justify the attribution of courage. Change them, and the quality of the courage changes, perhaps even its presence.

Consistent with this approach would be McDowell's suggestion that the criteria employed in applying moral terms like 'courageous' need not be recognizable from a point of view external to our moral practice. The features we use to judge an act courageous may themselves be moral features. Hence there is no derivation of the moral from the nonmoral, and morality maintains its autonomy.

In and of itself, this response does not solve the problem we face. What exactly is the relationship between the lower-level moral considerations and the higher-level judgments? The relationship is not one of entailment, in spite of the fact that the lower-level features fix the higher-level ones. The nature of this fixing remains a mystery. The response we are considering appears to do no more than transfer the difficulties we have in understanding the relationship between nonmoral and moral properties to the relationship between lower- and higher-level moral properties. The noninferential character of moral judgments still seems inconsistent with the demand that there be considerations that noncontingently justify them and hence fix the moral characteristics of concern to us.

Platts's next attempt to deal with the problem holds more promise. Moral situations, he tells us, do not "repeat themselves."[53] These situations are ordinarily quite singular and unique. The notion that there could be a set of properties, moral or nonmoral, entailing the moral features of a given situation presupposes that situations resemble one another to the extent that we can isolate the similarities giving rise to the same moral feature. It presupposes that we can formulate a universal proposition that logically links the moral feature to these similarities, a universal proposition to the effect that it is logically impossible to have these similarities without the moral feature. The singularity of moral situations shows this notion to be unacceptable. If moral situations do not repeat themselves, we cannot identify similarities that are and must be connected to the moral character of a situation. Given the uniqueness of moral situations, universal propositions relating moral features and

53. Ibid., p. 255.

those they are dependent upon are at best rules of thumb, useful but crude guidelines. Relying on them may well prevent us from seeing the unique way in which the properties of a particular situation give rise to its moral character. "In ordinary moral life, the problem is not that of squaring our present judgments with our previous judgments, but that of *attending* to the full, unobvious complexity of the present case. In ordinary moral life, determining our moral judgment about a particular case by means of some rule seizing upon non-moral aspects of that case will simply mean that we neglect the full complexity of that particular case."[54] If we do attend to the full complexity of a particular situation, we will see that a unique set of nonmoral or lower-level moral properties gives rise to or fixes its moral character. We must justify our claims about this moral character by appealing to this unique ensemble of features. The requirement, however, that any other situation having the same subvenient or base features shall also have the same moral value is in fact an empty requirement, for no other situation will have exactly the same base characteristics. Some of them, to be sure, will reappear, but always in combination with new ones. The set of base characteristics as a whole is unrepeatable, but it is precisely this entire set that fixes the moral feature we perceive.

One of the attractions of this way of looking at moral facts is that it allows us to handle cases in which there is an inherent conflict of values. We have seen that the realists are pluralists and that they foresee situations in which different moral demands will compete for our attention. In such a conflict, we may grant that were things different we would have an obligation to do x by virtue of the situation's features A, B, and C; at the same time we perceive that our real obligation is to do y, because of the situation's other features D, E, and F; hence, given the total ensemble of base characteristics, our obligation is to do y. It is not that D, E, and F impose an obligation that *always* takes precedence over the obligation imposed by A, B, and C. Another situation containing A, B, C, D, E, F, and M may be one in which we perceive x, not y, to be our obligation. No universal rules of precedence or weight can be formulated, and hence once again no entailment relations can exist between base and moral features. It is the total set of base properties which gives

54. Ibid.

rise to the moral one, and no extractable subset can ever be thought to entail the moral character of a situation or to entail the priority of one obligation or value over another.

We might sum this up by saying that the moral character of a situation is a toti-resultant property of the base features of the situation, not a parti-resultant one. If there is a change in the moral character, there must be some change in its base character, but not with regard to any determinate subgroup of the base features. The change must occur only with regard to the total, complex base character.

It should be noted that Platts's emphasis on the uniqueness of moral situations and the lack of entailment between base and moral characteristics which follows is consistent with McDowell's claim that moral knowledge is uncodifiable.[55] We discuss this claim in more detail later, but in the present context it is a way of saying that there are no universal principles or rules specifying the kinds of action or situation that always have a specific moral character: "As Aristotle consistently says, the best generalizations about how one should behave hold only for the most part. If one attempted to reduce one's conception of what virtue requires to a set of rules, then, however subtle and thoughtful one was in drawing up the code, cases would inevitably turn up in which a mechanical application of the rules would strike one as wrong."[56] McDowell also notes that "uncodifiability rules out laying down any general ranking (of values or obligations) in advance of all the predicaments with which life may confront one."[57] The moral world for the realists is highly complex and variable, a world in which the particular case has more weight and authority than any moral law or moral principle.

The doctrines of uncodifiability and situational uniqueness do explain why there is no entailment between moral and base characteristics. Entailment would require the truth of universal propositions linking the moral and base characteristics; the uniqueness of moral situations rules out such universal propositions. But do the doctrines of uncodifiability and situational uniqueness also explain how the base characteristics fix the moral ones? Do we not still have the same problem—namely, that if there is no entailment between the two sets of properties, they can only

55. "Virtue and Reason," p. 336.
56. Ibid.
57. Ibid., p. 344.

be related contingently? If so, it remains difficult to understand how the base features determine the moral one and how they can function as good reasons for claims about it. It is my own view that this problem has largely been solved. Nothing prevents the realists from claiming that the total set of base properties constitutes the moral feature of a particular case. The courage, for example, embodied in Washington's crossing of the Delaware *just is* his performing this action in the given military and social situation and in a certain frame of mind. It does not follow that we infer Washington's courage from these features—we could do that only if there were a universal, codifiable connection between these features and courage. Such, however, is not the case. These features constitute courage in the particular situation; in another context they might not constitute courage at all. So we can grant that the base characteristics fix the moral one without thereby turning the latter into an inferred feature. Moreover, the connection between base and moral characteristics, although not one of entailment, is nevertheless not contingent either. In a given case, the moral quality is identical with the base characteristics—they are not two things only contingently related.

It might be asked why the constitutive base characteristics, considered in relation to a particular context, cannot be said to entail the moral character of an act *in that context*. Why, for instance, cannot the social, historical, military, and psychological features constituting Washington's courage in crossing the Delaware be said to entail this instance of courage? We can answer these questions by reminding ourselves that entailments reflect universal logical rules or propositions. The base characteristics constituting Washington's courage in crossing the Delaware do so only in this particular context. It makes no sense to speak of one set of properties as occasionally, or on a single occasion, entailing another set. Hence base characteristics cannot be said to entail a moral property in a particular context, even though they constitute it on that occasion.

This interpretation of "fixing" as *constituting* amounts to a form of reductionism. Moral features of particular situations are reduced to the ensemble of base characteristics of those situations. This does not threaten the autonomy of the moral sphere, however, if we also adopt Platts's proposal that the base properties be seen as lower-level moral ones. There is some reason to believe that McDowell would go along with this proposal. In another context—a discussion of the relationship between the behavior on the basis of which we attribute psychological properties to a person and those psychological properties themselves— he insists that the criterial behavior cannot be identified in categories distinct from those in which we describe the psychological features themselves.[58] Pain-behavior, for instance, is not just bodily motion; it is the expression of pain. Extrapolating from this, if we think of the lower-level, moral base properties as the criteria for asserting the presence of a toti-resultant moral character, the base features must be understood in terms of the same categories we use in describing the moral character of the situation as a whole. And so they *are* understood if we treat them as lower-level moral features. Moreover, just as the pain is not something other than the pain-behavior (and only contingently connected to it), but is expressed, manifested, or present in the behavior, so our moral obligations and characters in particular situations are expressed in specific ensembles of base or lower-level moral characteristics.

Moral Facts and Moral Actions

Let us turn to another aspect of moral facts. What relation do they have to moral actions? The realists are especially sensitive to the fact that there is an intimate connection between moral judgments and actions, a connection that has led many nonrealist theorists to believe that moral judgments must make some reference to the desires of the agent to whom they are addressed. The reasoning that leads the nonrealists to this conclusion is as follows: a moral judgment always constitutes a reason for action; a reason for action must have motivational efficacy; only the desires of an agent motivate her; therefore moral judgments make reference to desires. The realists reject the conclusion of this argument, for in their view moral judgments register objective, independent moral facts that have no essential connection to desire. But they accept the first premise of the argument and appear to accept the second as well. In rejecting the third premise, they part company with a long philosophical tradition going back to Aristotle and having Hume as its high priest— the tradition that claims we reason in practical matters only in order to

58. John McDowell, "Criteria, Defeasibility, and Knowledge," *Proceedings of the British Academy*, 68 (1982).

assist our desires, the tradition that sees reason as the slave of the passions.

That desires alone motivate is a widely held dogma; but why should we accept it? the realists ask. Appealing to the work of Nagel, McDowell claims that many of the desires we attribute to agents are attributed *because* the agent intentionally and deliberately acts to achieve a certain end: thus the desire for the end cannot be an independent, causal condition of the act.[59] Attributing the desire is just a way of registering the fact that the act is intentional and has a certain end as its goal. And Platts asks why an objective moral fact bearing no relation to desire cannot be a motivating reason.[60] After all, if asked for one's reasons for acting, one often responds by stating independent, objective facts: *Question*—why did you run out of the building? *Answer*—Because my room was on fire. *Question*—Why did you withdraw from the race? *Answer*—Because the polls showed I had no chance of winning. Of course, a member of the tradition described above is likely to respond by claiming that one often does not mention a desire in reporting one's reasons simply because this desire is so obvious—everyone, for example, wishes to avoid fire and to avoid defeat. But why take these desires as prior causal conditions? Why not take them as identifying what the agent intentionally did, as opposed to conditions giving rise to what he did? As such, they are obvious because it is obvious that the agent intentionally did what he did.

Platts's question about why an objective moral fact cannot be a motivating reason for acting also implies a repudiation of the pseudopsychology that frequently operates in the traditional explanation of reasons for acting. The thesis that desires motivate amounts to the claim that only desires have the push-or-pull quality necessary to cause action. McDowell refers to this as the "quasi-hydraulic conception of how reason explanations account for action."[61] He rejects the conception on the grounds that reasons for actions justify actions; they are not forces that generate them.[62] To be sure, ascriptions of moral value are action-guiding, but this status does not have to be explained by connecting moral facts with affective/conative states of the agent. As Platts puts it,

---

59. "Are Moral Requirements Hypothetical Imperatives?" p. 15.
60. *Ways of Meaning*, p. 258.
61. "Non-cognitivism and Rule-Following," p. 155.
62. Ibid; also see "Virtue and Reason," pp. 342–45.

"Why should it not just be a brute fact about moral facts that without any such further element entering, their clear perception does provide sufficient grounding for action?"[63] There is no a priori reason to reject the idea that the clear perception of moral facts by itself leads us to act, and there is no empirical evidence counting against it either. Only metaphysical prejudices concerning human action stand in the way of accepting it.

In the life of a moral person, the perception of a moral fact provides a reason for action and a reason that motivates the person to act. In our moral language-game, moral facts serve as motivating reasons for action. Moreover, as Lovibond has argued, moral facts not only are reasons for action, they are overriding reasons for action, those that take priority over other reasons, including reasons that make reference to facts about what one desires.[64] Moral facts come to have this character for us, and we come to understand them as having this character, when we acquire mastery in the moral practice. People who act morally are those who are motivated by moral considerations, considerations that are often in conflict with their desires. Such people find moral facts to be decisive reasons for action. Thus the demand that moral facts be such as to have an intimate relation to action causes no problem for the realists' thesis that these facts are objective and independent of an agent's desires. Once we have identified and repudiated the pseudopsychology that requires motives to have the hydraulic force of desires, the facts about moral action and moral motivation can be seen for what they are.

Moral Knowledge

This brings us at last to epistemological considerations, attempts by the realists to explicate moral knowledge. How do we come to recognize the presence of moral features and to know moral facts? McDowell characterizes this knowledge as a sensitivity: "a kind person knows what it is like to be confronted with the requirement of kindness. The sensitivity is, we might say, a sort of perceptual capacity."[65] Platts insists

63. *Ways of Meaning*, p. 258.
64. *Realism and Imagination in Ethics*, p. 52.
65. "Virtue and Reason," p. 332. McDowell attempts to elucidate moral sensitivity as similar in some ways to an awareness of secondary qualities. He argues strenuously that the latter awareness is not subjective in a derogatory sense and hence that moral perception is not subjective in that sense. See his "Secondary Qualities and Values" in Ted Honderich, ed., *Morality and Objectivity* (London: Routledge and Kegan Paul, 1985).

that this knowledge is no different in kind from the knowledge we have of other sorts of facts: "we discover moral truths in the ways we discover most (if not all) truths: by attention, perception, and reflection."[66] Thus there is no need, he claims, to postulate a special and mysterious faculty of intuition.

The realists' view, then, is the following. Faced with a situation of a specific and complex kind, a (virtuous) moral agent can detect that it requires her to act, say, kindly. She detects this by examining the situation, attending to its details, and reflecting on them; doing these things she is able to see that she must act kindly in this context. If she then acts kindly, this fact in turn can be perceived by other moral agents who attend to and reflect on her behavior. In certain situations, a moral agent may be aware of factors that, were things different, would allow and perhaps require that she behave differently, but she perceives the necessity in this situation, with all its complex detail, of acting kindly. For example, a student has failed to meet a deadline for turning in a paper; his instructor might react sternly were it not for the despair that the student manifests concerning his abilities, together with the circumstances known to have produced this despair; so in this situation the only thing the virtuous instructor sees herself permitted to do is to be kind to the student. Another observer can see that the instructor is being kind, and not just lax or lenient, but he can see this only if he attends to all the details of the case. It is the toti-resultant moral property of a situation or action which he perceives, along with a recognition of the parti-resultant moral properties of specific dimensions of the situation, some of which, it is recognized, must be ignored on this occasion.

The challenge that immediately will be thrown at the theory—it has been urged against all forms of "intuitionism"—is that it is vulnerable to the skeptic's claim that *he* fails to perceive the moral qualities of acts and situations. The skeptic will grant, in our case above, that the student has missed a deadline, despairs over his abilities, and is the product of a deprived educational background—these things can be perceived. But in observing them the skeptic denies that he is *pro tanto* observing the requirement to be kind. Likewise, he will grant that we can observe the instructor allowing the student extra time, encouraging him, sympathizing with his difficulties, and so on; but to observe these things is not

66. "Moral Reality and the End of Desire," in Platts, *Reference, Truth, and Reality*, p. 72.

necessarily, he thinks, to see that the instructor behaves kindly. How can one justify the claim to have perceived a moral property when other persons like the skeptic, presumably as competent as oneself, fail to perceive it even though they are aware of all the relevant "base" properties of the situation?

The realists are not afraid of this challenge. They respond that the skeptical observer who fails to see the moral requirement of kindness is *not* competent, at least not on this occasion. His perceptual abilities are in fact impaired—perhaps "his failure occurs only because his appreciation of what he perceives is clouded, or unfocused, by the impact of a desire to do otherwise."[67] In other words, his failure of awareness is "explicable," the result of desires, fears, limited personal experiences, and so on.[68] Of course, it may be the case that *we* have seen the situation incorrectly, in which case *our* errors are explicable. And it may be that all of us exhibit a failure of clear perception. The moral situation is, as noted several times, exceedingly complex, and this complexity, together with the semantic depth of moral concepts, makes the moral truth difficult to obtain.[69] What must be rejected, however, is the suggestion that there may be, at the end of the day or the dispute, equally acceptable but different ways of seeing a moral situation. One of the parties to the dispute is wrong, and the other correct (unless both are in error). The one sees what really is there; the other fails to see it. The moral reality we seek to know exists in a fashion that is both determinate and independent of our perceptions; it is the standard against which these perceptions are measured.

If the skeptic continues to protest, it should be pointed out to him that with regard to properties like kindness and courage—those properties attributed by the use of thick moral concepts—the overwhelming majority of people do detect them and agree on them. There simply does not exist in this area or at this level of discourse the extensive disagreement the skeptic alleges to find in moral discussions, disagreement of which he tries to make so much. The widespread agreement that actually exists may permit us to speak of something comparable to color-blindness in the moral sphere. Assuming the skeptic is sincere and is not

67. McDowell, "Virtue and Reason," p. 334.
68. Platts, *Ways of Meaning*, p. 248.
69. See Platts, *Ways of Meaning*, p. 249.

under the influence of distorting desire, fear, or idiosyncratic personal experience, he may fail to see the moral aspects of acts and situations because he is morally blind.

It is possible to give a more elaborate explanation of this moral blindness. Although some desires may cloud our moral vision and prevent us from seeing the facts as they morally are, other desires may be required in order to see these facts. Perceptual concepts and the capacities involved in applying them are sensitive to distinctions and similarities we have an interest in noting and talking about. Perception is selective, and this selectivity is frequently a function of desire, need, or interest. This does not in any way impugn the objectivity of our perceptions—what we perceive is there to be seen, but we would have failed to see it if it had not been of concern to us. Detecting moral qualities, then, requires moral concerns and interests, and it is not at all implausible to suggest that some people do not have the affective dispositions required. Surely the psychopath, often referred to as a moral idiot, is lacking in precisely the sense of fellow-feeling and the capacity for guilt that normal human beings possess.[70] To a lesser degree, perhaps, the skeptic also may lack these qualities.

This explanation is connected to a point Wiggins has made concerning the relationship between moral features and desire. He expresses the realist conviction that we desire something because it is good (desirable); an object is *not* good (desirable) because we desire it, for there must be some reason for our interest in it.[71] But Wiggins admits that the desirability feature of objects may be accessible only to those who desire them—it is as if we come to know of these features through desiring them or as if they are "lit up" by the desire. This suggestion is unclear as it stands, for it is difficult to understand how desire could act as a conduit of knowledge. But it makes considerable sense if put in terms of the preceding paragraph. Only those who desire to be kind and are concerned that others be kind can detect kindness and the requirement of kindness, for this interest is the necessary selection device guiding the perception of this moral dimension. The desire itself is not a mode of perception; it is an affective/conative presupposition of any perception of this moral characteristic.

70. See Hervey Cleckley, *The Mark of Sanity*, 3d ed. (St. Louis, Mo.: C. V. Mosby, 1955).
71. "Truth, Invention, and the Meaning of Life," pp. 348–49.

It is reasonable to assume that, although some people are positively disposed by nature to kindness, most people are so disposed by nurture. We are trained in such a way as to develop dispositions favorable to kindness. This training, or moral education, is indistinguishable from the training we receive in the use of the moral concept of kindness. We learn to approve of kindness and to seek to be kind at the same time we learn what the concept of kindness involves. Thus our concern for kindness and our understanding of it are inextricably linked. Similar considerations hold for other moral concepts.

There is still another way to respond to the skeptic who maintains that he cannot detect the moral qualities of things in spite of being able to detect all of the so-called base properties on which the moral ones depend. Presupposed by this claim is the idea that the base properties are capable of being described and cognized in morally neutral terms. If we accept Platts's suggestion that the base properties are themselves moral ones, albeit of a lower level and higher degree of specificity, then the skeptic, in granting the perception of the base properties, is admitting that he can perceive moral features. Alternatively, if he denies as well that he can perceive the moral base properties, he indicts himself for being unaware of things that are plainly there for anyone to see. Consider again the case of seeing that a professor is kind to her student. The base properties in this situation include the fact that the student is in a state of despair and that his difficulties result from a deprived educational background. Despair and deprivation are not morally neutral notions: both refer to states of affairs that in certain contexts are morally significant and deserve sympathy, if nothing else. Still and all, these states of affairs are factual and in many instances obvious. The lower-level status of the notions of despair and deprivation may disguise their moral significance and mislead the skeptic into thinking he is aware of nonmoral characteristics only. But if he grants that he can perceive despair and deprivation, he grants all that the realist requires of him.

Lovibond has pointed out the similarity between this realist theory of moral perception and some things Wittgenstein has to say about the perception of psychological attributes.[72] Wittgenstein claims, for instance, that we can see emotion, and he notes that we can describe a

---

72. *Realism and Imagination in Ethics*, p. 47.

person's features as "sad," "radiant," or "bored."[73] In describing someone's countenance in these ways, we are not inferring the existence of
the emotion from the features; rather, we are noting the emotion *in* the
features, as manifested in or expressed by them. For Wittgenstein, Lovibond notes, psychological states such as emotion are not something hid-
den, not something separate from bodily features and only contingently
connected to them. Bodily countenance is not "evidence" for the existence of an emotional state; it is the embodiment of it. And thus we can
speak, as Wittgenstein puts it, of seeing how things stand with others.
Analogously, Lovibond thinks, moral aspects are manifested in rather
than evidenced by the observable properties of acts, persons, and situations, and this allows us to gather moral information directly by perception. If this be called *intuitionism*, so be it. Such intuitionism is simply
the view that "moral judgments are to be regarded as non-inferential."[74]
The credentials of the theory are obvious and persuasive: "an ethical
theory which was intuitionistic in this sense would be so simply by virtue of the fact that it did not disregard the license given to us by our
'naive language' to talk about 'seeing moral aspects of a situation'."[75]

According to Lovibond, in seeing or intuiting moral aspects like courage and kindness, one is not sensing something *supernatural*.[76] One is
simply aware of the moral features expressed in a person's behavior and
situation. These could be described without using the moral language,
and no entities would thereby be missed. If that happened, one simply
would not have brought the concepts and vocabulary of kindness and
courage to bear on the prevailing scene, whether deliberately or as a
result of not possessing these concepts. The description of moral aspects
requires moral concepts, which are not reducible to nonmoral ones. But
using the license of our naive language to describe things morally does
not "involve any ontological 'admissions' which need alarm the noncognitivist in his capacity as spokesman for the claims of natural science
to supply, within its own terms of reference, a total description of the

73. Wittgenstein, *Zettel*, trans. G. E. M. Anscombe (Oxford: Basil Blackwell, 1967),
§225.
74. Lovibond, *Realism and Imagination in Ethics*, p. 50.
75. Ibid., p. 49.
76. Ibid.

objective world."[77] The use of moral concepts is a matter of participating in a distinctive linguistic practice, from which no ontological claims or admissions follow. Nor is a special faculty required for detecting moral aspects of things in the world, and the realist is not obligated to introduce such a faculty: "For he need not concede that possession of a *sui generis* 'moral sense', a 'distinctive faculty of ethical intuition', amounts to anything more than possession of the specific range of discursive skills which enable us to report on moral features of the world."[78] Critics who accuse a realist intuitionism of inventing special faculties have failed to understand that all perception is impregnated with concepts and that moral concepts shape the observations of those who have mastered the moral language-game just as scientific concepts shape the observations of scientists.

It is unclear whether Lovibond's explanation of moral intuition and especially her claim that the use of a moral language carries no ontological baggage would be accepted by Platts and McDowell. They seem committed to an ontology of moral aspects, and their theory of moral knowledge may have to be framed accordingly. If so, they would be unable to accept Lovibond's Wittgensteinian characterization of moral intuition in terms of an ontologically uncommitted use of a distinctive moral language. As we have seen, Platts maintains that if someone fails to see the moral aspects of a situation, she has simply missed what is there. She has failed to grasp a real, independent dimension of the world. McDowell speaks overtly of conceptions of reality, and he rejects a "scientistic" conception:

> A scientistic conception of reality is eminently open to dispute. When we ask the metaphysical question whether reality is what science can find out about, we cannot, without begging the question, restrict the materials for an answer to those which science can countenance. Let the question be an empirical question, by all means; but the empirical data which would be collected by a careful and sensitive moral phenomenology—no doubt not a scientific enterprise—are handled quite unsatisfyingly by non-cognitivism.[79]

77. Ibid.
78. Ibid., pp. 49–50.
79. "Virtue and Reason," pp. 346–47.

This suggests that an adequate metaphysics would include moral aspects and facts and that a metaphysics based solely on scientific data would be incomplete. This view appears to oppose Lovibond's claim that science can give a complete description of things in its own terms alone. We shall return to this possible point of contention among the realists.

Uncodifiability

Continuing our discussion of epistemological themes, we need to look next at the striking doctrine of uncodifiability. Moral knowledge, according to this doctrine, is incapable of being formulated in universal propositions or moral rules. One knows what is courageous or kind *only in particular situations*. Thus moral knowledge cannot be represented as the application of a universal principle or standard to a situation via the specific, straightforward factual properties of the situation. "This picture fits only if the virtuous person's views about how, in general, one should behave are susceptible of codification, in principles apt for serving as major premises in syllogisms of the sort envisaged. But to an unprejudiced eye it should seem quite implausible that any reasonably adult moral outlook admits of such codification."[80]

Aristotle's authority is invoked at this stage, with regard to both moral generalizations holding only for the most part and moral judgments resting finally on perception.[81] We have already seen Platts's insistence on the complexity of the particular moral case and McDowell's stress on the need for appreciation of the particular instance. A virtuous person knows what to do here-now; he does not know, or pretend to know, what one always or even generally ought to do. "Occasion by occasion, one knows what to do, if one does, not by applying universal principles but by being a certain kind of person: one who sees situations in a certain distinctive way."[82]

The lack of codifiability manifests itself very noticeably with regard to the weight or priority of different moral demands or values in relation to one another. We have already discussed the realists' moral pluralism,

80. Ibid., p. 336.
81. Ibid., concerning Aristotle on generalizations, McDowell makes reference to the *Nicomachean Ethics*, I.3.
82. Ibid., p. 347.

according to which there are different, incommensurable values which cannot be ranked on a common scale by virtue of the degree to which they possess some "supervalue." Consequently, faced with the conflicting moral demands of a complex moral situation, an agent must see or appreciate which of the dimensions is the salient one. It is by virtue of his seeing this particular aspect rather than "that one as the salient fact about the situation that he is moved to act by this concern rather than that one. The perception of saliences is the shape taken here by the appreciation of particular cases."[83]

According to McDowell, an agent is also aware of the nonsalient dimensions of a conflict situation; he perceives *all* the requirements and values. But he does not weigh them against one another or see one as overriding the others, for this would require a common scale or lexical ordering, both of which are ruled out by the thesis of uncodifiability. Thus the moral agent is aware of the other dimensions, but as "silenced" by the salient feature: "the relevant notion of salience cannot be understood except in terms of seeing something as a reason for acting which silences all others."[84]

Moral perception, then, can turn out to be complex. A moral agent confronting a moral situation may perceive (a) various demands or values embodied in it; (b) the salient demand or value; and (c) the other dimensions as silenced by the salient one. Her knowledge of all these things is particular and specific, incapable of being guided by or articulated in a general formula. She is able to see these things and have this knowledge because, following McDowell, she is the kind of person she is, because she has a certain conception of how to live. But personal characteristics also resist formalization and express themselves only through particular sets of concerns and actions. One comes to have moral knowledge only by becoming a certain kind of person, and here again we should heed Aristotle: one becomes a good and virtuous person by following the example of other good and virtuous persons.

The uncodifiability thesis appears to generate a problem concerning consistency. If there is no universal formula capturing the kinds of things that have moral properties or give rise to moral demands, how can we be sure that a person applies moral concepts in the same way

83. Ibid., p. 344.
84. Ibid., p. 345.

from situation to situation? Given uncodifiability, is not everyone's use of moral concepts haphazard? If it were not haphazard and capricious, surely we could pick out the similarities among the applications and express them in a general formula. This possibility being rejected, how can we ever determine that someone, including ourselves, has mastery of a concept and can "go on in the same way" in the use of it?

McDowell meets this objection by claiming that it invokes a problematic assumption concerning consistency and rationality: "Rationality requires consistency; a specific conception of rationality in a particular area imposes a specific form on the abstract requirement of consistency—a specific view of what counts as going on doing the same thing here. The prejudice is the idea that acting in the light of a specific conception of rationality must be explicable in terms of being guided by a formulable universal principle."[85] He then cites Wittgenstein's attack on this assumption, as found in his reflections on following a rule. According to Wittgenstein, a rule should not be thought of as a psychological process or structure mechanically generating the right answers in particular cases, nor as somehow reflecting a transcendent system of rational connections.[86] A rule can be said to guide us only because there is a practice of rule-following. The practice encompasses numerous prior applications of the rule as well as uses of the rule to adjudicate controversy in particular instances. In learning to follow a rule, we learn to emulate these precedents, for it is they that possess normativity. These precedents, however, are themselves uses of rules, uses on which a linguistic community agrees; the rules are not transcendent standards that can be appealed to in order to assess the uses. Hence it is the human practice of rule use which constitutes the standard for our subsequent behavior. There is no justification for, or possible criticism of, this way of using rules. There is no sense to the notion, for instance, that the practice of rule use could be inconsistent—for this practice defines consistency.

As McDowell sees it, the implication of Wittgenstein's reflections is that subsuming a particular use of moral concepts under a general rule has only the appearance, not the reality, of *superior* consistency and rationality.[87] For, after all, the subsumption merely involves seeing one

85. Ibid., p. 337.
86. See *Philosophical Investigations*, I, §§185–242.
87. "Virtue and Reason," pp. 339–42; also see his "Non-cognitivism and Rule-Following."

application of the rule as the same as (consistent with) other applications—namely, those that constitute the practice of following the rule. And we cannot appeal to the rule itself to show that these applications are the same. So appeal to a rule does not provide a guarantee of consistency superseding or underwriting that of seeing particular cases as the same. Once this is granted, the alleged need to have a general rule or principle from which, in conjunction with an appropriate minor premise, one could deduce the proper application of a moral concept in a particular case is easily seen to be spurious. The absence of such a rule does not in itself endanger the consistency of our use of moral terms.

How do we know that this use of moral terms, unsupported by rules, is consistent? We *see* that it is. In seeing this, we are doing nothing different from what we do in seeing that one use of a term is the same as the uses constituting the precedent-setting rule uses. It is an ability most of us have, largely because we have been trained to use moral concepts. Similarly, we are trained to recognize the color red and to apply the concept of red, as a result of which we see that two red objects are the same color and that our uses of the concept are the same, even though we are totally unable to formulate a general rule to the effect that all things red are F, G, and H. If we can be consistent in calling things red, as surely we can, we also can be consistent in calling things kind or courageous. We have mastered the appropriate concepts by being educated into a particular language-game, the color one or moral one.

If we reflect on these features of the realists' doctrine, we can see that no other answer is possible to the question about consistency. The austere treatment of moral terms like courage assumes that the only answer we can give to the question "Why are all these actions called courageous?" is that they all *are* courageous—they all are seen to have this property. Given the claim that base properties do not entail moral ones, no general rule can be formulated that links base features and moral ones in such a way that we could appeal to the presence of the same base properties to justify our application (and consistent application) of the moral term. Given the uncodifiability doctrine, and the emphasis on the complexity and singularity of individual moral situations, we have no other recourse than to base the use of moral concepts on our perception of the unique ensemble of properties within a particular situation and on our perception of salience with respect to the members of this ensemble. Thus many of the features of moral realism come together here and show themselves to be consistent.

Moral Fallibilism

One final feature of moral knowledge needs to be discussed: the realist's insistence on moral fallibilism. This, too, at first sight seems consistent with what has been said about the complexity and uniqueness of moral situations. "It is not to be supposed that appreciation of the particular instance . . . is a straightforward or easy attainment on the part of those who have it."[88] Effort is needed to achieve this appreciation and often to get someone else to appreciate a situation in the same way. Effort and argument, for the fact that judgment finally rests with perception does not preclude using arguments to clarify a situation, to reveal its base qualities so that attention can be focused in the right direction. Moreover, "this process of attention to improve beliefs and understanding will go on without end; there is no reason to believe that we shall ever be justified in being certain that most of our moral beliefs are true, and no reason to believe that we shall ever be justified in being certain that we now completely understand any of the moral concepts occurring in these beliefs."[89] Given a "recalcitrant" and "infinitely complex" moral world,[90] we are but "tawdry, inadequate epistemic creatures."[91] We may hope to improve our sensitivity to moral features and hence improve our moral beliefs, but an approximation to the truth is all we can ever hope for. "Certainty plays no role in this form of intuitionism."[92]

Although the notion of fallibilism fits comfortably with the picture of complex moral situations and semantic depth, it does not fit comfortably with the idea of moral perception or intuition—not at least if this is understood on analogy with sense perception. Our ordinary concept of sense perception allows for certainty in the area of perceptual knowledge. Of course, sense perception as a faculty or ability is fallible: our vision and other sense capacities occasionally do deceive us, and the fact that a person has looked at an object does not in any way entail that she has correctly perceived it. On the other hand, however, if, by way of example, we grant that a person has *seen* a rat in the closet, it follows that there *is* a rat in the closet. It makes no sense, logically, to say, "S saw p, but maybe there is no p." Nor does it make sense to say, "I see that x is y,

88. Ibid., p. 342.
89. Platts, *Ways of Meaning*, p. 247.
90. Ibid., pp. 249, 252.
91. Ibid., p. 252.
92. Ibid., p. 247.

but x may not be y." So if one actually sees something, one cannot be in error about its presence or reality; in this sense, perception is infallible. (One might debate the question whether a person actually saw an object, but there clearly are contexts in which doubts about such matters make no sense.) Now the realists maintain that we have a perception-like access to moral features and moral facts. If we do have such intuitions, then on those occasions when they occur we have a form of knowledge that could not be in error. Such cases of knowledge would be inconsistent with the general thesis of moral fallibilism, which maintains that there is never any moral knowledge that is not subject to doubt and that could not in principle be in error. To assert the reality of moral intuitions is to introduce counterexamples to this thesis. The realists, then, must reject the analogy with ordinary perception, deny that moral perceptions ever really exist, or attenuate their fallibilism. The last seems the most attractive alternative for them.

Nothing precludes the realists from saying that moral certainty, though difficult to obtain and often not obtained, nevertheless does occasionally exist. Morally complex situations present special difficulties, but not all moral situations are overwhelmingly complex. In fact, most of our moral behavior does not seem to be problematical at all, being required by relatively simple moral situations. Desire, fear, and peculiar personal experiences always threaten the objectivity of our moral perceptions, but the influence of these factors can be assessed and often ruled out. There are, in other words, many moral situations in which we occupy the best conceivable epistemic position and in which it would be linguistically perverse to deny certainty. It is consistent with the complexity and singularity of moral situations to say on a particular occasion: "It is clear I must be kind" or "He is, beyond doubt, a courageous person." So something less than full-blown fallibilism is consistent with realism and seems to be called for by the facts of the moral life. (It must be questioned, however, if something less than full-blown fallibilism is consistent with a full-blown doctrine of semantic depth. Unqualified, however, this doctrine seems to constitute a bottomless bog. We need to know more about semantic depth.)

This concludes my presentation of the main themes of contemporary British moral realism. In the process of reviewing these themes, we have seen how the realists respond to one of the foremost challenges directed at their views—the claim that the logical feature of supervenience becomes unintelligible on their account. We turn next to another major criticism of the realist position.

The Problem of Moral Causation

Gilbert Harman has developed a powerful argument to the effect that moral perceptions need not be thought of as indicating the reality of moral properties because there is no need to postulate this reality in order to give a causal explanation of the perceptions.[93] His argument has been said to illuminate brilliantly the unarticulated reason many people today have for rejecting moral realism.[94]

Harman admits that there can be moral observations, given his understanding of what, even in science, an observation is. An observation occurs whenever an opinion is formed as a direct result of perception, without any intervening inference. In this sense, a scientist can be said to observe a proton in a cloud chamber, for he reacts to his perception of the vapor trail by saying "there goes a proton." Likewise, one can be said to observe that children who pour gasoline on a cat and set fire to it are doing something wrong, for one might immediately respond to the perception of the cat's being set on fire by saying, "What they are doing is wrong!" But granting that there are moral observations, does it follow that there are moral facts in the world which are revealed by these observations?

Harman's answer to this question is negative. In spite of the existence of both scientific and moral observations, there is, he thinks, a fundamental disanalogy between the two cases. Many scientific observations can best and most completely be explained by assuming that the observation statements are true and that the events or states of affairs they report are in part responsible for (i.e., cause) the observations themselves. To explain a moral observation, however, we never need to assume that the observation statement expressing it is true and that the moral fact it reports causes or is responsible for the moral observation. We can easily and fully explain moral observations solely in terms of the observer's mind set, psychology, or moral sensibility. These internal conditions alone suffice to render them intelligible.

---

93. See his *The Nature of Morality* (Oxford: Oxford University Press), chap. 1.
94. See Richard Werner, "Ethical Realism," *Ethics*, 93 (July 1983), 656–57.

Harman is even willing to admit that moral observations may be evidence for a moral theory or principle, just as scientific observations confirm a physical theory. The physicist's report that a proton passes through a cloud chamber confirms the theory of subatomic particles; the moral observation that in setting the cat on fire the children are doing something wrong confirms the moral principle that cruelty is wrong. But again, in spite of this similarity, there is a more basic disanalogy between the two cases. In the case of the scientific observation, we can trace a route from the observation to the physical theory, from there to a physical event, and then back again to the observation. The route looks something like this:

Scientific Confirmation

Making an observation $\xrightarrow[\text{for}]{\text{evidence}}$ a physical theory $\xrightarrow[\text{explains}]{\text{best}}$

a physical event $\xrightarrow{\text{explains}}$ the observation.

The moral case looks quite different.

Moral Confirmation

Making an observation $\xrightarrow[\text{for}]{\text{evidence}}$ a moral theory or principle

$\xrightarrow[\text{explain}]{\text{may}}$ a "moral fact" $\xrightarrow[\text{explain}]{\text{does not}}$ the observation.

The moral confirmation chart assumes, for the sake of argument, that there are moral facts—"certain moral principles might help to explain why it was wrong of the children to set fire to the cat."[95] What the chart shows is that even if moral observations confirm moral principles, and

95. Harman, *Nature of Morality*, p. 8.

they in turn explain moral facts, nevertheless "the explanatory chain from principle to observation seems to be broken in morality."[96]

In the case of scientific explanation, we count an observation as confirming evidence for a physical theory only if the most plausible explanation of the observation is that a physical event predicted and explained by the theory in fact caused the observation. But with moral confirmation, the theory or principle that is "confirmed" does not explain the observation, since the most plausible explanation of the observation is not some moral fact predicted by the theory but rather the psychology of the agent. So even if moral observations confirm moral theories, this provides no evidence for the reality of moral facts.

One way of interpreting Harman's argument highlights its use of the notion of explanatory simplicity. He tells us that we "do not seem to need to make assumptions about any moral facts to explain the occurrence of the so-called moral observations";[97] such assumptions are "irrelevant," since "all we need assume is that you have certain more or less well articulated principles that are reflected in the judgments you make, based on your moral sensibility."[98] Insofar as we can explain moral observations in terms of the agent's mind set or moral sensibility alone, it is unnecessary to postulate moral facts to explain them. The sufficiency of the alternative explanation makes any appeal to the truth of the observation "irrelevant" to explaining it.

Such an argument lacks the philosophical conclusiveness we might wish for, but it is in line with Harman's general methodological practice of inferring the best explanation of moral phenomena.[99] His reasons for thinking that a relativistic, social consensus theory of morality provides a better explanation of these phenomena than an appeal to moral facts are given in the next chapter of this book. But without going into these reasons, there is another way in which we could make an argument like Harman's considerably stronger.[100] We could argue that the postulation

96. Ibid.
97. Ibid., p. 6.
98. Ibid., pp. 6–7.
99. See his "Inference to the Best Explanation," *Philosophical Review*, 74 (1965).
100. Harman himself suggests this interpretation in *The Nature of Morality*, p. 8, and it is stressed in his "Moral Explanations of Natural Facts—Can Moral Claims be Tested against Moral Reality?" *Spindel Conference 1986: Moral Realism, The Southern Journal of Philosophy*, supp. vol. 24 (1986), 57–68—see especially pp. 62 and 64.

of moral facts, which appears to be a possible explanation of moral observations but one ruled out by a better explanation, is in fact no explanation at all.

What is impressive about scientific confirmation and explanation is
that the circle from confirming observation to explanatory theory back
to the observation is largely filled in. We understand how the physical
event postulated by the theory causes us to have the observation confirming the theory. The theory in question connects with other, independently confirmed theories that explain perception and provide a picture of the causal links between perception and the kinds of physical
events postulated. We understand how our observations mesh with the
world, and we understand the mechanism allowing these observations
to "track" the events in the world, that is, to provide a faithful guide to
them.[101] We may not understand all the links in the mechanism, but it
seems reasonable to assume that with advancing scientific knowledge
these lacunae will be filled in. Scientific observations confirm scientific
theories and give us information about the world because the inference
to the best explanation in this case contains, at least in principle, no
gaps.

Is this also true in the moral case? Let us for the sake of argument
postulate moral facts and hypothesize that they explain moral observations. There are, after all, some reasons for doing so that are prima facie
plausible. A critic of Harman might well say that appeal to the moral
sensibility of an observer is, in fact, not enough. The moral sensibility,
she might say, is simply a form of receptivity, an ability to appreciate and
respond to the moral features of people and events. In order for an
observation of these features to be made, this sensibility must be trig-
gered and put into operation. And is it not, she would ask, just the
presence of a moral feature or fact that does this? If so, a complete explanation of moral observations must appeal both to the moral sensibility
and moral facts—appeal to the former alone is not sufficient.

Is such a theory of moral causation plausible? Specifically, is it gap-
free? Exactly how do moral features or facts cause moral observations?
Surely we have no theory of the mechanism that allows the mind to
engage with moral facts. Moral facts must have some kind of causal

---

101. On "tracking," see Robert Nozick, *Philosophical Explanations* (Cambridge: Harvard University Press, 1981), chap. 3.

efficacy, but how normative moral facts could accomplish this is exceedingly puzzling. As Harman has pointed out, we have no idea how the wrongness of an act plays a role in generating belief—"there does not seem to be any way in which the actual rightness or wrongness of a given situation can have any effect on your perceptual apparatus."[102] It is questionable whether it even makes sense to postulate moral properties that give rise to (cause) moral perceptions. There are, then, significant and perhaps unbridgeable gaps in any alleged explanation of moral observations in terms of moral facts.

Some Responses

To see if the realists can answer this challenge, let us begin with the question whether it makes sense to speak of their "moral aspects" causing moral perceptions. The answer would seem to depend on the ontological status of these aspects. Platts and McDowell have no reluctance to speak of moral aspects as part of the furniture of the world, so that a metaphysic that did not admit them—for instance, a scientistic metaphysic including only scientifically observable or postulatable entities— would be incomplete and inadequate. Lovibond, on the other hand, claims that moral realism need not deny that a scientific conception of reality is complete; her brand of realism is not committed to any entities above and beyond the scientific ones—not committed, that is, to supernatural entities. As I understand her position, moral perception is simply a conceptually distinct way of seeing the natural features of things; it is not a matter of seeing features or entities of a distinct ontological realm.

Let us assume for a moment that Platts and McDowell are correct. How are we to understand the manner in which moral aspects give rise to moral perceptions? Remember that, as Platts tells us, no special sense is involved in this perception; normal observation, attention, and reflection are all that is required. But how can nonphysical moral aspects produce normal states of awareness, normal in the sense of being the same kind of states we have in ordinary sense perception? We understand the psychology and physiology of ordinary perception fairly well. It depends upon a mechanism that allows us to trace a physical path

---

102. Harman, *Nature of Morality*, p. 8; also see Harman, "Moral Explanations of Natural Facts," pp. 62 and 64.

from the stimulus object to the perception. How could such a physical mechanism be linked with nonphysical features, the moral features, of objects? We have no idea. In fact, the very notion of causality becomes quite mysterious here. If moral aspects have a distinct ontological status, we are hard pressed to understand how they could account for the perception of themselves. And then their very reality becomes suspect.[103]

But assume that Lovibond is correct. Our initial problem seems to be solved, for ordinary physical entities—the only ones in the world—can account for our moral perceptions in the way they account for all perceptions. That we have moral perceptions is simply a matter of our conceptually organizing our perceptions in a distinctive manner. But in solving the problem of causation this way, Lovibond's theory runs other risks. First, there is the risk of abandoning moral realism altogether. Moral aspects, properties, and facts take on the appearance of being only so many conceptual projections, not realities at all. Our moral way of talking involves no ontological admissions or commitments, we are told, so a noncognitivist need not feel that something mysterious is being smuggled into the universe. But a full-blown realism seems to need something mysterious, mysterious at least from the standpoint of a noncognitivist physicalism. Second, in denying that moral properties exist in addition to physical ones, Lovibond is conceding that moral properties do not cause moral perceptions. And then she appears open to Harman's objection that in this event we need not concede the reality of moral properties: the physical ones are all we need. Whereas a full-blown realism cannot explain moral causation, an attenuated realism of the type Lovibond develops seems to suffer from having no room for moral causation.

There is, I think, a way out of this dilemma. It involves accepting an extreme Wittgensteinian position that repudiates all forms of metaphysics on the grounds that they are just so many confused ways of projecting linguistic grammar onto the world.[104] From this perspective,

---

103. In his "Secondary Qualities and Values," McDowell himself seems to grant that moral aspects or "values" do not possess causal efficacy (p. 118). His main point, however, is a different one—namely, that the explanations of our moral experience we need are not causal, but rather ones that reveal if our moral responses are justified (see pp. 118–23).

104. It is unclear to me the extent to which Lovibond would be willing to accept this position.

both physicalism and a realistic moral metaphysics are misleading and unacceptable. Wittgenstein does not think that it makes sense to speak of science's providing us with an absolutely complete account of what there is in the world. The metaphysician who looks at the set of scientific statements and says, "That's it—that is an absolutely complete description of the world," is not speaking as a scientist. Lacking an intelligible notion of "absolutely complete account," it is questionable whether she is making any sense at all. All the scientist qua scientist can do is to list the empirical, scientific statements she wishes to make or accept—and nothing metaphysical follows from such a list. Likewise, the moral realist who proclaims that there are moral properties and facts in the world, in addition to scientific ones, is not speaking as a moralist. A moralist just tells us which people are kind, courageous, and so on, and when we are required to behave in certain ways. He normally does not speak of moral features or facts at all, but merely of its being right to do *x*, or kind to do *y*, and so forth. It is the moral metaphysician who says: given our moral talk, there are moral facts and features in the world which are different in kind from natural ones. But what does this mean? What concepts of fact, feature, and difference is he operating with? In ordinary life we may say that it is a fact that Achilles was courageous, but this adds little if anything to the statement that Achilles was courageous. If we say that Achilles' courage was his most outstanding feature, this is just to make a contingent moral judgment, not a metaphysical statement. And finally, as we ordinarily speak of facts, moral or otherwise, they cannot intelligibly be said to be "in the world," so that it is meaningless to affirm or deny that there are moral facts in the world.[105] Thus moralistic metaphysics is no more intelligible than scientistic metaphysics. Wittgenstein would reject both.

But by rejecting both, we see that the problem of moral causation begins to disappear. By avoiding all metaphysical descriptions of the world, we no longer face the problem of limiting the application of the causal relation to metaphysically similar, and metaphysically proper, entities. What things cause other things is now seen to be an empirical matter. There is no a priori obstacle to its being the case that, for exam-

105. For more on the conceptual grammar of 'fact' and on ways in which the realists violate this grammar, see the section entitled "Realism and Ontological Commitment," below.

ple, George Washington's courage caused him to succeed, even if the moral feature of courage cannot be reduced to a set of nonmoral features.

As it turns out, to the extent that the concept of causation has a place in our explanations of perception, it has been determined empirically to be applicable to the relation between chemical/physical events in the environment and physiological events in the observer. Moreover, these events and their connection are understood in terms that have little to do with the ways we normally talk about the objects of sense perception, whether physical objects like trees, cultural objects like money, or moral situations like those involving cruelty. For instance, assume that one observes a ten-dollar bill in one's wallet. *What* one observes, the ten-dollar bill, is an item in a highly complex, cultural system of currency and exchange, and its properties are defined by this system. It is not this set of cultural properties which has been found empirically to give rise to the physiological conditions of perception in an observer of the bill. It is a set of chemical and physical properties of the bill which empirically are known to cause this set of physiological conditions. Moreover, there is no way in principle that a description of an object as a ten-dollar bill can be reduced to or analyzed into a set of descriptions of this object in terms of its physical and chemical properties. Hence, in explaining the perception of a ten-dollar bill, one cannot appeal to the fact that the monetary properties of the object cause a perceptual response in the observer. Of course, an object described as a ten-dollar bill can also be described in terms of its chemical and physical properties, and these properties can be appealed to as a cause of the perceptual response. Talking about an object in cultural terms and talking about it in physical/-chemical ones are not incompatible, certainly not metaphysically incompatible; they are just different ways of describing it. And both are applicable. Explaining the perception of the object, however, requires appeal only to the physical/chemical properties of the object as the cause of the perception.

What about scientific observations themselves? Can they be explained as the causal products of their objects? If the objects of these observations are described in the terms of our everyday, common-sense talk of enduring, three-dimensional objects—J. L. Austin's "moderate-sized specimens of dry goods"—it is doubtful that they can be explained in this way.[106] The doubt arises for the same reasons. The language of moderate-sized dry goods is very different from the language of physics, chemistry, and physiology; indeed, it is different from the more psychological language of sensations, as the failure of all attempts to give a phenomenalistic reduction of the former to the latter demonstrates. If, on the contrary, the objects scientifically observed are already described in physical and chemical terms, then there is no problem in explaining how these objects have physiological consequences for perception. But the gap between the common-sense descriptions of physical objects and the scientific descriptions of them is no less than the gap between cultural descriptions of objects like money and scientific descriptions of them. And in both cases, additional descriptions of cultural and common-sense objects can be given in physical and chemical terms that allow for a proper scientific explanation of the perception of these objects. It must be reiterated, however, that this explanation is not given in terms of a causal relationship between the cultural or common-sense properties of the objects and physiological conditions in an observer.

Turning to the moral case, we can admit that it would be fruitless to attempt an explanation of the perception of moral states of affairs in terms of a causal relation between the moral properties defining these states and physiological conditions in an observer. But the moral case is not different in this respect from the cultural or common-sense case. And just as we can give physical/chemical descriptions of cultural and common-sense objects and link these properties causally with the physical state of an observer, we can do the same thing with moral states of affairs. Thus we are able to say that we see someone acting cruelly in spite of the fact that it is false to say that the cruelty itself caused us to have the perception. Cruelty cannot be reduced to chemical and physical properties, but any act having the property of cruelty will also have chemical and physical properties that *can* enter into a causal account of the perception of that act. Hence perceiving moral states of affairs is no different from perceiving cultural and common-sense facts. Undeniably all observations involve some physiological base—moral observations as well as other forms—but to require that moral features cause these observations is to misunderstand the nature of observation. There is no

---

106. J. L. Austin, *Sense and Sensibilia* (Oxford: Oxford University Press, 1962), p. 8.

causal relationship present in the cases of normal observation that is lacking in the case of moral observation. And hence there is no reason to question the objectivity of moral observation and to distinguish it in this respect from other forms of observation. Moral observations can be just as objective as the observations of ten-dollar bills and trees. The fact, then, that moral features and facts cannot themselves be described as causing moral observations does not in and of itself pose a problem for the realist. The problem is avoided, however, by jettisoning metaphysical conceptions of moral facts and causation, something some realists may not be prepared to do.

Supervenience, Perception, and Judgment

There is another problem with the notion of moral observation as the realists understand it, a problem I do not think it is possible for them to escape. It must be recalled that, according to the realists, the moral features observed are those that are fixed by the nonmoral or lower-level moral features of a situation or act. These subvenient properties are not just contingently related to the moral ones, even though they are not logically equivalent to them. The subvenient properties provide the reasons the situation or act has the moral features it has; indeed, they constitute the moral character of the situation or act. It is difficult, therefore, to understand how a person could observe the presence of a moral property and at the same time not observe the base properties that give rise to it. How can we see Washington's courage unless we can see the various features that fix this courage and make him courageous? If we here/now intuit this moral feature as characterizing Washington, would that not require that we here/now observe its subvenient base? But many of these base properties occurred in the past and hence are not within the purview of immediate observation. How can we observe them if, as is the case, many of them are embodied in an expansive historical and cultural context? How can we here/now see that John Smith is required to repay a debt if the debt was incurred in the distant past, far beyond the scope of our present observation? In all these cases, it needs to be remembered that, according to the realists, we do not infer the moral property from its subvenient base. We observe the moral property, and this property is fixed by its subvenient base. In the case of items with such an intimate relationship, how can we perceive one of them without perceiving the other? Given the frequent inaccessibility of the subvenient properties to immediate observation, the alleged observation of the moral property is highly problematic.

If we assume the realists' conception of the relationship between moral features and the features that fix them, perhaps a more plausible model of moral knowledge would highlight the role of judgment rather than observation. Given what we know about Washington—his personality and his history—and about the social and military context, we judge that he was courageous. Given what we know about John Smith's promises, we judge that he ought to repay his debt. Such judgments need not be thought of as inferences, if this means a derivation of the judgments from sets of premises only contingently related to them. Nor need the judgments be thought of as deductive derivations from the reason-giving premises. The relation of supervenience might be said to hold between the moral judgments and the reasons giving rise to them, in which case our judgments amount to affirmations of the reality of the moral situation in light of the nonentailing, noninductive reasons our minds comprehend. Prima facie, such a judgmental model of moral knowledge appears less paradoxical than the observational model. Much work would have to be done, of course, to explicate and render intelligible this notion of moral judgment. The American moral realists we study in the last section of this chapter offer us one account of the judgmental model, and the relativists we examine in the next chapter offer us another. My own theory, proposed in Chapter 6, provides still a different conception of it.

Realism and Ontological Commitments

To raise still another objection to realism, I wish to return to the suggestion I made above that statements to the effect that "There are moral facts" or "Moral facts exist" run counter to the rules governing our ordinary concept of a fact. We also noted that any theory not committed to such statements, as perhaps Lovibond's is not, can have its credentials as a *realist* theory questioned. Much hinges, then, on whether talk of moral facts as part of the furniture of the world makes sense. Perhaps it is easy enough to let such a statement as "There are moral facts" pass unchallenged; it does not come across at first sight as being unintelligible. Closer examination, I suggest, shows otherwise.

Moral realists give the appearance of thinking that the reality of moral facts follows from its being the case that we use the indicative mood in making moral judgments, that we use such locutions as 'It is a fact that. . .' in prefacing many of these judgments, and that we predicate 'is true' of numerous moral claims. In this context, we might recall that Quine has pointed out how some people take an ontological statement like "There are attributes" to follow immediately from "casual statements of commonplace fact" like "There are red houses" and "There are red roses."[107] Quine himself, of course, thinks that such an ontological claim follows only for a speaker who assumes a conceptual framework within which the bound variables over which he quantifies designate attributes. Another speaker with a different conceptual scheme in which no such quantification and designation occur could accept the commonplace statements without thereby swallowing the ontological claim. She could offer a paraphrase in which all references to the alleged ontological entities are removed. Likewise, many philosophers might reply to the moral realists that our ordinary moral judgments do not entail commitments to moral facts. Noncognitivists purport to find paraphrases of these judgments which show them not to designate or describe facts at all. And a contemporary projectivist like Simon Blackburn is quick to offer glosses on our uses of 'fact', 'true', and the like which give them a role in the evaluation of attitudes rather than one suited to a realist metaphysic.[108] Realists could respond, of course, by claiming that noncognitivists and projectivists have simply failed to understand the import of our moral discourse and that their paraphrases of it are mere caricatures.

Before we get too far into the debate over ontological commitment, we need to raise a prior question about whether ontological claims make sense. Quine seems to think that "There are attributes" makes sense whether or not he himself happens to accept it. My suggestion, to the contrary, is that "There are attributes," its denial, and similar ontological claims are idle utterances with no real use in our discourse. To see this with regard to "There are moral facts," we must ask whether there is a conceptual space or home within which we can locate this utterance

---

107. Willard Van Orman Quine, "On What There Is," in his *From a Logical Point of View*, 2d ed. rev. (Cambridge: Harvard University Press, 1980), p. 10.
108. Blackburn, "Moral Realism."

and thereby give it a use and meaning. It is difficult, I think, to identify such a home.

The statement "There are moral facts" seems to be an answer to the question, "Are there moral facts?" But what could this question mean? What kind of ignorance would it express? Would a person asking it be inquiring as to whether there are any particular moral judgments of the form 'It is a fact that x is right (wrong, good, evil)' which are true? It is unlikely that this would be his concern, since he may well be committed to the truth of many statements having this form and still not know whether this makes him a moral realist. Most of us are in just such a predicament. More likely, the person asking whether there are any moral facts wants to know whether, when such statements are true, they are true by virtue of there being something in the world (to which they correspond) which is a fact and is independent of human conventions, beliefs, and attitudes. It would appear that no examination of language practices alone could show this, since the question concerns what a segment of our moral language is about. If we want to answer this question, would we not have to look about in the world for moral facts, and would we not have to know what to look for? But just what would moral facts look like?

To see how strange "Are there moral facts?" is when understood as a question about things in the world, let us contrast it with questions like "Are there any Bengal tigers left in India?" or "Are there any insects with more than a thousand legs?" In these cases, we are inquiring whether we can find in the world creatures of a specific kind, and we can identify or define the kind by describing the properties it must have. Likewise, we can distinguish it from other kinds on the basis of its properties. In many cases, the properties identifying the kind are observational ones, but this need not be so. We can ask, "Are there any prime numbers between a million three and a million hundred thousand?" in which case we would identify the kind we are looking for in terms of certain mathematical operations.

Inquiring about the existence or reality of specific kinds makes sense, but ascending levels of abstraction quickly lead us into nonsense. If we ask, "Are there any numbers?" or "Are there any material objects?" we have no clearly intelligible question in mind. What are the properties that define a number? How do we distinguish numbers from, say, colors? If we say that we can add, subtract, multiply, and divide numbers, is this to suggest that we cannot add or subtract colors? We can, of course, add some yellow pigment to our palette, and we can even add some color to the room, that is, add some brighter colors. In these cases, however, we are not adding *colors* in the required manner. But it makes no sense to speak of adding or subtracting colors in the way we add or subtract numbers, and for this reason it makes no sense to deny that colors can be added or subtracted this way. We cannot conceive of adding colors so as to be able to rule it out. Likewise, colors do not have any properties that distinguish them from numbers—it is not that numbers do not have hues and colors do, since any talk of the hue of numbers simply makes no sense: "Numbers do not have hues" is meaningless. If it is thought that these general kinds can be distinguished by the fact that colors are seen and numbers conceived, then it must be asked how colors are distinguished from shapes: shapes too are seen. Furthermore, being seen and conceived cannot be essential properties of colors and numbers, respectively, for a particular color may not be seen, and a particular number may never be conceived.

In sum, color, number, shape, and the like do not designate discernible kinds with identifiable properties, kinds whose reality or lack of reality we can inquire about by asking whether the kinds we encounter in the world have these properties. Rather than designate types of things that may or may not exist, terms like *color* and *number* are what Wittgenstein thinks of as *grammatical concepts*.[109] They are presupposed by our talk of specific things and specific kinds of things, and they give sense to it by identifying the kind of discourse of which this talk is a part.

Much the same can be said about facts. What would we look for to determine if there are any facts at all in the world? And what would be the case if we found out that there are no facts in the world? What things other than facts would we find in it? It may be thought philosophically respectable to claim that there are no facts in the world, only objects. But surely this profundity is paradoxical. "There are only objects" should be greeted with the response: "Are any of them red?" If the

---

109. See his *Blue and Brown Books*, p. 19. Wittgenstein's thoughts on these matters pervade his philosophical writings and rank as some of his most obscure reflections. On the idea that kinds like color and number have no identifying properties, see his middle-period works, *Philosophical Remarks* and *Philosophical Grammar*, his *Zettel* (esp. §331), and his very late work, *Remarks on Color*. In the last-named we find him saying, "'The colors' are not things that have definite properties" (III, §127).

answer is either yes or no, then facts sneak back into the universe, since an object's being or not being red is equally a fact. Can we even conceive of a world without facts? If not, they are odd little buggers. Someone might say that they necessarily exist! We should say, more blandly, that the concept of a fact is a grammatical concept, conveying a host of activities and operations we perform on statements of the form "*s* is *p*." It does not designate an entity or kind of thing, but rather identifies discourse as being of a certain kind, in which certain linguistic equivalencies hold ("*p*" = "it is a fact that *p*") and in which talk of truth, correspondence, rational and objective belief, and the independence of truth from beliefs and attitudes is appropriate. To the extent that these forms of talk pervade our discourse, we cannot escape, evade, or deny the reality of "facts."

We can apply some of these lessons to the notion of moral facts. It, too, is a grammatical concept, directing our attention to certain linguistic equivalencies—"*x* is wrong (right, good, evil)" = "it is a fact that *x* is wrong (right, good, evil)"—and to the propriety of surrounding our talk of "*x* is wrong" with talk of truth, correspondence, rational and objective belief, and the independence of moral truth from beliefs and attitudes. And "moral facts" are just as difficult to evade as are "facts" in general. If we ask whether it is a fact that John Doe is a cruel man, we can entertain the thought that he is cruel and also the thought that he is not. If he is not cruel, *it is a fact* that he is not cruel. Hence showing the falsity of "It is a fact that John Doe is a cruel man" does not even begin to undermine "the reality of moral facts." This demonstrates how very different any talk of the existence of moral facts is from talk about the existence of kinds of things in the world. Denying the truth of "This insect has more than a thousand legs" does bear upon the reality of such insects, just as "One million four is not a prime number" correctly or incorrectly is part of a challenge to the reality of prime numbers between a million three and a million hundred thousand. Denying the truth of "It is a fact that *x* is wrong" does not diminish in the slightest the number of moral facts in the world and hence cannot be taken as undermining the claim that there are moral facts. Ontological claims about moral facts, then, are radically different from claims about the reality of specific kinds of things like insects, prime numbers, Bengal tigers, and so on. We have a firm grasp on the latter; the former quickly slip from our grasp.

Reflections of this variety should lead us to doubt whether there are any contexts—linguistic or nonlinguistic—within which "There are moral facts" or "There are no moral facts" finds a home and makes sense.[110] Consequently, such reflections suggest that realists cannot validly infer the reality of moral facts from the meaningfulness and truth of ordinary assertions about specific moral facts. They cannot do this because "There are moral facts" has no meaning. It appears to have meaning because it is patterned after other assertions that do. Metaphysical theories frequently take standard forms of expression out of their normal contexts and try, unsuccessfully, to use them without the sense-giving background provided by these contexts. They fallaciously take the mere form of an utterance to be a guarantee of its sense. Moral realism goes wrong by being a metaphysical theory.

American Moral Realism

I conclude this chapter by briefly examining another current form of moral realism. The discussion above has focused exclusively on British views, but a different theory of moral realism has been developed recently by some American philosophers.[111] The American version is an example of what I have called above a judgmental account of moral decision making. Seeing what the Americans have to say will further illustrate a judgmental model. The Americans' theory, however, is quite different from the judgmental account I myself develop in Chapter 6, so

110. Some philosophers who might accept much that I have said in this section would claim that statements like these really mean something about concepts and their grammar, but this, I suggest, is to invent a use, not to discover one. See Ilham Dilman, *Quine on Ontology, Necessity, and Experience* (Albany: State University of New York Press, 1984), esp. chap. 2. In spite of disagreeing with Dilman on this particular issue, I am indebted to him for many of the things he says about ontology in this work.

111. See Richard Boyd, "How to Be a Moral Realist," in Geoffrey Sayre-McCord, ed., *Essays on Moral Realism* (Ithaca: Cornell University Press, 1988); David O. Brink, "Moral Realism and the Skeptical Arguments from Disagreement and Queerness," *Australasian Journal of Philosophy*, 62 (June 1984), 111–25; William Lycan, *Judgement and Justification* (Cambridge: Cambridge University Press, 1988), chap. 11; John Post, *The Faces of Existence* (Ithaca: Cornell University Press, 1986); Hilary Putnam, *Reason, Truth, and History* (Cambridge: Cambridge University Press, 1981), chap. 6 ("Fact and Value"); Peter Railton, "Moral Realism," *Philosophical Review*, 95 (April 1986), 163–207; Nicholas Sturgeon, "Moral Explanations," in Sayre-McCord, *Essays on Moral Realism*; and Richard Werner, "Ethical Realism," *Ethics*, 93 (July 1983), 653–79. Also see the essays in Norman Gillespie, ed., *Spindel Conference 1986: Moral Realism, Southern Journal of Philosophy*, supp. vol. 24 (1986).

the present discussion also provides a contrast that should be helpful in illuminating some of the issues surrounding this model. I do not engage in detailed criticism of American moral realism, although I indicate where my objections to British moral realism can also be directed at it and, additionally, where some of the views to be elaborated in Chapter 6 are at odds with it.

American moral realism is modeled after the philosophy of scientific realism currently popular in the English-speaking world, especially in the United States and Australia. This influence is evident in the causal relation the American thinkers often postulate between nonmoral and moral features. David Brink, for instance, speaks of moral properties being "causally realized" by the natural or physical properties of objects and events, and he describes the relation between them as one of "causal constitution or dependence."[112] Another scientific-realist strategy is to postulate the reality of moral properties and facts on the grounds that they explain certain features of experience: "Moral facts exist . . . in the sense that I am using the phrase, just in case the most reasonable explanation of reports of moral observations includes the positing of the existence of the moral entities mentioned in the reports."[113] Although these realists may countenance talk of moral observations, they do so in a way quite different from the British thinkers, and consequently they distance themselves from intuitionism. Whereas the British realists think we have direct observational access to moral facts, the Americans contend that we have to infer their existence by means of an explanatory theory. In this respect, they view our knowledge of moral entities as similar to the knowledge we have of the entities endorsed by a scientific theory of the world. As Richard Werner has put it, "Both moral and scientific entities are posits which provide the inference to the best explanation given what we do observe."[114]

One of the central features of American moral realism is its vigorous commitment to naturalism. According to this theory, moral facts are part of the natural world: they are not mysterious nonnatural or supernatural entities. Moral features can be understood as grounded in natural properties in the same way many biological and psychological charac-

---

112. Brink, "Moral Realism and the Skeptical Arguments," pp. 119 and 120.
113. Werner, "Ethical Realism," p. 653.
114. Ibid., p. 667.

teristics are grounded in more fundamental physical and chemical ones. Another central theme is the claim that by positing moral facts we are in a position to explain some key aspects of human experience and history which could not be explained, or explained as well, by theories not making such posits. Werner has claimed, for instance, that the realist hypothesis is needed in order to explain moral conversions.[115] And Peter Railton has argued that a realist is able to provide an explanation of certain observable trends in history—for example, the trend among human communities toward according the status of "humanity" to larger and larger groups.[116] Moreover, he thinks it possible to develop a realist theory that provides an understanding of the progressive changes in the moral structure of a society. This understanding is to be achieved through an explanation that appeals to a feedback mechanism linking social inequities with a resulting expression of social discontent which in turn generates pressure toward social arrangements embodying higher levels of objective rightness (objective rightness being for Railton a matter of social rationality).

Philosophers who accept the general themes defining American moral realism may have considerable disagreements among themselves as to specific dimensions of a realist theory of moral features and facts. They may dispute, for instance, the precise relationship between nonmoral and moral properties as well as what properties constitute the natural base for the moral ones. Furthermore, some realists would deny that at this time we are in a position to articulate a specific moral theory (such as the one proposed by Railton)—all we can do, they would claim, is appeal to general considerations and arguments in defending realism against its critics and appeal to common examples of moral rightness and wrongness in order to begin the development of a specific realist theory. In spite of these divergent views, it is profitable to examine in more detail the themes that unite the American realists.

Most of these thinkers approach the topics of moral knowledge and moral truth from a methodological perspective quite different from that of the British realists. Whereas the latter have been influenced by the later Wittgenstein, the former draw their inspiration from Quine. They accept Quine's "naturalization of epistemology," according to which

115. Ibid., p. 677.
116. Railton, "Moral Realism," p. 197.

there are no a priori or conceptual truths to which philosophers have special access and which can constitute the basis of philosophical moral reflection.[117] Contrary to moral philosophers who appeal to conceptual necessities, the American realists claim that all of our moral beliefs and our philosophical views about them are revisable in the light of ongoing experience. They are revisable, however, not individually, but as part of a corpus or web of belief—as part of a moral theory. Our everyday moral beliefs form a part of this corpus, but they and other aspects of ordinary moral experience stand in need of explanation. Such explanations also will be part of our moral theory, and they will invoke whatever existential hypotheses and systematic considerations are necessary to provide an understanding of why we have the moral beliefs we do as well as why our moral experience takes the shape it does. What philosophical theory of morality is correct or most worthy of acceptance cannot be determined by a priori conceptual considerations or by straightforward empirical verification. Rather, epistemological merit must be accorded on the basis of the explanatory virtues of the theory along with some other pragmatic considerations.

Most of the American moral realists admit that there are moral observations, but they understand this notion in a special way, much the same way that Harman understands it: a moral observation occurs if and when a moral judgment is made on the basis of sensory stimulation rather than as a result of inference.[118] The Americans do not attribute much epistemic weight to moral observations in and of themselves. They do not see them as providing immediate or direct access to moral reality. The observations, or observation statements, need to be explained; the making of the statements needs to be explained, and their content as well. If the best explanation of an observation (statement) is one that involves taking it to be true, the observation can be understood to provide us with information about moral reality. If, that is to say, we can best explain why a person makes a moral observation by positing a moral entity (a moral feature or moral fact) in the external world which the observation reports and which is causally involved in the person's making the observation, we have grounds for believing that the moral

117. See Willard Van Orman Quine, "Epistemology Naturalized," in his *Ontological Relativity* (Cambridge: Harvard University Press, 1969).
118. See Harman's *Nature of Morality*, chap. 1.

observation is true. And, in turn, the ability of the theory to explain moral observations in this way gives us reason to accept the theory. If, in addition, the theory provides us with an understanding of other aspects of moral experience by positing moral realities responsible for them, we have further reasons for accepting it—and hence for accepting moral realism.

A prima facie case for this brand of moral realism can be made by taking note of the frequency and high visibility of moral explanations in our everyday discourse.[119] Most of us would acknowledge that Hitler behaved as he did because he was morally depraved. We would agree that a judge may be activated by a sense of compassion in assigning a light sentence to a convicted criminal. And we would entertain as at least plausible the hypothesis that serious opposition to the institution of American plantation slavery arose when it did because American slavery was, as forms of bondage go, particularly vicious. In putting forward or accepting these explanations, we are entertaining causal hypotheses to the effect that particular moral qualities gave rise to (caused) actions or events. And many of us would go on to say that often we have the moral beliefs we do about certain alleged moral facts because these facts exist and enter into the causal production of our beliefs. We form the belief, for example, that teenagers torturing a cat are doing something wrong because they *are* doing something wrong.

Opponents of realism might reply that appeals to moral properties and facts to explain our beliefs about the moral character of behavior are totally unnecessary.[120] As we have seen, Harman would claim that such beliefs can be explained solely by the psychological set of the individuals doing the observing and perhaps by the socialization process that leads to this psychological set. According to this line of thought, a person will judge Hitler to be depraved because of the way that person has been socialized to have certain attitudes and feelings toward the kind of behavior Hitler exhibited. Such a highly plausible explanation makes no reference to moral facts. Consequently, a critic like Harman replies, appeal to moral facts in explaining our moral observations is "totally irrelevant."[121]

119. See Sturgeon, "Moral Explanations."
120. See Harman, *Nature of Morality*, chap. 1.
121. Ibid.

In response, a realist maintains that the posit of moral features and facts as explanatory causes is perfectly reasonable, perhaps even more plausible than the competing hypothesis, and hence not irrelevant.[122] This is true, first of all, with regard to the explanation of events in the world other than moral observations and judgments, as can be seen from the fact that we accept certain conditional statements about what would have happened if the moral facts to which we appeal had not existed. We find it perfectly reasonable, for example, to claim that if Hitler had not been morally depraved, he would not have done the things he did—only a morally depraved person, we think, could have done that. Likewise, we find quite plausible the conditional to the effect that if Southern plantation slavery had not been so morally vicious, serious opposition to it would not have arisen when it did. Second, the plausibility of conditional statements of this type also justifies our conviction that there are moral explanations of our moral observations and beliefs. If we take teenagers who torture cats to have behaved in a morally wrong manner, we can justify the moral explanation of our judgment—namely, that we judged their act wrong because it was wrong—by appeal to the conditional that we would not have made the judgment if the act had not been wrong. Not all such conditionals are in fact true: a person might judge that the teenagers are doing something wrong because he hates teenagers and hence would have made the judgment even if the act had not been wrong. But in many cases we can have legitimate confidence that conditionals such as these are true, and this provides support for the conviction that moral facts are relevant to the explanation of our beliefs.

A persistent critic still might not be convinced. She could argue that it is possible to accept these conditional statements and nevertheless not be drawn into the realist camp.[123] One way to show this would be to claim that the conditionals hold true not because the moral properties have the effects postulated, but rather because the nonmoral properties on which the moral ones supervene have these effects. It was, for instance, the natural features grounding Hitler's alleged depravity that caused him to do what he did. The moral property of depravity need not enter into the picture at all.

Realists of the American persuasion have several ways to answer this

122. See Sturgeon, "Moral Explanations."
123. See Harman, "Moral Explanations of Natural Facts."

objection. As noted above, they view themselves as naturalists and happily accept the idea that moral properties supervene on nonmoral, natural features. This leads some of them to view the moral properties as causally constituted by the nonmoral ones and to see the moral ones as having in turn causal effects on other things. As Nicholas Sturgeon has expressed it:

> Since we find it plausible to attribute causal efficacy and explanatory relevance to moral facts, why should we not conclude . . . that their supervenience on nonmoral facts is . . . like the supervenience of biological facts on physical and chemical ones, or (on a physicalist view) of psychological facts on neurological ones—a kind of "causal constitution" of the supervening facts out of the more basic ones, which allow them a causal efficacy inherited from that of the facts out of which they are constituted?[124]

Other realists might claim that moral properties are in fact type-identical with nonmoral, natural properties.[125] If moral properties can be reduced in this manner to nonmoral ones, then to the extent that the properties constituting the reduction basis have causal effects on human behavior and beliefs, *so too do the moral ones.*

At this time, most realists would admit that we do not have an altogether clear picture of what natural properties the moral ones supervene on.[126] Many would deny that we are in any position to talk about the reduction of moral facts to nonmoral ones. Sturgeon has argued that at this stage of our moral development—in the development of our moral theory—we must rely on everyday examples with which we feel comfortable: teenagers do something wrong in setting fire to cats because it is the needless infliction of pain on a sentient creature; Hitler was depraved because he attempted to eradicate an entire race of people; and so on.[127] These examples give us a sense of the place of moral facts in the natural world and hence an assurance that moral facts do fit into the natural scheme of things and are not mystical, nonnatural entities. Furthermore, we can use these examples to build a more general and com-

124. Sturgeon, "Harman on Moral Explanations of Natural Facts," in Gillespie, *Spindel Conference 1986: Moral Realism*, p. 75.

125. See Lycan, *Judgement and Justification*, p. 206.

126. Railton, "Moral Realism," gives what is perhaps the most detailed theory currently available as to what these natural properties are.

127. Sturgeon, "Harman on Moral Explanations of Natural Facts."

prehensive moral theory—they constitute part of the basic data against which we can test moral theories (using something like Rawls's procedure of seeking reflective equilibrium). A moral theory will attempt to specify in general terms the kind or kinds of nonmoral facts that give rise to moral ones, through supervenience or outright identity. As our moral theorizing improves, we will be in a better position to understand the precise manner in which moral facts take their place in the world.

In principle, a highly confirmed moral theory would be able to establish a necessary connection between the subvenient natural and the supervenient moral properties, just as science has established a necessary connection between water and H_2O, lightning and charged particles, and so on.[128] All of these latter necessary connections are a posteriori, not a priori. Our grasp of them results from advances in scientific knowledge. Likewise, as our moral knowledge develops through the articulation and testing of moral theories, we can hope to achieve an insight into the truth of necessary, a posteriori moral truths. Then we would be in position to understand in detail the causal mechanisms that give rise to moral states of affairs and the mechanism that in turn produces our observations of these states of affairs. We would be in a position to provide detailed, articulated moral explanations of why things happen in the world.

So much, then, for a general profile of American moral realism. This profile shows us how the American realists view moral facts and their relationship to the natural world and to our moral convictions. It also conveys an idea of the form a more specific or substantive realist theory would take. Finally, it identifies some of the differences separating American and British moral realism.

It is clear that the American theory of moral realism could be subjected to some of the same objections I brought to the British approach. It speaks of moral facts as entities and has no hesitation in postulating their existence. It therefore is a metaphysical theory that runs afoul of our ordinary concept of a fact. Furthermore, it forthrightly describes moral features and facts as causing moral observations, and I have urged above that it is empirically false to speak this way. It does, however, reject talk of moral intuitions and hence avoids one of the main objections I had to British moral realism. But after repudiating intuitionism

128. See Lycan, *Judgement and Justification*, pp. 205–7.

and going on to interpret moral judgments as hypotheses about the-oretical moral properties and facts, the theory, I suggest, goes too far.

When we say that a person acted wrongly in telling a lie, are we pos-tulating a theoretical property—wrongness—and forming a hypothesis to the effect that this property attaches to the act in question? It is diffi-cult to know what weight belongs to the notions of a theoretical prop-erty and a hypothesis. If they suggest only that we do not observe the wrongness, and that our moral judgment is not just a report of the ob-servation, that much can be granted. But if these notions are taken to suggest that moral features are unobservable entities identified by means of definitions found in a general moral theory, objections are in order. We do not use, and do not need, a general theory in order to know that a person acted wrongly in telling a lie. All we need to know is that the person told a lie and that he did not do so in order to avoid a more serious moral error. In making the judgment that a person who told a lie acted wrongly, we may be said to appeal to the rule or principle that it is always wrong to tell a lie unless doing so is necessary in order to avoid a more serious moral infraction. But neither this rule nor the particular moral judgment we make in light of it can be interpreted as the Ameri-can moral realists would have it. This can be seen from the following considerations.

For the realist, both the principle against lying and the particular moral judgment that a person acted wrongly would have to be taken as revisable. They are both to be understood as part of a moral theory, and this theory is always subject to revision. But the moral principle we have identified is not one that is subject to revision: it holds come what may. Moreover, the particular moral judgment, although frequently the sub-ject of considerable doubt, can on occasion be known to be true beyond doubt. Reservations frequently occur as to whether on a given occasion there is some moral infraction a person would commit by deciding not to lie, an infraction more serious than lying. But there are occasions and circumstances in which no reason exists to think that this is the case. In these instances, we can be certain that the person who lied acted wrongly. Both the unrevisability of our principle against lying and the potential certainty of our particular moral judgment that an act of lying is wrong go against the grain of the naturalized epistemology of the American realists. That it is wrong to lie unless . . . is, I claim in Chapter 6, a matter of a priori necessity, a conceptual matter, what some would call a conceptual truth. The realists, we have noted, reject a priori conceptual truths. And the fallibilism and pragmatism accompanying their notion of a theory go in opposite directions from the notion of moral criteria I develop in Chapter 6. That a person has lied is a criterion of his having acted wrongly. Judgments based upon the satisfaction of criteria are defeasible, but this defeasibility permits the occasional achievement of moral certainty.

In elaborating their theories of moral realism, some of the American thinkers bump up against the reality of principles that are unrevisable or "necessary." Werner adopts a quasi-Wittgensteinian approach to certain "basic moral beliefs" such as "pain and anguish are intrinsically bad" and "people are moral equals."[129] These are beliefs he claims to "know best"; they are "the ones that stand fast for me."[130] And Sturgeon maintains that the proposition that an act is one of deliberate, pointless cruelty but not for that reason wrong is necessarily false.[131] It is difficult to see how these admissions do not constitute an embarrassment for the realists. The basic beliefs Werner cites are not the results of a highly confirmed moral theory possessing superior explanatory value (or at least he does not show them to be).[132] Nor is the necessary proposition implied by Sturgeon's remark a component of a highly confirmed moral theory possessing superior explanatory value. Sturgeon, after all, does not think we are as yet in possession of such a theory. The perspective on moral truths I develop in Chapter 6 can easily accommodate such propositions, and I take that to be a mark in its favor. I am in agreement with the realists in adopting a judgmental model of moral decision making, but the model I propose allows for current moral necessity and certainty—and theirs does not.

129. Werner, "Moral Realism," p. 676.
130. Ibid., p. 674.
131. Sturgeon, "Moral Explanations," p. 69.
132. It seems that he has to appeal to them in order to show that we know the truth of the basic tenet of moral realism: the objectivity of moral facts—see B. C. Postow, "Werner's Ethical Realism," *Ethics*, 95 (1985), 286.

5 / Relativism

OVER the centuries of philosophical reflection on morality, relativism seldom has failed to find an advocate. Although the theory always has been faced with strong opposition and powerful criticism, it nevertheless continues to attract philosophers who are skeptical of claims to moral universality and who wish to deny the existence of an independent realm of moral facts. Relativism has had a particularly strong resurgence recently. Sophisticated forms of the theory have been developed which bear little resemblance to the crude forms so often pilloried by philosophers. Given this recasting, relativism stands today as a major option in moral theory.

Notoriously, relativism is difficult to pin down. Philosophers disagree over what the term 'relativism' means, and often they are at odds over what an acceptance of this kind of theory entails. It is helpful to begin our discussion by positioning relativism, by seeing where it stands vis-à-vis certain doctrines in moral philosophy and observing what options are open to it. This is not to be construed as an attempt to define a particular form of relativism—that task will be left to the authors we discuss. Rather, our goal is to see the kinds of philosophical stances, epistemological and otherwise, usually associated with relativism.

Positioning Relativism

First of all, relativists traditionally have seen themselves as the opponents of absolutism. Perhaps without exception, relativists repudiate the idea that there are absolute moral truths. They deny, that is to say, that there are universal standards of moral value true for all human beings or universal principles of moral duty and obligation binding on all. They may allow that some standards and principles can be rejected on rational grounds, but they deny that there is any one set of them which legitimately dictates how all human beings should behave. Absolutism being the view that there *is* a set of moral standards or principles governing how all rational human beings should behave, relativism and absolutism are generally taken to be polar opposites. As we shall see, however, absolutism and relativism are ambiguous philosophical positions, and their relationship is hardly straightforward.

More often than not, relativists also reject objectivism. Objectivism in moral theory is, in the first place, the metaphysical doctrine that true moral judgments describe a subject matter that is independent of the thoughts and feelings of finite sentient beings, and hence a subject matter that would exist even if no one believed in it or had certain feelings or attitudes toward it. Additionally, many objectivists make the epistemological claim that at least some moral judgments can be supported by evidence that any knowledgeable and rational individual would have to accept. The realists we studied in the last chapter clearly are objectivists on both counts. Relativists, on the contrary, usually deny one or both of these objectivist theses. Some claim that a part of the subject matter of moral judgments is a set of human artifacts—mores, conventions, rules—resulting from human invention or dependent on human beliefs or attitudes; others maintain that an appeal to such artifacts is an essential presupposition or part of any moral justification. Each assertion is an expression of the thesis of nonobjectivism. Mores, conventions, and rules, relativists hold, are human creations which, from a metaphysical point of view, are obviously not part of the objective furniture of the world. Moreover, from an epistemological perspective, these mores, conventions, and rules have no ultimate claim on human reason. Although they are subject to the demand that they be consistent and the requirement that they not be based on false factual beliefs, a person who rejected a set of mores or rules possessing these virtues could not be accused of error or irrationality. Relativists, then, can be metaphysical nonobjectivists, epistemological nonobjectivists, or both.

Objectivism and absolutism are closely related doctrines. Frequently they are found together in the writings of the same philosopher and are not always distinguished from one another. The universally binding set of moral principles and standards touted by the absolutist is easily thought to be one that any rational thinker would have to acknowledge. Moreover, it is natural to think of it as part of a moral law existing independently of human thought and practice. In fact, it is difficult to know what absolutism is if it is not just an expression of objectivism. When the absolutist says that there is a set of principles binding on all human beings or true for all of them, what do these terms 'binding on' and 'true for' mean? Do they not mean that any person not accepting the principles would be in error or would be irrational? If so, absolutism just *is* objectivism.

There is, however, another way to express and understand absolutism. If a person says, "It is true that all human beings should tell the truth" and "It is true that all human beings should keep their promises," she is in effect asserting that these principles legitimately dictate how all human beings should behave. Is she not, therefore, an absolutist? It appears that absolutism in this sense captures all that many relativists have wanted to deny. They have claimed only that there is no true principle that prescribes how everyone should behave.

There are, then, at least three forms of absolutism. The first of these, *moral absolutism*, maintains that certain propositions about how all human beings should behave are true; the second, *epistemological absolutism*, maintains that these propositions are binding on or true for all human beings; and the third, *metaphysical absolutism*, claims that these propositions reflect a moral law or moral reality independent of human cognition and sentiment.

Let us concentrate for the moment on moral and epistemological absolutism. The difference between them may be a subtle one, but it is substantial nevertheless, as we can see by asking what the denials of the two positions entail. To deny the moral absolutist thesis is to say that it is not true that all human beings should, for example, tell the truth, and this entails, at a minimum, that it is morally permissible for some of them to lie. To deny the epistemological absolutist thesis is to assert that a person could refuse to accept a principle like "All human beings should tell the truth" without thereby making an error or manifesting irrationality. The denial of the first claim indicates what moral proposition(s) would be true if "All human beings should tell the truth" is false. The denial of the second claim indicates something about the epistemic credentials of those who do not accept the truth of "All human beings should tell the truth." These are different matters.

Relativists who reject moral absolutism often do so on the grounds that different societies subscribe to different moral principles. Such relativists argue that individuals have obligations to act only on principles accepted by their society. Given the variation in moral codes, it follows for these relativists that there are no true moral propositions prescribing how all human beings should behave. A moral absolutist will respond by insisting that whether or not a person has an obligation to behave in a certain way does not depend on whether or not she accepts a principle enjoining this behavior. Here we have a disagreement over the truth conditions of moral principles. Furthermore, it is (or yields) a moral disagreement, a disagreement over what moral principles are true and hence over how human beings ought to behave.

Relativists who think that one may refuse to accept "All human beings should tell the truth" without being in error or irrational are making an epistemological claim, not a moral one. They are not saying that it is morally permissible for some people to lie. Whatever their reasons, they believe it is possible to reject any moral claim without being epistemologically at fault. According to this view, a person could equally reject "All human beings should tell the truth" and "It is permissible for some persons to lie" without transgressing epistemological standards concerning reasoning, evidence, and rationality.

Moral relativism, then, is distinct from epistemological relativism. The latter is a nonobjectivist position equivalent to the repudiation of epistemological objectivism: it rejects the objectivist thesis that one can refuse to accept some moral propositions only on pain of error or irrationality. Moral relativism has nothing to do with nonobjectivism, being equivalent as it is to the repudiation of the moral absolutist's thesis that there are true moral propositions ascribing moral obligations to all human beings. In light of these distinctions, it is in principle open to one to be a moral absolutist and at the same time an epistemological relativist. The position I develop in Chapter 6 could be characterized in precisely these terms. A similar constellation of views (but certainly not mine) would grant that, although the universal moral principles expressing God's will are true, the evidence telling us what these principles are is not so compelling as to require assent from all rational human beings.

Where does the relativist stand regarding metaphysical objectivism/absolutism? Obviously, many relativists reject this point of view, since they see humanly created rules and other artifacts as part of the subject matter of moral judgments. Denying the objectivist/absolutist doctrine that moral values or moral laws are part of the objective furniture of the world, these thinkers are metaphysical relativists.

It is important to observe, however, that epistemological relativists need not be committed to the view that moral judgments describe customs, rules, or other human artifacts, and hence they can divorce themselves from the metaphysical relativism thought to follow from this conception of moral judgments. One could take the subject matter of these judgments to be something perfectly objective and yet deny that the evidence favoring them is rationally compelling for all agents. Clearly, though, a conception of the subject matter of moral judgments may have implications for moral epistemology. Finally, moral relativism, being a theory about what moral propositions are true, is also logically independent of any thesis of metaphysical relativism. Nevertheless, the two often go hand in hand.

The complex set of relationships among the theories of absolutism, relativism, objectivism, and nonobjectivism can be represented as in Table 1. This chart helps us to understand some of the possibilities for a relativist theory of morality, but it is not yet a complete picture of the positions open to the relativist.

Although relativists are almost always nonobjectivists of one kind or another, they need not be subjectivists. Subjectivism itself covers a varied terrain. Some subjectivists claim that moral judgments have a subject matter consisting of the states of mind of human beings: beliefs, feelings, attitudes, and the like. Others maintain that noncognitive states of mind are the sources of moral judgments. Subjectivists who interpret "x is good" as equivalent to "I like (approve of, desire) x" or "People of society S approve of x" (or even "I believe that x is good") fall into the first category. Emotivists or prescriptivists who take moral judgments to be the expression (rather than the description) of attitudes or decisions fall into the second. Also falling into the second category are subjectivists who think that moral judgments, even though descriptive (and descriptive of matters other than human beliefs or feelings), are motivated primarily by feelings, emotions, or attitudes. Such subjectivists attach no cognitive weight to moral judgments because they think of them as the causal product of noncognitive, affective/conative states of mind rather

Table 1. Relationships among Philosophical Positions

Absolutism (A)	Relativism (R)	Objectivism (O)	Nonobjectivism (N)
Moral (A_1)	Moral (R_1)	Metaphysical (O_1)	Metaphysical (N_1)
Epistemological (A_2)	Epistemological (R_2)	Epistemological (O_2)	Epistemological (N_2)
Metaphysical (A_3)	Metaphysical (R_3)		
$A_1 = {\sim}R_1$	$R_1 = {\sim}A_1$	$O_1 = {\sim}N_1$	$N_1 = {\sim}O_1$
$A_2 = O_1 = {\sim}R_2$	$R_2 = N_2 = {\sim}A_2$	$O_2 = {\sim}N_2$	$N_2 = {\sim}O_2$
$A_3 = O_1 = {\sim}R_3$	$R_3 = N_1 = {\sim}A_3$		

than the result of facts or evidence independent of such states. Relativists, on the contrary, often picture moral judgments as describing, as depending on for their justification, or as being the response to moral customs or rules that are independent of how the individuals making these judgments actually believe or feel about the subject matter of the judgments. In fact, relativists of this persuasion are able to show ways in which moral judgments are relative to rules that are independent of the current beliefs and feelings of the group or culture governed by the rules. Although nonobjectivists, these relativists are not subjectivists. Relativism may, it is true, take on a subjectivist form. The most extreme example of this kind of theory is the view that interprets a moral judgment as being true if the person making it *believes* it is true—"*x* is good" if and only if "I believe that *x* is good." This subjectivist form of relativism has few supporters today. Most current versions of relativism testify to the possibility of a theory that is both nonobjectivist and nonsubjectivist.

Everyday moral (and nonmoral) debates frequently include discussions concerning whether a certain point of view, conviction, argument, set of considerations, or criticism is objective or subjective. Those who claim that it is objective are claiming that it is based upon evidence and sound reasoning. A point of view, conviction, argument, set of considerations, or criticism is usually said to be subjective if it is thought to depend for its force on an appeal to feelings, emotional concerns and attachments, or the interests of those who put it forward. It needs to be emphasized that this everyday distinction between objective and subjective matters is largely independent of the philosophical distinction between objectivist and subjectivist theories. These theories involve characterizations of entire ranges of discourse. Some subjectivists, for example, claim that all moral judgments are descriptions of the feelings of individuals or groups. The everyday subjective/objective distinction, on the contrary, is a way of classifying individual judgments. Based on this distinction, some moral judgments turn out to be subjective and others objective. It is noteworthy that some subjectivists can easily claim that many moral judgments are perfectly objective. If a moral judgment is, as they think, a claim about the shared feelings or beliefs of a group, and if we make a judgment of this kind on the basis of evidence (polls, observations of group behavior, etc.) rather than on the basis of our own feelings concerning the issue, our judgment would be objective. Likewise, current forms of relativism can accommodate the objective/subjective distinction even while they propose global theories of nonobjectivism. If, as some affirm, moral judgments make reference to customs or rules created by human beings, we can make such judgments in either an objective or subjective manner. The distinctions among objectivist, nonobjectivist, and subjectivist theories are just that—distinctions among theories. The ordinary objective/subjective distinction can usually be preserved regardless of the moral theory we accept. One exception is the case of the subjectivist who thinks that all moral judgments are based upon feelings and the like and hence are subjective in the manner conveyed by the ordinary use of the term.

The situation is complicated even more, however, by the fact that philosophers frequently speak of moral judgments, rules, and so on as objective or subjective, meaning this not in the everyday sense but rather in a philosophical or theoretical sense. Epistemological objectivists think of moral principles as being objective because they believe that one cannot refuse to accept them without making an error or manifesting irrationality. Similarly, some subjectivists characterize moral judgments as subjective on the grounds that they are descriptions of feelings or attitudes. In this chapter and the next, context usually makes it clear in which sense 'objective' and 'subjective' are being used; otherwise I speak of "subjective/objective in the everyday sense" and "subjective/objective in the theoretical sense."

Finally, in order to position relativism in the scheme of philosophical doctrines, we must note that relativists need not be noncognitivists. To be sure, during the middle part of this century many of them were. They based their rejection of the idea of absolute moral truths on their radical claim that moral judgments have no truth values whatsoever. These judgments, they maintained, are mere expressions of psychological states having no cognitive significance. In general, however, relativism is not inconsistent with a cognitivist metaethical perspective. In fact, the forms of relativism most recently developed by philosophers are cognitivist in nature. These theories picture moral judgments as being either true or false, but only relatively so. Such theories claim that the truth of a moral judgment is relative to the conventions accepted by the individual who formulates it or to some conventional aspect of his society. More specifically, most contemporary relativists make moral truth relative to the rules adopted by an individual or his society. These rules themselves need not be thought of as true or false. Nevertheless, such relativists will argue, when we formulate a moral judgment we are attempting to state some fact about these rules—for instance, the fact that an act accords or does not accord with one of them, or the fact that, in light of a rule applicable to us, we have a good reason to behave in a certain way. Hence our judgment has a truth value, and often we can know what it is. But as the rules of an individual or a society vary, so too will moral truth. A truth about moral values for one person or society may well be a moral falsehood for another person or society adopting different rules. There is moral truth, but it is relative and variable.

Recent moral relativism, then, is nonobjectivist (in either a metaphysical or epistemological sense, or both), nonsubjectivist, *and* cognitivist. Nonsubjectivist, cognitivist theories of relativism are far more attractive than other, more traditional varieties. They are less paradoxical, being able to acknowledge and account for many, if not all, of the cognitive locutions found in moral language. In this chapter I examine two recent nonsubjectivist and cognitivist theories of moral relativism, one put forward by Gilbert Harman and the other by David Wong.

Standard Criticisms

As we approach the examination of these theories, it is well to have in mind some of the standard criticisms that have been directed at relativism in the past.[1] Insofar as relativism has been criticized more often than

1. Excellent critical discussions of relativism are to be found in Richard B. Brandt, *Ethical Theory* (Englewood Cliffs, N.J.: Prentice-Hall, 1959); Richard B. Brandt, "Introduction" to the chapter on "Ethical Relativism" in his *Value and Obligation* (New York:

defended, any new theory of this sort is under an obligation to present its credentials by responding in a plausible fashion to these objections. I argue that the theories of Wong and Harman are able in large part to deflect these standard criticisms, thereby achieving considerable credibility. In the end, however, I find other faults with them.

The following six objections are frequently raised against relativism: (1) It is difficult, as we have already noted, to know exactly what 'relativism' means. There are so many different theories calling themselves (or charged with being) relativistic that the term carries no clear connotation. At a minimum there is the traditional distinction between cultural relativism and ethical relativism, the former amounting to the empirical thesis that different individuals or social groups believe different basic moral propositions, the latter being a philosophical characterization of these moral propositions. Ethical relativists have claimed—to use my moral, epistemological, and metaphysical categories—that none of these propositions truly ascribes moral duties to all human beings, that none of them is true for all rational human beings, or that moral values are not a part of the objective furniture of the world. There are variations on all of these versions—for instance, individual relativism (which relativizes morality to individuals) and social relativism (which relativizes it to social groups). Any theory offered for serious consideration must specify where among these and other possibilities it stands.

(2) The relativist invalidly derives an ethical thesis that all moral values are relative from the factual thesis that societies and individuals have different moral beliefs. Disagreement and diversity of moral beliefs never entail that one ought to obey only the rules of one's society, that no moral belief is true for all rational human beings, or that no moral belief pictures objective facts.

Harcourt, Brace and World, 1961); W. T. Stace, *The Concept of Morals* (New York: Macmillan, 1937); Paul W. Taylor, "Social Science and Ethical Relativism," *Journal of Philosophy*, 55 (1958), 32–44; Carl Wellman, "The Ethical Implications of Cultural Relativity," *Journal of Philosophy*, 60 (1963), 169–84; selections from the book by Stace and the articles by Taylor and Wellman are reprinted in Paul W. Taylor, ed., *Problems of Moral Philosophy* (Belmont: Dickenson, 1967); Bernard Williams, *Morality: An Introduction to Ethics* (New York: Harper & Row, 1972), pp. 22–26; David Lyons, "Ethical Relativism and the Problem of Incoherence," *Ethics*, 86 (1976), 107–21; Charles L. Stevenson, "Relativism and Nonrelativism in the Theory of Value," in his *Facts and Values* (New Haven: Yale University Press, 1963); and Thomas L. Carson, *The Status of Morality* (Dordrecht and Boston: D. Reidel, 1984), esp. chaps. 3 and 4.

(3) Frequently a relativist concludes that people ought to obey the rules of their society or group without realizing that this is in fact an absolutist thesis. This position, therefore, is incoherent. Sometimes the relativist inconsistently derives the claim that one should be tolerant of those who disagree with one on moral issues—another absolutist thesis—from the claim that no set of moral beliefs is more correct than any other.

(4) The relativist has difficulty identifying the group whose opinions, attitudes, mores, or moral standards determine what is right or wrong for an individual. It is essential, however, that this be done if the truth of a moral judgment depends on its being in accord with the mores or standards of this group or, alternatively, if people ought to obey the rules of their social group. If a person is a member of a group *by virtue of* sharing its moral principles and standards, then any person disagreeing with those moral convictions would ipso facto not be a member of that group. This would make it impossible to condemn people for having beliefs out of accord with those of their society, as some relativists wish to do.

(5) The relativist position becomes incoherent by virtue of entailing that some acts are both right and wrong and that some moral judgments are both true and false. If an act is right when it accords with the principles of the speaker or appraiser, a particular act may be right by virtue of according with one speaker's principles and wrong because it fails to accord with another speaker's principles. Or if a moral judgment is true when it accords with the standards of a group and false when it does not, the same judgment may be true with respect to the standards of one group and false with respect to the standards of another—hence, for the relativist, both true and false. Such a position, it is argued against the relativist, is incoherent.

(6) If the relativist escapes the kind of incoherence described in (5), it is often in such a way as to turn genuine moral disagreements and conflicts into disagreements that are not genuine. Incoherence is sometimes avoided by interpreting moral judgments as containing in their meaning some essential reference to a particular person, group, or set of standards. Moral judgments that apparently conflict but in fact make reference to different persons, groups, or sets of standards are judgments that do not really conflict. They could all be true, each with respect to a distinctive set of standards or principles. This is implausible, the critic of

relativism contends, in that it would turn genuine conflicts between in-dividuals and cultures into so many confused instances of "talking past one another." Cannibals who eat their victims think such acts are mor-ally obligatory, and so they are, according to their principles. We Ameri-cans think cannibalism is morally repugnant, and so it is, according to our principles. In the relativist interpretation, there is no genuine dis-agreement here; the two positions are logically compatible. But surely, the critic claims, we do disagree with the cannibals, just as we disagree on many other issues with people from other cultures. The relativistic analysis of moral judgments is therefore false.

Gilbert Harman

One of the most widely discussed recent theories of moral relativism is that of Harman.[2] Harman develops a limited or restricted form of rela-tivism and incorporates it into a more general social custom theory of morality. He characterizes the general theory as follows: "We can define social custom theories loosely as theories that say that morality derives from the rules or customs that society enforces in a certain way."[3] These rules or customs are conventions that have been accepted by members of a social group and passed on to other members and generations by means of social and psychological forms of acculturation. Judgments of right and wrong are made by appeal to the principles expressed in these conventions or rules. The relativistic aspect of Harman's social custom theory pertains to the range of individuals on whom someone may pass moral judgment. Such judgments are restricted to the group of individ-uals sharing the moral principles of the person formulating the judg-ments. According to this theory, when the subject of a moral judgment is considered to have accepted, at least tacitly, the principles the speaker accepts, the speaker is justified both in claiming that the other person ought to act as the conventions require and in judging that it was mor-ally right or wrong of the person to act as he did. Contrariwise, if a

2. See Gilbert Harman, *The Nature of Morality* (Oxford: Oxford University Press, 1977); "Moral Relativism Defended," *Philosophical Review*, 84 (1975), 3–22; and "What Is Moral Relativism?" in A. I. Goldman and J. Kim, eds., *Values and Morals* (Dordrecht and Boston: D. Reidel, 1978).

3. *Nature of Morality*, p. 93. Further chapter and page references to this work are indicated parenthetically in the text.

person does not accept the conventions of a group, it is logically improper for members of that group to pass judgment on what he ought to do or what it is morally right for him to do. Hence moral judgments are relative to the set of rules, conventions, or principles shared by the person formulating the judgment and the person who is the subject of the judgment. Relative to this shared set, a judgment may be true or false, depending upon whether or not it, or the act it refers to, accords with the rules. Judgments made about individuals or societies not sharing the principles of the speaker are not so much false as logically improper. Moral truth *and* falsity are relative to a shared set of social norms.

Harman is insistent that his relativism is a limited one. It is restricted to judgments concerning what one morally ought to do or what is morally right or wrong. In contrast, it does not apply to evaluative judgments about good and evil or about what would make the world a better place. These judgments, Harman implies, although made with reference to the principles or standards of the speaker and her social group, are not restricted in any way with respect to their subject matter. Any thing or any person can be judged to be good or evil, to make the world a better or worse place. It is only when we make a judgment about what a person morally ought or ought not to do that we are restricted to those who share our principles. These judgments are what Harman calls *inner judgments*—they pertain to the relationship between an agent and her act, and they involve what Harman calls the *moral ought* (p. 59).[4] He warns us that in addition to the moral ought, with its relativistic restrictions, there is an *evaluative ought*, which is not so restricted. We can say of a person who does not share our moral principles that she ought not to have acted as she did if we mean by this that evaluatively the world would have been a better place had she not so acted. In such cases we are evaluating the act and not passing judgment on the moral relationship between the act and the person who engages in it. Harman's relativism, then, is not simply a claim that moral judgments are made relative to conventional rules; in fact, given his view of evaluative judgments it would appear he does not think that relativity to social standards is sufficient to make a judgment relative. The only relative judgments are those

4. On "inner judgments," see "Moral Relativism Defended," reprinted in M. Krausz and J. W. Meiland, eds., *Relativism: Cognitive and Moral* (Notre Dame, Ind.: University of Notre Dame Press, 1982)—see esp. pp. 190–95 of the reprint.

moral *ought*-judgments or judgments of moral rightness and wrongness dependent upon, and hence relative to, a set of shared principles.

Harman's theory develops out of two very strong intuitions. The first is that morality must be conceived of as having a source external to the individual; otherwise, Harman thinks, we would be forced to defend a counterintuitive form of subjectivism. The second intuition is that it is contrary to the proper use of moral language to say that a person (morally) ought to do something unless he has reasons for doing so, reasons deriving from the principles he himself accepts. The first requirement, what I call the *externality requirement*, is satisfied by locating the source of morality in social conventions, those of a group transcending the individual. The reasons-for-acting requirement, or what I call the *motivation requirement*, is met by restricting the scope of moral judgments about agents to those agents who at least tacitly accept the speaker's conventions. Let us look more closely at each of these intuitions and the theories developed to accord with them.

Harman feels that a moral theory should be as consistent as possible with our common intuitions about morality, and one of the strongest of these is that matters of right and wrong are not "up to the individual": "We are ordinarily inclined to suppose that a person's intentions, goals, plans, and projects are one sort of thing and morality is another. We do not ordinarily suppose that right and wrong are determined by a particular individual's decisions and principles. We are inclined to think that morality has an external source, not an internal one" (p. 92). He notes that we have no reluctance to speak of moral truth, facts, and knowledge, and he thinks these linguistic practices count against the theory of emotivism, which turns a moral judgment into a noncognitive expression of the individual speaker's attitudes. Moreover, Harman does not believe that moral principles describe attitudes and feelings. Hence he is not, to use my term, a subjectivist. A subjectivist theory for Harman would be inconsistent with our ordinary moral discourse (chap 1).

Before one can pass from the externality requirement to the social custom theory, it is necessary to show that alternative ways of meeting the requirement do not work, or do not work as well. To this end Harman surveys and criticizes ethical naturalism and rationalism (chaps. 2 and 6). We shall not follow him in this effort but shall content ourselves with noting the results. Naturalism, he argues, fails in its attempt to equate moral facts with a specific set of natural facts because of the likelihood that different people morally approve and disapprove of quite different natural features and facts. Furthermore, naturalists frequently ignore, or fail to explain, the important role that principles play in the moral life. Rationalists, on the contrary, do stress moral principles, and a rationalist like Kant thinks that the moral life consists of following principles derived from reason itself, principles that are binding on all rational agents. Harman tells us that, according to Kant, "if you are to act morally, your basic principle or maxim must be a principle that you accept as a principle for all rational beings" (p. 73). Such a view, Harman thinks, rests on an ambiguity in the notion of accepting a principle. He grants that if we act from a certain principle we must acknowledge that it would be rational for others to do so as well, and in this sense we accept the principle as binding on all rational agents. But although we grant that it would be rational for others to follow our principle, it does not follow, Harman argues, that we must *want* them to do so—in this sense we need not accept our principle as binding on all rational beings. We can accept our principle simply as our own and allow that others may have different ones.

Many of Harman's arguments against the naturalists and rationalists are less than convincing and hardly amount to refutations. But Harman is not really interested in refuting these philosophers, for that is not his philosophical strategy. He points to weaknesses in emotivism, traditional naturalism, the naturalist ideal-observer theory, Kantian rationalism, and the contemporary rationalist theory of Thomas Nagel and suggests that his own social custom theory can explain in a better fashion the phenomena of morality. Here he uses his well-known methodological strategy: making an inference to the best explanation.[5] Hence he can deny Kant's assumption that basic moral principles are binding on all rational beings, not by refuting it but by pointing to an alternative conception that he urges is a more plausible explanation of the facts. The alternative he proposes is "a more relativistic conception of morality, in which each person's moral principles are his own and rational beings do not necessarily assume that they all share the same fundamental principles" (p. 77). As we have seen, when this relativism is formulated as a social custom theory, it satisfies the externality requirement; according to Harman, it has the added virtue, not shared by rationalism and other

5. See his "Inference to the Best Explanation," *Philosophical Review*, 74 (1965).

objectivist theories, of satisfying the motivation requirement. We can now turn to the way in which he develops this latter requirement.

Harman's intuition that we cannot pass moral judgment on another agent who does not share our moral principles is most clearly expressed in one of his criticisms of R. M. Hare (pp. 80–90). Hare maintained that a person's morality is his system of moral principles. These principles are "general imperatives" addressed to everyone, and as Harman expounds the theory, to accept a principle is to intend to adhere to it and to intend to try to get others to accept it. There are no constraints on what principles a person can accept other than that they must be universalizable, and early Hare (as opposed to the Hare of *Moral Thinking*) assumed that different, equally rational people can have different principles.

It follows from Hare's theory that one could say of another person that he ought to do an act D even if that person does not accept any principle implying that he should do D. If person A accepts a moral principle requiring D, he must universalize it in the sense of prescribing that all other similarly situated persons do D. If person P does not accept this principle, it follows, Harman claims, that A prescribes that P engage in an act P has no reason to engage in. "The objection is that this is an odd thing to say, given that P has no reason to do D, at least none that derives from his principles. It is part of our ordinary view that P ought to do D only in cases in which P has reasons to do D. And, it is unclear where those reasons might come from, except from P's principles (pp. 83–84). Given this oddity, Harman rejects Hare's view that we can make moral judgments concerning anyone whomever, judgments prescribing what they morally ought to do. On the contrary, he thinks, we can say that it is morally right or wrong for a person to act in way D only if that person shares our principles, principles from which it follows that he ought or ought not to do D.

The motivation requirement plays a crucial role in Harman's distinctive relativist theory; it also is one of the most controversial aspects of his theory. For these reasons, it bears a closer look. Harman argues for his thesis largely by way of examples (pp. 97–98, 105–9).[6] Consider, for instance, a group of cannibals. Does it make sense for us to say that they ought not to eat human flesh and that it is morally wrong of them to do so? Obviously they do not see anything wrong with doing this, which

6. See also "Moral Relativism Defended," in Krausz and Meiland, pp. 192–93.

indicates that they do not share our moral principles prohibiting cannibalism. We might well think, and say, that the world would be a better place if there were no cannibalism in it, and we might express this by using the evaluative *ought*, namely, there ought to be no cannibalism in the world. We might even say that cannibalism is wrong, passing judgment on this practice simply as a part of the world. But to say that members of a primitive tribe are *morally wrong* to eat human flesh is to judge them in relation to their act, and such an "inner" judgment presupposes that they have good reasons not to eat human flesh. What good reasons do the cannibals have? They do not view cannibalism as wrong; their society does not endorse a principle condemning it. On the contrary, they most likely possess principles that make it morally right, even obligatory, for them. At a minimum we can agree that under such circumstances we should not *blame* these people for their act of cannibalism. And if it is impossible in the nature of the case for them to see or understand that their act is wrong, in what sense is it wrong of them to do it? Surely they cannot be said to have an obligation to refrain from cannibalism, and if not, it follows that it is wrong to say that they ought not to engage in it.

Take as another example the case of Hitler. Was it morally wrong of Hitler to attempt to exterminate the Jews? Ought he not to have done it? Harman grants that Hitler was an evil man, and that the world is infinitely worse off for having had him in it. But Hitler was so evil, he maintains, that it is impossible for us to think of him as having the slightest appreciation of our standards of right and wrong—he was, as it were, beyond the pale. To say that he ought not to have murdered Jews implies that he could recognize that this was wrong. But not being able to appreciate the standards in relation to which we judge his act wrong, how could he recognize this? In contrast to Hitler, Harman suggests, Stalin may have appreciated the moral enormity of his purges and may have ordered them only because he thought them necessary to achieve the higher goals of the Communist revolution. If we do not rule out the possibility that Stalin had a reason to order the purges—even if in the end not a good reason—we have a right to judge that it was morally wrong of him to kill so many people. But if we think that Stalin too was beyond the pale and incapable of appreciating our moral standards, it once again makes no sense to speak of him as being morally wrong in his actions.

Harman's motivation requirement has not been accepted by many of his critics, most of whom think that a different interpretation can be given of his examples. It has been said, for instance, that our refusal to judge Hitler or the cannibals to be morally wrong in their actions is the result simply of our acknowledged inability to convince them of this.[7] We think it was morally wrong of them to do what they did, but we realize the pointlessness of saying as much to them. Harman likely would reply that if we really are unable to convince these moral monsters that what they did was wrong, it follows that they could not come to understand that their acts were wrong. If they could not understand this, they could not have a reason to refrain from performing the acts, in which case it is logically improper to say that it is morally wrong of them to engage in them.

In spite of defending the motivation requirement on the basis of its intuitive appeal, Harman realizes that it may well conflict with one aspect of our moral beliefs. If we accept the motivation requirement and deny that all human beings have the same moral principles, it appears that "something is wrong with our ordinary view that we can make moral 'ought' judgments about anyone, no matter what their principles" (p. 90). This is to suggest that our ordinary moral intuitions are in conflict. Another possibility, not considered by Harman, is that the *ought*-judgments we make about "anyone, no matter what their principles" are really evaluative *ought*-judgments rather than moral ones. This would allow Harman to defend his relativism without coming into obvious conflict with our moral common sense. And indeed it is unclear whether many of the judgments we make about what everyone ought to do are moral "inner" judgments rather than evaluative ones—we could very well be expressing our view of what would make the world a better place. We shall inquire later on whether this maneuver is really satisfactory.

To summarize our discussion thus far, the social custom theory of morality with its attendant limited relativism meets both the externality requirement and the motivation requirement. Morality derives from social customs and rules that are socially enforced and transmitted to the members of the group. These rules and customs are external to the indi-

---

7. See the editors' introduction to "Moral Relativism Defended," in Krausz and Mei-land, pp. 186–88.

vidual; hence they have a degree of objectivity that the individual's goals and feelings do not have. The fact that society provides sanctions for violating the rules enhances their objective character. But although the rules are external to the individual, they are also in many instances internal, since most members of society have internalized them. It is because of this fact that the theory satisfies the motivation requirement. A member of a society who has internalized the society's rules ipso facto accepts these rules and consequently has a reason provided by them to act in certain ways. The members of the same society, at least those who share the moral rules, engage in moral assessments of one another's behavior. They may legitimately regard a fellow member as having done what she morally ought not to do, for they may assume that she too accepts the rules under which it is morally wrong to act in this way. If they cannot reasonably assume this, as in the case of hardened criminals, they cannot legitimately speak of its being morally wrong of such individuals to act as they do (p. 113). Furthermore, the vital importance of social rules in moral assessment ensures that the theory acknowledges the importance of principles in moral life, another desideratum for Harman. These principles are essential, for "morality is constituted by the rules, whatever they are, that society enforces" (p. 94).

Another important dimension to Harman's theory is its interpretation of the moral rules of a society as being conventionally adopted by the members of society because they benefit from the fact that everyone acts in accordance with the rules (chap. 9). Moral rules, according to Harman, are at least tacitly accepted by the members of society, and they reflect an actual, if nevertheless tacit, agreement among them. Each member is seen as having actually agreed to follow the rules on the condition that the others do so as well. No *hypothetical* agreement is at work here, Harman claims; the rules of a society do not reflect what the members *would* agree to were they, say, behind a Rawlsian veil of ignorance. By participating in a society, its members show that they intend to obey its rules on the condition that the other members reciprocate. The rules as it were reflect a tacit bargain struck among the members, who have agreed (in intention, not in any ritualistic way) to abide by the rules because doing so is the best way for them to benefit from, and not be harmed by, one another's actions.

For Harman, this hypothesis concerning the origination of moral rules has immediate explanatory value. It serves to explain why our society has rules against murder, theft, lying, and so on (pp. 105, 110–12). Society has an obvious interest in such rules, which is to say that each member of our society has such an interest. If moral rules are the reflection of a tacit agreement in intention among the members of our society, the above rules are precisely the ones we would expect to emerge from a conventional agreement. Thus the social custom theory together with the theory of implicit bargaining serves to render intelligible the content of our morality.

Harman's theory also has a more specific pay-off with regard to the content of our morality. Why is it, he asks, that we feel that it is more wrong morally to harm someone than to refrain from helping that person? Why do we have a moral injunction against harm, but no strong requirement that we help others? (p. 112) The distinction between harming and not helping others is deeply embedded in our moral thinking, and Harman believes he can explain why. Imagine the members of a group attempting to agree on the rules that would govern their behavior. Insofar as we are talking about an actual process of bargaining, not a hypothetical one from a Rawlsian original position, we must imagine the members of this group to possess different levels of wealth, power, and ability and to bargain with their own advantages in mind in light of their relative and specific degrees of wealth, and so on. Everyone engaging in this process of bargaining would agree on a rule prohibiting one person from harming another, but not everyone, specifically not those possessing favorable amounts of wealth and power, would favor a rule requiring them to help others, since they would stand to lose far more than they would gain by its implementation. Given this situation, a compromise might be reached. The rich and powerful, although in need of not being harmed by others, need a rule to prohibit this harm less than do the weak and dispossessed. But they might agree to such a rule on the condition that everyone not require another rule demanding positive help, for, as we have seen, this latter rule would be to their disadvantage. The wealthy and powerful might agree, therefore, to accept the "harm principle" only if a much weaker "help principle" were adopted. Thus the bargaining that goes on among the members of our society would produce exactly the set of rules we have regarding help and harm.

Harman spends a considerable amount of time defending his notion of implicit agreement and bargaining, for the most part trying to show that it does not commit him to the absurd notion that there occurred a ritualistic, dateable agreement giving rise to the moral rules.[8] As noted above, the agreement he hypothesizes is one "in intention" and as such does not require a specific act of agreement; nor does it require explicit awareness or acknowledgment. It is enough that the members of a group show through their behavior that they are disposed to obey moral rules on the condition that others do so as well, and Harman thinks the evidence for the existence of this disposition is quite favorable.

Criticism of Harman

Let us assume that Harman is correct about this. The problem I have with the implicit bargaining aspect of his overall theory is that (a) it is not an essential part of his relativism, and (b) it sits uncomfortably with his relativism. In the first place, the view that moral rules are social customs enforced by society and passed on through acculturation to its members requires no specific theory as to the origins of these rules. It can comfortably accept different accounts, indeed, different accounts for different rules. The rules might originate from ecclesiastical authority or from a strong, Hobbesian sovereign. They might even have a biological origin. All that the social custom theory need insist on is that the rules are seen as binding because they are enforced by society. If relativism requires that different societies have different rules, this diversity could easily be explained in terms of rules having different ecclesiastical, political, or biological origins.

In fact, and this leads to my second point, if relativism does require the notion of alternative moral customs, the implicit bargaining theory is a threat to relativism. If we make what seems to be the plausible, safe assumption that all societies have members with varying degrees of wealth and power, and if, with Harman, we view their moral principles as emerging from a process of bargaining, we might reasonably expect all of them to come up with the same bargain concerning the balance struck between the harm and help principles. If this balance is reasonable for us to agree to in the face of differences of power, surely it is reasonable for members of, for example, primitive societies to agree to in the face of similar conditions. And although different circumstances among

8. See "Moral Relativism Defended," in Krausz and Meiland, pp. 196, 201–2.

societies and different personal or social interests might lead to some different moral principles, it seems likely that the moral rules prohibiting lying, murder, and other forms of harm would be universally attractive. After all, the rules against lying and murder would reflect basic interests that all human beings are likely to have, and these are the interests that would be most dramatically affected by a person's relative degree of power. Thus the implicit bargaining theory would predict that principles proscribing lying and murder would be common—that is, that there would be widespread agreement on basic moral matters. Relativism, on the other hand, seems to be based on the conviction that there is widespread moral disagreement. At a minimum, it is committed to the likelihood that different social groups subscribe to different basic moral principles. Hence relativism and the implicit bargaining theory go in opposite directions.

It is true that Harman's implicit bargaining theory in and of itself does not entail widespread agreement on basic moral principles; in and of itself it is compatible with either agreement or disagreement. But put together with the assumption about widespread disparities of power— an assumption Harman appears to endorse—the theory does predict extensive agreement on basic moral principles. Furthermore, Harman's social custom interpretation of relativism does not in and of itself imply widespread *dis*agreement on moral matters. Conceivably, most societies could have the same customs. But Harman's emphasis on the limit surrounding the use of the moral *ought*—that it can be used to prescribe actions only with regard to agents who agree with the speaker about moral principles—strongly suggests that there will be many individuals who do not share the principles of any given speaker. Harman himself uses the cases of Hitler and cannibals to make his point, and surely these examples are intended to be representative of many individuals who hold moral principles different from our own. Given this presumption in favor of widespread diversity of principles, it is difficult to see how Harman can consistently claim that moral bargaining yields moral principles, when such bargaining would, in our world, produce widespread moral agreement.

Furthermore, there is a sense in which the implicit bargaining theory embodies a full-blooded objectivism. Consider the process of bargaining that is supposed to yield the moral rules—specifically, the harm/help rules. Would not any rational person in a bargaining position agree to these principles? Would it not be irrational not to do so? And when similar bargains are struck yielding other moral principles, would they not reflect what any rational person would agree to? The principles of practical rationality would seem to be applicable to the kind of moral bargaining Harman describes. And if moral bargaining produces a result that can be evaded only by being irrational, do we not have a basis for morality that is independent of custom and opinion—moreover a basis that is likely to yield the same set of principles, or largely overlapping sets, for most people? Such a view is not far removed from Kant's claim that moral principles are binding on all rational agents. Even if Harman were willing to grant that there is widespread agreement among societies concerning basic moral principles, it would still be difficult for him as a relativist to grant that these principles have a rational foundation. Thoughts such as these prompt one to say that relativism sits very uncomfortably with moral bargaining theories.

But a relativist, social custom theory need not, as we have seen, accept the implicit bargaining account of moral rules. These rules may be thought of as having other origins, some of them—the ecclesiastical and political, for instance—being far more likely to yield a highly variable set of rules and hence being far more compatible with relativism. Let us separate, then, the implicit bargaining hypothesis from the remainder of Harman's theory and turn to an examination of its relativistic core.

First, how does Harman's theory fare with respect to the six common criticisms of relativism mentioned at the beginning of this chapter? The first of these criticisms protests the lack of clarity involved in the use of the term 'relativism'. Is it possible to say precisely what it is that makes Harman's theory relativistic?

Harman's use of this term is a bit unusual. He is not claiming that moral judgments are relatively true simply on the ground that they are made relative to a set of standards and principles, since we have seen that he does not call evaluative *ought*-judgments relativistic in spite of the fact that they make appeal to standards of goodness. His thesis is relativistic because it limits the moral *ought*-judgments an individual can make to those directed at persons who share a set of moral principles with that individual. (If we think in the terms of his implicit agreement or bargaining theory, the only moral *ought*-judgments a person can make are those directed at persons with whom she has made an agreement or bargain.)

But, we might object, is this relativistic enough? If a moral *ought*-judgment can be true only by virtue of being in agreement with the principles shared by a speaker and her subject, does not this requirement uniquely define the set of applicable principles and hence render the moral judgment objectively true (or false)? Would not everyone have to agree that the judgment accords with the relevant principles?

Harman can reply to this objection by pointing out that the principles relevant to the truth or falsity of a particular moral judgment are not themselves required by reason or experience (he can, at any rate, say this if he abandons his implicit bargaining theory, for we have seen how this involves rational constraints on what can be accepted by a rational person). If the principles are not so required, a person can, without error or irrationality, refuse to accept the truth of a moral judgment by refusing to agree to the relevant principles. Harman's theory, then, is relativistic in an epistemological sense because moral truth is a function of something any person could refuse to accept without error or irrationality.

With respect to the second criticism, does Harman derive his theory of relativism from the factual thesis that individuals and societies have different moral beliefs? Decidedly not. He derives it from a logical claim about one of the conditions under which it makes sense to issue a moral *ought*-judgment about an individual—namely, when that individual has a reason for acting in the way he ought to act and this reason is a principle he accepts and shares with the person making the *ought*-judgment. To be sure, it appears that in addition to being an epistemological relativist Harman is also a moral one. His relativism can be taken to comment on the conditions under which a moral judgment is logically proper (and hence true or false), and if, as seems to be the case, he thinks there are alternative moral customs, this should lead him to deny that there are any true moral principles prescribing how all human beings should behave. His moral relativism, however, does not follow directly from the factual claim about alternative moral customs, but only from this together with his claim about the truth conditions of moral judgments.

The third criticism charges the relativist with inconsistently adopting the (moral) absolutist thesis that people ought to obey the rules of their society. Is Harman guilty of this inconsistency? Nowhere does he make the claim that individuals ought to obey the rules of their society.[9] Furthermore, it would be inappropriate, given his theory, for him to say that an individual B should act in accordance with the (B's) group's standards unless he, Harman, was a member of this group. Harman would be prevented by his theory from telling any person B who does not accept the same rules he himself accepts that B should obey the rules of Harman's society or B's own. Harman's analysis of the truth-conditions of moral judgments, that is to say, prevents him from endorsing the moral absolutist thesis in question.

Does Harman have difficulty, as the fourth criticism would suggest, in identifying the group whose moral standards are relevant to determining how a given individual ought to act? The answer is no. The group whose standards are applicable to individual A is the group this individual is in by virtue of accepting its standards (through acculturation, bargaining, or what have you). It is the group whose standards this person has internalized. If a person does not accept the standards of a particular group, she has, according to Harman, no reason to act as these standards require, and consequently no one has the logical right to demand that she do so.

The fifth criticism of relativism charges that the theory incoherently entails that some moral judgments are both true and false, or that some acts are both right and wrong. Is Harman's theory incoherent in this fashion?

In general, it seems that it is not.[10] If a person B shares a set of moral principles with person A, then, according to Harman's theory, B may say, and say truly, that it was wrong of A to do x. Only those who share

9. He does come close to saying this, however, in "What Is Moral Relativism?" (pp. 152–56), where he argues for what he calls *normative moral relativism*, the theory that two or more people can be subject to different moral demands and not subject to some more basic demand accounting for this. One assumption of his argument is that a moral demand applies to a person "only if" that person accepts the demand or fails to do so because of ignorance, confusion, etc. If this 'only if' were changed to 'if and only if', Harman would have to grant that any person accepting a moral demand is subject to that demand.

10. Again one must hedge, since in "What Is Moral Relativism?" (pp. 159–60) he argues that really conflicting moral judgments can both be right *if* they are judgments involving a nonrelativist's usage of moral language; really conflicting moral judgments cannot both be right if these judgments involve the *relativist's* usage of moral language. It is unclear why Harman wants to allow the nonrelativist's usage, involving as it does universalizability. Why is this usage not deemed irrational or incoherent?

these principles with A can make such an inner judgment about A, and hence all those who share them would have to agree that it is true (or, as the case may be, false) that A was morally wrong to do x. Of course, someone sharing these principles may think that the standards allow A to do x, but that person would simply be in error. It cannot be the case, then, that for those accepting this set of standards it is both true and false that A ought to do x. And someone not accepting these standards can make no judgment at all about what A ought to do. Hence there is no possibility that conflicting truth values will be assigned to a moral judgment.

It is possible, as Harman notes, for an individual to hold more than one set of standards, and it may be the case that one set requires him to do x and another permits him to do not-x.[11] In this case, would it not be both true and false that he ought to do x? Harman's reply is that "superficially conflicting moral judgments about that agent . . . made in relation to different moralities can both be true if the agent accepts both moralities relative to which each of the judgments is made."[12] These moral judgments only superficially conflict because each is made relative to a different set of standards. Relative to set M, it is true that A ought to do x; relative to set N, it is false that A ought to do x. These judgments are not logically contradictory, so that if A (or Harman) grants that both are true, A (or Harman) is not incoherently accepting two logically inconsistent judgments.

But this response raises the sixth objection considered above. If the judgments that A ought and ought not to do x are not logically inconsistent because they are made relative to different standards, they are not really in disagreement with one another. Similarly, if two people have different standards, and if one of them, A, says in light of her standards that she ought to do x, and another, B, says in light of *his* standards that A should not do x, it is misleading to describe them as disagreeing. They are not expressing logically inconsistent propositions and hence cannot be in real disagreement. But they certainly appear to disagree! Is not Harman's theory to be faulted by virtue of so construing the two judgments that A and B do not in fact disagree?

Although Harman is not very clear on this point, he could respond by

11. Ibid., p. 159.
12. Ibid.

reminding the disputants that they can pass moral judgment on one another only if they have the same standards. Hence, in the case above, person B, who says that A ought not to do x, is speaking in a logically improper way, given that he does not share A's standards. If he did share those standards, he and A would be in real disagreement, and one of them at least would be wrong. So, either two individuals are in real disagreement (sharing standards as they do) or the superficial disagreement is really a case in which one of the judgments is logically improper.

Harman's theory is therefore capable, I maintain, of making plausible responses to the six standard objections to relativism. But his theory is not yet out of the fire. There are other serious problems endemic to its specific formulation, and to these we now turn our attention.

It must be granted that there is some intuitive appeal to Harman's claim that we would not readily say *to*, or even *of*, a group of cannibals that it is morally wrong of them to eat human flesh. To say such a thing would imply that they are to be blamed for what they do, and it would indeed be absurd to blame them for doing something they have no reason not to do. All of the reasons they, in fact, have suggest to them that eating human flesh is something they are morally permitted, and probably obligated, to do. Blaming them for their action makes utterly no sense, for they are not responsible for doing something wrong. They are not responsible because they do not know that it is wrong and could not be expected to know this. So to the extent that Harman is saying that cannibals should not be blamed for their actions, he is on sound ground.

But to put the matter this way, to say that cannibals should not be blamed for what they have done, is to imply that they have done something morally wrong; it is just that they cannot be held culpable for these wrong actions. Is there anything counterintuitive about saying that cannibalism is morally wrong? Surely most of us believe this. And missionaries have no reluctance whatsoever to say it to the cannibals, hoping thereby to change their practices. So perhaps we should distinguish the proposition "It is morally wrong of the cannibals to eat human flesh" from "Cannibalism is morally wrong." Harman may be correct in claiming that the former proposition is odd, but the latter proposition is not odd at all. And the former proposition can be thought of as odd because it attributes moral culpability when such an attribution makes no sense. The proposition that cannibalism is morally wrong is not about culpability but rather about the moral character of cannibalism.

These considerations suggest that Harman has misunderstood the reason that a proposition like "It is morally wrong of you to eat human flesh" is appropriately said only to someone who shares the speaker's moral principles. This reason has nothing to do with moral relativity, with the notion that there are logical limits on whom one may pass judgments of moral wrongness. It has to do rather with the fact that moral culpability entails responsibility, a fact that no absolutist would wish to deny. The intuition, then, on which Harman builds his relativism is shared by moral absolutists and is as consistent with absolutism as with relativism.

Harman might reply to this argument by reminding us of the evaluative *ought* and suggesting that "Cannibalism is morally wrong" is equivalent to a proposition in which this evaluative *ought* is used. This would be a way of defending his claim that the moral *ought* cannot be used with reference to individuals who do not share the speaker's principles. "Cannibalism is morally wrong," he could say, is to be taken as equivalent to "People ought not to eat human flesh," in which 'ought' occurs evaluatively, that is, as expressing the notion of "the world being a better place." Thus "People ought not to eat human flesh" interpreted as involving the evaluative *ought* would mean the same as "The world would be a better place if people did not eat human flesh."

It seems counterintuitive, however, to suggest that "Cannibalism is morally wrong" means nothing more than "The world would be a better place if there were no cannibalism in it." For one thing, we may not have a moral obligation to make the world a better place, but we surely do have a moral obligation not to engage in cannibalism. In asserting that cannibalism is morally wrong, part of what we are asserting is that everyone has an obligation to refrain from this kind of behavior.[13] Cannibals, to be sure, do not recognize this obligation, largely because of their cultural traditions and lack of moral education. But many of us,

---

13. Some obligations are incurred just by our being human. Others are incurred by virtue of a special act or status, and many of these acts must be done knowingly and voluntarily. Yet some special obligations do not require the voluntary assumption of a role or acknowledgment of it—for instance, the obligation of parents to their children—and universal obligations are also of this kind. All human beings have an obligation not to kill one another and not to treat one another with disrespect, whether they know this or not. We would not blame them for not fulfilling these obligations if they were not aware of them, but we would still think they have them.

certainly the missionaries, feel morally required to improve the can- nibals' moral education. When we tell them that cannibalism is morally wrong, we are informing them of one of their obligations—one of the obligations of all human beings. "Cannibalism is morally wrong," then, is a statement about (everyone's) obligation. If Bernard Gert is correct, however, and it seems likely that he is, we do not have a moral obliga- tion to make the world a better place. This is not the sort of thing that everyone can do, which is one of Gert's conditions for a moral obliga- tion.[14] (Refraining from cannibalism, on the contrary, is something that all human beings can do). Hence "The world would be a better place if there were no cannibalism in it" is not a statement about obligation or one that entails any claim about obligation. This being the case, Harman cannot legitimately equate it with "Cannibalism is morally wrong." It follows that he has not shown us a way to make sense out of "Cannibal- ism is morally wrong" which avoids proscribing conduct of those who do not share our principles. Our propensity to proclaim to everyone in the world that cannibalism is morally wrong constitutes evidence against Harman's claim that we can issue moral 'oughts' only to those who share our moral principles.

Let us examine another locution Harman frequently employs in expli- cating his relativism: the notion of what one morally ought not to do (p. 106). He maintains that, just as it is counterintuitive to say that it is morally wrong of the cannibals to eat human flesh, it is also counterin- tuitive to say that they morally ought not to do so. It should be noted, however, that the sentence 'These people morally ought not to eat hu- man flesh' is slightly odd, just as is the sentence 'You morally ought not to eat human flesh'. Less odd would be 'Morally, these people ought not to eat human flesh' and 'Morally, you ought not to eat human flesh'. These latter sentences seem equivalent to 'These people's eating of hu- man flesh is morally wrong' and 'Your eating human flesh is morally wrong'. As we have seen, propositions of this sort do not equate with propositions incorporating Harman's evaluative *ought*; moreover, they are propositions we feel no compunction in expressing to people whom we know do not share our moral convictions. Thus, in what appears to be their most natural rendering, propositions containing the phrase

14. See Bernard Gert, *The Moral Rules* (New York: Harper & Row, 1966), pp. 66– 75.

'morally ought not to' do not obey the relativist restrictions that Harman would place on them.

Finally, let us look at Harman's notion of the evaluative *ought*. Judgments containing this *ought* are not inner judgments, according to him, and they are not said to be relativistic. Only judgments of what one morally ought to do are claimed by Harman to be relativistic, not judgments about what one evaluatively ought to do. But this distinction has an artificial air to it. If, as Harman suggests, we use the evaluative *ought* to say something equivalent to "The world would be a better place if there were no cannibalism in it," we might wonder why Harman's relativistic argument would not apply here as well. This judgment seems to commend a world without cannibalism. Commending something usually means that we recommend that people prefer or choose that thing, which in turn presupposes that the people to whom it is addressed have some reason to prefer or choose it. Could we not say, in Harman-like fashion, that these reasons can only come from the standards of goodness of the people addressed? If so, it would follow that if the people addressed do not share our standards, they have no reason to prefer or choose what we commend. In that case, it would be improper for us to commend it to them. So if it is improper for us to make an inner judgment about what a person morally ought to do when that person does not share our moral principles, it should be equally improper for us to make a judgment using the evaluative *ought* when addressing a person who does not share our standards of goodness. Thus, on the kind of grounds Harman himself adduces, his distinction between relativist and nonrelativist judgments becomes suspect.

Of course, most of us would feel quite comfortable telling someone whose standards are different from ours that the world would be a better place without cannibalism (Nazism, slavery, etc.) in it. In saying this, we feel that we are correcting or enlightening them. Equally, when we tell people with whom we disagree that cannibalism or Nazism or slavery is morally wrong, we see ourselves as putting them straight. And that we can quite properly say these things and at the same time stop short of saying that it is morally wrong *of them* to engage in such actions shows only that correcting/enlightening is one thing and blaming another. Blaming, as we have seen, is relativistic in an innocuous sense; correcting does not seem relativistic in any sense. The relativity of blaming affords no grounds for a doctrine of moral or epistemological relativism.

David Wong

David Wong's *Moral Relativity* is the most recent major attempt to develop a relativistic theory of morality.[15] Unlike Harman, Wong extends his relativism to judgments of moral goodness as well as to judgments of moral obligation. His theory is also novel by virtue of its use of recent developments in the philosophy of language: specifically, truth-conditional semantics and the causal theory of reference. In my opinion, however, Wong's analysis can be presented and understood without the trappings of these semantic theories, and I shall attempt to expound his views without appealing to them.

Early in his book, Wong tells us that one of the main tasks of moral theory is to account for both the subjective and the objective characteristics of moral experience.[16] The widespread and often irresolvable disagreements among people over moral issues speak in favor of the subjective status of morality; moral commitments seem to have the variability one would expect from matters pertaining to feelings, emotions, and interests. At the same time, however, human beings use a highly cognitive vocabulary to express their moral views, claiming as they do that their views are true and well-argued, whereas those of their opponents false and unsubstantiated. Is it possible, Wong asks, to construct a theory that acknowledges that moral judgments have truth values but at the same time pictures these judgments as resting on a subjective basis? He thinks the theory of relativism does precisely these two things. His doctrine of relativism grants the following "absolutist" theses:

(1) Moral statements have truth values;
(2) There are good and bad arguments for the moral positions people take;
(3) Nonmoral facts (states of affairs that obtain in the world and that can be described without the use of moral terms such as 'ought', 'good', and 'right') are relevant to the assessment of the truth value of moral statements;
(4) There are moral facts (which may or may not be claimed to be reducible in some way to nonmoral facts). (p. 1)

15. David Wong, *Moral Relativity* (Berkeley: University of California Press, 1984).
16. Ibid., p. 1. Further chapter and page references to this work are indicated parenthetically in the text.

Wong's relativism, however, does not concede two other absolutist claims:

> (5) When two moral statements conflict as recommendations to action, only one statement can be true;
> (6) There is a single true morality. (p. 1)

As a relativist, Wong is committed to the view that two conflicting moral recommendations can both be true. And there is for him no single true morality but rather a plurality of true moralities.

How are we to accommodate theses 1–4 while denying 5 and 6? We must, in the first place, interpret moral judgments in such a way that they can be seen to correspond or fail to correspond to facts and hence be true or false; but in the second place, they must correspond to facts that are the product of "social creation" and hence may vary from one social context to another. For Wong, the facts to which moral judgments correspond or fail to correspond are relationships among acts, persons, and *rules*. A morality comprises a set of rules developed to guide action and to help the members of society avoid internal and interpersonal conflicts resulting from competing goals and interests. Contrary to Harman's view, a morality need not contain only those rules on which there is "implicit agreement" resulting from a process of bargaining by the members of a society; it contains, rather, any rules that a society's members are committed to as conflict-resolution devices, whatever the origin of this commitment. Most of us, Wong thinks, simply inherit our morality from our parents and other members of society; most of us engage in no explicit agreement or implicit bargaining. Wong subscribes to the view that, although human nature and natural resources place some constraints on the ways in which internal and interpersonal conflicts can be avoided, human nature is plastic enough to allow alternative resolutions of conflicts and hence permits the development of alternative sets of moral rules—that is, alternative moral systems. Accepting the possibility of alternative, equally legitimate moralities, we can then interpret the truth or falsity of moral judgments as a function of whether or not these judgments accurately describe the relationships among actions, persons, and the moral rules contained in the morality or moral system of the individuals formulating them. Moral truth is thus relative to a moral system which arises from the subjective needs and interests of people and which, being one among several such systems, cannot claim to be the only legitimate morality.

Let us look, then, at the way Wong analyzes the judgment 'A ought to do X'. He takes it as equivalent to: "By not doing X under actual circumstances C, A will be breaking a rule of an adequate moral system applying to him" (p. 40).

This is a fairly complex analysans, and we need to go into it in some detail, especially with regard to the notion of an adequate moral system. For the moment, however, let us concentrate on the manner in which the analysans provides truth values for moral judgments. It would appear to be a straightforward matter of fact whether or not in not doing X under circumstance C person A will be breaking a rule that is applicable in this case. This fact is a relational one in which the terms of the relation are the appropriate rule, the action, the person, and the circumstances. The relation is one of consistency or inconsistency, a matter of whether or not the action in context accords with the rule. Even if the rule is thought of as a prescription, it is still a fact whether or not the action accords with the demands of the rule. There may be some disagreement over whether or not doing an act in fact breaks a moral rule, but we can expect that further argument would resolve the disagreement. A good argument would be one proving that not doing an act did, or did not, follow from a moral rule and a description of the prevailing circumstances. Hence interpreting an *ought*-judgment as a statement about the relationship between a rule requirement and an act allows us to understand exactly how and why cognitive locutions enter into our moral discourse. And it allows us to see how there can be moral facts and some degree of moral objectivity—for it is an objective matter of fact that an act in a certain context does or does not accord with a rule requirement.

At the same time, Wong's analysis of 'A ought to do X' reveals to us the source of what he identifies as the subjective aspects of moral experience. Rules are matters of social creation, and different societies may operate with different ones, reflecting their different ways of resolving internal and interpersonal disagreements. Assume that societies M and N have different moral rules. In that case 'A ought to do X' might reflect the fact that, in not doing X, A would be breaking a rule of society M. At the same time, it might be false that, in not doing X, A would be breaking a rule of society N. So, relative to society M, A ought to do X, whereas relative to society N this is not so. Members of society M could say truly that A ought to do X, and members of society N could say truly that A is permitted not to do X. Here we have incompatible moral claims, both of which are true. (We discuss below the manner in which these judgments are incompatible and their authors in disagreement.) Furthermore, with certain qualifications to be considered later, no amount of argument could resolve the disagreement, and irresolvable disagreement is one of the hallmarks for Wong of moral subjectivity. And if among different societies we find numerous sets of conflicting rules, we encounter the diversity of moral opinion which is another of his criteria of subjectivity. Hence Wong's account is capable of accommodating the subjective dimension and explaining it.

With this overview in mind, let us look more closely at some of the elements of Wong's analysans. We see that various kinds of relativity are built into it. First of all, the fact that A ought to do X is relative to actual and specific circumstances C. These might include the fact that A promised to do X, or entered into a contract that involves doing X, or that X would have certain predictable consequences. All obligations are relative to such specific conditions. Additionally, however, there is built into Wong's analysans a relativity of moral obligation to general circumstances. For instance, our moral rules governing marriage in a society containing approximately the same number of males and females may be quite different from the moral rules we would accept in a society in which the men greatly outnumber the women. Or our rules prohibiting interference with certain freedoms may vary with the availability of resources: in circumstances of scarcity we may feel that people should no longer be free to take what they can but rather that distribution requirements severely restricting freedom should be instituted. Wong takes note of this variability by speaking of the rule of an adequate moral system *applying* to A. If A were in one set of circumstances, one rule would apply, but in another general circumstance of the sort above, a quite different moral rule might apply.

The distinctive part of Wong's relativistic analysis involves his use of the phrase 'adequate moral system'. First of all, it allows him to avoid at the outset a criticism often leveled against relativistic theories. This is the objection that, contrary to relativism, people who claim that A ought to do X cannot be seen as merely reporting what the rules of their society require, because those people may very well repudiate these rules. Wong grants this (pp. 29, 39–40). We do not attribute authority to just any of the rules of our society, for we recognize that some of them may be the result of superstition, prejudice, or error. When we make moral judgments, we do not operate with the idea of our own or our society's *prevailing* moral rules, but rather with the idea of *adequate* rules. Adequate rules are those meeting the standards that define for us our *moral ideal*. Hence when we say that an act would break a rule of our adequate moral system, we are saying that it would break a rule warranted by the moral ideal of this system, a rule meeting the requirements set forth in its standards for moral rules. The actual rules of our society or the ones we normally follow may not do this. So in making moral judgments we are not making claims about what accords with actual rules; we are making claims about what accords with ideal rules, those of our adequate moral system.

The fact that moral judgments make reference to ideal as opposed to actual rules shows that one popular argument for relativism will not work. The fact, if it is a fact, that different social groups operate with different moral principles or rules does not entail that no one of these principles or rules is correct. Of course, as critics of relativism have been quick to point out, a conclusion about the correctness or incorrectness of principles cannot validly be derived from premises about agreement or disagreement among those who accept these principles. In the context of Wong's theory, the conclusion also fails to follow because the various sets of conflicting rules may be held by people who in fact subscribe to the same moral ideal. If so, one of the sets of rules might well be more correct than the others—it might be more in accord with the shared moral ideal. It is quite possible that a society as a whole can make a mistake about what its moral ideal requires in the way of rules. Actual disagreement in rules among societies is consistent, then, with agreement on a moral ideal by the members of these societies—and given this common ideal, the same warranted rules follow for all, whether they are recognized or not.

Wong's notion of a moral ideal and ideal moral rules clearly distinguishes his theory from those relativistic theories equating a moral principle's being true with its being believed or accepted by a society. His theory is not a subjectivist one in this sense. For Wong, a society can have false beliefs about morality because it can make mistakes about its moral ideal. Rational criticism of a society's actual moral beliefs is therefore possible.

But what about the moral ideal from which we derive a set of adequate rules—can it be rationally criticized? Wong's answer is not an unqualified yes or no (pp. 73–79). Rather, he points to respects in which rational criticism of the ideal is possible, and at the same time he indicates the limits of this criticism. In the first place, some moral ideals may be based upon factual errors, and to this extent they are subject to rational criticism. But it is possible that different societies operate with different moral ideals and that none of them is based on false factual assumptions. In the second place, there may be constraints on what a society can choose to be its moral ideal, constraints relating to the very function of moral rules, to what is possible or impossible in general for human beings to do, and to what resources are available for human life. Any moral ideal is subject to criticism if it fails to satisfy these conditions. An ideal that does not promote the function of moral rules—resolving internal and interpersonal conflicts—or that does not take into account the limits of human endeavor and the limits of human resources is legitimately open to rational censure. But if, within these constraints, human beings produce alternative moral ideals based on no factual errors, there is nothing that requires us to accept one of them rather than the others. Different moral systems with their distinctive moral ideals may represent equally valid ways of resolving personal and interpersonal conflicts. There need be no rational or factual ground for choosing between them. Hence, although rational criticism of moral ideals is possible, Wong thinks that in the end this criticism will not yield one moral ideal that all rational individuals must accept. In this sense, a moral ideal is not objective. A person could without error or irrationality refuse to accept a moral ideal that passes the above tests because he accepts another one that is equally rational.

Wong also repudiates the absolutist view that when two moral statements conflict as recommendations to action, only one can be true. Given his analysis of the meaning of the moral judgment "*A* ought to do *X*," it is possible that when two individuals make this judgment they are referring to the rules of two different adequate moral systems. The extension of the term 'adequate moral system' would therefore be different for each of them: these extensions would contain different moral ideals and different moral rules derived from the ideals. Whether or not it is true that a person ought to do a certain thing depends on whether the act is permitted or disallowed by the rules of the speaker's adequate moral system. Therefore the truth conditions of "*A* ought to do *X*" are relative to the adequate moral system of the speaker: "A speaker *B* may say of *A* that he ought to do *X* under condition *C*. A speaker *D* may say of *A* that he ought not to do *X* under the same condition. If 'adequate moral system' has different extensions in the ideolects of *B* and *D*, both statements may be true, and there is no conflict between the statements generated by their truth conditions" (p. 45). If two speakers refer to different rules, via their respective notions of an adequate moral system, their moral judgments will be logically independent. The conditions that make the one true do not make the other false. It is in this way that we arrive at the relativistic view that when two moral statements differ in their recommendations to action, both can be true. For *B*, it is true that *A* ought to do *X*, given the extension of 'adequate moral system' for him; for *D*, for whom 'adequate moral system' has a different extension, it is not true that *A* ought to do *X*.

If '*A* ought to do *X*' and '*A* is permitted to do not-*X*' can both be true, how can they be said to conflict with one another? The conflict, according to Wong, is not logical but pragmatic (p. 45). The two judgments require different actions that cannot both be undertaken. It is impossible for *A* both to do and not to do *X* (at the same time and/or in the same circumstances). So the requirements imposed by the two judgments cannot both be followed, although the judgments are logically independent of one another.

In this light, we are able to see how Wong could respond to four of the standard criticisms brought against relativism. First, he need not concern himself with a precise definition of 'society' or 'social group', since he relativizes the truth conditions of a moral judgment to the speaker's own moral rules. This move also allows him to avoid the criticism that the relativist inconsistently asserts the absolutist thesis that one ought to obey the moral rules of one's society—Wong makes no such assertion. Third, by relativizing moral judgments in such a way as to have them refer to the speaker's own adequate moral system, Wong avoids the incoherence of claiming that a moral judgment can be both true and false. If two or more speakers share a moral system, any conflicting judgments they make will be logically inconsistent and at least one will be in error. If two speakers do not have the same moral system, 'adequate moral system' will denote something different in each of their apparently conflicting judgments, which will be logically independent. Given the rules of moral system M, a person A ought to do X; given the rules of moral system N, A ought not to do X. Although there is no logical disagreement here, the two speakers are not just talking past one another. One of them requires A to do X, and the other requires A not to do X. Such conflict is genuine, but it is pragmatic rather than logical. Hence Wong is able to repudiate the criticism that by relativizing the meanings of moral judgments the relativist must deny the obvious fact of real disagreement among people adopting different moral systems. Wong does not deny such disagreement; he simply gives a particular interpretation of its nature.

We should emphasize again how very far removed this version of relativism is from the one that often is held up as an example of the theory and subjected to derisive criticism—namely, the view that a moral judgment is true if the speaker believes that it is true or if it seems true to the speaker. On Wong's account, a speaker can make numerous errors with regard to his moral judgments. He may mistakenly think that an act would violate one of the rules of his adequate moral system, or he may mistakenly think that the rule the act would break is part of his adequate moral system, that is, that it meets the standards of his moral ideal. Hence the fact that a speaker believes that A ought to do X by no means entails that it is true for him that A ought to do X. Wong's relativism is consistent with the conceptual distinction between *true* and *appears true* so often stressed by absolutists. He shows how we can accommodate this distinction within relativism.

It was noted above that Wong extends a relativistic analysis to statements of moral goodness as well as to statements of moral obligation. Let us look briefly at this application. Wong's general analysis of 'X is a good Y' is: "Under actual circumstance C, X satisfies those standards for Ys contained in adequate moral systems applying to X" (p. 69). Here again there is a relativity to specific conditions (actual condition C) and to the set of standards applying to X by virtue of the general conditions in which X occurs. That we might have one set of standards for general conditions F and another for general conditions G leads Wong to speak in the plural of adequate moral *systems*, each one of these systems being considered adequate by the speaker for a certain kind of general condition. Wong's analysis also makes X's goodness relative to the speaker's standards for the kind of thing X is, that is, for Y things. This opens up the possibility that different speakers may refer to different standards of moral goodness, standards derived from the moral ideals of different adequate moral systems. If two speakers do refer to different standards, it might be true for one that X satisfies his standard and false for the other that it satisfies her standard. Hence the judgment 'X is a good Y' would be true for the first speaker and false for the second.

Once again, incoherence is avoided by virtue of the fact that 'X is a good Y' has one set of truth conditions for one of the speakers and another set for the other. Pragmatically, however, the two speakers are in conflict, for one recommends the choice of X and the other recommends against it. And, once again, considerable error is possible on the part of people who judge that X is morally good. They may think incorrectly that X satisfies the standards of their adequate moral system, or they may think incorrectly that the standard they apply to X is one of the standards of their adequate moral system (it might, for instance, merely be the standard prevailing in their society at the time). And a speaker's moral ideal may itself be based upon false factual assumptions. Rational criticism of relativistic judgments of moral goodness is therefore possible in many different forms.

Nevertheless, it is Wong's view that there is no one set of standards of moral goodness that reason and/or experience will inevitably lead people to adopt (pp. 113, 158–59, 175). Some such standards may fail to perform the assigned task of resolving conflicts, but more than one standard will perform it. Indeed, what constitutes balance—the resolution of conflict—may vary from group to group, and, especially relevant in the case of moral goodness, what constitutes human fulfillment also may vary. According to Wong, "such variation results in different extensions for 'adequate moral system' as the term is used among different groups and societies" (p. 79). Moral goodness is no less relative than moral obligation.

Wong is not content just to claim variability of moral rules and standards; he wishes to demonstrate actual variation. To do so, he argues that we can find throughout history at least two radically different ways of conceiving an adequate moral system. There are, in the first place, what he calls *virtue-centered moralities*, and in the second place, *rights-centered* ones (chap. 9). The former operate with the concept of a good common to a community of persons, and they identify as virtues those modes of character and action necessary to achieve this common good. The notion of social roles and duties also functions as an important part of virtue-centered moralities. Rights-centered moralities, on the contrary, start with a conception of the interests individuals have prior to or independent of their participation in a community. They attribute rights or entitlements to individuals as a means of protecting and promoting these interests. These rights allow individuals to pursue their private interests with maximum freedom, balanced only by a consideration of the freedom of others and (at times) considerations of equality.

Wong argues at length that these two concepts of morality are distinct from and irreducible to one another. If he is correct, individuals who adopt a rights-centered morality refer to something different by 'adequate moral system' than do those who adopt a virtue-centered morality. Moreover, Wong maintains that there is variation (and, on occasion, indeterminacy) in the extension of 'adequate moral system' even within one of these general perspectives. Rawls and Nozick, he claims, present different standards for moral rules, although both operate within a rights-centered morality (pp. 139–41). Nozick is committed to a moral ideal that makes an absolute of the right of a person to her just entitlements; Rawls is committed to an ideal that emphasizes both freedom and a fair method for the distribution of goods. When Rawls and Nozick disagree on an issue, then, it follows that they both may be correct, each relative to his conception of an adequate moral system.

We now can determine how Wong could respond to the two other common criticisms of relativism. What meaning does he assign to the term 'relativism', and does he infer any normative theses from the diversity of moral belief?

Wong claims that different individuals and social groups refer to different rules and ideals in their use of the term 'adequate moral system' (or an equivalent phrase). Moreover, he argues that given the plasticity of human nature it is possible that different sets of rules can equally well perform the task of resolving internal and interpersonal conflicts. Hence he is in a position to conclude that it is not necessary from the standpoint of rational choice to adopt any one set of moral rules as opposed to any of the other sets of equal value. Different people refer to different sets of rules in talking of morality, and it is not necessarily more or less rational for them to use the term to refer to one set of rules rather than to some other set or sets. This is a form of nonobjectivist, epistemological relativism. Given that the rules are human artifacts, Wong's relativism also can be classified as metaphysical.

Does Wong derive his relativism from the (alleged) fact that people have diverse moral opinions and disagree in a basic way over moral issues? He derives part of his thesis from this kind of evidence—namely, the claim that people refer to different sets of rules with the phrase 'adequate moral system'. It is questionable, however, that any invalid derivation of a normative proposition from a factual one is involved. That people refer to different things by 'adequate moral system' or 'morality' is a non-normative, metaethical claim, and radical differences in moral beliefs among people are precisely the kind of evidence one should use to infer a difference in the extension of 'morality' for these people. The other part of Wong's thesis is a normative claim, the claim that different sets of rules are equally valid by virtue of performing equally well the task of moral rules. It would be logically inappropriate to infer this thesis from the fact of moral disagreement. Presumably Wong would not wish to do so—rather he would wish to present evidence indicating the equal success different sets of moral rules have in resolving internal and interpersonal conflicts (although I think it is fair to say he does not actually provide this evidence, and he gives us no clear indication of what it would look like). Prima facie, then, Wong is able to counter effectively the criticism that his derivation of ethical relativism is invalid.

Returning now to the exposition of Wong's theory, we need to consider one other component. Wong, like Harman, argues that relativism provides the best explanation of our moral experience. Both argue for their position by way of an inference to the best explanation. Wong uses this strategy with particular effectiveness in regard to the issue of moral disagreement. Which of the two theories—absolutism or relativism—gives us the best explanation of the frequent and apparently irresolvable disagreements we encounter in morality? The absolutists contend that the most obvious explanation of diversity in moral belief among different groups or societies is that the difference is caused by at least one group's error in perception or reasoning or its ignorance of some crucial fact (p. 117). The relativist has quite a different explanation: "Relativists may admit that there *are* errors or ignorance to be found in many of these disagreements, but would claim that the errors or ignorance are not the fundamental cause of at least some of them. Instead, they would claim that some of the disagreements would occur simply because the two sides have opposing interests and desires that lead them to adopt opposing moral positions" (p. 146). The major problem Wong sees with the absolutist's argument is that it is not able to explain the error or ignorance it attributes to at least one party to the dispute. Absolutists may tell us that one party fails to see (or to see clearly) the objective moral facts, but to say this is only to "wave a hand" in the direction of an explanation: "This story suffers from a lack of any detail about how we perceive this property, clearly or unclearly. . . . The story need not be scientific, but it needs to be a story with some real content" (p. 152). Absolutists who appeal not to perception but rather to rationality have, in Wong's opinion, failed to identify "the relevant standards of rationality," and neo-naturalists who appeal to a notion of benefit as the basic moral desideratum have failed to make this notion sufficiently determinate to constitute an objective measure that can be used to decide between the different conceptions of benefit and fulfillment found in different moralities (p. 153). All these attempts to explain diversity and disagreement, then, are woefully incomplete and unconvincing.

By way of contrast, the relativist explanation of diversity and disagreement invokes notions that have considerable plausibility and weight:

> By rooting morality in rules and standards intended to fulfill the human needs for the resolution of internal and interpersonal conflict, by allowing for indeterminacies and variations in the extension of 'adequate moral system' with respect to certain rules and standards, and by explaining the existences of these indeterminacies and variations by reference to conflicting needs and interests . . . they help us explain apparently irresolvable disagreements while preserving much moral objectivity. (p. 153)

Moreover, appeal to social differences can explain moral differences, for "a social and cultural environment can influence the degree to which a person experiences an activity as rewarding" (p. 158). Even if human nature is fixed and invariant across social environments, it is still a reasonable hypothesis that this nature "is not sufficiently determinate to justify the claim that there is a determinate good for man, a complex of activities arranged in an ideal balance, which any rational and informed person would find the most rewarding" (p. 158). Notions such as these, highly plausible if not in fact obvious, make it easy to understand moral disagreement and diversity. There are no gaps in the explanation, for it is easy to fill in the details concerning the manner in which social influence is exerted and the way in which needs and interests give rise to rules for preventing internal and interpersonal conflict.

Relativism, Wong concludes, is simply the best explanation of our moral experience. It allows for individuals and indeed societies to make mistakes with respect to moral issues, and it justifies the other cognitive locutions pervading moral discourse. At the same time, it can accept and explain what Wong thinks is apparent to everyone, that individuals frequently disagree on moral matters. This explanation shows how morality is based on interests and attitudes that can make no claim to objectivity. Hence relativism accommodates truth but makes it relative. It thereby reconciles the subjective and objective dimensions of our moral experience.

Criticism of Wong

Although Wong's theory has a great deal of initial plausibility, some questions must be addressed before one can conclude that it does in fact provide the best explanation of our moral experience. Some of these questions relate to problems endemic to Wong's own theory and call either for clarification or emendation. Others reflect the alternative conceptions of morality we have discussed in previous chapters and hence call for a decision to be made between such conceptions and Wong's point of view.

Wong's moral relativism directly confronts the problem that has served as a common theme throughout this study: the problem of interpreting the cognitive locutions pervading moral discourse. As a cognitivist, he takes these locutions seriously and attempts to show why they are justifiably used in our moral talk. At the same time, he offers us a theory that retains a definite nonobjective component in its interpretation of morality (he would call it a subjective component, but his characterization of it does not fall directly under our subjectivist categories above). For Wong, moral beliefs may be true, but they are not true of an independent moral reality. True moral beliefs are truths about social creations—moral rules and standards. Moreover, they are always truths relative to one among many of these social creations, and hence there is no one true morality but rather many true moralities, among which there can be no rationally necessitated choice. The question we must confront is whether this blend of cognitivism and nonobjectivism works.

We can begin, not with criticism, but with two points of contrast. First, it is clear that Wong attributes far more importance to rules and to the notion of deduction from rules than do many of the philosophers we studied in Chapter 1. In fact, the idea of an act's being consistent or inconsistent with one of the rules in a speaker's moral system is essential to his analysis of a moral judgment. Any skepticism about general moral rules or about the deduction of specific duties and obligations from them would therefore cast doubt on Wong's form of relativism. Contrariwise, to the extent that Wong's theory seems plausible, he will have shown that these doubts about rules and deduction are without foundation. We address this issue in the next chapter.

Second, from the vantage point of moral realism, Wong's cognitivism is artificially purchased. Wong makes it possible for moral judgments to have truth values by turning them into claims about the relationship between an act in context and what is required by the rules of the speaker's moral system, or into claims about an object of a certain type and the standards of goodness for that type contained in the speaker's adequate moral system. At several points he remarks that his analysis provides an understanding of moral ideas and judgments in terms of nonmoral notions—namely, acts and rules. It is this very reduction of the moral to the nonmoral that would be questioned by a realist. Moral judgments are interpreted by Wong as being statements, not about irreducible and independent moral facts, but about actions (objects) and human artifacts—moral rules and standards. The realists would contend to the contrary that moral judgments are intended to be descriptions of independent moral facts in the world. For example, they would say that, in judging that a person ought to perform a certain act, one is claiming that the moral property of obligation attaches to the person and the act. And they would interpret the judgment that some person is morally good as a description of him as possessing the property of moral goodness. From the standpoint of the realists, it is inadequate to claim that a moral judgment is only about a moral rule, for they take moral rules merely to reflect our (limited) experience of moral facts, facts that would exist even if there were no moral rules. Using the truth-conditional analysis of meaning that both Wong and the realists accept, the realists would say that an act's being wrong is a relevant dimension of the truth conditions of a moral judgment that describes the act as being wrong. For Wong, the truth conditions of such a judgment contain only the act and the rule proscribing it. The realists therefore would say that Wong has inaccurately characterized the truth conditions of moral judgments.

In response to this challenge from the realists, relativists of Wong's persuasion could argue that the evidence available from an appeal to ordinary moral discourse is no more favorable to realism than to relativism. To be sure, we speak of its being a fact that murder is wrong, but this is or may be as much a fact for the relativist as for the realist, for it is a fact that in many societies murder is inconsistent with their moral rules. As we saw in our criticism of realism, it is doubtful that "There are moral facts" means anything more that "It is a fact that murder is wrong," "It is a fact that one ought to keep one's promises," and so on. The statement "Moral facts exist" is a conceptual howler, for facts cannot sensibly be said to exist, in the world or anywhere else. To say "There are moral facts," then, is just a confusing way of assenting to specific moral judgments like "Murder is wrong." A relativist could accept many of these specific moral judgments, and to that extent he accepts the claim that there are moral facts in the world.

Nor is it obviously the case that relativism is in a position inferior to that of realism with regard to talk of moral properties. Relativists can recognize moral properties—they simply take them to be *relational* properties, relations between an act and a moral rule. The property of being wrong is a property an act has if a rule proscribes it. The realists take moral properties to be nonrelational, but further argument would be necessary to show that ordinary moral discourse favors the realists' account as opposed to the relativists' one (or whether it favors either). Perhaps the best reading of ordinary use is that it is silent on this issue.

What the realists and relativists provide us, then, are two different interpretations of moral facts and moral properties, or two different interpretations of the way we talk about facts and properties in this area of discourse. Both interpretations are compatible with the locutions that appear to make moral discourse "factual," and at this stage it is an open question as to which (if either) of these interpretations is correct.

At another point, however, Wong's analysis may conflict with ordinary moral discourse. It is also a point at which Wong's criticism of another philosopher may come back to haunt him. According to Wong's interpretation of R. M. Hare and his noncognitivist theory,

Hare allows particular moral judgments to be true or false by virtue of their correctly or incorrectly subsuming a particular act under a universal quasi-imperative, that is, a standard or principle accepted by the speaker. Unfortunately, Wong argues, Hare is unable to accommodate the fact that we also speak of standards and principles as true or false, since interpreting them as prescriptions precludes their having a truth value (pp. 14–15). Wong rejects Hare's theory precisely because it is out of accord with ordinary usage on this point. I suggest that he may be in a similar predicament himself with respect to his own notion of rules and standards and, more fundamentally, with his idea of an adequate moral system.

Moral rules are characterized by Wong as having the logical form 'A is to do x' or 'If C, everyone is to do x' (pp. 37–38). Likewise, both standards of goodness (p. 69) and standards of adequacy for rules (p. 39) have the logical form 'x is to be F', where x stands for either an object or a rule that is being evaluated. Can utterances of the form 'A is to do x' or 'x is to be F' have truth values? They too are quasi-imperatives, and it seems inappropriate to think of them as being true or false. Any problem, then, that Hare has with standards and principles, Wong also has with rules and standards. If Hare's noncognitive characterization of principles runs counter to our normal tendency to reject some principles as false, then Wong's characterization of rules and standards may equally run counter to our habit of denouncing alternative moral systems, particularly their rules and moral ideal.

To be sure, one could interpret Wong to take a universal principle of the form "All acts of type A are wrong" as a way of saying, truly or falsely, that all acts of type A would be inconsistent with a rule of the speaker's adequate moral system. Hence Wong's principles need not have the same logical status as those of Hare, and Wong's theory need not be open to the same criticism at this point. Moreover, Wong allows that one's actual rules and standards of goodness can be in or out of accord with one's moral ideal and hence can be subjected to rational criticism on the grounds of logical inconsistency. But when we turn our attention to the adequate rules of this system and the moral ideal that generates them, then, as we have seen, there are features of the ideal and the set of adequate rules which are acknowledged by Wong to be subjective (nonobjective). A moral system is a social creation, something deriving from "human invention and choice" (p. 72). Wong explicitly denies that moral standards reflect an independent moral reality, and he is insistent on taking them to be the variable responses people make to their needs, purposes, and interests. Conflicting moral judgments made within different moral systems can both be correct, and instead of there being one morality true for all rational beings, there are many different true moralities, no one of which must be chosen in order to avoid error or irrationality. At the level of the moral ideal, then, we encounter certain nonobjective dimensions, and we must consider what consequences they have for Wong's theory as a whole.

At least prima facie, the nonobjective aspects of Wong's theory are problematic. As Wong himself grants, "we criticize as false the morality of another group of language users, even when that morality is a coherent system of moral beliefs very different from ours" (p. 73). He means by this that we translate the judgments of the other morality into our own language and then evaluate them as false in terms of our own rules and ideal. But if it is the case that a moral system is just a social creation and that other systems can be just as valid as our own, what right have we to do this? Both moral and epistemological questions can be raised with respect to our doing so. Are we not imposing our moral system on others, thereby raising questions of fairness and tolerance— questions that arise within our own moral system? And are we not assuming the superiority of our moral system when in fact our system may have no epistemological advantage over the other system? How, in light of the nonobjective dimensions Wong attributes to morality, can we defend the use of our system to criticize those who adopt a different system?

It is true, of course, that we frequently criticize the moral judgments and the behavior of people who do not share our moral system and that in doing so we appeal to our own moral rules. Most of us feel no impropriety whatsoever in doing this. Furthermore, we feel no need to justify our moral system or to show that it is superior to the different set of rules adopted by the people we criticize.[17] But if there are many different valid moral systems, should we not be more concerned to demonstrate the credentials of our own? Should we not pay more attention to the issue of whether other systems of rules are or are not valid as systems? Should we not assure ourselves, before criticizing the behavior

---

17. The basis of these attitudes is described in the next chapter.

and rules of others, that our system is "more valid" than theirs? And should we not be brought up short by the fact that moral systems are social creations rather than competing descriptions of some independent moral reality? If a moral system has the nonobjective features Wong attributes to it, our attitudes toward our system and those we criticize should be different from what they are—given our own moral and epistemological norms. Either we are unaware that our morality is just a social creation and that there are many true moralities (or we incorrectly believe otherwise), or Wong is incorrect in his nonobjective characterization of moral systems. Either we are in substantial ignorance or error with regard to morality—thinking it to be in no need of justification vis-à-vis other sets of rules—or Wong himself is in error. If, however, consistency with our actual moral experience is a desideratum for a moral theory, as Wong seems to think, the attitudes we actually have toward our morality tend to speak against his nonobjectivist characterization of it.

There are, of course, cognitivist and objectivist components of Wong's theory blended with the nonobjectivist ones. Perhaps the former dimensions will give us the ability and right to criticize alternative moral systems. After all, Wong pictures absolutism as the doctrine that there is only one true morality and relativism as the denial of this, namely, the claim that there is more than one *true* morality. This suggests that, although we cannot settle on a single true morality, we can distinguish true moralities from those that are not. Furthermore, we have seen that one of the constraints on acceptable moral ideals is that they must promote the very purpose of moral rules: the resolution of internal and interpersonal conflict. At one point Wong argues that a rule permitting torture for amusement would not serve this purpose and therefore could not be a rule of an acceptable moral system (p. 60). It appears, then, that in the notion of reconciling conflicts of interests we have an objective criterion for distinguishing acceptable from unacceptable moral systems—one that makes no appeal to what we believe or what attitudes we have. Perhaps Wong uses the notion of a "true morality" in an unusual way to refer to a set of rules that is effective in realizing its purpose, that is, one that in fact reconciles internal and interpersonal conflicts. Such a set of rules also might appropriately be called *valid*, for its rules have been validated. Describing a moral system as valid or true, however, is passing a cognitive judgment on it, and considerations of purpose-fulfillment might allow us to assess some moral systems (perhaps those of the Nazis or conservative Moslems) as invalid or false.

Insofar as Wong feels that a moral system can be valid or true and that a true moral system is one that satisfies the criterion of resolving internal and interpersonal conflicts, his relativism is objectivist in spirit. According to such objectivist relativism, we may be thoroughly justified when we condemn some alternative morality as being false, for that morality may not do an adequate job of reconciling conflicts of interests. Objectivist relativism would not take moral judgments to represent an independent moral reality if 'independent' means 'distinct from human needs and interests'; it would, however, take them to represent a reality that is independent of human convictions, attitudes, customs, and mores. Hence we could repudiate a moral system customarily accepted by other people because it is in fact out of accord with the reality of human need. So, it seems, Wong's views need not conflict with our practice of judging alternative moralities to be false or otherwise unacceptable.

But there are problems with this kind of objectivist relativism. First of all, it is questionable whether it is still a form of relativism. It seems very close in spirit to the ethics of a naturalistic philosopher like Aristotle, who granted that the Principle of the Golden Mean might yield different results for different people in different circumstances. In a similar vein, Wong claims that differences of history, present conditions, and human and material resources determine what moral system it would be rational for a group of people to adopt (p. 75). And there are psychological constraints on what moral system an individual would be rational to accept (p. 75). But the criterion of rational acceptability is one and the same for all these groups and individuals—namely, the successful resolution of internal and interpersonal conflict. Does not this criterion convert the judgment that a moral system is true or valid into an objective judgment, one that no one could deny without error or irrationality? Furthermore, the judgment that a moral system is true or valid (or false or invalid) is one that is true for everyone, since it is true (or false) for everyone that any given moral system successfully resolves conflicts. But this is absolutism—epistemological absolutism. One might not have to accept a moral system that was true, because there could be another, equally true system one could adopt. But one would have to grant that the alternative had as much merit as the system one adopts. Thus

Wong's objectivist relativism is at least quasi-absolutist in nature. Furthermore, even though there may be different true or valid moral systems, they are all true or valid with respect to the same criterion: the resolution of internal and interpersonal conflict. This very criterion becomes a universal principle that prescribes how all human beings and societies should behave. This is moral absolutism. Is not Wong's relativism, then, really a form of epistemological and moral absolutism, chastened, perhaps, because it realizes that there is more than one true moral system but absolutist nevertheless because these moral systems are true for everyone and true with respect to a universal moral principle?

In the second place, however, Wong's objectivist relativism still falls short when it comes to accommodating our practice of condemning alternative moralities in light of our own. Granted, Wong's theory allows us to condemn some moral systems as false or invalid on the grounds that they do not adequately perform the task of reconciling conflicts of interest. But what about a moral system that is valid in this way but nevertheless is pragmatically inconsistent with our own system? On Wong's account, we would have no grounds for condemning it—we should be just as willing to admit that it is true or valid as that our own system is true. But then why should we prefer our own system to this alternative one and why should we feel ourselves justified in doing so? Surely many adherents of a rights-centered morality take their rules and ideals to be justifiably preferable to those of a virtue-centered morality. But if Wong is correct (and a virtue-centered morality in fact does an adequate job of resolving conflict), there is no justification for their doing so. Conversely, that we feel within our rights in condemning systems of rules that cannot be viewed as false in Wong's sense speaks against his form of relativism, even when we take into account the objectivist elements he incorporates into it. His theory is inconsistent with an important dimension of our ordinary moral experience. In light of its objectivist dimensions as well as its nonobjectivist ones, then, Wong's relativism still runs afoul of our conviction that our moral system can legitimately be used to criticize the behavior, rules, and ideals of others and that it requires no comparative justification for this purpose.

But this is not the end of the difficulties encountered by Wong's relativism. Still other objections can be raised against it.

One unconvincing aspect of the idea of objectivist relativism is that it operates with a notion of reconciling internal and interpersonal conflicts which is suspiciously neutral with respect to the different systems of rules to which Wong applies it. One might well question whether at this level of abstraction there is any meaning to this notion. Wong himself notes that different moral systems rest on different conceptions of human fulfillment (p. 79). These different conceptions likely imply different senses of 'conflict' and 'resolution'. A conflict understood as competing pressures (desires, needs), for instance, is quite different from one understood as insubordination by one element of the personality or society against another element having natural authority. Is there a general notion of conflict that subsumes these concepts and hence allows us to identify the solutions to each specific kind of conflict as equally being moral solutions? Considerable doubt must be expressed as to whether there is.

In a similar vein, one can question whether some of what Wong refers to as *alternative moral systems* (all of which are said to be moral systems because they attempt to reconcile internal and interpersonal conflict) should be thought of as moral systems at all. For many of us contemporary Americans and Europeans operating within what Wong calls a rights-centered morality, the ancient Greek notion of virtue has little if anything to do with what we mean by *morality*. For us, the Greeks' set of rules centering on the notions of virtue and community good is not an alternative morality, but rather an alternative form of social structure and control distinct from morality. We do not look upon it simply as an equally valid way of reconciling personal and interpersonal interests and (therefore) as an equally valid or true morality. We might grant that the Greek concept of virtue signifies an important dimension of individual and social life; it is not, for all that, the same dimension we think of as moral. Where, for instance, are we to find in Greek culture the notion of individual rights, an essential ingredient in our understanding of morality? As Wong himself has argued, a rights-centered morality is distinct from and irreducible to a set of rules emphasizing human potentiality and excellence, social roles, and the common good. Participants in a rights-centered morality, as many if not most of us are, therefore must have some difficulty in thinking of the set of rules embodied in ancient Greek culture as being moral rules, given what they mean by morality. And as we pass on to more exotic cultures, removed even further from our own, their rules for social control and resolution of conflicts of interest look even less like the rules of morality.

It must be granted, of course, that frequently we do hear talk of "Greek morality," just as we hear of "the morality of the nineteenth-century South Sea Islanders," "the morality of the Ik," and the morality of many other cultures dramatically different from our own. Such a way of talking is foremost to be found among philosophers and social scientists, particularly anthropologists, and it must be wondered whether 'morality' as used this way is not a term of art invented by the specialists in these disciplines. At a minimum, we must ask what is meant when they speak in this fashion of Greek morality or Ik morality. And does 'morality' as they use it mean the same as what we ordinarily mean by it? It seems clear that this specialist's sense of 'morality' is a value-neutral one—what Hare calls an *inverted-comma* use of the term.[18] It is possible that in referring to another morality these social scientists are merely referring to what the inhabitants of another culture *believe* to be moral rules, whether or not they *are* moral rules. Another possibility is that in speaking of "the Greek morality" these specialists are referring simply to the set of rules the Greeks believed to have overriding importance. Given the use of the term 'morality' to signify rules believed by a people to have overriding importance, it is likely that in fact there are many different moralities.

Even if this is so, it does not follow that there are many different moralities in the ordinary sense of this term as opposed to the specialist's sense. When we use 'morality' and 'moral' in ordinary contexts—in referring, for example, to what is demanded of us by morality, or to violations of morality, or to our moral obligations—the terms are not value-neutral. Rather, they are highly charged terms, referring to something to which we are deeply committed. Our moral rules *are* of overriding importance; they are not just believed to be so. With the possible exception of the amoralist—who knows what morality requires but is unmoved by it—those who speak of morality refer to something they acknowledge as having authority over them. In this sense, there are no alternative moralities, and the rules of people like the ancient Greeks are not moral rules. And if it is insisted, nevertheless, that the virtue-oriented rules of the Greeks constituted *a morality*, it must be concluded that 'a morality' is a technical, non-normative term coined for special purposes. In this usage 'a morality' is a general term; 'morality' as we use it is a singular one.

18. R. M. Hare, *The Language of Morals* (Oxford: Clarendon Press, 1952), p. 124.

Although Wong speaks frequently of a morality as a set of rules for resolving internal and interpersonal conflict, he does not actually say that this is what 'morality' means.[19] Nevertheless, given his willingness to refer to different sets of rules having this end as *moral rules* or *moralities*, it appears that he is indeed taking 'morality' to mean this. He could be understood to say that although the term refers to different rules for different people, all of these rules aim at resolving internal and interpersonal conflicts. Hence ancient Greeks, nineteenth-century Polynesians, and contemporary Americans all mean the same thing by *morality* even though they pick out different rules with this term. Consequently, contemporary Americans must admit that other people have different moralities. Some of these other moralities may be invalid, but some may be valid: they may in fact achieve the end of reconciling conflicts. In any event, they are all moralities because they all contain rules aimed at achieving this end.

To the contrary, I would urge, contemporary Americans and Europeans who are speaking nontechnically do not mean by the term 'morality' a set of rules for reconciling internal and interpersonal conflicts. This use of the term, though it might be greeted with favor by social scientists, has little to do with the ordinary sense of 'morality'. "What morality requires of us" is not equivalent to "what a set of rules for reconciling internal and interpersonal conflicts demands of us." We acknowledge morality as having authority over us, but we do not, and have no reason to, acknowledge the authority of any given set of rules for reconciling conflicts of interest. In fact, from the standpoint of morality we most certainly reject some of the rules that have this function—for example, the virtue-centered rules of the Greeks which promoted totalitarianism. It is no contradiction to say that a set of rules serves to reconcile internal and interpersonal conflicts but is nevertheless an immoral set of rules. A highly efficient, and perhaps lucky, fascist regime might be successful at reconciling conflicts of interest, but at a terrible moral cost.

At this point I do not want to go into the question of what 'morality' does mean for us. That is a task for the next chapter. But we might note that philosophers frequently use the term in its ordinary sense when they refer to theories of morality, for they normally imply that one and only

19. But in Appendix A of *Moral Relativity*, Wong explicitly opts for this kind of material definition of 'morality'.

one of these theories is correct—namely, the one that correctly describes what morality is. From this perspective, utilitarianism and deontology are competing moral theories, and one of the important questions of philosophy is to determine which of these theories is correct, which one adequately captures the singular nature of morality. But it is easy for philosophers to shift from this sense of the term 'morality' to a different one, as they do when they speak of the utilitarian morality and of a deontological morality. A transition has taken place from talking of theories about that dimension of life we acknowledge to have authority over us—and about which we urgently need a correct description so that we can get it right—to talking of a set of rules accepted by someone and identified as moral on the basis of its functional or formal properties.

It is instructive to consider the question of what 'morality' means from the standpoint of the Kantian deontologists, who argue that the ideal of act utilitarianism might commit one in certain circumstances to slavery or murder. Such deontologists are not going to admit that the utilitarian is simply operating with another moral ideal; they certainly are not going to grant that the utilitarian system is an equally valid moral system. Rather the deontologists claim that the utilitarian ideal of maximizing happiness or preference satisfaction has little if anything to do with morality. Morality for them is the set of rules specifying universal, absolute duties; nothing far removed from these duties will be allowed by them to be a *moral* system. There is for the deontologists no alternative morality. Utilitarianism, rather than being an alternative morality, is for them either an erroneous theory about the nature of morality or a set of actual rules and practices distinct from morality.

What has just been said about the deontologists could equally be said about the utilitarians. Rather than admit that the deontological position reflects a different morality, the utilitarians are likely to say that it is a false, confused picture of morality, based as it is on factors that do not take the maximization of happiness properly (centrally) into account. For the utilitarians, morality is the set of requirements for the improvement of life by means of the elimination of pain and suffering and the enhancement of contentment and satisfaction. These requirements, they think, are imposed on us by reason, experience, and human nature. Any alternative, competing set of requirements amounts to irrational obfuscation.

It follows from such considerations that most of us, whether deontologists or utilitarians, think there are fairly narrow, well defined limits to what can be called 'morality'. For most contemporary Americans and Europeans, there is one set of rules or ideals constituting morality. We may disagree over the nature of these rules or ideals, but from the standpoint of each disputant, the factors taken to be moral are the only ones that can properly be called 'morality'. They are the referent of the singular term 'morality'. The rules and ideals of others are not alternative moralities, certainly not alternative true moralities, but rather false conceptions of morality (or forms of social control distinct from morality). To be sure, the boundaries between morality and those other aspects of life which do not pertain to it are often not sharply defined. Some utilitarians and deontologists, for instance, may have no difficulty in accepting as marginal components of morality some of the rules identified by the other party. Widely dissimilar ideals and rules, however, would at best be deemed a "so-called morality" or a "pseudomorality"—something incorrectly believed by some moral philosophers, or by entire groups of people, to be the substance of morality.

If Wong takes 'morality' to mean any set of rules for resolving internal and interpersonal conflicts, then in his sense of the term there may well be alternative moralities. But he would be in error if he thought his sense of the term was shared by those who speak in everyday contexts of morality. Wong's use is consistent with there being alternative moralities; the normal use is not.

Wong's claim that the extension of 'adequate moral system' or 'morality' varies across individuals and groups could be taken to suggest that these individuals and groups mean different things by the term. It may in fact be true that they mean different things by it. It is not difficult to see the utilitarian and deontologist, for example, as disagreeing about what 'morality' means. But from the fact that there are different meanings of this term, it does not follow that there are different moralities and certainly not that there are different true moralities. Let us take Wong to assert the thesis: "There is more than one true morality." What does he mean by 'morality' in this statement? Very likely 'a system of rules for reconciling internal and interpersonal conflicts of interest'. Wong's statement could be true, given what *he* means by 'morality', but it would not be a statement that everyone else would or must accept. Given what many of them mean by the term, they could legitimately repudiate Wong's claim. So we must sharply distinguish the metaethical claim that people mean or refer to different things by 'morality' from the substantive claim that there are many true moralities. The latter is substantive because it rests on a particular (and contestable) concept of morality. The former, metaethical, claim does not use the notion of morality at all and hence does not presuppose a specific meaning of the term. Nothing said on the metaethical level about what people mean by 'morality' or 'adequate moral system' entails anything said on the substantive level which involves the use of these terms. Hence Wong cannot draw his relativistic conclusion—there are many true moralities—from the metaethical claim that the extension of 'adequate moral system' varies among people and cultures.

Lessons and Goals

As we leave this discussion of relativism, what lessons should we take with us? First, we have seen that relativism can be formulated in ways that are not open to the standard criticisms of this kind of theory. Both Harman and Wong avoid these criticisms, and this fact alone should lend new credibility to the general idea of a relativist conception of morality. Second, the ease with which relativists like Harman and Wong can explain normative diversity stands as one of the major advantages of their theories. Even if, as I have argued, it makes no sense to speak of alternative moralities (given our ordinary concept of morality), it can still be granted that different people and different cultures may operate with different normative rules or mean different things by 'morality'. It is an empirical question whether this kind of diversity actually exists, but there is every initial appearance of such diversity. A relativist can explain how people could disagree or go in different directions with regard to their requirements for human behavior without some of them being guilty of irrationality or significant errors of perception or fact. A widely shared reluctance to impute such cognitive imperfections to large numbers of people speaks in favor of relativism. Third, however, we have seen how difficult it is to be or remain a relativist. The theories of Harman and Wong teeter on the brink of objectivist, epistemological absolutism. In conclusion, we must ask whether it is possible to develop a theory of relativism which avoids this pitfall, which is able to withstand the standard criticisms directed against relativism, and which can maintain the advantage of explaining how fundamental normative disagreements can occur without at least one party to the disagreement falling into cognitive disrepute. The assumption behind the next chapter is that such a theory is possible. In it I offer a proposal designed to meet just these desiderata.

6 / Conceptual Relativism

Is it possible to form a conception of relativism that is free from the major difficulties found in the theories of Gilbert Harman and David Wong? In this chapter a preliminary and tentative effort is made to describe such a relativist view—a view I call *conceptual relativism*. It is my conviction that, in addition to improving on current forms of relativism, conceptual relativism is able to accommodate many of the insights of the rationalists and the realists, and to do so without falling victim to the problems inherent in those theories. Hence I view it as preferable to the other forms of contemporary moral epistemology we have studied.

A difficulty common to the theories of Harman and Wong is their tendency to lapse into forms of epistemological objectivism or absolutism. This arises from the fact that both theories offer explanations of how the rules of a social group come into being, and these explanations make the rules susceptible of an objectivist/absolutist interpretation. Harman sees the rules as resulting from a process of bargaining; Wong sees them as instruments developed by groups of people to resolve internal and interpersonal conflicts. In both cases these rule-generating activities are constrained by standards either of truth or of rationality. Harman's rules, adopted as a result of bargaining, are those a rational person would accept given his own circumstances of power and wealth and those of his fellows. But what a rational person would accept is a mark of objectivity, and insofar as any rational person in the same circumstances would be constrained by reason to accept the same bargain, we have a case of epistemological absolutism. Harman's moral rules become bargaining rules valid for all rational human beings. Wong's rules, being conflict-resolution devices, are assessable in terms of their success or lack of success in attaining the goal for which they are produced. Even if different rules can equally pass the test, any person constrained by truth would have to grant that any given set of rules does, or does not, pass it, in which case these rules are justified (or invalidated) absolutely, not relatively. Their justification would be relative only if it rested on factors that some individuals without error or irrationality might refuse to accept, something like variable feelings, tastes, or arbitrary customs. Both Harman and Wong, then, picture rules in such a fashion as to convert what purport to be relativist theories into at least quasi-absolutist ones. If this is relativism, absolutists have little to fear.

If a relativistic theory like that of Harman or Wong did not lapse into objectivism, however, it would face an even greater problem. Failing an objectivist justification, the kind of social rules involved in these theories would have to be characterized as arbitrary or subjective. Harman and Wong show us ways in which these rules could be justified rationally—through a process of bargaining or by virtue of their function in resolving conflicts of interest. Since we can imagine them as justified, a failure on the part of objectivists to show us that in fact they are justified could easily lead us to a subjectivist interpretation of them, one that takes them to be nothing more than the result of emotional tendencies or customary practices. Relativism, or what I henceforth call *social-rule relativism*, risks becoming either an objectivist or subjectivist theory. Though the versions proposed by Harman and Wong veer toward objectivism and absolutism, more traditional conceptions of social-rule relativism come across as subjectivist.[1]

---

1. And some contemporary ones as well. Sabina Lovibond's peculiar brand of realism can easily be interpreted as a concealed form of social-rule relativism. According to Lovibond, social practices give rise to moral standards and principles, and the participants in these practices maintain their norms through social coercion. She says, for instance, that "the laws of inference—and the same applies to all norms of meaningful behavior . . . — are social laws, enforced by human agency" (*Realism and Imagination in Ethics* [Oxford: Basil Blackwell, 1983], p. 56). Furthermore, she claims that "the compulsion exerted by logical laws is grounded in the coercion exerted by the linguistic community upon its individual members" (p. 57), and clearly she would make the same assertion regarding moral laws or rules. Faced with such a view, we should ask what could justify a society in enforcing its moral norms. For Lovibond, there is no practice-transcendent norm to which one could appeal, and we are left with the uncomfortable feeling that the social coercion and the rules backed up by it are arbitrary and unjustified, just as legal rules

Another Form of Relativism

To avoid objectivism and subjectivism while remaining relativistic, we must look for a kind of relativism that is not of the social-rule variety. Moral judgments must be found to be relative to something for which a rational justification is not possible—indeed, for which such a justification is inconceivable. If, furthermore, this relativity base is something for which no justification is needed, it cannot be viewed as arbitrary or subjective, since these terms of reproach signal the lack of a desirable or required warrant. Conceptual relativism proposes just this kind of relativity base: basic moral concepts. As a consequence, it is firmly entrenched as a nonobjectivist theory and does not risk collapsing into a subjectivist one.

To begin our search for this kind of relativism, let us ask whether moral rules must be thought of as instruments adopted to achieve some higher end, such as the resolution of internal and interpersonal conflicts or the production of a society in which agreement in intention is sufficient to allow for stability and predictability. Do not moral rules have their own intrinsic end—namely, the promotion of morally correct behavior? Many societies have rules prohibiting cruelty, but is this because cruelty is seen as promoting conflict and instability or because it is seen as an immoral way for one person to treat another? Is injustice denounced simply because it upsets a balance of interests or rather because it is unfair and wrong? If morality is truly autonomous, as many philosophers have urged throughout this century, then moral rules have *moral ends*, and whether in fact they promote still other ends is irrelevant to their justification.

What are our moral ends? Here we can learn quite a lot from the rationalist philosophers, for as I suggested in Chapter 3, they have come

---

backed only by force have no de jure authority. The kind of social rules that are, in our experience, enforced by coercion but nevertheless are justified are those—legal rules, for instance—backed up either by considerations of the type Wong introduces or by moral considerations. Insofar as Lovibond's theory is a theory of morality, she cannot appeal to moral rules to justify her social practices and the norms arising out of them. And she would have to label Wong's justifying conditions as standards transcending moral practices. Hence Lovibond's socially enforced moral practices and norms come across as in need of justification but lacking in it, and thus in the last analysis as subjective and provincial. She can easily be seen, then, as presenting a social-rule form of relativism of the subjectivist variety.

closer than many other thinkers to characterizing accurately the content of morality. At least provisionally we can accept most of Bernard Gert's ten rules as being moral rules. Furthermore, Alan Gewirth's emphasis on the right to freedom clearly falls within the sphere of morality. And we could borrow a notion from a rationalist we have not studied: Alan Donagan. According to Donagan, the ends of morality are not producible ends deriving from contingent desires and brought into being by our actions. Rather they are ends in themselves that already exist and require acknowledgment and preservation.[2] We can concur with Donagan that many of the rules we in the western world today consider to be moral rules aim at preserving the integrity and autonomy of persons. Many of them promote respect for persons as ends in themselves.

If moral rules have moral ends of this kind, then, in the language that was popular some years back, these rules should be thought of as constitutive rather than regulative.[3] They do not aim at producing ends that are identifiable independently of them. On the contrary, ends like moral integrity and autonomy are defined only in terms of the rules prohibiting cruelty, deception, and so on—that is to say, one respects the integrity of a person by not deceiving her, not being cruel to her, and so forth. More generally, one respects other persons by following the moral rules in one's interactions with them. Hence achieving our moral ends just *is* behaving in accordance with the moral rules. These rules do not merely contingently lead us to our moral ends. It is no happenstance, for example, that we acknowledge the integrity of others by not lying to them; this in part is what "acknowledging integrity" means. To adapt Gert's approach, in determining what morality is we must identify the rules we commonly and paradigmatically accept as moral rules. These rules constitute what we call morality. They may share some formal features, but these features do not exhaust what we mean by *morality*—morality is given its substance by the specific rules we take to be moral rules.

At this point someone might object that in other groups, societies, or cultures, people do not have the same moral ends or moral rules. If interpreted correctly, this suggestion is not implausible, but caution must be exercised as well. As I argued in Chapter 5 in criticizing Wong,

2. See Alan Donagan, *The Theory of Morality* (Chicago: University of Chicago Press, 1977).
3. See John Rawls, "Two Concepts of Rules," *Philosophical Review*, 64 (1955), 3–32.

we members of a rights-centered culture cannot say that the virtue-centered rules and ends of the ancient Greeks are constitutive of morality. By *morality* we mean a set of rules and rights preserving individual autonomy and integrity. We can say that the Greeks had *a morality*, and even an alternative morality, if we use the term 'a morality' in a value-neutral way, that is, different from the way we use it when *we* talk about morality, since *morality* has substantial value for us. To say that the ancient Greeks had *a morality* would only mean that they had a set of rules satisfying some value-neutral descriptive conditions (e.g., formal or functional ones). It also might turn out to be the case that they referred to their virtues and their ideal of a common good *as morality*—they may have used the word 'morality' or a closely related one in talking about such matters. This fact, together with the fact that their normative concerns, though not identical to ours, nevertheless do overlap with our own, might lead us to say that the ancient Greeks had a different concept of morality. We would be even more inclined to say this if their rules shared some formal or functional features with ours. We do not operate with their concept today, and we may even wish to repudiate many features of it (e.g., its tendency toward totalitarianism). But we can admit that instead of what we call morality they had another set of ends and social practices and that they called them moral ends and practices. We can grant, that is to say, a metaethical statement to the effect that other people like the Greeks *mean* something else by 'morality' than we do.

Our use of the term 'morality'—our concept of morality—is undoubtedly a vague, fluctuating, and flexible one. There is no precise specification of the rules encompassed by this concept, and some of us will use it in such a way as to include rules that others would not. We can still recognize one another as operating with the same concept of morality by virtue of our accepting overlapping sets of rules. In spite of this vagueness, there are limits to what we are willing to call morality. Morality has to do with personal autonomy and integrity, respect for persons, avoidance of harm to persons, and similar notions. If a person or society uses the word 'morality' to refer to matters distinct from these, we are not willing to grant that they are talking about *morality*, what *we* mean by 'morality'. In that event, we encounter a use of the word 'morality' which goes beyond the bounds of legitimate vagueness and must be identified as a distinct concept.

The practical or pragmatic differences resulting from different concepts of morality may be extreme, and we may be led to denounce as *immoral* the behavior, beliefs, and attitudes of those using a concept other than our own. While acknowledging that people of another society have a different concept of morality, we may be prepared nevertheless to say that their society is immoral, that the activities it condones have nothing to do with being a moral person. If this is our reaction, we may be prepared to say in a derogatory fashion that the other society has a "so-called morality." And if its concept of morality involves a perversion of what we ourselves understand by morality, we may refer to the practices of the other group as a "pseudomorality." Some would say that the so-called hippie morality and Nazi morality were mere pseudomoralities. A pseudomorality usually exists among people who *know better*, who know what morality really is and are making capital with the word 'morality' in order to further their own corrupt or depraved interests. Finally, we also should allow for the possibility of other normative systems (embodying a different concept of morality) that are *amoral* but not immoral. We can grant, then, considerable flexibility with regard to what morality requires, but we must also respect the limits imposed by our concept of morality and see those normative practices falling outside these limits as being something other than moral practices.

Another problem we had with the relativism of Wong was its inability to explain why we reject what, from his perspective, are alternative "true" moralities. Equally, his theory is inconsistent with our assumption that the commitment we have to our own moral system, rather than to the alternatives, is in no need of justification. From Wong's point of view, some of the alternative moral systems could be just as valid as our own: they could equally well resolve conflicts of interests. In response to Wong, we noted that to criticize other "moralities" from the vantage point of our own is to assume that we have the moral and cognitive right to do so. If some of these "moralities" are as valid as our own, this criticism would merely beg the question in favor of our moral rules and moral ideal. The possibility of equally valid moral systems also would require us to justify our system by showing it to be at least as valid as the others. Thus if Wong is right about there being many true moralities, some aspects of our actual moral practices—namely, our condemning other sets of rules and feeling no need to justify our own—become suspect.

We now have a way to avoid this predicament. The sets of rules characterized by Wong as alternative moral systems are not *moral* systems at all—they are not alternative *moralities*. Morality is defined for us by our moral rules, and any set of rules significantly different from these will not be part of morality. Such a set may, as Wong argued, be equally successful in resolving conflicts of interests, but this does not make it an equally valid competitor. Our rules are not moral *because* they resolve conflicts, and hence they are not matched in validity by some other system of rules that resolves conflicts in an adequate manner. Morality does not compete on that ground. In fact, it does not compete on any ground external to itself; it exists only to promote morally correct behavior. So a moral person is never faced with Wong's predicament: the difficulty of needing to justify her commitment to morality in the face of equally valid competitors. For the moral person, there are no competitors; for her, only her moral rules constitute morality. To be sure, one might still raise the question whether a person's commitment to a particular concept of morality as opposed to some other one is not a subjective affair. We confront this issue shortly. But for the moment, defining morality in terms of our basic moral rules allows us to avoid the predicament of Wong's agent. Our moral system constitutes morality; nothing else does.

Defining morality in terms of our basic moral principles or rules also allows us to see why a person can justifiably criticize others who operate with a different set of rules they call moral. If our moral rules and standards define for us what morality really is, and other concepts of morality designate merely so-called moralities, pseudomoralities, or amoral normative systems, we need feel no concern that others are in wholesale *moral* disagreement with us. Hence we need feel no impropriety in universalizing, as we are wont to do, our moral demands. We are not, that is to say, in the uncomfortable position of having to assert "Although relative to your moral standards you have an obligation to do *x*, relative to my moral standards you should not do *x*—therefore do not do *x*." Our standards define morality, so other people do not have *moral* obligations that conflict with our moral demands. Accordingly, we are not imposing our morality on them in arrogant defiance of their morality. The attitude of tolerance for sincerely held moral (and religious) convictions with which we disagree—a part of morality for most of us—makes us hesitant to impose our views on those who are at odds morally with us. But if the "alternative moral systems" are not moralities at all, no considerations of tolerance for other moral convictions need call into question the propriety of our universalizing our moral demands.

Expressing what is morally required of everyone, we say, for instance, that all human beings should respect the integrity and autonomy of others. We may refuse to blame people in other cultures if they do not live up to this fundamental moral rule, since in many instances they are ignorant of what is right and wrong. But this does not prevent us from demanding that they change their ways and become moral persons. Given what morality is, it is either right or wrong for all individuals in the same circumstances to engage in certain activities, not right for some and wrong for others. Nor is there any real point in saying that what is right and wrong is so relative to our standards of morality, since our standards are the (only) standards of morality. In light of the standards of morality, we criticize other people for both behaving immorally and subscribing to principles that lead to immoral behavior. Thus moral absolutism is an essential part of our moral outlook. To participate in morality is to believe that some propositions about how all human beings should behave are true.

But if we grant that other people mean something different by 'morality' than what we mean—that they have a different concept of morality—can we find a way to justify our concept and invalidate theirs? This is not to ask whether we can repudiate and condemn their practices. As we have seen, we can do this, but in doing so we are judging their practices in light of our moral rules and ends, thus presupposing those rules and ends. The question we now raise is whether this presupposition can be justified. And the answer appears to be negative. If moral rules have their own internal ends, there is nothing independent of them that can be appealed to in order to determine if they are justified or not. That moral rules succeed in attaining or fail to attain some independently identified, nonmoral end in no way bolsters or undermines their legitimacy as moral rules, as rules promoting moral ends. And if different sets of rules—equally called "moral" by their adherents—have significantly different internal ends, the sets will have nothing in common to constitute a basis of comparison in light of which we can judge one of them to be superior to the others. (Of course, one set might be judged superior on the basis of considerations of self-interest, the reconciling of conflicts of interests, or some other nonmoral end, but this is irrelevant to the legitimacy of our rules as promoting their internal, moral ends.) We accept our moral rules and ends, and they define for us what morality is and hence what morally we must do. Operating with another set of rules and ends, another culture will consider different actions to be "morally" required. At the end of the day, all we can do is to support our ends and rules and judge others in light of them. This is not, of course, to justify our practice but only, again, to presuppose it, to *engage* in it.

Our discussion has shown, however, that there is nothing wrong or problematic in our presupposing the rules of morality. These rules cannot be justified, but they do not need to be. They and their correlative ends are simply what we mean by *morality*.

Here we have what may be called a form of conceptual relativism.[4] Different people, cultures, or societies mean (or at least may mean) different things by 'morality'. Each judges persons, actions, and events in light of—relative to—the rules and ends definitive of its concept of morality. None of these concepts can be justified or rationally criticized; we simply have different basic and autonomous forms of life. Likewise, no concept of morality can be demonstrated to be superior or inferior to another. Faced with the reality of other so-called moralities, we are reduced to saying something like "*This* is morality! *This* is what we must do." At the same time we should acknowledge that others may mean something different by the term 'morality' and consequently may behave differently. We may not approve of the way they behave and indeed may bitterly oppose it; we may think their so-called moral behavior decidedly immoral. But we cannot say that they have made an error or engage in irrational behavior—they are simply different, and their lives revolve around a different concept of morality. Hence justification in morality rests on something—a concept of morality—that is not itself objective: it is not the case that any person constrained by truth and rationality would have to accept this concept. Neither reason nor empirical evi-

---

4. There are obvious affinities between conceptual relativism and the views of D. Z. Phillips and H. O. Mounce in their book *Moral Practices* (London: Routledge and Kegan Paul, 1969). Although I acknowledge the influence, I am unhappy with the way they express some of these views, perceptive criticisms of which can be found in Roger Beehler, *Moral Life* (Totowa, N.J.: Rowman and Littlefield, 1978), Introduction and passim. I particularly wish to distance myself from their claim that there are many different moral practices.

dence requires that we adopt or reject a concept, certainly not one as basic as the concept of morality.[5] This is the repudiation of epistemological objectivism and the assertion of relativism. It is *conceptual* relativism in that our moral claims are made relative to our concept of morality (rather than to customs, mores, attitudes, or social rules designed to resolve conflicts of interests, etc.), and this concept has no ground in truth or reason. It is beyond proof and beyond refutation.

A turn to conceptual relativism thus avoids the tendency of many social-rule relativist theories to collapse into concealed forms of epistemological absolutism. It involves no reference to any ulterior function of moral rules and hence does not require that these rules be evaluated in light of such a function. Conceptual relativism renders moral judgments relative to something—a basic concept—that may be rejected without error or irrationality, something, therefore, unlike the rules of Harman and Wong, whose construction is constrained by canons of either truth or rationality. No set of substantive moral principles is such that it is binding on all human beings: a person might refuse to accept these principles by virtue of refusing to use the concepts employed in them.

Conceptual relativism no less than social-rule relativism can accommodate the fact that we frequently use cognitive locutions in moral discourse. Within the moral life, judgments about right and wrong and good and evil are straightforwardly cognitive. If rules prohibit certain modes of conduct, a judgment to the effect that one ought not to engage in this conduct on a particular occasion results from an application of the rule to the occasion. Arguments can be engaged in to demonstrate that the rule does or does not apply on this occasion. Thus participants in a practice can be justified in judging and acting as they do. Later we shall see in more detail what such moral knowledge involves.

Conceptual relativism, then, is a cognitivist, epistemological, nonob-

---

5. I am willing to grant that some concepts may be developed for special purposes and may be successful or unsuccessful in achieving these purposes. Such cases, however, presuppose a conceptual scheme or language-game with its own internal purposes. The conceptual scheme of morality falls into the latter category. It is one of the fundamental ways in which we think *and act*, and involves its own goals and ends. See Ludwig Wittgenstein, *Philosophical Investigations*, G. E. M. Anscombe and R. Rhees, eds.; G. E. M. Anscombe, trans., 3d ed. (New York: Macmillan, 1969), I, §132; and his *The Blue and Brown Books* (New York: Harper & Row, 1965), p. 59.

jectivist moral theory. Insofar as it grants that in operating with our concept of morality we are obligated to regard as true some principles about how all human beings should behave, it is also a theory that accepts *moral* absolutism. But does it escape subjectivism?

If the rules and ends constitutive of morality cannot be justified, are they not in some way subjective? And does the fact that the concept of morality which we employ cannot be justified not show that all of our moral judgments are subjective? We can begin to answer these questions by noting that if the rules and ends constitutive of moral practices define morality for the participants, and hence what it means for an act to be morally right or wrong, moral judgments are no more subjective than ordinary empirical judgments, which, after all, are true or false relative to the rules defining the meanings of their constituent terms. Furthermore, what is presupposed by our moral judgments is not (or not just) some set of interests or attitudes or desires, but rather a set of concepts, the concepts embedded in our moral talk. Concepts themselves are neither true nor false, but this does not make them subjective. They are, in the everyday senses of these terms, neither subjective nor objective. In the ordinary way of speaking, a conviction, point of view, argument, set of considerations, or the like is properly called subjective when it is based upon feelings or desires rather than upon evidence. Concepts are not statements or beliefs, but rather are presupposed by them. And that concepts are not objective simply reflects the fact that, rather than being based upon evidence, they help to define what can be evidence for the statements that employ them. They do not *fail* to be objective, for there is no sense to the notion that a set of concepts is not (or is) backed up by evidence. Concepts set the stage for the everyday distinction between objective and subjective convictions—hence they are prior to that distinction.

It should also be clear that conceptual relativism is not subjectivist in either the theoretical or the everyday sense with respect to moral judgments. It does not, in the first place, picture these judgments as being descriptions or expressions of subjective feelings and attitudes. On the contrary, it pictures them as frequently representing facts that have nothing to do with feelings or beliefs. Nor does conceptual relativism, in the second place, view moral judgments as resulting from bias, desire, or self-interest. It sees them as frequently made on the basis of the best available evidence and hence as objective.

Although it avoids subjectivism, conceptual relativism remains a non-objectivist view. It renders moral judgments relative to something that could be rejected without error or irrationality: basic moral concepts. These concepts cannot be justified or invalidated, and a person might refuse to employ them without falling into error or irrationality. The relativity of moral judgments to concepts, then, is a source of their non-objectivity but not their subjectivity.

The most fundamental challenge to nonobjectivist conceptual relativism comes from an opposing, objectivist view of moral concepts (some might call it a realist view). It would claim either that our concepts reflect an independent moral reality or that they are useful in attaining an independently specifiable and valuable end. This "concept objectivism" would maintain that the concepts we employ in moral discourse are justified and hence cannot be rejected without transgressing the bounds of truth or reason. Our conceptual relativism, to the contrary, rejects the metaphysical idea that we can meaningfully speak of there being something—moral properties of right and wrong, and moral facts incorporating them—that is independent of our moral concepts and practices, something that could be ascertained independently of these concepts and determined to be in or out of accord with them. It also rejects the idea of a practical or instrumental validation of moral concepts.

To support these views, a conceptual relativist can muster several of Wittgenstein's arguments in defense of the autonomy of grammar.[6] First, he can repudiate the very notion of determining whether moral concepts correspond to or mirror extralinguistic reality. What the facts are—moral or otherwise—to which the objectivist would compare our moral concepts is a matter that would have to be described for us. If moral language were used to describe these facts, the very idea of a justification of the concepts would be specious; such justification would involve an inescapable begging of the question, a use of moral language to describe the reality that is to justify the moral language. If moral

---

6. For the development of the first argument we consider, see Ludwig Wittgenstein, *Philosophical Remarks*, R. Rhees, ed.; R. Hargreaves and R. White, trans. (Oxford: Basil Blackwell, 1974), pp. 53–55; and Ludwig Wittgenstein, *Philosophical Grammar*, R. Rhees, ed.; A. Kenny, trans. (Oxford: Basil Blackwell, 1974), p. 186. For a development of the second argument, see Ludwig Wittgenstein, *Zettel*, G. E. M. Anscombe and G. H. von Wright, eds.; G. E. M. Anscombe, trans. (Berkeley: University of California Press, 1970), §320; and Wittgenstein, *Philosophical Grammar*, p. 184.

reality were described in terms distinct from our moral terms, the question would be begged against morality, since it is not moral reality against which moral language is being tested. If the claim that moral concepts mirror reality cannot be verified or falsified by describing reality in either moral or nonmoral terms, the very idea of such a test of correspondence becomes suspect. Is it not just an empty, meaningless notion?

Second, using another Wittgensteinian argument, the conceptual relativist can reject the objectivist claim that moral concepts can be justified pragmatically or instrumentally through a demonstration that their use allows us to achieve some end that we value. Wittgenstein makes a distinction between rules like cooking rules and the rules of language. Cooking rules are judged in light of their ability to produce edible food, an end that can be identified independently of whether it has been produced in accordance with any given set of rules and hence one that can be employed to test these rules. In contrast, the rules governing the use of moral concepts, like most rules of language, themselves serve to identify their goals. As we have seen, moral rules have their own internal moral ends, and their ability or inability to promote other ends is irrelevant to their validity as *moral* rules. To impose some other end on moral practices and to demand that they attain it in order to be justified amounts to a practical begging of the question.

Morality, then, can receive neither a metaphysical nor a practical justification. Morality is autonomous. In defending a nonobjectivist view of moral concepts, a conceptual relativist is asserting the autonomy of moral language.

If persons or societies operate with a set of concepts different from ours, we cannot prove that they are wrong and we are right. We might, however, find their way of talking, their standards of evidence, and especially their actions to be so different from our own that we cannot share the same physical space with them—or even the world. Their way of life under those circumstances would be pragmatically inconsistent with ours, and it could become intolerable to us. If we cannot live in the same space or the same world with them, we may reject their way of life not only by condemning it but also by attempting to eradicate it. To make our way of life possible, it may be the case that theirs must go. The result would be open conflict, perhaps war.

In such a situation of radical opposition, we cannot be said to disagree over the truth or falsity of judgments about what is right or wrong, since, having different moral concepts, we do not use their concepts even to the point of denying that one of them has an application. Such a denial would require us to conceive of circumstances in which the concept would apply and to maintain that these circumstances do not exist; it would commit us to the use of their concept. In refusing to accept someone else's concept of morality, we are not in logical disagreement with them, for we do not share the same logical or conceptual space. Our practice is pragmatically incompatible with theirs—ours commits us to actions that physically cannot take place if the actions required by their practice are to occur. We butt heads in the realm of action, not in the realm of logic.

But what about the claim made in my criticism of Harman that in rejecting the so-called moralities of others we attempt to correct or enlighten those with whom we disagree and that we think of our moral ideal as the true one? Conceptual relativism may appear to be inconsistent with these aspects of moral experience. Before we reach this conclusion, however, let us consider once again the implications of the view that our moral rules and ends define morality for us. There is no alternative morality and so there is no need to defend our morality or moral concepts as true and condemn those of others as false. From the vantage point of morality, we condemn other so-called moral practices as being immoral or, at best, amoral. Hence, if we attempt to correct or enlighten others, our aim is to show them that they are not behaving in a moral manner. To claim as much is not to maintain that morality is true and more valid than their so-called morality—it is simply to point out that the practices of the so-called morality are not moral. To be sure, we might say something like "It is true that one ought to respect the integrity and autonomy of human beings." But this is just an emphatic way of saying that one ought to respect the integrity and autonomy of human beings. In other words, in stating that this moral principle is true, we are simply articulating that principle and expressing our commitment to it.

Moreover, when we repudiate a practice that conflicts with morality, we frequently do so by saying, not that it is false, but that it is revolting, or morally repugnant and perverse, or inhumane—or, simply, evil. Such language suggests that what we encounter and reject is seen as alien to our very way of life; we are not just rejecting conflicting opinions and beliefs. And if we do say something like "It is false that one ought to seek to purify the race by reducing it to pure Aryan stock," this can be understood as a negative evaluation of the Nazi ideal from the vantage point of morality. In taking issue, then, with a practice that pragmatically opposes morality, we need not be interpreted as making truth claims about our concept of morality—saying that it is true and other concepts of morality false. We express our concept of morality (our basic moral rules), and we evaluate the activities in the opposing practice in light of this concept. We may even decry the inhumanity of those who do not acknowledge the demands of morality, thinking them subhuman (not in error) because they fail to do so. None of this amounts to a pragmatic or rational defense of our concept of morality. In fact, very few people talk in the language of concepts at all, but most people in our culture are ardent moralists. They take their stands, frequently expressing the principles of morality and condemning practices that violate these principles.

This form of relativism has a significant feature related to the issue of alternative "moralities." Whereas conceptual relativism can easily accommodate alternative concepts of morality, it is also compatible with the possibility that all human beings agree in some ultimate or basic way as to what they would call moral rules and moral ends (any disagreements among them being the result of differences in nonmoral beliefs or circumstances). Even if this were so, a conceptual relativist still could maintain that the moral judgments of people are relative to a practice, that is, a set of rules or concepts, that cannot itself be justified or cognitively repudiated. Morality, even if universal in this sense, could not be thought of as true or rational qua practice. In being presupposed by all moral judgments, the unique autonomous practice or conceptual scheme renders these judgments nonobjective. Even if we all in fact agree on these judgments, or would agree at the end of ideal moral inquiry, morality would still remain nonobjective, since if some people were to reject the conceptual scheme, they would not be in error or irrational.

At this point, we may wonder how different morality is from common-sense and scientific beliefs. As noted above, all empirical judgments are relative to the concepts governing their constituent terms and hence to the rules of evidence embodied in these concepts. If basic concepts per se cannot be true or false/rational or irrational, empirical judgments in common sense and science are as nonobjective as moral judgments. The real difference between common sense/science and morality appears to be a matter of the extent of conceptual agreement within them. Whereas scientists appear almost always to agree on their basic scientific concepts, most of us harbor the suspicion that moralists disagree on their concepts. Scientists, of course, may disagree more than we expect—the recent historical approach of Kuhn and Feyerabend suggests that they do.[7] Alternatively, disagreements and variations in the moral sphere may be fewer or more superficial than the typical relativist thinks. Nevertheless, if science and morality both presuppose conceptual schemes, both moral and empirical statements are relative, whatever the facts about conceptual change and variation in science and morality. And if scientific judgments are relative, the relative status of moral judgments need not disturb us.

Let us briefly note the ways in which our conceptual relativism could respond to the six common objections to relativism we identified in the previous chapter. First, it offers a clear and precise concept of relativism, defining it in terms of relativity to concepts presupposed in making moral judgments; these concepts or rules are not in principle susceptible of justification or criticism and hence might be rejected without error or irrationality. Second, no attempt is made to derive the thesis of relativism from the diversity of moral beliefs. Indeed, as we have seen, conceptual relativism is consistent with the possibility that all people agree on basic moral principles. Third, there is no inconsistent espousal of a normative thesis that one ought to obey the norms of one's society (or only those norms), since the thesis of conceptual relativism is a purely metaethical one with no normative components. The moral absolutism accepted by the conceptual relativist—the thesis that there are true moral principles stating how all human beings should behave—is a consequence not of conceptual relativism per se but rather of the concept of morality. In elucidating the concept of morality, the conceptual relativist demonstrates how it entails moral absolutism, and if he uses this concept, he will advocate moral absolutism. Participating in the moral life obviously involves making normative claims, but it is as a moralist, not as a metaethical theorist, that one propounds the normative thesis of moral absolutism. The conceptual relativist, denying that basic moral concepts can be justified or invalidated, hardly can claim that

---

7. See Thomas Kuhn, *The Structure of Scientific Revolutions*, 2d ed., enlarged (Chicago: University of Chicago Press, 1970).

this thesis of moral absolutism is false or unjustified. He must leave morality as it is.

Fourth, the conceptual relativist does not need a precise definition of 'social group'. Contrary to many so-called Wittgensteinians, the conceptual relativist does not make truth relative to social customs or the standards of a group.[8] Moral truth is relative to concepts, and a person's concepts need not be identified with those of any social group. Fifth, conceptual relativism avoids the charge of incoherence because it does not entail or sanction the statement "'A ought to do x' is both true and false" or the statement "It is both right and wrong to do x." Relative to the set of concepts presupposed by it, any given moral statement will be true or false, or at worst indeterminate. Those individuals not using these concepts will be unable to say that this moral statement is either true or false. Sixth, the one charge that might cause trouble for the conceptual relativist is the claim that relativism incorrectly characterizes some moral disagreements as pseudodisagreements. Perhaps people using different concepts of morality are to some degree talking past one another when they debate the "morality" of an act or person. But these disagreements, we have seen, are not moral disputes. Moreover, Wong's notion of pragmatic inconsistency can be used here as a means of explaining the true nature of the disagreement.

We have seen how relativism can be formulated in such a way as to acknowledge and accommodate the cognitive locutions of moral discourse while remaining relativistic. We also have observed how the relative status of moral discourse is indistinguishable from that of common-sense and scientific discourse, thereby reinforcing the conviction that morality, albeit relative (nonobjective), is not subjective. Having removed from its interpretation both the objectionable subjective elements and the inconsistent objectivist tendencies, we are able to see relativism as a doctrine that is thoroughly cognitivist, but also as one that allows for variability in what is meant by 'morality' and hence variability in what are called by their participants "moral practices." Thus con-

---

8. For a treatment of Wittgenstein's thought which does not interpret him as taking social customs and practices to be the criterion of truth, see G. P. Baker and P. M. S. Hacker, *Scepticism, Rules and Language* (Oxford: Basil Blackwell, 1984). Here again we find a significant difference between my views and those of Lovibond in her *Realism and Imagination in Ethics*—Lovibond subscribes to a theory that makes moral truth relative to standards arising out of social practices.

strued, conceptual relativism may be attractive to someone committed to cognitivism in ethics but suspicious of the doctrine that there are moral facts in the world independent of human practices. Specifically, it is a theory that may appeal to someone as a plausible alternative to moral realism.

To ascertain if the appeal is justified, we must observe how the theory would respond to some of the objections it can expect from the realist camp (and from elsewhere as well). In doing so, we can also identify ways in which conceptual relativism can be developed so as to borrow some valuable points from realism. We also can note advantages of this form of relativism over realism. The result will be a theory of relativism that is arguably superior both to realism and to other contemporary forms of relativism.

Realism or Relativism? The Issue of Rules

One of the central features of moral realism is its insistence on the uniqueness of moral situations and its denial that rules play more than a secondary "rule of thumb" role in moral decisions. Social-rule relativists, on the contrary, place rules at the very heart of the moral life. For them, morality consists in following rules, and for a relativist like Wong the truth value of moral judgments is a function of whether the actions referred to by these judgments are consistent with the rules accepted by the speaker. The relativists' conception of moral rules is close to that of noncognitivists like Hare; the realists' conception of them is more in line with the thought of those philosophers studied in Chapter 1 who reject the notion that moral judgments always involve the subsumption of particular cases under general rules.

The realists make what appears to be a sound phenomenological point when they deny that moral judgments are simply the conclusions of deductive inferences from general principles or rules. This deductive conception seems to be a simplistic, artificial way of picturing moral decisions. What we are to do in a specific situation seldom can be determined just by consulting a general rule. Rather, as the realists suggest, we must attend to the fine-grained detail of the situation, and we require perception, or something akin to it, to ascertain the moral features arising out of this detail. Given the complexity of most moral situations, it rarely will be the case that one principle alone will apply to them and determine their moral character. Moreover, the sheer difficulty of arriving at moral decisions and the weight of uncertainty attending most of them speak against a simple, straightforward deductive construal of moral decision making.

At the same time, however, it is possible to feel that the realists have gone too far in picturing moral situations as unique and in disparaging the applicability of general rules to concrete cases. There simply *are* commonalities among moral situations. Perhaps no two such situations are exactly the same, but they share dimensions, and these shared dimensions frequently are what we find morally relevant about them. Moreover, as we have noted throughout this study, rules do appear, phenomenologically, to have an important role in the moral life. We are taught moral rules, we inscribe them in our moral tracts, and we appeal to them in practice. They seem, in short, to be more than rules of thumb that merely summarize some common features of our past and limited moral experience. Thus the realists' rejection or disparagement of rules seems as excessive as the relativists' reliance on them in a simple deductive model of moral decision making.

In our discussion of realism, I questioned the perceptual model of moral experience to which many realists are committed. Complex moral situations, I argued, contain elements that frequently are unavailable to perception. It is difficult to understand, for example, how we can *see* the courage involved in a situation if that courage is a function of features in the past or embodied in a complex social context. I suggested that a judgmental model of moral decision making might be more appropriate than the perceptual model.

Relativists who use the notion of deduction from rules as central to their conception of moral decision making accept such a judgmental model. Unfortunately, for the reasons given above, the notion of deduction from general rules does not appear to be altogether satisfactory. Is there a way, however, in which a relativist might modify his ideas about the way moral rules operate which will allow him to retain the judgmental model while avoiding the artificialities of a simple deductive construal of it? Such a modification is indeed possible.

One of the major differences between moral realism and relativism arises from the way they interpret moral judgments. The realist takes these judgments to describe moral facts consisting of objects, acts, or events having certain moral characteristics. A relativist like Wong sees them as describing a relationship between an act or object and a rule adopted by the speaker. For instance, such a relativist would take people who say that abortion is wrong to claim that acts of abortion would be inconsistent with a rule of their adequate moral system. The realist would take these people to predicate the property of moral wrongness of acts of abortion.

Who is correct on this issue? It is not easy to decide. A relativist like Harman argues that morality requires something like the notion of a moral law, and he interprets this notion in terms of rules that are socially enforced and transmitted. From this perspective, moral obligation is an obligation to obey a law, but a law consisting of rules created by human beings. In a similar fashion, a relativist like Wong takes morality to be essentially a matter of action-guiding rules. According to Wong, we ourselves create these rules, and we do so on the basis of our interests and needs and with a view to resolving conflicts. In focusing on the importance of lawlike practices and action-guiding edicts in the moral sphere, relativists provide support for the idea that moral judgments amount to statements about the relationship between the subject matter of these judgments and things like rules.

Furthermore, the relational analysis of moral judgment renders them analogous to another type of judgment with which they obviously have something in common: legal judgments. It is plausible to take many legal judgments to be statements about the relationship between an act or person and some legal rule. This gives at least prima facie credibility to the claim that moral judgments also have this relational structure.

Finally, the relational analysis can take credit for being an ingenious way of explaining how truth values become attached to moral discourse. It allows relativists to accommodate the fact that moral judgments can be true or false without committing themselves to a realm of independent moral facts.

But there are also disadvantages to the relativists' relational analysis of moral judgments. It makes sense to speak of man-made legal rules because we can point to them, because they have been created at a particular place and time or are inscribed in statute books. There is nothing quite like this in the moral sphere. Even if we can agree on a set of moral rules—which is not always the case—we certainly cannot locate them in statute books or identify their author or the time and place of their origination. Furthermore, legal rules have a provincial scope as well as origin: most of them govern behavior within a certain political domain. Moral injunctions, on the contrary, have a universality of scope built into them: they apply to all human beings.

The relational analysis of moral judgments also carries with it a degree of artificiality. It is, to my mind at any rate, unconvincing and unintuitive to claim that in making a moral judgment we are comparing an act, person, or object with a rule we accept (or ought to accept, given our standards for moral rules). Rules do not have quite this kind of ubiquitous involvement in moral discussions. Even if we grant the reality of moral rules, their role in the moral life seems more restricted than the relational analysis implies: we appeal to moral rules on occasion, and on occasion we teach them to others, preach them, and preach about them. But they are not part, overtly at any rate, of the subject matter of every moral judgment. Moreover, it makes more sense phenomenologically to say that moral judgments are about the referents of their subject terms than to say that they are about these referents in relation to something that does not get explicitly mentioned—moral rules. Additionally, rules have a dependence on human invention and creation. If they are involved as ingredients in all moral judgments, their status as artifacts sits uncomfortably with the apparent independence of moral facts from human creation and invention.

The relational analysis seems particularly artificial when applied to those moral judgments incorporating the realists' "thick concepts": courage, loyalty, cowardice, cruelty, and so on. What rules pertain to these matters? Do we have a rule that tells us to be courageous, and another that tells us not to be a traitor? Even if we have such rules, what do they have to do with the fact that George Washington was courageous in crossing the Delaware, or that Judas was a traitor? It is most implausible to suggest that in saying that Washington was courageous we are saying that he was acting in a way consistent with one of our rules. We are talking about Washington, not about Washington in relation to ourselves. And if to say that Washington was courageous were to mean only that he was acting in a way consistent with one of our rules, what we mean would be no different from what we would mean, on the relativist view, when we assert that he was honest. Both judgments would claim only that he acted in ways consistent with one of our rules—both would, absurdly, mean the same thing.

The relational analysis is perhaps a bit more plausible when applied to moral judgments like "*A* ought not to lie to *B*" or "It is wrong of *A* to lie to *B*." For in these cases, something like a rule seems to be implicitly involved in the judgments—namely, "It is wrong to lie" or "One ought not to tell a lie." But are these rules? They seem more like general principles. Perhaps the rules the relativists talk about are what other philosophers have called moral principles. If "It is wrong to tell a lie" is taken as a rule, however, it could not be thought of, as a relativist like Wong wishes to think of it, as having a truth value. As a rule, it would be part of the situation described by a true particular judgment; it would not itself be a description of a relationship between a kind of action and another rule. Or is it the case that, in the relativist's analysis, a judgment like "It is wrong to tell a lie" sometimes functions as a rule—in relation to a particular moral judgment—and at other times as a true or false moral principle—which describes a *kind* of act as being consistent or inconsistent with a higher rule? Not wishing to speak for the relativists on this issue, I shall simply rephrase our main question: Are rules or general moral principles part of the subject matter of such moral judgments as "*A* ought to do *x*"?

I wish to argue that *substantive moral rules or principles*—universal rules or principles forming a set of moral beliefs we feel capable of defending and justifying—are not part of the subject matter of all true or false moral judgments. My reason for this claim is simply that not all individuals who make moral judgments subscribe to such rules or principles, and certainly not on all occasions of judgment. At the same time, I want to argue that another kind of rule is presupposed by moral judgments. It is not a substantive moral rule, but rather a *rule of moral grammar*; and it is not incorporated into the content of moral judgments, but rather is part of the background of such judgments. By developing these two lines of argument, I am able to reject the relativists' relational analysis of moral judgments in favor of something like the realists' nonrelational account, but at the same time I am able to show how realism errs in its extensive repudiation of rules, having failed to notice or acknowledge the rules of moral grammar. In sum, conceptual relativism, shorn of the unfortunate relational analysis of moral judgments, becomes closer to realism than it has heretofore been pictured to be, while it retains a relativist conception of the importance of rules (rules of grammar) in the moral life. Hence we have a convergence of two views which corrects an implausible component in each, the result being a conception of morality that is superior to either realism or relativism as they are frequently understood.

What are we to make of such propositions as "One ought to keep one's promises," "One ought to tell the truth," "Harming other people is wrong," and "Being disrespectful of others is wrong"? Are they substantive moral convictions with the weight of proof or evidence behind them? Could there be legitimate *moral* disagreement over these propositions? Could we be wrong in subscribing to one of them? In fact, can we even be said to believe them? Is this the proper way to describe the mode in which they figure into our moral deliberations? It is only by answering such questions that we will be able to understand the logical status of these propositions.

Realists, to the extent that they allow for such propositions at all, must take them to express substantive moral principles. Given the realists' perspective on moral life, it would be necessary for them to consider these principles to be true or false claims, true if they correspond to moral reality and false otherwise. The realists are skeptical of our ability to formulate such general principles, as they believe that moral properties are situation-specific and that principles at best generalize from a limited sample of particular moral contexts. Hence for the realists, anyone who accepts the principle "One ought (always) to tell the truth" subscribes to a proposition that very likely is in error, and subscribes to it as an inductive generalization that is probable at best. It would surely be appropriate, from this perspective, to speak of a person's *believing* that one ought to tell the truth; and it would be equally appropriate to insist that any such belief can be challenged.

A relativist like Wong can be understood to interpret the logical status of "One ought to tell the truth" in a similar way. If he takes it to be a true/false principle, and not a rule, he would hold that it is a statement concerning the relationship between acts of the kind *telling the truth* and a rule of the speaker's adequate moral system—specifically, a statement to the effect that doing this kind of act is consistent with the rule. The proposition so construed is a contingent one—it could be true or false, and its truth value would depend on whether it accurately characterizes the (relational) fact it purports to characterize.[9] Given the various kinds

9. It must be granted that Wong does allow for the possibility of moral propositions that are necessarily true—see *Moral Relativity* (Berkeley: University of California Press, 1984), p. 59. He does not, however, put this notion to any significant use. Moreover, his

of error possible when one makes this kind of claim (errors clearly delineated by Wong), it also would be the case that the speaker could easily be in error with regard to the proposition and that at best she could be said to believe strongly and for good reason that it is true. Finally, two speakers sharing a set of rules could disagree morally over whether it is true that one ought to tell the truth. And if they do not have the same rules, they could still disagree over whether "One ought to tell the truth" accurately describes the facts relative to either speaker's adequate moral system.

Both realism and relativism, then, take a moral principle like "It is wrong to tell a lie" to be a contingent proposition that could be false and could be the subject of legitimate moral disagreement between speakers who believe differently with regard to it. Such a position, however, is implausible. As Robert Coburn has argued, it is counterintuitive to think that we could be in error in thinking that it is wrong to torture and kill innocent people "just for the hell of it."[10] Likewise, I propose, it is counterintuitive to suggest that we could be in error about "It is wrong to tell a lie." This is as certain as anything can be in the moral sphere; indeed, it seems absolutely certain. If it is not wrong to tell a lie, and to kill and torture innocent people, what *is* wrong from the moral point of view? If there is nothing wrong with harming others and being disrespectful of them, what is morally wrong? It is difficult to see how we could remain in the moral camp and debate, much less reject, the morality of such actions as telling the truth and being respectful of others.

Of course, we can easily debate whether one ought to tell the truth or keep one's promise on a particular occasion. This is not to debate the general principle of truth telling or promise keeping, but rather its applicability to the given circumstances or its priority over other principles that also may apply. The principles of truth telling and promise keeping will be trumped on occasion by the principle requiring that we not take

---

analysis of the truth conditions of moral judgments shows that he takes the vast majority of these judgments to be contingent, and he says nothing to indicate that "it is wrong to tell a lie" and the other grammatical rules are among the exceptions. To be sure, Wong could develop his theory so as to say more about noncontingent moral propositions, but then his theory would be more like mine. As it stands, Wong's theory does not turn at all on the contingent/noncontingent distinction; such a distinction is central to my theory.

10. Robert Coburn, "Morality, Truth, and Relativism," *Ethics*, 92 (July 1982), 661–69; see esp. p. 662.

the lives of innocent persons, and they not infrequently will be overridden by the principle that we not harm others. This should not be seen as invalidating the principle that it is wrong to break a promise or that it is wrong to tell a lie, but rather as warning us that what we ought to do on a given occasion may be something that is in some respects morally dubious. Regrettably, we may be forced to tell a lie because another moral obligation takes priority over the obligation to tell the truth. But we do not feel that the principle of truth telling is weakened every time it is trumped. Our reaction is more along the lines that, unfortunately, we had to tell a lie on these occasions, that is, we were forced to do something that remains morally dubious. On the realist and the relativist interpretations of such principles, the fact that one principle can override another on a given occasion should tend to weaken the beliefs we have in them. For on both of these interpretations the principles are generalizations—for the realist, generalizations about moral reality; for the relativist, generalizations about certain kinds of action relative to a rule. But if our commitment to "It is wrong to tell a lie" and "It is wrong to break one's promises" is not weakened by the fact that on a given occasion one of these moral strictures overrides the other, these principles are not generalizations. Hence our commitment to them is not to be adjusted according to the degree to which they are adequate generalizations.

How are we to get a hold on the logical and epistemological status of these propositions? First of all, we need to ask whether certain questions about them are appropriate.[11] If a proposition like "It is wrong to tell a lie" is contingent, it would be appropriate to ask when this truth was discovered. It also would be appropriate to inquire whether there is any kind of *experimentum crucis* that could be devised to prove it. It would make sense to inquire what evidence we have for the proposition and to ask whether some people merely believe the proposition whereas others know it, the latter having adequate evidence for it. Is the proposition one that we could on occasion forget, an item in our store of knowledge that momentarily slips from memory? The inappropriateness of all of these questions strongly suggests that "It is wrong to tell a lie" is not a contingent proposition that we can be said to know, and come to know,

11. I am indebted here to suggestions by P. M. S. Hacker.

through something comparable to empirical procedures. And we have already questioned whether it makes sense to claim that we could be wrong about "It is wrong to tell a lie" or that such a proposition could be false. But if it cannot be false, it is also unclear what it means to say that it is *true*. Perhaps "It is wrong to tell a lie" and its like are not propositions that we know at all, or fail to know; perhaps they are neither true nor false. But if not, what are they?

To give a constructive account of the logical/epistemological status of the propositions in question, it is advisable to look for the contexts in which they are expressed and to note the jobs they do in these contexts. If we attempt this search, it is immediately noticeable how rare these contexts are. We incessantly discuss and debate the morality of things like abortion, euthanasia, war, and advertising, but do we ever discuss the morality of telling the truth or keeping promises? About the only kind of person who would call the latter actions into question and prompt us to discuss them is the moral skeptic, a person outside the moral fold altogether. The skeptic has no interest, for instance, in establishing that it is morally obligatory or permissible to tell lies or break promises. Such a person questions *all* talk of moral rightness, wrongness, and permissibility. Those "moralists" inside the fold do not themselves disagree over promise keeping and truth telling. They seldom if ever talk about these matters, much less debate them. In what contexts, then, would a moralist utter "One ought to tell the truth" or "It is wrong to break one's promises"?

One such context is that in which we give children moral instruction. We repeat over and over again to them: one ought not to tell a lie—it is wrong to do so. We use basic history lessons—for example, about George Washington and the cherry tree—for reinforcement. In such moral instruction, it is not the case that we are trying to persuade children to believe one thing rather than another; we are not trying, for instance, to get them to believe that it is wrong morally to tell a lie rather than that it is morally permissible or right to do so. The children are not debating moral issues with us. At their stage of moral development, children do not have established ideas of moral rightness and wrongness such that we could be attempting to give them reasons to apply the former, and not the latter, to telling the truth, keeping promises, and so on. In instructing them that one ought not to tell a lie and that one ought to keep promises, one is introducing them to morality. One is, as it were, characterizing moral space—the moral dimension of life—and training them to live and operate within it.

Similarly, a missionary uses these propositions when preaching to "heathen savages." Such a missionary is trying to convert the savages, to bring them to give up a way of life involving, say, cannibalism, and to adopt a way of life in which one does not harm other people. The missionary is not arguing morally with the cannibals, not trying to get them to see that cannibalism is morally wrong rather than morally right. The missionary and the cannibals do not agree in general terms about morality while disagreeing about the specific moral issue of cannibalism. The cannibals are outside the moral fold, and the missionary is trying to bring them within it—to convert them, to change their lives, to introduce them to a new way of thinking about things.

There is still another kind of context in which propositions like "It is wrong to tell a lie" can be found. Sometimes, in the midst of an argument, we will say something like "You can't do that—that's lying." The kind of argument I have in mind is not one about whether one should lie or, say, keep one's promise, but rather (typically) about whether one should or should not do something that obviously would be in someone's self-interest. If a friend, for instance, tries to talk me into a scheme by means of which I will save myself thousands of tax dollars, I might say to him, "I can't do that—that would be to lie." In such an argument, I am bringing the moral perspective to bear on an issue that my friend (friend until now) considers only from the standpoint of self-interest. I might express the moral dimension of the situation by saying that it is wrong to lie. My friend, being neither a cannibal nor a child, does not need to be introduced to the moral dimension of life for the first time, but he certainly may need to be reminded of it.

Finally, we sometimes feel called upon to defend our way of life by taking extreme action, occasionally by going to war. On these occasions we are likely to see our way of life as incorporating the moral dimension and the way of life of those we oppose as not including it. The Nazis, we believe, had no respect for others, cared nothing about harming them, and made breaking promises and lying a way of life. We go to war against them when we realize that they cannot be convinced by rational means of the moral impropriety of their actions. We realize that they are beyond the pale, not simply in moral disagreement with us over the morality of certain actions. We fight them when we come to understand that they have no morality at all. In engaging them in combat, we are upholding morality itself against modern barbarianism. Part of our arsenal of war slogans will be those moral propositions we have been concerned with: It is wrong to lie! and so on. We use these slogans to define the way of life for which we stand and to contrast it with the way of life we oppose.

What picture emerges, then, of the function of propositions like "It is wrong to lie" in the contexts we have identified? We use these propositions to identify a way of life, to introduce people to it, to remind wayward ones of it, and to proclaim it as a cherished possession. Such propositions are being employed, I would like to say (following Wittgenstein), as grammatical propositions. They serve to define morality, to define the morally relevant dimensions of life. They are, in reality, rules of moral grammar, rules for talking and thinking about morality.

The rules of moral grammar, like all grammatical rules, are a priori and "necessary," not empirical and contingent. We do not pick them up or generalize them from experience. We need them in order to describe any moral experience from which we might learn and generalize. Hence they are presupposed by the experience rather than derived from it. Nor can such rules of moral grammar be thought of as true or false. It is inconceivable that it is morally right to tell a lie, even though we may tragically be forced to do so on a particular occasion because another, higher, duty takes precedence. The following kind of necessity attaches to these grammatical propositions: we must subscribe to them if we are to participate in the moral way of life, and within the moral life their denial is incoherent. It is not that they are necessarily true, whatever that could mean; their function is not to be a true, as opposed to a false, picture of the moral way of life. Their function is to define it, to identify it, to proclaim it. Given these functions, it makes no sense to say that we *believe* these grammatical propositions, for if we did so we might incorrectly believe them. And it makes no sense to say that we could be wrong about them; anyone who rejects them simply does not understand what morality is or simply rejects morality. Hence they are not debatable from within morality—it is inconceivable that there could be moral disagreement about them.

If propositions like "One ought to tell the truth" have the functions and logical characteristics identified above, it is to be expected that their role in the moral life will be different from that of moral judgments we make about individual persons and acts, and different as well from generalizations we make about moral matters. Rules of moral grammar are not to be found among the objects of our moral beliefs or expressed by our everyday moral judgments. Rather, they are presupposed by those beliefs and judgments, giving sense to them and identifying the kind of evidence that can be adduced in support of them. The rules of moral grammar identify the morally relevant dimensions of experience; hence they instruct us as to the kinds of things we are to look for in order to decide what we morally ought to do on particular occasions. They tell us to investigate, for instance, whether a situation involves a promise or a lie, or whether doing a certain action has as its consequence hurting someone or treating people disrespectfully. And if we find that a situation does involve such a feature, or has such a consequence, we are in possession of a bit of information that is vital for the purpose of deciding what to do or assessing the morality of what has been done. A rule of moral grammar establishes a presumption to the effect that individual circumstances having the morally relevant feature identified by the rule will have a certain moral character. "It is wrong to tell a lie" establishes the presumption that anyone who has lied has acted wrongly. This presumption may be overridden by the application of a rule dictating a higher duty to the same act. Even so, however, the rule against lying would have established a morally relevant feature of the act.

Are the grammatical propositions definitive of morality properly called *rules* or *principles*? There is nothing wrong with speaking of them in these terms if it is understood what they signify in this context. It must be clear that grammatical principles or rules stand in contrast to other moral principles and rules concerning which there can be legitimate moral disagreement. Take, for instance, the principle that premarital sex is wrong. Many people subscribe to this principle, but many do not. Likewise, many subscribe to the more general rule "No sex outside marriage," but others find those who impose this rule (and many who follow it) to be hypocritical and morally suspect. Thus there are those who believe that premarital and extramarital sex is wrong and others who do not believe this. And both sides ought to admit that they could be wrong about the matter. Hence "Premarital sex is wrong" stands in contrast to "Breaking a promise is wrong" with respect to its logical status. The former is what I call a substantive moral principle; the latter is a rule or principle of moral grammar.

It is noteworthy that in a debate over substantive moral principles like "Premarital sex is wrong" the evidence adduced on both sides of the issue frequently makes appeal to those moral dimensions identified by the rules of moral grammar. Those who think premarital sex wrong are likely to defend their position by arguing that this practice shows a lack of respect for the other person and also runs a grave risk of bringing substantial harm to those who engage in it. Those who think there is nothing in general wrong with premarital sex frequently point to the harmful effect its prohibition has on young people—how, for instance, it frustrates natural desire. Furthermore, they would argue that the prohibition actually drives young people to engage in furtive sexual relations, thereby reducing the respect the participants have for one another and the integrity they bring to the practice. In other words, the evidence advanced on both sides of the debate is dictated by those considerations identified by the rules of moral grammar as being morally relevant.

Having distinguished a grammatical rule from a substantive principle, we nevertheless must recognize that "It is wrong to tell a lie" and the like can be, and for some people are, substantive moral principles. Some individuals believe that one should *never* tell a lie, and they may hold firmly to this principle and defend it robustly. What this shows is that one cannot identify a rule as grammatical simply from its verbal form; rather, one must consider the role and status it has in a person's life. Consider the case of someone who sincerely believes that it is always wrong to tell a lie. She may have come to such a belief as a result of considerable experience, which reveals to her that although one could frequently condone telling a lie on the grounds that another duty conflicts with the possibility of telling the truth, the moral consequences of lying usually have been disastrous. She may have noted new and unexpected ways in which mendacity undermines the integrity and autonomy of human beings in community. Thus her experience and reflection lead her to the position that, appearances notwithstanding, one ought never to tell a lie. Or a person affirming this substantive principle may have lived in a simpler age, or perhaps just led a simple life, in which no conflicts arose among his various moral duties. Such a person can see no justification for admitting any exceptions to the rule against lying. In both cases, these individuals view themselves as having reasons for their principle. Hence for them it is a defensible principle, one that can be justified, one that in theory could be in error but that in fact is demonstrably, or at least probably, correct. Here we have the markings of a substantive moral principle. A rule of moral grammar has been converted into a contingent proposition.

Frequently we admire people of high principle, those who subscribe to and live by such dicta as "It is always wrong to tell a lie" or "Extramarital sex is always wrong." We sometimes admire them because we see them as having a vast and deep experience of the world, particularly of its moral dimension. Sometimes we simply admire their strength of will. People of high principle frequently are "men for all seasons," individuals who, we suspect, will prevail morally by dint of their experience, their insight, or their decisiveness—those who will either prevail or come to some tragic denouement. We can admire them for their moral experience and courage even if we think them wrong. But we also can be deeply suspicious of people of high principle, believing that they often confuse deep moral truth with willfulness and that they may well sacrifice the lives or well-being of themselves and others in order to maintain their principles. A life of high moral principle is debatable—morally debatable.

Much the same thing can be said of moral rules. Some people live by moral rules that tell them never to do such and such, or never to do it except in specifiable conditions. Parents frequently try to impose upon their children the rule "No premarital sex!" And some individuals live by the rule "Never tell a lie!" In defense of their rule-governed approach to life, they may argue that it is necessary in order to preserve respect for moral principles or that it is required if we are to have fair practices. On the other hand, many individuals, frequently those who are wise to the ways of the world, are suspicious, on moral grounds, of such rule-governed behavior. They will point to its inflexibility, with its own pernicious consequences. They argue that such behavior dulls the moral sensibility and often produces lives that are narrow in scope and mean in effect. Once again, then, we are dealing with rules that are contingent and debatable. What in one context can be taken as a rule grammatically defining a relevant moral dimension can be taken in another context as a substantive moral rule. The grammatical rule is unexceptionable, but the substantive rule requires considerable defense.

What is to be said about those of us who are not people of high principle and who do not live our lives according to strict rules? It is certainly not the case that, by virtue of these facts, we fail to live a moral life. Most of us, I suggest, live our moral lives piecemeal, dealing situation by situation with the moral dimensions that confront us and trying to decide in each case where our duty lies. Such a life is not easy. We have few substantive general rules or principles to fall back on. Judgment and decision are always necessary, and given the complexity of the moral life, error seems a constant likelihood. But we muck along, doing the best we can. And we resist the simple solution proffered by the universal principle or rule, thinking that it fosters more moral harm than good.

Such a piecemeal approach to moral judgment and the moral life is not, however, a matter of constant compromise and pragmatic meandering. Nor is it a blind, existential leap of faith. We who adopt it have our guideposts; we have our feet planted firmly on moral ground. This support is provided by the rules of moral grammar. They stand firm for us; they provide direction and guidance and ensure that we are occupying moral space. What they do not do is provide us with simple rules or principles that tell us what we always ought to do. They establish presumptions about what we should do in particular circumstances; they tell us what dimensions we must take into account if we are to arrive at a moral judgment or take moral action. But all of our judgments can be in error, and more often than not we risk doing the wrong thing. At the same time, if we persevere, if we are diligent and attentive to the details of the moral life, we may get it right, in judgment and in action. The rules of moral grammar tell us what to look for, but they do not tell us what we will find. Each moment of judgment or decision must be approached in its fullness; we must determine what the moral dimensions of our situation are, and what order of priority, if any, they have in this situation. The risk we run is the risk of making *moral* mistakes, of erroneously thinking that we have identified all the moral dimensions of our situation or that we have correctly ascertained their order of priority. Only a person occupying moral space can make moral mistakes. And if we make an error, we are at least fortunate to be able to recognize it and hence be in a position to feel the proper remorse or shame. We can recognize our errors because, firmly in command of the rules of moral grammar, we can recognize the evidence that we failed to see before.

It must be granted that the piecemeal approach to the moral life is not a glamorous one. It is likely to be ignored, even derided, by those who are in full possession of a set of substantive moral principles. And frequently it is subject to caricature and abuse by those armed with an arsenal of political goals and ambitions, especially those with a new all-encompassing ideology. As Milan Kundera put it in his novel *The Book of Laughter and Forgetting*, describing the Communist takeover in Czecho-slovakia: "They had a grandiose program, a plan for a brand-new world in which everyone would find his place. The Communists' opponents had no great dream; all they had was a few moral principles, stale and lifeless, to patch up the tattered trousers of the established order. So of course the grandiose enthusiasts won out over the cautious compro-misers."[12] Moral principles concerning telling the truth and keeping promises may appear stale and lifeless, and a matter of compromise, to those who ignore them, especially to those who operate with "higher" goals. But we have learned from sad experience that putting aside these grammatical principles out of preference for "newly discovered" sub-stantive principles or totalizing ideologies often leads to moral catas-trophe.

I would venture to say that most human beings engage in piecemeal moral efforts, that they assess given moral situations, not on the basis of general, substantive principles, but solely on the basis of grammatical rules and the facts they encounter and discover. If this is so, then, con-trary to the relativists' relational analysis of moral judgments, our moral judgments do not consist in a comparison between an act or situation, on the one hand, and our substantive rules or principles, on the other. In most instances, we simply do not have such rules or principles to apply to the cases at hand. It follows that the relational analysis has badly misconstrued the nature of moral judgments.

It remains for an advocate of the relational analysis to insist that what I have called the rules of moral grammar function as one of the *relata* in all moral judgments. For though I have questioned the presence of sub-stantive rules and principles in all moral decision making, I have at the same time insisted upon the ubiquity of these rules of grammar. Perhaps a moral judgment that a person ought to do *x* is a statement to the effect that not doing *x* would break one of the speaker's rules of moral gram-mar.

To decide whether this is in fact the case, we need to examine other,

12. Milan Kundera, *The Book of Laughter and Forgetting*, Michael Henry Heim, trans. (New York: Alfred A. Knopf, 1980), p. 8.

nonmoral contexts in which grammatical rules operate. We need to determine whether in these contexts grammatical rules are part of the relational content of judgments incorporating terms that the rules serve to define or whether the rules have some other kind of connection to the judgments. Take, for instance, the attribution of colors. We say of an object that it is yellow. Are we saying that so describing it is consistent with the rules of color grammar? It seems obvious that we are not—our judgment is not a reflexive one. Moreover, most of us seldom think of color rules. And yet there are such things: they are to be found on color charts, where a color name is coordinated with a color sample. The color chart not only indicates what color a term designates, it also relates this color to the others and hence relates the meaning of the color term to the meanings of other color terms. All of this constitutes an expression of the grammar of color terms.

Furthermore, we give a rudimentary expression of the grammar of a particular color term by providing an ostensive definition of it. These ostensive definitions and the color chart express the grammatical rules of color. The grammatical rule governing 'yellow' is at work when we say that a particular object is yellow, but it is not at work as part of the content of that judgment. We are not saying that the object has the same color as is found beside 'yellow' on some color chart. We are speaking only of the object. But our judgment does presuppose the rule of grammar governing the word 'yellow'. If someone asks us what we mean when we say "The sofa is yellow," we explain our meaning by producing the color chart or giving an ostensive definition. Thus the rule explicates the meaning of what we say, rather than being a part of what we say. We are assuming that 'yellow' has this meaning when we use it to describe the sofa, and in this clear sense the rule of grammar is presupposed by our judgment. Furthermore, if there were a debate over the color, we could produce the sample to settle the matter. The sample is thus presupposed as defining the set of epistemic possibilities surrounding the use of the color term.

These illustrations also show how these rules of grammar are referred to and used. Perhaps their main use is to teach someone the color language, particularly a child. In the contexts of teaching the meanings of color words, explaining their meaning, and debating whether their application is correct, our rules of color grammar become explicit, and as such they sometimes serve as a component of the content of our judgments. At other times, when we are simply using the color words these rules define, the rules are part of a presupposed background, not part of the literal content (overt or covert) of our judgments.

We have seen above how the rules of moral grammar are used to introduce a person to the moral dimension. And we have seen how these rules are appealed to in moral debate, how they define the kind of evidence that can be brought to bear on an issue. Hence their function is quite similar to that of color rules. It seems plausible to conclude that the rules of moral grammar, like those of color grammar, function as an element of the presupposed background of moral discourse and not, for the most part, as ingredients in its content. As part of this background, they define moral terms and are available when the need arises to explain the meanings of these terms.

Moral Concepts and the Concept of Morality

Let us test this hypothesis by asking whether the rules of moral grammar can be used to instruct people in the meaning of moral terms. And let us start with those thick moral concepts like courage and loyalty. It seems obvious enough that these words have definitions, both verbal and ostensive, and that these definitions are used to explain the meanings of the words. Courage, we say, is the control over fear which allows us to function effectively in difficult and dangerous situations, and we might go on to point out that George Washington's crossing of the Delaware was an act of courage. Furthermore, we might add something like "One should strive to be courageous—it is a highly desirable character trait." These grammatical remarks serve to identify the conditions under which we call someone courageous and to express the moral import of this trait. To use the terms of the noncognitivists, they serve to characterize the descriptive and the evaluative meaning of 'courage'. These two components are not, however, identified independently. As we saw in Chapter 2, it is much more plausible to think of them as inseparable, as forming a tightly fused union. Such seems to be the case with terms like 'courage'. There seldom if ever would be a point to identifying the conditions of their application without at the same time providing a lesson in their moral import. The rules presupposed by thick moral concepts like courage, then, do serve to explicate the meanings of these terms.

But consider such propositions as "It is wrong to tell a lie," the kind of proposition we identified above as a rule of moral grammar. In what sense does it serve to explain the meaning of moral terms? How does "One ought to keep one's promises" constitute an explication of meaning? I wish to suggest that such propositions can fruitfully be compared to grammatical rules like "Red is a color."[13] The latter defines 'red' by saying that it designates a color. But equally it partially defines 'color'. As we saw in Chapter 4, we have no general concept of color allowing us to discover that red is a color. Color is a determinable property and one that is defined through its determinants—color is red, yellow, green, blue, and so on. Generally we are taught that red is a color at the same time we are taught that yellow is a color, green is a color, and so forth. These definitions jointly define color and thereby introduce us to the color dimension of experience.

Likewise, "One ought to keep one's promises" and "It is wrong to tell a lie" simultaneously serve to define, on the one hand, 'keeping one's promises' and 'lying' and, on the other hand, the moral notions of obligation and wrongdoing. "Morally what we ought to do" and "what it is right for us to do"—as well as "what we ought not to do" and "what it is wrong to do"—are determinable notions. They have no identifiable content in addition to such notions as keeping one's promises, telling the truth, breaking promises, lying, and so on. So in saying that one ought to keep one's promises, one is defining the sphere of moral obligation by means of identifying one of its determinants. One does not understand *morality* by grasping a general definition of it; one understands it by knowing that we are morally obligated to tell the truth and keep our promises, as well as to avoid harming others and to respect them. Ronald Milo has expressed such a view of morality in the following way:

> I do not see how anyone who claims to know what it means to say that it is *morally* wrong to do something can deny that an act's causing pain, injury, or death to someone is at least *a* reason for judging it to be morally wrong. Indeed, it is in terms of such criteria as these that most people are taught the meaning of "morally wrong." . . . We are not first taught the meaning of "morally wrong" and then taught that such acts are morally

13. See Phillips and Mounce, *Moral Practices*, p. 9.

wrong; rather, such criteria define, for the ordinary person, what it means to say that an act is morally wrong.[14]

As we learn more and more of these principles ("criteria"), we come into more complete possession of the concept of morality.

The concept of morality is undeniably open-ended: there is no absolutely complete set of determinants serving to define it. Thus it is impossible to list all of our rules of moral grammar. And the concept of morality is "fuzzy around the edges." It is difficult to tell whether some principles help define morality or are substantive ones derived from a combination of grammatical and empirical considerations. For some individuals, "One has a moral obligation to be patriotic" may serve as a rule of grammar definitive of morality; for others, it may serve as a substantive moral principle; for still others, it is a moral falsehood.

But while propositions like "One ought to keep one's promises" help to define the moral dimension of experience, they also serve to define such notions as *keeping one's promises*. The concept of keeping one's promises is morally laden. It designates a kind of action we ought to engage in. If a person takes the notion of keeping one's promises—indeed, the notion of a promise—as morally neutral, she has failed to understand it. *Keeping one's promises* is a determinant of the determinable notion *moral obligation*. We no more understand it if we fail to grasp that it is a moral obligation than we understand *red* if we can identify it but fail to grasp that it is a color.

It might be argued that 'color' does have a meaning independent of its determinants—it is, for instance, a perceptible quality of objects. This is true, but a similar thing can be said about right and wrong—they are features of action identifiable through conscience, the moral sense, or a sense of decency. We might add that 'right' and 'wrong' connote highly important and action-guiding features of experience. They signify dimensions of life we should be concerned about, dimensions that should figure prominently in how we act. Morality shares these features with other, nonmoral dimensions of experience—the dimensions of etiquette and law—just as the property of color shares with the property of shape the feature of being perceptible. Perhaps moral features have some more

14. Ronald Milo, *Immorality* (Princeton: Princeton University Press, 1984), pp. 195–96.

general traits that they alone possess and share—perhaps they are of overriding importance, or perhaps they are features that everyone should acknowledge. But none of these general connotations of 'right' and 'wrong' is sufficient for understanding these terms, just as 'a perceptible property of objects that varies in hue and brilliance' is not sufficient for understanding 'color'. We know what color is, and hence what varies in hue and brilliance, when we come to know what red, yellow, blue, green, and so on are. And we know what features of action are of overriding and universal importance when we know that it is wrong to tell a lie, to break a promise, and so forth.

The idea of treating propositions like "It is wrong to tell a lie" and "One ought to treat others respectfully" as rules of moral grammar which serve to define the moral realm runs counter to a philosophical tendency, especially common around 1970, to seek a definition by genus and difference of the term 'morality'.[15] It was proposed by some— *formalists*, they were called—that a morality is any set of rules or principles that are prescriptive, universalized, and overriding. Others suggested a material definition in terms of content, urging that the only set of principles we would consider moral are those that serve, or are intended to serve, the interests of people in community. These "materialists" claimed that we would not consider a set of principles moral unless it took the interests of others into account, even if for someone these principles were prescriptive, overriding, and universalized. W. K. Frankena, for instance, has proposed the following definition of morality: "*x* has a morality . . . only if it includes judgments, rules, principles, ideals, etc., which (d) concern the relations of one individual . . . to others, (e) involve or call for a consideration of the effects of his actions on others . . ., not from the point of view of his own interests or aesthetic enjoyments, but from their own point of view."[16] Hence for Frankena, any rules, in addition to being (a) prescriptive, (b) universalized, and (c) overriding,[17] must also satisfy his material conditions (d) and (e) in order to qualify as moral rules. Formalists like R. M. Hare objected to

15. A useful collection of essays on the topic is G. Wallace and A. D. Walker, eds., *The Definition of Morality* (London: Methuen, 1970).

16. W. K. Frankena, "The Concept of Morality," in Wallace and Walker, *Definition of Morality*, p. 156.

17. Frankena expresses some reservations about the claim that moral considerations are overriding or supreme; ibid, p. 170.

such material accounts of morality on the grounds that they amounted to ways of settling substantive moral disagreements by means of linguistic fiat.[18] An egoist or a Nazi, he suggested, is in substantive disagreement with those who adopt a material definition of 'morality' requiring a concern for others, and the egoist or Nazi should not be summarily dismissed as not having a moral point of view. Hare also objected that materialist accounts tended to make something like utilitarianism true by definition, an unfortunate consequence since utilitarianism, correct or incorrect, is a substantive moral theory and the principle of utility a substantive moral principle, not an empty, verbal tautology. The theory and the principle have implications for behavior, Hare insists, not just for the way we are to talk.

The search for a comprehensive definition of morality was not successfully concluded. No general agreement was reached over the necessary and sufficient conditions a set of rules or principles must meet to be moral. If the notion of grammatical moral rules being put forth here is correct, it is not surprising that this search was unsuccessful. Designating a basic and irreducible domain of experience, 'morality', like 'color', can only (or only for the most part) be defined in terms of its determinate features. Certain general features (universality, prescriptiveness, and overridingness) possibly can be identified—although each of them is controversial—but none of them singly or jointly is sufficient. What remains to give substance to the notion of morality are the specific moral dimensions: telling the truth, keeping promises, avoiding harm to others, respecting others, and so on. These dimensions do not lend themselves to any general formula, and they frequently conflict with one another. Moreover, they can come into conflict with requirements springing from "moralities" satisfying one of the material definitions of 'morality'. Taking the interests of others into account, for instance, is compatible with a Nazi perspective (as Frankena himself has noted), but Nazism certainly is incompatible with morality. What must be added to such a material account is that the interests of others must be respected and that the integrity of others must not be undermined by lying to them, breaking promises to them, and harming them. Our specific

18. See R. M. Hare, *Freedom and Reason* (Oxford: Oxford University Press, 1965), pp. 146–49 and 162–66.

moral duties to others, and they alone, give substance to the notion of taking the interests of others morally into account.

The definition of morality I am proposing here is extremely narrow, some might say excessively so. It equates morality with a set of specific moral demands, although it is an open-ended set and fuzzy around the edges. Given this account of morality, the notion that there could be alternative moralities basically makes no sense. At best it would be the notion that there are demands and rules that other people incorrectly take to be moral ones. A formal definition in terms of universalizability and overridingness would allow for alternative and incompatible moralities. Likewise, material definitions like the one considered above—taking the interests of others into account—would allow, as some of their authors grant, for alternative, incompatible moralities. Frankena has remarked, for instance, that such a definition is compatible with both a utilitarian and deontological morality.[19] And a functional definition like the one Wong proposes, equating morality with rules that reconcile internal and interpersonal conflicts, clearly would allow for alternative, incompatible moralities. But the narrow conception offered here rejects this possibility. Any set of rules making no reference to, or being incompatible with, the obligation to tell the truth, keep promises, refrain from harming others, and respect others is at best a set of amoral rules, at worst a set of immoral ones.

It needs to be emphasized that these remarks aim at characterizing the concept of morality that is central for most contemporary Americans and Western Europeans. From this perspective, there may be many other so-called moralities which operate with totally different sets of rules or incorporate concepts of morality defined in general material, functional, or formal terms. Furthermore, the concept of morality shared by most Americans and Western Europeans will admit of variations from subculture to subculture, and indeed from individual to individual. Such variation is easy to explain in terms of the open-ended and fuzzy nature of the concept, which highlights the fact that the grammatical rules comprehended by the concept cannot be enumerated with any finality or absolute precision. It should not be surprising, then, that the set of rules defining morality need not be exactly the same for any two individuals.

19. Frankena, "Concept of Morality," p. 156.

This fact can be the source of unending philosophical controversies over the "true" or "essential" nature of morality. It also can provide an explanation for many of the disagreements we encounter in the moral realm, an explanation, I suggest, that is at least as plausible as the one put forth by Wong.

Objections

It might be objected that this account renders unclear the scope of the rules of moral grammar. I have argued (a) that it is compatible with the necessity of "It is wrong to tell a lie" that there may be specific occasions on which telling a lie would be morally permissible or excusable, and (b) that "It is wrong to tell a lie" is sometimes converted into a substantive moral principle by which it is claimed that one ought *never* to tell a lie. Does it follow that the grammatical rule has only restricted generality, that it tells us only that it is sometimes (or even more often than not) wrong to tell a lie? As I am interpreting the rule, this does not follow. The rule informs us that it is always morally questionable to tell a lie, that a moral stigma always attaches to doing so. Hence when another rule is judged to take precedence over and is in conflict with the rule proscribing lying, the lie that we are morally forced to tell, and which in the circumstances it is morally excusable to tell, is nevertheless something about which we properly feel uncomfortable, about which we appropriately feel remorse. A morally ideal world would be one in which this kind of conflict of duties never took place and hence a world in which lying was never permitted. In our actual world, we are sometimes required to infringe the rule against lying, but even then lying remains morally problematic, less than ideal, the lesser of two evils. The rule of grammar "It is wrong to tell a lie" establishes a presumption against lying; we are always to presume that lying is to be avoided, and we should persevere in this stance unless a morally defined reason overrides the presumption on a particular occasion. Only a higher moral reason can trump the requirement that we refrain from lying.[20] We might build these conditions into the grammatical rule by rephrasing it to read "It is

20. If for some people moral considerations are not supreme or overriding, if, for example, they would subscribe to a Kierkegaardian "teleological suspension of the ethical," then for them nonmoral considerations can trump moral ones.

always morally questionable, and a matter of grave moral import, to tell a lie, and it is morally excusable to do so only when a higher moral obligation demands it." This rule has no exceptions; it is one we hold to in all cases. Likewise, "One ought to keep one's promises" establishes a presumption in favor of keeping promises. We are always to presume that keeping a promise is morally commendable, and we should always keep our promises unless another moral consideration takes precedence and requires that we break one of them. Even when we are forced by moral considerations to break a promise, we should feel morally uncomfortable in doing so.

The strength of the presumption established by a rule of moral grammar varies from rule to rule, and rules usually have a built-in index of priority. "It is wrong to kill an innocent human being" establishes not only that murder is morally questionable and grave but also that it is a moral atrocity of the highest order. This presumption trumps just about all others on almost all occasions. It is reflected in the fact that we often use the stronger "must" rather than the weaker "ought" to express our rule against murder—"One must not intentionally take the life of an innocent human being." "It is wrong to harm another person" usually takes priority over "It is a good thing to help another person," so that if we find ourselves in a situation whereby we can help someone only by harming someone else, the indices of priority built into these two rules make it likely that we should not attempt to help the other person. But it is evident from a case like this that the order of priority among rules is seldom clear-cut and stable. If the harm we must do to another is small, and the help we thereby can extend to others great, it becomes an open question morally whether the harm is justified on such an occasion. And with many of our rules, there is no initial presumption of priority among them. If we can keep a promise only by telling a lie, or tell the truth only by breaking a promise, what are we to do? There is, I think, no general answer to these questions, which is a way of saying that there is no a priori order of priority between the two rules of moral grammar concerned with lying and keeping promises.

The order of priority among our moral rules, then, is limited, flexible, and imprecise, and it is the source of many of our moral puzzles and our most intractable moral dilemmas. Sometimes the rules and the facts together do not (seem not to) dictate an answer, and there is on these occasions a dimension to the moral life requiring personal judgment and decision. This is the case in Sartre's famous example of the young Frenchman during the war who is torn between an obligation to help his mother and an obligation to defend his country.[21] Sartre's solution to the dilemma—the young man must decide for himself—is correct, but it cannot be generalized as Sartre wishes. Personal decision is required in situations in which there is no clear answer to the question which of several conflicting duties should take priority—but we are not always in such situations. On some occasions the order of priority among the prevailing moral dimensions is clear.

Our situation in the moral sphere is in this respect not altogether different from the predicament we frequently confront in the law. The law contains many clear and rigid rules that judges must apply uniformly and mechanically. But the law also contains many imprecise and flexible rules, such as those governing, say, the severity of crimes, and when these rules are applicable, considerable discretion is placed in the hands of judges—discretion with respect to sentencing, for example.

Furthermore, there may be genuine indeterminacy in the moral sphere, cases for which there is no fact of the matter concerning what one must or ought to do. But indeterminate cases can sit comfortably with determinate ones—not all moral questions have to be resolvable in order that some can be. One has the suspicion that hard cases like abortion are in fact morally indeterminate. Our rules simply do not tell us whether it is morally permissible to take the life of a fetus if in doing so one would avoid great physical and psychological harm to the mother. Perhaps what we need to do here is to revise and augment our rules rather than to continue looking for an answer in our current set.

The fact that our rules have an order of priority and that each serves to establish a moral presumption that can be overridden by the application of another, higher-priority rule may mislead some philosophers into thinking that the rules of moral grammar are contingent and the proper objects of belief and debate. But this does not follow. We often disagree over and debate whether a particular rule is to override another on a particular occasion, but this is because there is no a priori order of priority between these two rules. The debate does not challenge either rule as establishing a moral presumption. What the debate focuses on is what

21. J.-P. Sartre, *Existentialism and Human Emotions* (New York: Philosophical Library, 1957), pp. 24–27.

we should do on a particular occasion, given the fact that the two conflicting, nonprioritized rules apply. Whatever we decide may be debatable, but the rules themselves are not debatable—they establish the terms
and conditions of the debate. Furthermore, when grammatical rules do
have an order of priority among them, this order is as necessary and
certain as anything else in morality. That killing a person is a more serious offense than lying to him is not a matter we ever debate. It is a
given of the moral life. And finally, as we have noted before, the fact that
a moral rule may be trumped by another, higher-priority rule does not
turn it into a contingent proposition, one that is debatable and possibly
false. As an indicator of a moral presumption, it remains unchallenged
even when it is trumped. The rules of moral grammar are universal, a
priori, and necessary, not contingent, debatable generalizations that are
matters of mere belief.

Two additional and related objections to the account of the rules of
moral grammar offered here can be expected from followers of Hare.
Hare and disciples would contend, in the first place, that my account
converts substantive, action-guiding principles into empty, linguistic
tautologies. And in the second place, they would claim that my denial
that principles such as "It is wrong to tell a lie" are substantive principles
is in error.[22]

First, is a grammatical rule an empty, verbal tautology? "It is wrong to
tell a lie," I have said, serves to define both 'telling a lie' and 'wrong'. To
this extent, it certainly is a proposition about words. Furthermore, it has
a kind of necessity attaching to it: one cannot deny it and still understand what morality is all about. It is not a contingent proposition that
can be backed up by reasons. Does it follow from these characteristics
that it is empty, merely linguistic, and fails to guide action? Does my
characterization of the rules of moral grammar "empty moral practices
of life," as one critic of the type of view I am defending has argued?[23]

Following a line of argument developed by Renford Bambrough and
discussed in Chapter 2, we can note that a grammatical rule guides action to the extent of telling us how to talk; talking, after all, is a kind of
action. Furthermore, we have seen how a grammatical rule guides us in

22. See R. M. Hare, *The Language of Morals* (Oxford: Clarendon Press, 1952), chap.
5; and *Freedom and Reason*, chap. 2.
23. Beehler, *Moral Life*, p. 13.

our debates over substantive issues—it indicates a form of evidence relevant to a moral disagreement. Hence it also guides us in our moral
thinking. And finally, insofar as 'telling a lie' is defined as a matter of
grave moral import, a kind of action of significant concern to us, the rule
obviously has implications for our attitudes (toward lying) and also our
actions. Talk about right and wrong, as Wittgenstein might put it,
meshes with our lives. A grammatical proposition is not about *mere*
words, but words as they function in our activities and midst the attitudes and feelings we bring to these activities. If a person understands
the moral rule "It is wrong to tell a lie," she knows that lying is morally
objectionable, she knows that she is being told to refrain from it, and she
knows that telling a lie is a presumptive ground for moral censure. A
grammatical rule helps define for us a way of life, not just a way of
speaking. It does not merely guide the application of moral words, but
rather guides us in the use of these words to issue moral injunctions and
condemnations. Thus it is not a mere, empty, linguistic tautology. It is a
rule with momentous ramifications in our discourse, our states of mind,
our behavior, and our institutions and practices.

We might note that it is only if one sharply distinguishes evaluative
and descriptive meaning that one would be tempted to take a moral rule
as doing nothing more than indicating the application of words. And it
is only if one thinks of the meaning of a sentence as constituted by its
truth conditions that one would be tempted to interpret a moral rule as a
tautology. We have seen reasons in Chapter 2 for repudiating both the
separation of evaluative and descriptive meaning and the analysis of utterances into truth-conditional propositions with added-on illocutionary forces. Setting aside such philosophical confusions, it is easy enough
to take "It is wrong to tell a lie" as telling us both how to apply words
and how to behave and feel.

Hare's second objection would likely be that "It is wrong to tell a lie"
is in fact a substantive moral principle, one we adopt as a result of argument and decision. We have seen how this sometimes is true: some
human beings do argue themselves into thinking that it is always wrong
to tell a lie. What the present account denies is that this rule is always, or
even generally, a substantive one. This can be seen from the fact that
most of us do not believe that one ought never to tell a lie—we can
think of too many occasions on which doing so should not invoke moral
censure. Hare might reply that, to be sure, most of us do not accept "It

is always wrong to tell a lie" as one of our substantive moral principles; rather, he would maintain, we build exceptions into it.[24] Most of us, he would claim, do accept something like "It is always wrong to tell a lie except when one is a prisoner of war, or when doing so would involve putting someone in grave risk, and so on." What I have called the rules of moral grammar, he would suggest, are *when properly qualified* substantive rules of action.

To respond to this charge, we need to distinguish cases. "It is wrong to tell a lie except when telling the truth would put someone in grave risk" sounds very much like a proposition about the relative order of priority of the rules "It is wrong to tell a lie" and "It is wrong to bring harm to another person." As such, it does not need defense; it is as basic, as necessary, and as a priori as "It is wrong to tell a lie." Thus it does not qualify as a substantive moral principle. On the other hand, "It is wrong to tell a lie unless one is a prisoner of war" sounds very much like a substantive moral principle which some people do accept. But as such, it is highly contestable, indeed dubious. One should ask a person subscribing to it whether the only permissible occasion for telling a lie is when one is a prisoner of war. If the answer is yes, the principle is one we surely ought to reject. If the answer is no, we must know what other exceptions are built into the principle. Any such list of exceptions is going to be limited, and we can legitimately doubt whether it is exhaustive. How can we determine whether to add another exception to the list? In fact, we must argue for each and every exception, and this argument will of necessity involve bringing the presumption of moral wrongness to bear on a hypothetical case of lying and seeing how this presumption bears up against the pressures created by the other moral dimensions of the case. This means that we decide an exception *on the basis of* an application of the rules of moral grammar. Thus a principle like "It is wrong to tell a lie except in cases where one is a prisoner of war, etc." presupposes a commitment to the rules of moral grammar "It is wrong to tell a lie," "It is wrong to bring harm to other people" and so on. People who subscribe to substantive moral principles with exceptions built into them do not arrive at these principles simply by decision, as Hare sometimes suggests. They must argue for the exceptions—as he

24. See Hare, *Language of Morals*, chap. 4, esp. p. 62 and passim; and *Freedom and Reason*, chap. 3.

often grants—and doing this requires appeal to something that needs no argument: rules of grammar with their built-in orders of priority. Thus even when a person adopts a principle of the sort described by Hare, another principle is operating—a grammatical one—which is not a substantive principle. Therefore, he is wrong in thinking that all moral principles are of the substantive type.

A final objection relates to the question whether there is a plurality of autonomous moral rules, as I have claimed, or whether, on the contrary, these rules can be unified by being derived from more basic moral considerations. If there is a more basic principle, datum, or concern, then not only is there a unity among our moral rules, but they also have a foundation and justification—namely, the fact that they derive from the basic principle or support the more basic concern. A view of this sort has been developed by Roger Beehler, who thinks it makes perfect sense to ask why we ought not to lie or to break promises and who claims that the answer to these questions lies in the contingent fact that lying and breaking promises cause harm or hurt to other individuals.[25] According to Beehler, the *given* in morality is not a set of rules of the kind I have identified, but rather a basic attitude of care or concern for others. This attitude leads us to engage in moral activity and judgment, and it leads us to condemn acts of lying and breaking promises when we come to realize that they cause harm to others. Caring for these others, we are opposed to those forms of action that bring harm to them. It is this care and concern for other persons which delineates the moral sphere and distinguishes it from other spheres; moral considerations, as opposed to prudential or aesthetic ones, are those that bear on the well-being of others and, conversely, the harm done to others.

Beehler's theory has some surface plausibility, because we do in fact have an obligation not to harm others. This, it will be recalled, is one of the basic rules of moral grammar. But this rule has a more specific intent than that expressed by Beehler's repudiation of harm. When we are told not to harm others, we are instructed not to cause them pain or injury. A different kind of harm is in question when we are advised not to lie to others. Lying need not cause them pain or injury, but it is an assault on their moral integrity. Similarly, breaking a promise to another person produces a distinctive form of moral harm, and acting disrespectfully

25. Beehler, *Moral Life*, chaps. 1–3.

yields still a different kind of moral assault or harm. Although we may refer to all of these consequences of wrongdoing as forms of harm, this general notion has no content of its own but is merely a place marker for the variety of specific results of specific kinds of moral wrongdoing. The general notion of harm is certainly not equivalent to the notion of physical pain or injury we have in mind in enjoining people not to harm others. Thus neither the specific sense of harm as pain or injury nor the more general notion yields a result that we can tie contingently to all forms of wrongdoing.

Beehler tells us that we can harm another person in at least two ways: "when the action is itself an injury to them in some way, or when the action realizes some disappointment or vexation to them."[26] Presumably the first way amounts to our notion of causing pain or injury. The second way is far more difficult to fathom. Beehler gives us an example of wrongdoing in which this sort of result is said to occur. It is the example of a brother who lies to his sister when she asks if he has seen her boyfriend arrive home next door. When he says "No," his sister "shudders with disappointment and the tension of waiting." And Beehler asks, "What now? *Can't* we seriously ask: why is this wrong?"[27] In fact, if we do ask this question, the answer certainly is not "because as a result the sister felt disappointment." She would equally have felt disappointment if her brother had told the truth when he said the boyfriend had not returned home. The brother's act was wrong because it was a lie, whatever the feelings the sister may or may not have felt. Her feelings do not make the lie wrong; it would have been wrong even if she had not felt the disappointment and tension. Thus Beehler's example does not provide us with a case in which an act is wrong because it contingently results in a form of harm. The moral harm the act of lying results in is not just contingently related to it; it is precisely the harm of being lied to.

It is risky to generalize from a single case, but the problems with Beehler's argument do show us how difficult it is to "get behind" the rules of moral grammar and find some type of consideration that justifies them and brings unity among them. And we must remember the effort of Gewirth to discover and prove the truth of a fundamental prin-

---

26. Ibid., p. 49.
27. Ibid., p. 88.

ciple of morality—an effort we found in Chapter 3 to fail. It is not implausible to think that many philosophical moral theories that attempt to identify a fundamental moral principle or a basic, all-encompassing moral consideration in fact end up only either (a) selecting one of the rules of grammar and attempting without success to force the other rules into its mold, or (b) identifying a form of moral good or evil which has no real content of its own but serves merely to collect the goods and evils respectively promoted and denounced by the various moral rules.

This concludes my discussion of rules. We have seen how the relativist's relational account of the way rules operate in moral judgments needs to be rejected in favor of an alternative account. Substantive moral rules are not a part of the content of moral judgments for the very good reason that frequently people make these judgments without subscribing to substantive principles or rules relevant to the cases at hand. Rules of the grammatical sort are presupposed by moral judgments; they are not part of the (covert) content of these judgments. In characterizing the nature and role of grammatical rules, I also have said enough to rebut the realist's charge that rules are not central to the moral life. Thus I have rejected the relativist's analysis of rules and also rejected the realist's skepticism over rules. Conceptual relativism, wedded to a conception of rules of moral grammar, provides a perspective on moral judgments superior to that of both social-rule relativism and realism.

The Judgmental Model of Moral Decision Making

As we have seen, some moral rules can be thought of not as substantive general principles but rather as grammatical statements of the moral dimensions of experience, as indicators of factors that are relevant to the determination of what we ought or ought not to do. (This approach, we might note, is similar to Harman's way of looking at rules.[28]) "Lying is wrong," we say, and we mean by this that the fact of a lie occurring is an important, morally negative aspect of a situation and one that must be considered in making up our minds about the moral character of this situation. Seen in this light, moral grammatical rules provide us with reasons

28. See Gilbert Harman, *The Nature of Morality* (New York: Oxford University Press, 1977), pp. 115–16.

for judging that something wrong (or right) has been or will be done. Often these rules have a built-in index of strength or priority, allowing us to determine which is to prevail in circumstances in which they conflict, which is to provide the overriding reason that determines what we ought to do. Taking grammatical rules to be the indicators of morally relevant dimensions of situations, allowing for the flexibility frequently built into these rules, granting the possibility of indeterminate cases, and insisting on the necessity of interpreting a situation in light of all the rules applicable to it, the conceptual relativist is thereby in a position to elaborate a judgmental model of moral decision making which bears only faint resemblance to the simple deductive model according to which moral arguments subsume particular cases under general principles. The newer, more elaborate model does contain a deductive component: knowing that performing or not performing an act would be consistent or inconsistent with one of the grammatical rules applicable to the case involves a grasp of the logical implications of these rules. But much more is also involved. Assessing the often vague and imprecise order of priority among rules is an activity that can seldom be cast in the deductive mode. Nor can the need to determine that there are no other (overriding) rules applicable to a case be a matter of deduction from rules: how can we deduce from rules that there are no other rules applicable? These features suggest that the moral judgment concluding a process of moral argumentation and decision making might well be thought of as a "judgment call." Such a judgment does not report a moral perception, nor is it merely the conclusion of a deductive inference. It reports what we think to be the overall moral character of a situation, given all our rules and all the information we have about the situation. It is an intellectual, nondeductive, summary judgment. It might well be called a *deliverance of conscience.*

This nondeductive judgmental model of moral decision making allows the conceptual relativist to accommodate a number of insights of the realists (shorn, to be sure, of their perceptual interpretation). For instance, such a relativist can accept many of the things the realist has to say about supervenience (see Chapter 4). He can take the overall moral character of a situation to supervene on its base features, its nonmoral or lower-level moral features. The overall moral character is a matter of whether a certain action is required in light of all the moral rules applicable to the case. The base features are those characteristics identified by the moral rules as morally relevant. (Because these base characteristics are identified by moral rules, it is much more appropriate to speak of them as lower-level moral characteristics than to call them nonmoral ones.) The presence of any one of these characteristics does not entail the supervenient moral character of the situation—what one ought to do or must do—because the rule that renders this characteristic morally relevant may take secondary status to another rule that also is applicable. But even when there is no other morally relevant dimension present, the moral character of the entire situation is not entailed by the presence of its one moral dimension. It is the presence of this dimension and the absence of other morally relevant features which makes the situation one in which there is, or is not, an obligation to act in a certain way. It is the applicability of one rule and the inapplicability of other rules which determine what we ought to do.

Although the applicability of a moral rule and hence the presence of a morally relevant feature do not entail the supervenient moral character of a situation, the applicability of the rule is not just contingently related to its overall moral character. If the morally relevant feature is unique or overriding, it becomes the dimension that *makes* it morally right or wrong to act in a certain way in the circumstances at hand; referring to this feature is a matter of providing a noncontingent reason for an act's being right or wrong. Such a theory does not become a reductionistic naturalism, however, for what one ought to do is not a function solely of the natural features of things; these features are morally relevant for us only via the normative rules we accept—via, that is, the rules of moral grammar.

Following up on an (undeveloped) suggestion by Ronald Milo (a suggestion also voiced some years earlier by Mounce and Phillips) we could refer to the rules of moral grammar as identifying the *criteria* for determining the moral character of a situation.[29] I propose to use this notion of criteria in what I take to be the Wittgensteinian way.[30] In general, criteria provide noncontingent but nonentailing reasons for asserting the existence of a certain state of affairs; the satisfaction of the criteria generates a presumption that the state of affairs exists, and this

---

29. Milo, *Immorality*, pp. 195–96; Phillips and Mounce, *Moral Practices*, pp. 11–12.
30. For an excellent recent discussion of criteria, see the revised edition of P. M. S. Hacker's *Insight and Illusion* (Oxford: Oxford University Press, 1986), pp. 307–22.

presumption can be overridden only by the presence of special, defeating conditions, no complete list of which can be identified. In a situation in which we have ascertained that the criteria are satisfied, and in which there is no reason to believe that a defeating condition exists, we have every right to believe that the criterially indicated state of affairs in fact exists. We have satisfied our share of the burden of proof and have no obligation to defend our position by adducing additional grounds. The burden of proof shifts to someone who would deny that or question whether the state of affairs exists, and a defeating condition must be identified if doubt continues to make sense. In the absence of such identification, we can be certain of the state of affairs. Insofar, however, as the satisfaction of the criteria does not entail the existence of the state of affairs, and insofar as there can be no complete list of defeating conditions—and hence no checking off of the items on the list to ensure that no defeating conditions exist—the claim that the state of affairs exists is never entailed by the evidence at hand. In ideal circumstances—satisfaction of the criteria and no evidence of defeating conditions—we have the right to be sure of the state of affairs, but the proposition describing it could still be false.

Take a situation s in which a person P has made a promise to do x. By virtue of the rule of grammar "It is wrong to break a promise," one criterion for its being wrong for P not to do x has been satisfied in s. This rule of grammar identifies P's *having made a promise to do x* as a criterial reason for its being wrong in the situation for P not to do x. Hence P is completely justified in doing x unless some defeating condition is present of which he should be aware. If it is clear that in keeping his promise, he also would harm a great number of people in rather severe ways, he should realize that the judgment "I ought to do x" is defeated in spite of its resting on criterial grounds. But if he has no reason to believe that this or any other overriding moral consideration is present, he has every reason and right to believe that he ought to do x. Nevertheless, the satisfaction of the criterion "It is wrong to break a promise" together with the absence of a reason to believe that a defeating condition exists does not entail that he ought to do x. Some defeating condition may be present which neither he nor anyone else has a reason to believe exists, and there is no way to rule this out (there being no complete list of defeating conditions). Hence "I ought to do x" could be false even though the criterial rule "It is wrong to break a promise" has been satisfied and there is no reason to believe that an overriding moral consideration prevails. There is no reason to question *P*'s judgment that he ought to do *x*—neither *P* nor anyone else has such a reason—and yet for all that *P*'s judgment may be in error.

It is worth emphasizing that the conditions that can override a criterially justified moral claim are themselves indicated by rules of moral grammar, rules that identify conflicting moral reasons of higher priority. We have seen how these rules are frequently imprecise and flexible; we also have noted that the class of such rules is open-ended—new rules may enter the set and old ones disappear. These facts about our moral rules are pertinent to the issue of defeating conditions. Satisfaction of the rule prohibiting harm to others may override the satisfaction of a rule prohibiting the breaking of a promise if the harm is extensive or severe enough, but we have no precise measure of extent or severity to which we can appeal. In some situations, then, disagreements could exist over whether the obligation to keep a promise is overridden. In these cases it would be inappropriate to claim certainty, for considered judgment is the best one can hope to achieve. (But it is equally important to note that in many other situations it will be clear that the obligation is, or is not, overridden.) Furthermore, if we are to have the epistemic right to be totally confident of one of our moral judgments, we must have no reason to believe that any of our other moral rules apply to the situation and override the satisfaction of the rule on which we base our judgment. But insofar as the set of moral rules we usually operate with is open-ended and changing, it will be no easy matter to determine that there is no applicable rule that defeats our claim. Once again, in many such cases we have no right to be sure of our judgments.

Another difficulty with defeating conditions arises from the fact that many of them are, in the situations at hand, unknown. We are unaware of many facts about our actions. Some of these facts we could be expected to know or to find out about; others we could not possibly know. These unknown facts frequently have moral importance, and indeed such importance that, were we aware of them, we would see that they defeat our moral claims. If we have not done our moral homework and not ascertained all the facts we could be expected to uncover, our moral judgment will not have been made in an ideal epistemic situation and we will have no right to any great confidence. If, on the contrary, we have done our homework (as defined contextually) and it has revealed no reason to think there are defeating conditions, then, in the presence of a satisfied moral criterion and in the absence of a reason to think there is a defeating condition, we have the right to be confident in our judgment. In such a situation we have the strongest conceivable grounds for believing that we ought to do *x* and no reason to believe otherwise.

The conceptual relativist position sketched here largely supports the realists' thesis of fallibilism (see Chapter 4). Attending to all the rules applicable to a situation, measuring their order of priority, and determining that there is no reason to think other rules are applicable—such a complex process is fraught with the possibility of error. The realists, it will be recalled, had difficulty reconciling their fallibilism with their notion of moral perception, since perceptual statements carry with them an implication of certainty. An intellectual judgment of the sort postulated by the conceptual relativist's model carries no such implication, and to this extent the judgmental model of decision making is consistent with fallibilism. All contingent moral propositions could be in error, not simply because they are contingent and hence logically capable of error, but because their evidence or grounds are, even at best, nonentailing. Consequently, even in ideal circumstances we could always make a mistake in asserting one of them. The only moral propositions that cannot be in error are the rules of moral grammar, but they are not contingent.

At the same time, however, this judgmental model allows for the possibility of certainty. There may be, indeed there are, instances in which only one morally relevant dimension needs to be taken into account in assessing a situation. This dimension may be known to exist beyond any shadow of a doubt, and there may be no reason to think another relevant and overriding feature exists. In this case, we can be said to know and to know with certainty what the moral character of the situation is. We are in the best conceivable epistemic position with regard to it. One of the real virtues of this judgmental model is that it allows for both occasional certainty and normal uncertainty with respect to our contingent moral convictions.

A cognitivist, judgmental theory of moral discourse needs to be able to display the variety of epistemic situations in our moral lives. It is not enough to argue that there is moral knowledge and that some of our moral propositions are true. If the cognitivist theory and the judgmental model are in general correct, we might expect to find the same epistemic and logical distinctions among moral judgments we find in nonmoral contexts. We might expect, for instance, to encounter judgments that we know with certainty, and others, many others, that cannot be grasped with certainty; likewise, we might expect to find some propositions that are necessary and others that are contingent. We have seen that this is in fact the case. It is appropriate at this point to recall the different logical and epistemic modes of moral judgment we have identified in this chapter. In doing so we also can point to one additional kind of moral judgment and, in light of the distinctions introduced, illuminate the specific mode in which it enters the stock of moral knowledge. Consider, then, the following logical/epistemological classification of moral judgments, together with some examples:

1. Grammatical Propositions—Basic Moral Principles

> "It is wrong to tell a lie."
> "One ought to keep one's promises."
> "One ought not to harm other people."
> "It is wrong to treat others disrespectfully."
> "One must not take the life of an innocent person."

2. Grammatical Propositions Concerning Order of Priority among Basic Principles

> "One ought to tell the truth unless doing so would cause grave harm to others."
> "One ought to keep one's promises unless doing so would involve taking the life of a innocent person."

3. Substantive Moral Principles

> "Premarital sex is wrong."
> "One ought to be patriotic."
> "Mercy killing is wrong."
> "One ought to live a simple and frugal life."
> "One ought to give a quarter of one's income to charity."

4. Grammatical Propositions Converted into Substantive Moral Principles

> "One ought never to tell a lie."
> "One ought always to keep one's promises."

"One should never kill another human being, in war, peace, or self-defense."

5. Principles of Moral Permissibility

General formula: "There is nothing wrong about doing *x*, but one is under no obligation to do it."

"It is morally permissible to put money into tax shelters."

"Suicide is morally permissible."

"It is morally permissible to let a deformed fetus die."

"It is morally permissible to let another person die, but not to take a life."

6. Statements of "The Lesser Evil"

"You ought to lie to her; otherwise she will be deeply hurt."

"I had to tell the truth, so I could not keep my promise."

7. Exceptions to Moral Principles

"One ought always to tell the truth, unless one is a prisoner of war."

"One ought to turn the other cheek, unless one's family honor is at stake."

8. Particular Moral Judgments

"You ought to pay him back."

"It was wrong of you to cheat on him."

Undoubtedly this classification is far from complete. But it does succeed in demonstrating how varied are the kinds of moral judgments we make and what different kinds of epistemological status they have. Propositions falling into categories 1 and 2 are necessary; the remainder are contingent. The defense of those contingent propositions will invariably make reference to one or more of the necessary propositions, the rules of moral grammar. Statements in categories 6, 7, and 8 concern particular circumstances, and their defense will appeal to the nature of these circumstances in addition to both substantive and grammatical principles. Of special interest are the principles of moral permissibility, a form of moral judgment we have not hitherto discussed. These are contingent propositions. It would appear that there are no grammatical propositions about moral permissibility, only an abstract definition of the term. Moral space, it would seem, is defined by the principles of good and evil, of obligation and moral wrongdoing. That which is morally permissible can be determined only among the general facts that obtain within this space. A knowledge of the moral domain as a whole requires a geometrical understanding of the definitive contours of moral space, a scientific grasp of the general principles of moral geography, and a novelistic acquaintance with the accidental twists and turns that here and there are to be found in it, in its nooks and crannies, as it were.

A theory of conceptual relativism is able to provide a judgmental model of moral decision making which maps the moral cognitive territory better than competing theories. It improves upon British moral realism in important ways, particularly with respect to its questionable notion of moral perception and its inconsistent thoughts on certainty and doubt. And by virtue of allowing for the possibility of moral certainty, it offers a picture of moral judgment superior to the one of the American moral realists. We also have seen how this relativist theory avoids the difficulties inherent both in the deductivist account of moral reasoning and in the relational account of moral judgment offered by social-rule relativists like Wong. If next we can demonstrate that the autonomy thesis of conceptual relativism is to be preferred to the objectivism of metaphysical realism and to the peculiar, unstable nonobjectivism of social-rule forms of relativism, we will be in a good position to conclude that conceptual relativism is the preferred theory among the cognitivist alternatives available. We can then claim with reason that it does the best job of accommodating the cognitive locutions in moral discourse and therefore takes us closer to the truth about morality.

Moral Facts, Moral Autonomy, and Moral Change

Moral realists believe that there are moral facts which exist independently of human beliefs, attitudes, or artifacts like rules. Social-rule relativists claim to the contrary that there are no independent moral facts. Although most of these relativists would grant that moral facts do exist, they see them as having some essential connection to human thoughts or sentiments. In this section we consider once again the issue of moral facts, specifically with a view to determining if there can be an intermediate position between moral realism and social-rule relativism. I claim that the form of epistemological, nonobjectivist conceptual relativism developed in this chapter provides just such an intermediate position. It neither asserts nor denies that there are independent moral facts and hence is a theory neither of metaphysical objectivism nor of metaphysical nonobjectivism, to use the terms introduced in Chapter 5. But it puts us at ease philosophically with our everyday discourse about moral facts, truth, and knowledge. And contrary to what some philosophers might think, its doctrine of the autonomy of moral concepts in no way implies a subjectivist, historicist, or idealist view of moral experience, these being specific forms of metaphysical nonobjectivism.

In discussing the realist view in Chapter 4, I pointed out that it is a conceptual howler to say that *facts exist*, be they moral facts or scientific ones. Objects and persons exist, but facts are not objects or persons. It is a fact that a person weighs two hundred pounds; it also is a fact that a person is good, or evil. But the fact that a person is good cannot be said to exist. "The fact that Gandhi is good exists" is so much nonsense. "There are moral facts in the world" just generalizes this nonsense. We also observed in Chapter 4 that moral facts are difficult to avoid. If we deny the truth of the proposition "It is a fact that Gandhi was a good man," we have not taken a single step toward reducing the number of moral facts in the world, since if our denial is correct it follows that it is a fact that Gandhi was *not* a good man. And "There are no moral facts" was seen to have a very odd status, quite unlike that of "There are no Bengal tigers in India." It is difficult if not impossible to understand how "there are no moral facts" could be verified, facts—and ipso facto moral facts—having no defining properties that could fail to be detected.

Although it makes no sense to assert or deny that there are moral facts, we can reflect on exemplary statements like "Washington was courageous" and "It is a fact that Washington was courageous" and try to display what we are saying in making these statements. Thus a conceptual relativist can point to the grammatical rules presupposed by such statements and can describe the process of justification leading us, in light of these rules, to accept the statements as true. One can, that is to say, describe the epistemic environment in which we make moral statements, debate them, and hold to them. Such a description highlights the involvement of grammatical rules in moral discourse, and it also highlights some of their characteristics—how, for example, they have a necessity attaching to them which substantive, contingent principles do not have. Consequently such a description allows us to raise certain questions about these rules: why, for instance, do they have their unquestioned role in our moral lives? Can they be given some kind of demonstrative proof? Can they be justified at all? Does their presence in moral discourse speak in favor of some sort of moral idealism, moral subjectivism, or moral historicism? In asking the last question, we are inquiring whether human beings, through their commitment to rules of moral grammar, somehow *create* moral reality, somehow infect moral facts with human subjectivity, or render them historically provincial. So, although we cannot deny the reality of moral facts, perhaps we can raise questions about their ontological status.

In the first section of this chapter, it was claimed that grammatical rules and the concepts they define are autonomous, that they cannot be justified or invalidated. Two arguments were sketched to demonstrate this. First, any effort to compare the concepts with reality begs the question; second, any effort to demonstrate that they are successful or not in attaining an independent goal imposes on them an end that is foreign to their intrinsic purpose and hence begs the practical question. If arguments of these types are successful, grammatical rules and basic moral concepts are without foundation; they provide the framework within which justification of particular moral judgments is possible, but they themselves cannot be justified.

If moral judgments are relative to such foundationless rules of moral grammar, then what, if anything, does this have to say about these moral judgments? Does it show that the moral facts they represent are essentially mental in nature or origin—the product of mental thoughts, concepts, or acts of will? Does the autonomy of moral grammar, that is to say, entail moral idealism? Or does it show that the judgments themselves are subjective—the product, expression, or description of emotions and attitudes? Is subjectivism the consequence of the autonomy of moral grammar? Finally, is "relativity to grammatical rules" a form of historicism that denies that moral facts are universal and "hard," there for anyone, at any time, to ascertain? Does conceptual relativism render moral facts a matter of provincial social customs and practices?

Conceptual relativism does imply that in defending a claim about moral facts we appeal to grammatical rules; it does imply that these rules dictate the kind of evidence that can be used to demonstrate that a moral judgment is true. It also entails the claim that the meanings of the moral terms we use to describe actions and persons are defined by these rules. But these are innocuous consequences philosophically. They amount to saying that we would not know what the moral facts are, and could not describe or even conceive of them, if we did not have these grammatical rules. It is tempting, however, to look for more profound philosophical significance in these truths about the relationship between moral judgments and moral grammatical rules. It is tempting, first of all, to think they show that the moral facts themselves depend on or are created by the grammatical rules. Is this true? Is conceptual relativism an idealist position?

Whether it is true that moral facts depend on grammatical rules can be determined only after ascertaining what 'depend on' means in this claim. There are at least two possibilities: the dependence could be causal or logical. In discussing whether moral facts causally or logically depend on grammatical rules, we must be careful how we phrase the question. It will not do to ask whether the existence of moral facts causally or logically depends on these rules, since this would require us to speak of the existence of moral facts. But perhaps we can ask if the actual moral facts are as they are as a result of the rules. Is it the case, for example, that Jones acted wrongly because of the moral rules?

If it is a causal dependence we have in mind, it is clear that most moral facts do not depend on moral grammatical rules. What made Washington courageous was his state of mind, character, history, and situation, all of which can be described without any appeal to the causal efficacy of rules of grammar. What makes a particular act wrong is the fact that it involved a lie or a broken promise or harm to another person, and grammatical rules seldom if ever have anything to do causally with the fact that the act involved such things.

Perhaps, however, 'depend on' means some kind of logical rather than causal dependence. Unfortunately, the notion of logical dependence is itself unclear. A grammatical rule might be thought of as either a logically sufficient or logically necessary condition of a moral fact. Let R stand for the rule "It is wrong to lie" and let F stand for "It is a fact that Jones, in lying, acted wrongly." If the grammatical rule is a logically sufficient condition of the fact, then "If R, then F" would have to be a logically necessary proposition—its denial would have to be self-contradictory. If the rule is a logically necessary condition of the fact, then "If F, then R" would have to be logically necessary and its denial self-contradictory.

It seems clear that "If R, then F" is not a logically necessary proposition, since "It is wrong to lie" and "It is not the case that Jones, in lying, acted wrongly" are hardly inconsistent. As we have seen, a moral rule, even when applicable to a particular situation, may be overridden by some other moral rule. The satisfaction of a moral rule is the criterion for the truth of a moral proposition, but it does not entail this proposition. A moral rule, then, is not a logically sufficient condition of a moral fact.

Is it perhaps the case that the rule against lying is a logically necessary condition of its being a fact that Jones, in lying, did something wrong? Is it contradictory to assert that Jones, in lying, did something wrong but that it is not a rule that lying is wrong? It does not appear so. Jones could have acted wrongly in lying not because lying is wrong but because there was some other rule applying to the case which showed his act to be wrong. It might be wrong, for instance, because it hurt someone.

Still another option is that moral facts would not be as they are unless there were some rules of moral grammar. A moral fact is not logically dependent on any particular moral rule, but it might be dependent on there being moral rules, some of which would make it a fact in a given situation. Is, then, "If Jones, in lying, acted wrongly, then there are some moral rules" a necessary proposition? Is "Jones, in lying, acted wrongly, but there are no moral rules" self-contradictory?

It must be granted that the latter proposition does sound odd. But there is a way of explaining its oddity without taking it to be logically incoherent. If there were no moral rules, we could not provide a reason for claiming that Jones acted wrongly. Even more basically, we would not be in a position to assert it, since we would not have the concept of moral wrongness. But the conditions that constitute Jones's acting wrongly (his telling a lie in circumstances in which there are no other, morally overriding factors) could exist even if we were in no position to assert that he acted wrongly or give a reason for believing it. Thus "Jones, in lying, acted wrongly, but there are no moral rules" is odd because the conditions for asserting the first conjunct are denied by the second conjunct. It is not odd by virtue of its being inconceivable that Jones could have acted wrongly in the absence of moral rules.

There is another, more fundamental problem surrounding the suggestion that grammatical rules are the logically necessary conditions of
moral facts. Take the proposition, "If F, then there are some R." What
would happen if we transpose this, so as to get "If there are no R, then it
is not the case that F"? Thus: "if there are no moral rules, then it is not
the case that it is a fact that Jones acted wrongly." The consequent of
this hypothetical proposition could be reduced to: it is not a fact that
Jones acted wrongly. But if it is not a fact that Jones acted wrongly, it *is* a
fact that Jones acted either rightly or in a morally permissible manner.
This leads us to the conclusion that, if there are no moral rules, it is a fact
that Jones acted rightly or in a morally permissible manner. In either
event, his doing so would be a moral fact. Consequently, the conclusion
hardly expresses the proposition that moral facts are morally dependent
on grammatical rules; it seems to suggest just the opposite.

It is very difficult, then, to generate philosophical idealism out of the
fact that moral judgments are constructed relative to the rules of moral
grammar. Nor can a thesis of subjectivism be derived from it. It might
be suggested, for example, that we have the grammatical rules we do
because of the way our human sentiments operate. Given the variability
of human sentiments, it would be easy on this hypothesis to explain why
different people operate with different "moral" rules: different feelings
yield different rules. Several things can be said in response to this suggestion. First, even if the conjecture turned out to be true, it would not
in any way impugn the rules. Their origin is one thing; their epistemic
or logical status is another. We have seen reasons for denying that grammatical rules can be justified or invalidated. Given such autonomy, it is
simply irrelevant whether they have their origin in human emotions or
not. Second, the picture lurking behind the suggestion that our moral
rules are subjective shows certain dimensions of experience being picked
out by our rules as morally significant because we have some kind of
emotional reaction to them. We say lying is wrong because we dislike it,
and we say that keeping promises is right because we view promise keeping with favor. But this presupposes that we can detect these kinds of
action prior to having our rules. We have seen, to the contrary, that
'lying' and 'promise-keeping' are in part defined by the rules. It makes no
sense, then, to speak of our responding unfavorably or favorably to
them prior to our forming the rules.

Third, the affective/conative origin of grammatical rules, again assuming that such is their origin, does not entail that moral judgments made in accordance with the rules are in any way subjective. As noted above, a judgment is normally said to be subjective if it is the product of feeling or emotion rather than evidence and sound reasoning. To the extent, however, that we back up our moral judgments by appeal to the kind of evidence dictated by the rules of moral grammar, these judgments are perfectly objective. Grammatical rules define what appropriate evidence is for judgments incorporating the terms defined by the rules, and hence they are the presuppositions of moral objectivity. Fourth, the feelings or attitudes conjectured to be the causes of grammatical rules are not easily identified. Most of the emotions we are familiar with in the moral sphere are those which we understand in the context of certain moral situations. Just as pride is a feeling for a certain kind of accomplishment (as Philippa Foot showed us in Chapter 2), concern for others and out-rage over what happens to others are affective states that can be under-stood only in terms of their objects—namely, the integrity, autonomy, and dignity of others (and the violation of these moral conditions). And these objects are precisely what we aim at or avoid in obeying moral rules. Thus most of the emotions we might appeal to are internal to morality and cannot be postulated as external causes of morality.

One other objection to subjectivism can be registered. The idea that we could generate grammatical rules by approving of general kinds of action (like telling the truth) and disapproving of others (like breaking promises) assumes that it makes sense to approve in general of telling the truth and to disapprove in general of breaking promises. It does not. Philippa Foot has observed that approval can take place only under cer-tain conditions,[31] and we might add to her set of conditions the follow-ing one: if we can approve of something, it also makes sense to disap-prove of it. Approval and belief are parallel in this respect, since if it is possible for someone to believe a proposition, it is possible for someone to disbelieve it as well. We have already seen how it is impossible either to believe or disbelieve that lying is wrong or keeping promises right. These are grammatical facts about the rules of moral grammar, and they are related to the fact that the moral rules in question cannot be false. Such grammatical facts also rule out our approving or disapproving of

---

31. See Philippa Foot, "Approval and Disapproval," in P. M. S. Hacker and J. Raz, eds., *Law, Morality, and Society* (Oxford: Oxford University Press, 1977).

the acts in question. It is possible to approve or disapprove of telling the truth on a particular occasion, because it may or may not be the case that this is the right thing to do on that occasion. It is not possible to approve of telling the truth in general (unless one has adopted a substantive and contingent principle commending truth telling), because it cannot be false that it is right to tell the truth. "I approve of telling the truth" and "I disapprove of breaking promises" have an odd air about them. They would be, for one thing, highly presumptuous—as if it mattered whether the particular person who asserted them approved or disapproved of these matters. At best their utterance might have a comic effect, prompting the kind of ironic chuckle that greets Coolidge's remark made when he was asked what he thought of sin: "I'm agin it."

If it makes no sense to say one approves of telling the truth, it cannot be the case that one ought to tell the truth because one approves of it. Hence the classic subjectivist, emotivist account of how we come to have our basic moral principles is essentially flawed.

But although idealism and subjectivism do not follow from the autonomy thesis, certain less impressive consequences can be noted by attending to the relativity of moral judgments to grammatical rules. We can ask whether all human beings operate with the same set of rules, and we can entertain as highly probable the hypothesis that they do not. We can note how the rules of moral grammar change in our own lives, some disappearing and new ones entering the scene. "It is wrong not to be patriotic," one might think until one reads and absorbs Voltaire, at which time patriotism may come to take on a morally unsavory air. And after a convincing reading of Sartre, one may add the rule "It is wrong to live in bad faith" to one's list of grammatical rules. The briefest experience with history reveals how moral rules and categories change over time—for example, the concept of personal honor so central to the concept of morality operating in the western world during the last several centuries has almost disappeared from view. How many of us today are sufficiently concerned about our honor to be willing to fight duels to defend it? And if we go to court to protest slander or libel, we usually are more interested in our rights (or the financial settlement) than in the vindication of our honor.

The existence of rules of moral grammar, then, is contingent. These rules may come in and out of existence. The course of history is ever-shifting, and just as different forms of life incorporating alternative concepts of morality likely existed before us, others equally diverse from our own are likely to follow.

These considerations may suggest to some that moral judgments and moral facts are provincial, that they are relative to historical periods and to the cultures that exist during them. Consequently, one might argue, moral facts are not "hard," not there for anyone to observe or discover, not incapable of being denied. Can conceptual relativism distinguish itself from this historicist view?[32]

What are we to say if a rule of moral grammar does disappear during the course of history? Take, once again, the rule that places personal honor at the center of our moral concerns. Does it follow from the near disappearance of this rule that the honor the inhabitants of the nineteenth century talked about was somehow chimerical? Were there no hard facts about honor in the last century? Can we today say that it was not a fact that, contrary to the best opinion of the time, person P's honor was affronted by person R? Such consequences do not follow. If we no longer operate with the concept of honor, we cannot say "It is not a fact that P's honor was affronted by R," since to say this involves a use of the concept of honor. If, however, we still have immediate access to this concept, or if through historical and anthropological research we can reappropriate it, then we can make statements about honor in the nineteenth century. In that case, we might even want to use new historical evidence to reject some of the heretofore accepted facts about honor (and this evidence might allow us to ascertain new instances in which honor was manifested or affronted). But we can hardly deny that all previously alleged facts about honor really were facts. The evidence would hardly show that!

Having granted as much, can we say, nevertheless, that these facts about honor were facts only because of the grammatical rules these Europeans operated with? Given that the rules are no longer operative, are not the facts tainted with historical relativity and hence are facts *only for the nineteenth-century Europeans*? Here we must be very careful. We must distinguish between propositions' being true, on the one hand, and their being true *for someone*, on the other. Facts are facts, we need to remind

32. The kind of historicism I have in mind is similar to that developed in the early part of this century by Ernst Troeltsch and Karl Mannheim. See "Historicism" by Maurice Mandelbaum in Paul Edwards, ed., *The Encyclopedia of Philosophy*, vol. 4 (New York: Macmillan, 1967), pp. 22–25.

ourselves, and something is a fact if the proposition describing it is true. And if this proposition is true (and does not contain indexical expressions), it is true for all times. To the extent that we today can use the concept of honor and can talk about the facts of honor in the last century, it is because we can grasp that, in light of the grammatical rules operating then and appropriated by us today, such and such factual propositions were true and are still true today. The propositions were (are) not true because nineteenth-century Europeans believed them or because the propositions were customarily accepted. What made the propositions true were the facts of the case; what allows anyone to know they were (and are) true is an appeal to evidence in light of the grammatical rules defining 'honor'. The facts described by these true propositions are as hard as any can be. Given what was meant by 'honor', it is a fact for all time and for anyone who cares to look into the matter that, on a certain date and in a certain place, Count A's honor was affronted by Count B. Anyone using the concept of honor would have to grant such a fact, and anyone not using it would be unable to deny the fact. We who have lost interest in honor, and those multitudes today who do not even have the concept of honor, are not in a position to acknowledge historical facts about honor. But from our disinterest or ignorance nothing follows about the nature and course of social relationships in years past.

Hard facts about personal honor can still be nonobjective in the theoretical, epistemological sense introduced in Chapter 5. If we do not operate with the concept of personal honor at all, it cannot be claimed that we have made an error or have acted irrationally. We can refuse to talk of honor without being cognitively defective. There is no way to demonstrate that the property of honor really exists (properties do not exist!) and that the nineteenth-century concept accurately represents it. And it is hardly irrational of us in light of our moral ends not to speak of honor and dishonor: being concerned about honor is not a required means for achieving *our* moral ends. Conceptual relativism, then, can claim that although moral judgments frequently are true, and moral facts hard, they are for all that nonobjective in the theoretical sense. The judgments are nonobjective because the rules they presuppose could be put aside without error or irrationality. No one is constrained by canons of truth or reason to use any set of concepts. If we today do not use the concept of honor, it is not true for us that Count A had his honor offended in 1803 and subsequently defended it. Hence facts about honor may be facts for nineteenth-century Europeans and not facts for us today. We are not able to deny these facts, but we are under no obligation to grant them, refusing, as we might, to talk about honor at all.

The fact that our set of moral concepts is historically contingent and likely to be just one among numerous sets of normative concepts embodied in different historical circumstances may cause some to feel that moral absolutism is inappropriate. If other people operate with different concepts of morality, with what right should we judge these people in terms of our own? With what right should we apply our moral principles universally—to all human beings regardless of their normative practices and concept of morality? Should not conceptual relativism be taken to imply a principle of tolerance whereby other cultures are respected for their uniqueness and allowed to engage in their distinctive practices without fear of censure, correction, or alteration from us?

Such a line of thought sounds attractive until we ask for specifics. Are we being urged to allow people from cultures not using our concept of morality to tell lies, break promises, harm one another (and us), and show disrespect for human beings? This is what would follow from an agreement not to apply the rules of moral grammar to other cultures. For most of us, I suggest, the very thought of withdrawing our moral demands with respect to these basic moral actions is highly repugnant. It must be realized that the issue here is not whether we should blame the members of these other cultures for not following our moral rules. As we saw in our discussion of Harman, we can easily agree that they should not be blamed, since many excusing conditions can be found—most basically their ignorance of what morality requires. But not to blame them is not to withdraw our claim that in killing and lying to others they are doing something morally wrong, something they ought not to do. A proper spirit of tolerance would require only that we treat another culture's violation of moral principles with understanding, forgiveness, and compassion, realizing that the members of this culture are not to blame for their actions and should be reformed through educative measures rather than through punishment and coercion.

Morality, then, with its basic moral principles and its moral absolutism, is not something most of us would be willing to give up or to limit in its application. That it is a practice arising at a certain time and place and beset with all the threats imposed by its contingency is no reason to be bashful about it. In spite of its historical contingency, we can celebrate it without reservation, just as we celebrate one of our other civilized but historically contingent activities—modern science.

This discussion of the implications of relativity to grammatical rules reveals how very close moral realism and conceptual relativism are. Both acknowledge moral truths that are untainted by subjectivity and resistant to idealist appropriation. Both consider these truths to be uncontaminated by historicist reduction and hence to be as hard as truths can be. But there are crucial points of difference between the two theories. The conceptual relativist avoids the conceptual blunders the realist commits in talking about the existence of, and independence of, moral facts and moral properties. Moreover, the conceptual relativist proposes a nonobjectivist theory allowing us to acknowledge different normative practices without having to conclude, as a realist with his objectivist perspective must, that large segments of mankind are cognitively at fault for failing to recognize the rules that define and the truths that describe the moral universe. But in spite of these differences, the spirit of conceptual relativism is very realistic—in a nonmetaphysical way. It dissolves any philosophical objections we might have to our talk of moral truth, moral facts, and moral knowledge. Consequently, it removes any philosophical temptation we might feel to derogate, discourage, or condemn such talk. It allows us to engage in the moral life without philosophical doubts. Conceptual relativism, we might say, maintains that moral discourse and experience are empirically real even while being transcendentally relative.

Index

Library of Congress Cataloging-in-Publication Data

Arrington, Robert L., 1938–
    Rationalism, realism, and relativism : perspectives in
contemporary moral epistemology / Robert L. Arrington.
        p.   cm.
    Includes index.
    ISBN 0-8014-2302-3 (alk. paper). — ISBN 0-8014-9563-6 (pbk. :
alk. paper)
    1. Ethics.   2. Ethics, Modern—20th century.   3. Knowledge, Theory
of.   4. Rationalism.   5. Realism.   6. Ethical relativism.
I. Title.
BJ1031.A77   1989
171—dc20   89-42874